PERGAMON INTERNATIONAL LIBRARY
of Science, Technology, Engineering and Social Studies
The 1000-volume original paperback library in aid of education,
industrial training and the enjoyment of leisure
Publisher: Robert Maxwell, M.C.

Humanism and Behaviorism: Dialogue and Growth

THE PERGAMON TEXTBOOK
INSPECTION COPY SERVICE

An inspection copy of any book published in the Pergamon International Library will gladly
be sent to academic staff without obligation for their consideration for course adoption or
recommendation. Copies may be retained for a period of 60 days from receipt and returned
if not suitable. When a particular title is adopted or recommended for adoption for class use
and the recommendation results in a sale of 12 or more copies, the inspection copy may be
retained with our compliments. If after examination the lecturer decides that the book is not
suitable for adoption but would like to retain it for his personal library, then a discount of
10% is allowed on the invoiced price. The Publishers will be pleased to receive suggestions for
revised editions and new titles to be published in this important International Library.

PERGAMON GENERAL PSYCHOLOGY SERIES

Editor: Arnold P. Goldstein, *Syracuse University*
Leonard Krasner, *SUNY, Stony Brook*

TITLES IN THE PERGAMON GENERAL PSYCHOLOGY SERIES
(Added Titles in Back of Volume)

The terms of our inspection copy service apply to all the above books. A complete catalogue of all books in the Pergamon International Library is available on request.

The Publisher will be pleased to receive suggestions for revised editions and new titles.

Humanism and Behaviorism: Dialogue and Growth

Edited by

ABRAHAM WANDERSMAN
PAUL J. POPPEN
DAVID F. RICKS

PERGAMON PRESS
OXFORD · NEW YORK · TORONTO · SYDNEY
PARIS · FRANKFURT

U.K.	Pergamon Press Ltd., Headington Hill Hall, Oxford, England
U.S.A.	Pergamon Press Inc., Maxwell House, Fairview Park, Elmsford, New York 10523, U.S.A.
CANADA	Pergamon of Canada, P.O. Box 9600, Don Mills M3C 2T9, Ontario, Canada
AUSTRALIA	Pergamon Press (Aust.) Pty. Ltd., 19a Boundary Street, Rushcutters Bay, N.S.W. 2011, Australia
FRANCE	Pergamon Press SARL, 24 rue des Ecoles, 75240 Paris, Cedex 05, France
WEST GERMANY	Pergamon Press GmbH, 6242 Kronberg/Taunus, Pferdstrasse 1, Frankfurt-am-Main, West Germany

First Edition 1976

Library of Congress Cataloging in Publication Data

Main entry under title:

Humanism and behaviorism.

(Pergamon general psychology series; PGPS-62)
1. Humanistic psychology.   2. Behaviorism (Psychology).   3. Personality change.
4. Psychotherapy.   I. Wandersman, Abraham.   II. Poppen, Paul J.   III. Ricks, David F.
[DNLM: 1. Behaviorism.   2. Personality development.   3. Behavior therapy.
4. Psychology.   BF204 H918]
BF204.H85   1975   150'.19'2   75-23300
ISBN 0-08-019589-X
ISBN 0-08-019588-1 pbk.

Printed in Great Britain by A. Wheaton & Co. Exeter

THIS BOOK IS DEDICATED TO

Sidney Jourard and Gilda Gold

WHO EXEMPLIFIED THE MAGNIFICENCE

OF PEOPLE WHO HELP PEOPLE GROW

Contents

Preface

This book is the result of stimulus, response, feedback, encouragement, and hope for growth. The stimulus was a symposium on Behavioristic and Humanistic Approaches to Personality Change held at Cornell University and organized by the Psychology Coordinating Committee, a group of psychologists from various departments and colleges at Cornell. The symposium featured distinguished spokesmen for the humanistic and behavioristic approaches, Sidney Jourard and Joseph Wolpe, as well as a series of introductory and concluding sessions. The response was the interest of the Cornell community and the editorial staff of the *Cornell Journal of Social Relations* in obtaining a record of the session and discussing the issues that were raised. The *Cornell Journal of Social Relations* then published a special issue, "Behavioristic and humanistic approaches to personality change," which Wandersman and Poppen edited, consisting of the original symposium and several additional papers addressed to issues in humanistic and behavioristic approaches to personality change. The symposium and the articles by Lambert and Bergin, Harding, and Alker are reprinted in this book with the permission of the *Cornell Journal*. The Jourard therapy session is reprinted with the permission[1] of the American Academy of Psychotherapists.

Feedback to the *Cornell Journal* issue from colleagues and other readers was extremely favorable and we were encouraged to expand it into a book which would broaden the issues covered and further the dialogue. At this point Ricks was enlisted as an advisor and eventually an editor. Our hope for this book is similar to the one we first expressed in the *Journal* issue—to further understanding and critical evaluation of each

---

[1] We wish to thank the American Academy of Psychotherapists for their permission to reprint this therapy session. Catalogs and tapes can be ordered from: AAP Tape Library, 1040 Woodcock Rd., Orlando, Florida 32803.

approach and facilitate integration and novel syntheses of the two approaches. The additional articles by Poppen, Wandersman, and Wandersman; Rychlak; Mischel; Goldstein; Curtiss; Gold; Ricks and Fleming; Devereux; Alexander, Dreher, and Willems; and Ricks, Wandersman, and Poppen were written expressly for this book.

Albert Bandura's article is a revised version of his American Psychological Association presidential address in 1974. It is the only article in the book that is not original to the *Cornell Journal of Social Relations* issue on "Behavioristic and humanistic approaches to personality change" or the book. This exception was made because the article is so relevant to the book that it could have been expressly written for it—it integrates many points made in the book and adds significantly to the dialogue.

We have attempted to create an evolving dialogue for the purposes of: (1) clarifying ongoing controversies between the two approaches, (2) evaluating the strengths and weaknesses of each approach, and (3) demonstrating the potential of syntheses between parts of each approach to develop new and useful integrations. The following is an outline of the evolving dialogue as it develops in the book. Parts I and II describe the present state of humanism and behaviorism and the controversies that have divided them. A comprehensive review of the present status of each approach would have required two volumes, and many fine reviews of each approach already exist. (Good reviews of the behavioristic approach include Ullman and Krasner (1969), Wolpe (1973), Yates (1970), Lazarus (1971), Bandura (1969), Kanfer and Phillips (1970), and Franks and Wilson (1973, 1974). Good reviews of the humanistic approach include Jourard (1974), Maslow (1970), and Bühler and Allen (1973).) Therefore, our intention in Part I is to provide readers who know of one approach exclusively, or have relatively little knowledge of either approach, with a brief description of the contrasting theories, philosophy, and techniques that have divided humanists and behaviorists, and the possible frameworks for combining the two. In Part II, the views of two major figures in humanism and behaviorism, Sidney Jourard and Joseph Wolpe, are presented in a symposium. Jourard and Wolpe describe their views of the person, techniques of therapy, and therapist control. Then questions similar to the ones the reader might want to ask are answered by Jourard and Wolpe. Therapy sessions are presented so that the reader can go beyond the theoretical language of humanism and behaviorism. The viewpoints expressed by Jourard and Wolpe serve as a reference point for many of the articles that follow.

One of the greatest areas of controversy and misunderstanding between humanism and behaviorism concerns their views of the person. This includes the issues of the definition of the self, the person as active vs. passive, and freedom. In order to encourage the dialogue between humanism and behaviorism, we asked a behavioral theorist, Mischel, and a humanistic theorist, Rychlak, authors who are creative rather than extreme in their theoretical positions, to describe their view of the self and to discuss the commonalities and incompatibilities between their views (Part III).

Part IV is an evaluation of the effectiveness of humanistic and behavioristic approaches to personality change. A major conclusion of Lambert and Bergin is that while both approaches have demonstrated limited effectiveness, new approaches are needed. Part V discusses the question of compatibilities between the two approaches and suggests the potential value (Harding) and problems (Alker) in combining parts of them.

Part VI contains articles by practitioners which demonstrate the effectiveness, potential, and problems of synthesizing parts of humanistic and behavioristic approaches in three different types of settings. Goldstein describes the use of appropriate expression training to teach individual clients to make their feelings and behavior more congruent, with a therapy of behavioral origin. Curtiss describes her experience as a consultant in a state mental hospital in which she attempted to "humanize" and increase the effectiveness of a behavioristic token economy program. Gold describes her theory of affective behaviorism and its application to effectively teach children with behavior problems to develop self-control.

Part VII opens the dialogue to several authors who view humanism and behaviorism from broader perspectives. They question the effects (anticipated and unanticipated) of the approaches on the individual and his society and the limitations of each approach in understanding and changing individuals and societies. Ricks and Fleming discuss the values and limitations of humanistic and behavioristic interventions when viewed in terms of the person's life history. Using a sociological perspective, Devereux discussed the societal implications of the two approaches. Alexander, Dreher, and Willems view the two approaches from an ecological perspective and discuss such issues as the delicate balance between systems and consequently the need to intervene with caution. Bandura reviews the whole range of current behavior theory and shows its consequences, not only for individual change, but for public policy.

The last Part (Part VIII), written by Ricks, Wandersman, and Poppen, presents a summary of the issues and discusses the implications of the ideas and research presented in the book. We try to evaluate the conceptual and practical syntheses between humanism and behaviorism and to discuss practical implications for the layman, researcher, and therapist interested in understanding the person, and assessing the effects of therapy and other efforts toward psychological change. Finally, we suggest some possible directions for the future of humanism and behaviorism.

We realize that the book has many limitations; it does not cover all of humanism and behaviorism or all the new developments and relevant psychosocial perspectives. Our aim was to demonstrate the value of a dialogue between humanism and behaviorism. It is our hope that the dialogue will continue to evolve and include areas that we did not include.

Undergraduate students and others interested in clinical psychology, personality, and educational psychology as well as those concerned with understanding ethics, the person, and planning for individual and social change should find this book relevant. It should be useful to graduate students in clinical and personality psychology and to those who intend to do research in and/or practice psychotherapy. The book is also intended for the academician and professional in psychology, philosophy, psychiatry, social work, and counseling. Often the concepts and philosophy of one's teachers tie the professional to one school and create stereotypes of other schools as ineffective, dictatorial, incorrect, etc. Schools change. We believe that the usefulness of openness and dialogue will become apparent. We hope that those who have been exposed to only one approach will gain a working understanding of the other. The possibility of useful change was demonstrated to us by the change in therapeutic approach of a psychiatrist of neo-Freudian bent who attended the Jourard–Wolpe symposium. It was the first time he was exposed to behavior therapy beyond the stereotypes of manipulation, surface behaviors, and elimination of stuttering. He eventually adopted some behavior therapy methods in his psychotherapy. This example also demonstrates that the book should be useful to all who are interested in man and psychological change and not only to humanists and behaviorists.

We owe gratitude to many in completing this book. We believe our first thanks belong to the hard work and creativity of the contributors who made this dialogue possible. Special thanks are owed to Lois Pall Wandersman for her valuable suggestions and comments on many of the articles. Her ability to analyze an article for strengths and weaknesses and for organization were demonstrated repeatedly. We would also like to thank the following colleagues who made valuable suggestions on several of the articles: Henry Alker, Gilda Gold, and William Lambert.

As a final note, we would like to express our feelings about the two contributors, Sidney Jourard and Gilda Gold, who died while the book was in preparation.

Sidney Jourard was a major creative force in the development of a humanistic psychology. His discussions of human feelings, behaviors, and strivings will continue to be important and provocative, and his own very striking personal humaneness gave ever more meaning to the concepts he espoused.

Gilda Gold was a young psychologist whose creative growth was stopped by cancer. In her practice of therapy she effectively integrated her knowledge of psychoanalysis, behavior modification, and humanistic therapy. Her research career was oriented toward the development of a program for children which was a synthesis of humanism and behaviorism. We believe that this exciting synthesis was just a beginning for her. Before her death she told A.W. that she hoped others would continue the work of developing syntheses between humanism and behaviorism. In addition, Gilda Gold was a wonderful friend and a remarkable person.

This book is dedicated to the magnificence of Sidney Jourard and Gilda Gold whose work truly represent a major aim of this book—to help the person better relate to himself and to others.

The Editors

ABRAHAM WANDERSMAN (PhD Cornell University) is research scientist in social ecology and community processes at the John F. Kennedy Center for Research on Education and Human Development and Assistant Professor of Psychology at George Peabody College, Nashville, Tennessee. Dr. Wandersman's major area of interest is social ecology. Specific interests include the effects of participation in planning environments, humanism and behaviorism as theories of the person-environment relationship, adaptation and adjustment of families to newborn children, and exposure and voting behavior.

PAUL J. POPPEN (PhD Cornell University) is Assistant Professor of Psychology and Director, Graduate Program in Social Psychology, The George Washington University, Washington, DC. His major research interests are in the areas of the development of sex differences and moral judgment, and population psychology.

DAVID F. RICKS (PhD University of Chicago) is Professor of Psychology at the City University of New York. His major interest is in psychological development through the life span and the discovery of effective methods for intervention into ungratifying life patterns. Dr. Ricks is co-author of *Mood and Personality* and an editor of *Life History Research in Psychopathology*, Vol. I and Vol. III.

Contributors

JAMES L. ALEXANDER
Department of Psychology
University of Houston
Houston, Texas 77004

HENRY A. ALKER
Department of Psychology
Cornell University
Ithaca, NY 14850

ALBERT BANDURA
Department of Psychology
Stanford University
Stanford, California 94305

ALLEN E. BERGIN
Department of Psychology
Brigham Young University
Provo, Utah

SUSAN CURTISS
Department of Counselor Education
Boston University
Boston, Massachusetts

EDWARD C. DEVEREUX
Department of Human Development
  and Family Studies
Cornell University
Ithaca, NY 14850

GEORGE F. DREHER
Department of Psychology
University of Houston
Houston, Texas 77004

PATRICIA FLEMING
Counseling Center
Queens College
Flushing, NY 11367

GILDA H. GOLD*
c/o Dick Gold
Department of Psychology
University of Massachusetts
Amherst, Mass. 01002

ALAN GOLDSTEIN
Eastern Pennsylvania
  Psychiatric Institute
Henry Avenue
Philadelphia, Pa. 19129

JOHN HARDING
Department of Human Development
  and Family Studies
Cornell University
Ithaca, NY 14850

SIDNEY JOURARD, PhD*
Formerly of Department of Psychology
University of Florida
Gainesville, Florida 32601

MICHAEL J. LAMBERT
Counseling Center
Department of Psychology
Brigham Young University
Provo, Utah 84601

WALTER MISCHEL
Department of Psychology
Stanford University
Stanford, California 94305

PAUL J. POPPEN
Department of Psychology
George Washington University
Washington, DC 20006

DAVID F. RICKS
Psychological Center
City University of New York
New York, NY 10031

* Deceased

JOSEPH F. RYCHLAK
Department of Psychological Sciences
Purdue University
West Lafayette, Indiana 47907

ABRAHAM WANDERSMAN
Center for Community Studies
George Peabody College
Box 319
Nashville, Tennessee 37203

LOIS PALL WANDERSMAN
DARCEE Box 51
George Peabody College
Nashville, Tennessee 37203

EDWIN P. WILLEMS
Department of Psychology
University of Houston
Houston, Texas 77004

JOSEPH WOLPE, MD
Temple University and
Eastern Pennsylvania Psychiatric
   Institute
Henry Avenue
Philadelphia, Pennsylvania 19129

PART I

What are Humanism and Behaviorism and What Can They Say to Each Other?

What Are Humanism and Behaviorism and What Can They Say to Each Other?

PAUL J. POPPEN

Department of Psychology, George Washington University, Washington, DC 20006

AND ABRAHAM WANDERSMAN

Department of Psychology, George Peabody College, Nashville, Tennessee 37203

WITH LOIS PALL WANDERSMAN

DARCEE Box 151, George Peabody College, Nashville, Tennessee 37203

Are humanistic and behavioristic approaches to personality change fundamentally irreconcilable? Or, are they merely complementary theories and styles of specialized therapeutic treatment? The question of the relationship between humanism and behaviorism is widely debated in personality psychology and psychotherapy. This introductory article is intended to sensitize the reader to the humanistic and behavioristic positions so that he can more fully understand and better evaluate this possible controversy between them. Most importantly, we are concerned about the comparability, compatibility, and future relationships between the approaches.

What is the humanistic approach and what is the behavioristic approach? In the first section of this article we discuss some of the major features and defining characteristics of the approaches. We hope to show the complexity and scope of each approach. This section is a selective review of humanistic and behavioristic approaches as related to the important topics of personality and personality change, mental illness, and techniques of therapy. We will argue that it is difficult to summarize the positions because of their breadth and diversity. Thus, we choose to speak about the positions of several major representatives for each approach.

What are some of the major current views about the relationships of humanistic and behavioristic approaches? The second section contains seven

3

commonly held views which we term "characterizations". We use this term to reflect our belief that these views *may* be based more on stereotyped impressions of the approaches than on careful analysis. Nonetheless, we do wish to set the stage for the debate.

Are the approaches really irreconcilable? The third section deals directly with the issue of compatibility of the approaches. We discuss several types of compatibility and incompatibility. Subsequent articles in this volume will be addressed directly or indirectly to the same question.

I. HUMANISTIC AND BEHAVIORISTIC APPROACHES

We deliberately chose the term "approaches" to describe the humanistic and behavioristic positions because the generality of this term allows us initially to be quite open about the character of humanistic and behavioristic psychology. Each approach includes theories formulated to guide and to explain personality change as well as techniques of affecting change that have been related to the theory. Each also has implicit or explicit views on certain philosophical matters, such as what constitutes human nature, towards what ends personality change should be directed, and what kinds of explanation constitute a sufficient explanation of behavior.

Currently there is no one type of behaviorism that represents the behavioristic approach. There are a wide variety of theories, assumptions, and techniques. Some behaviorists examine animal behavior in highly controlled environments while others work as human counselors and therapists. We will be most interested in behaviorism as applied to human behavior, although many of the principles derived from animal study may be relevant. Behaviorism is commonly associated with the study of learning in psychology. The behavioristic approach presents several different views on the principles that best account for the learning of behavior. Behavior therapy is an attempt to devise techniques to alter behavior based on any or several of these principles of learning.

Is there anything in common to all the behavioristic positions? Perhaps what characterizes all behaviorists is their use of experimental evidence in systematic factual inquiry. There is concern for objectivity, replication of results, and the use of a rigorous scientific method (Child, 1973). Additionally, there is a common focus on the environment as contrasted with inner causes or states as an important determinant of human action (Thoresen, 1973). Some behavior therapists note (e.g., Krasner, 1971a; Lazarus, 1971; Wolpe, 1969) that behavior therapy is actually a combination of empirically derived objective techniques and elements of social influence such as expectancies and trust.

Similarly, there is no one type of humanism[1] that represents the humanistic approach. The humanistic approach has been influenced by a wide variety of philosophical and religious thought and only in the past few decades has made efforts to become a humanistic psychology. What is clearly common to all humanistic thought is an insistence on a human model for a human psychology which is distinct from models which account for animal or mechanical behavior (Child, 1973). Humanists study man as a conscious agent with feelings, ideals, and intentions, and believe that these factors are crucial to the understanding of behavior. Such a view of human beings has led to a concern with human growth, personal fulfillment, and self-actualization. Humanistic therapy is an effort to fulfill the individual's potential by exploring the behavioral characteristics and emotional dynamics that can lead to personal development.

There have been clear differences of emphasis between humanistic and behavioristic approaches. The next sections examine the approaches in more detail. We wish to compare humanistic and behavioristic approaches with regard to their development as schools of psychology and as therapeutic techniques, and their views on selected aspects of personality and personality change. Neither approach has a single definitive position and spokesman. Rather, each approach has a variety of views on these issues. We will present the central thrust of each approach and some of the variations within each. In these comparisons, psychoanalytic theory and concepts occasionally serve as a background for discussion, since a major impetus to the development of behavior therapy was a belief in the ineffectiveness of psychoanalysis and a major impetus to the development of humanistic psychology was the reaction against the philosophy and techniques of both behavior therapy *and* psychoanalysis.

---

[1] Humanism is often confused with humanitarianism. Humanitarianism refers to a concern for the interests of mankind, for instance, in solving human problems and relieving suffering. In this way both behaviorism and humanism can be humanitarian, and in most instances are. But there is nothing about the two positions which logically requires a behaviorist or a humanist to be humanitarian. Humanism refers to a focus on distinctively human interests, but this focus need not be humanitarian. This distinction is important because a number of claims for combination of behaviorism and humanism are in actuality combinations of behaviorism and humanitarianism.

Personality and Personality Change

It is crucial to understand the views of personality held by the behavioristic and humanistic approaches, since they strongly influence how each approach views illness and the development and administration of treatment techniques. These latter issues will be discussed in later sections.

An ideal-type continuum[2] will be used in this section and several other sections in the introduction to help explicate the humanistic and behavioristic positions. In comparing the behavioristic and humanistic approaches to personality, the ideal-type continuum of personality consists, at one extreme, of a radical behaviorist ideal-type which concentrates on external and behavioral factors and avoids internal constructs; at the other extreme is the humanistic ideal-type which concentrates on internal, subjective, and experiential dynamics.

The Behaviorist Approach.   Many behavior therapists eschew internalized constructs such as motives and needs, and as the name implies, concentrate on the behavior itself. Their view of personality is based on models of learning and behavior influence. For example, Wolpe defines personality as the person's totality of habits or learned S–R bonds. Most behavior therapists take the position that the behavior indicates the real person and all we can really know about a person is his behavior in the context of the situation.

Taking the behavioral viewpoint, Krasner and Ullman (1973) and Mischel (1968, and in this volume) feel that it is unproductive to talk about general personality traits, such as dominance, dependence, and competence. The correlation, and therefore prediction, between behaviors relevant to traits across situations is very low, averaging 0.30. Behaviorists prefer to discuss specific behaviors in specific situations such as dominance with peers in play,

---

[2] An ideal-type may be defined as the pure state of a concept and is rarely approached in reality. Ideal-types are generally used to describe dichotomous variables, e.g., folk and urban societies. A continuum is defined as a continuous extent or series. The concepts of ideal-type and continuum are generally used separately. We think that the combination of ideal-type and continuum is useful here because it indicates that, although several representatives of each approach have taken the extreme (ideal-type) position, a dichotomy would be unfair to those members of each approach who are beginning to integrate humanistic and behavioristic concepts.

with leaders at work, with parents at home, and so forth, rather than to discuss generalized traits.

Although behavior therapists share a common focus on behavior when they discuss personality, some differences exist between behavior therapists in their emphasis on how behaviors are learned and maintained.

Skinner's radical behaviorist views on personality (1953, 1971) typify the ideal-type position that focuses on external contingencies of behavior and eschews internal constructs. Skinner and most behavior therapists involved with the operant conditioning paradigm view genetic and cultural influences and the near environment as shaping forces of the individual. According to Evans (1968) ". . . in Skinner's experimental analysis of behavior he has integrated all these three conceptualizations into a purely empirical system, in which generic bases of behavior vis a vis *biological, social or self-determinism* are less important than arranging contingencies of reinforcement in the organism's immediate environment so that the probability of a given response is heightened" (p. 129, italics added). In the Skinnerian orientation, the culture through parents, peers, and other socializing agents shapes the individual by reinforcing the behavior it desires and punishing behavior it does not desire, conditioning anxiety reactions to some situations but not to others, teaching norms of acceptable social behavior, shaping the person's standards of art and morality, and so forth. Attention is focused on contingencies of reinforcement rather than individual dynamics of personality. In brief, Skinner prefers to deal with the properties of behavior and avoids mental constructs such as habit, ability, motive, needs, and cognition. He believes that a small number of learning concepts such as reinforcement, extinction, and counterconditioning can account for complex human behavior.

In contrast to the Skinnerians, whose causal analysis of behavior emphasizes external forces, several influential behavior therapists take a social learning view which places greater importance on cognition, imitation, and self-reinforcement. The social learning view can be seen as falling closer to the midpoint in the continuum of control by external contingencies vs. control by a subjective self.

Bandura (1971a) discusses several features of social learning theory which distinguish it from radical behaviorism and traditional learning theory (operant and classical conditioning). First, there is an emphasis on observational learning and modeling as an important basis, along with direct experience, for learning about consequences of behavior and the environment. Second, there is an emphasis on man's cognitive capacity enabling him to solve problems symbolically. Therefore, man can think about the consequences of alternative actions without actually having to perform them. This may be called insightful and foresightful behavior. Third, there is an emphasis on man creating self-regulating influences. Man can manipulate stimuli in order to produce certain consequences, thus allowing people to control their own behavior to a certain degree. Mischel presents part of his cognitive social learning view in more detail later in this volume.

Bandura (1971a) considers the radical behaviorist position as incomplete rather than inaccurate. By avoiding the study of inner causes, the radical behaviorists have neglected the determinants of behavior which are due to man's cognitive functioning. "In the social learning view, man is neither driven by inner forces nor buffeted helplessly by environmental influences. Rather, psychological functioning is best understood in terms of a continuous reciprocal interaction between behavior and its controlling conditions" (Bandura, 1971a, p. 40). The concept of reciprocal interaction between behavior and environment does not allow one to say that the control of behavior is one way, either behavior determining environment or environment determining behavior. Rather, "behavior partly creates the environment and the resultant environment, in turn influences the behavior" (p. 40).

The Humanist Approach.   The humanists typify the other extreme end of the continuum by focusing on internal, subjective, and experiential dynamics. The humanists attempt to investigate human potential rather than to define personality with these characteristics. Their domain of study does include behavior, but the emphasis is on subjective experience. Through the study of experience the humanist focuses on the uniquely human aspects of people such as intentionality and creativity. While the humanistic view of personality is frequently not explicitly defined, personality is implicitly conceived as an internal force which organizes human experience.

Maslow, Jourard, and other members of this humanistic school have pointed to the relationship between the characteristic assumptions of human nature and personality, and the original population of subjects for each of the schools of psychology. Freud studied neurotics, and therefore viewed human personality as inevitably conflictual, with life at best a compromise. Behaviorists studied species that were without the ability to report on introspective experiences, and therefore studied the properties of those species that were available as data, namely, their behavior. Although some behaviorists (e.g., Bandura, Mischel) are now paying some attention to intrapsychic experience and reports (while studying humans, of course), this is a recent change, and an admission of cognitive features into a behavioristic system. Humanists, on the other hand, have focused on human experience as the uniquely human. (See Jourard in this volume for additional discussion on this point.) Rather than studying neurotics, or animals, their subjects have been frequently those who are functioning at the fullest possible level of their potential. Maslow, for instance, spent much of his career studying those he characterized as self-actualizers, those who were pushing towards the actualization or expression of inherent potentialities.

The humanists' study of personality has not been especially concerned with how internalized traits or structures cause people to behave in certain ways. Although they would probably admit a belief that certain personality characteristics are associated with certain behaviors, they are not interested in those behaviors as manifestations of some internal traits.

Mischel's (1968) analysis of the low intercorrelations between measures of the same personality trait, and between traits and behavior, is also taken by humanists as supportive of their position. In the extreme case, these low correlations represent the uniqueness of persons, according to Buhler and Allen (1973), since personality characteristics of people are manifested in different ways. Mischel (1973a) also seems to agree on this point. If supposedly stable traits do not relate consistently to behavior, then perhaps a more individualized approach to the study of persons is warranted, rather than a contrasting of persons with each other. (These are generally referred to as the idiographic and nomothetic methods of study. In an idiographic approach, characteristics of a person are compared with himself, rather than with other people as is done in the nomothetic approach.) Humanists are interested in how a person organizes his own experience and how certain aspects of his personality relate to other aspects.

For many humanists, the self-concept, or how the person sees himself, is a central personality construct. The self-concept is not seen as a static structure of personality, nor as a trait, but rather as an organizing principle of a person's experience. There is much dispute over the nature of the self, and to some (e.g., Allport, 1937) each person has many selves. But in general, the self denotes the organized gestalt of a person's awareness of his perceptions, values, and other aspects of life.

There are other elements that are important in the humanists' study of personality. They all deal with subjective experience, and many of them also relate to a notion of the self. Some of these elements are feelings and personal meanings, intentions, mode of experiencing, congruence between affect and expression, communication, self-actualization and authenticity.

Rather than describing personality traits or the effects of personality, humanists have focused more on the development and change of personality. What factors are responsible for producing optimum growth of human potential? What blocks this growth? These questions reflect the humanistic interest in understanding the process of attaining the highest levels of functioning. Humanists, therefore, are interested in personality as a process of change and development. Humanists do not describe static structures of personality or traits, but rather a process of becoming fully functioning, which has been thwarted in certain particular individuals.

What thwarts personality development? Humanists such as Maslow and Rogers believe that humans are born with an inner nature—comprised of needs, capacities, talents, physiological balances, anatomical equipment— which if allowed growth and expression will develop and continue to grow in productive and healthy ways. This inner nature is certainly not evil and perhaps it is even inherently good, according to the humanists. Thus, these inherent potentialities are set upon a course for expression unless blocked. They may be blocked, altered, or destroyed by environmental factors— culture, family, friends, and so forth. For instance, Rogers speaks of conditional positive regard. Conditional positive regard refers to the selective awarding of approval and disapproval contingent upon the occurrence of desired behaviors. A child thus treated will develop a sense of being worthy *only* if he performs these behaviors which others desire. Unfortunately, what others desire may conflict with one's inner nature. Thus the environment and those important people in a person's life may interfere with the expression of one's inner nature. According to Rogers, unconditional positive regard should be given to the child, providing an environment of approval and respect for what the child is, and allowing for expression of this inner nature.

In short, the environment exerts a major impact on personality development and change. Commonly, humanists have described it more in terms of its detrimental effects than its potential ameliorative effects.

Model of Mental Illness or Abnormal Behavior

The Behavioristic Approach.   The behavioral model of abnormal behavior has grown largely out of dissatisfaction with the "infectious disease" medical model of mental illness. In the "infectious disease" medical model, which was largely developed during the nineteenth century, a person's behavior is considered abnormal or diseased because of an underlying disturbance, which is usually physical. Major concepts of psychoanalytic theory, such as underlying cause and symbolic symptom formation, are derived from the medical notions of a closed system with combinations of forces which attract and repel. Ullmann and Krasner (1969) note several important implications an infectious disease medical model holds for treatment, including: (1) maladaptive behaviors cannot be treated directly because they are the result of an underlying cause; (2) a change in behavior alone is not important since it is merely a symptom or symbol of the " real " problem; (3) the causes of behavior may be hidden from sight, blurring the distinction between the patient's overt behavior and the clinician's expectations or beliefs about what is happening within the patient. All of these imply the need for clinicians to dig deeper.

Mischel (1968, 1973b) discusses several reasons for dissatisfaction with this medical model. Inferences based on hypothesized traits, dynamic forces, or motives have had little predictive power. Skilled clinicians disagree about which particular dynamics, motives, and dispositions characterize a given individual; therefore, there is skepticism about the value of helping the patient get insights into dispositions. Perhaps most important is the relative lack of success of psychotherapy related to this medical model (e.g., Eysenck, 1952). However, this may be a misreading of the data (see Lambert and Bergin, pp. 174–175, in this volume).

Behavior therapists prefer to deal with the behavior itself rather than searching for "underlying" variables which they do not believe exist. Many behavior therapists have adopted a social learning view (e.g., Bandura, Mischel) or sociopsychological view (e.g., Ullmann and Krasner) of abnormal behavior. The sociopsychological view argues that "abnormal behavior is no different from normal behavior in its development, its maintenance, or the manner in which it may eventually be changed. The difference between normal and abnormal behaviors is not intrinsic; it lies rather in the societal reaction to them " (Ullmann and Krasner, 1969, p. 92). In the social learning view, "such terms as mental illness, maladjustment, and abnormality all refer to social judgments about a person's behavior rather than to hypothesized diseases or to traits or states that reside in the person who displays the behavior " (Mischel, 1968, p. 198). Problem behaviors are viewed as responses which have disadvantageous or aversive consequences for others in the society or for the person who exhibits them. Believing that the behavor and its consequences should be the focus of treatment, the behavior therapist, as Mischel notes, avoids social judgments about the client's behavior or speculations about origins and motives of the behavior, and attempts to select reasonable and specific treatment goals. The question in the therapist's mind is what requires change and what is the best way to change it.

Mischel (1968) has distinguished several major categories of problem-producing stimuli which may lead to behavior with disadvantageous consequences. (Actually it appears to be the responses that are problem producing.) These distinctions are useful in classifying types of problems dealt with in behavior therapy. The first category deals with stimuli that are problematic primarily because they evoke disadvantageous emotional reactions in the person. Stimuli may produce aversive reactions, e.g., muscle tension and anxiety, and avoidance in an individual, although these stimuli may be neutral or positive to many other people. Examples are fear reactions to dogs, heights, or common interpersonal situations. In his clinical practice and research, Wolpe has dealt primarily with this type of problem. The concept of anxiety is generally avoided by behavior therapists who follow the operant conditioning approach which avoids cognitive concepts (Skinner, 1971, Krasner, 1971b), and who tend to work with problems in the following categories of stimuli.

In a second category of stimuli the individual's response to particular stimuli is incorrect, inappropriate, or otherwise deficient, but the stimuli do not necessarily evoke a disadvantageous emotional reaction in the individual. Examples of this behavior are the psychopath who shows lack of guilt at societal transgressions or the child who is consistently unresponsive and aggressive in the classroom.

The third category, closely related to the second one, deals with behavioral deficits in the presence of certain stimuli. The person is at a disadvantage because he has never learned the appropriate educational, social, or interpersonal skills for a particular situation. This often results in avoidance of the situation. For example, a boy may refuse to go to dances because he does not know how to talk to girls.

In summary, behavior therapists (e.g., Wolpe, 1973) make the assumption that if an unadaptive habit or behavior can develop through learning, it can be changed through learning. In this view behavior change does not merely remove the "symptom" without curing the "disease" as the medical model asserts. Rather, behavior change removes the problem at its actual sources: behavior. This does not mean that behavior therapists do not recognize the possibility of organic and hereditary factors contributing to problem behavior. They do. Even in these cases some behavior therapists look at the behavior of the individual and attempt to re-educate him by teaching him whatever skills are possible.

The Humanistic Approach. Humanists have also rejected the infectious disease medical model of mental illness. However, they are somewhat less specific than behaviorists regarding which model they suggest to replace it. As a matter of fact, there do not seem to be distinct categories of mental illness for humanists. There is no humanistic diagnostic classification of types of disturbed persons. Rather, humanists seem to envisage a continuum of functioning, with self-actualization at one end, mere adjustment near the midpoint, and unadaptive ways of functioning at the other end.

Self-actualization is a goal rarely reached, but it refers to the actualization of inherent potentialities of one's inner nature. A self-actualizer is one who has true psychological health. He is aware of whom he is and what controls him, but also of what he could become. He is in touch with his inner self. His expression is consistent with his feelings, rather than distorted. He is empathic and compassionate, able to communicate clearly and intimately with others, and in ways that are helpful. Such a person experiences (Jourard, 1964) the possible, and is searching for a more liberated mode of existence. He is responsible for his actions, and acts in accord with his values.

How does one become a self-actualizer or psychologically healthy? As mentioned earlier, this is the natural expression of the self. If the environment is repressive, if it exacts too many rules and expectations, then problems may develop.

Most people are probably more "adjusting" than "actualizing". Such people conform to cultural expectations and values. They fear to express their inner selves. Their existence is dependent upon approval by others. While a person who has merely adjusted could be more healthy and fully functioning, he/she rarely is a client in psychotherapy. However, many of the encounter groups (discussed later) have as members people who are adjusted: those who are not suffering from problems but feel a need to be more open and candid in expression and to be in greater touch with their inner feelings.

Unadaptive ways of functioning represent the opposite actualization. Rogers speaks of the ideal self and the actual self. The ideal self refers to what a person ideally would like to be, while the actual self refers to what a person believes he is. If there is gross discrepancy between the ideal and actual selves, there is maladjustment. A related conception is incongruence between feelings and behavioral expression, reflecting the view that feeling is prepotent and expression should be consistent with it.

Jourard speaks of an impasse in life, a time when old solutions no longer can deal with current problems of meaning. Such a view is more adequate as a description of unadaptive ways than as an explanation for how one becomes unadaptive.

In large part, humanistic therapists have ignored behavior problems, since their focus is on problems of experience. Humanistic therapists, like behavior therapists (other than Wolpe), have largely ignored the diagnostic and classification schema which has a classical psychiatric origin.

Techniques of Therapeutic Treatment

We will briefly describe the major techniques of therapy used by behaviorists and humanists.

BEHAVIOR THERAPY

There are four major kinds of treatment techniques in behavior therapy: operant conditioning, systematic desensitization, modeling, and aversive therapy. In practice, several techniques may be combined. Each of these techniques is assumed by behavior therapists to be derived from a theory of learning and will be briefly defined and described below. (London, 1972, has argued that this belief of derivation from learning theory is more ideology than fact.) In addition, an illustration of each technique will be provided.

Operant conditioning. Operant conditioning techniques generally use systematic positive reinforcement to obtain desired behavior. The paradigm is derived from Skinner's work on operant conditioning and is the most widely researched technique in behavior therapy. The operant model is described in the following example of a child learning to write for his father. If an organism (child) performs a response (writes his name) which is rewarded (praise) the probability that the organism will repeat the behavior increases. If the target behavior is initially too complex for the organism to perform, the organism can be *shaped* by reinforcing approximations to the desired behavior (e.g., first copying one letter at a time, copying name, writing name from memory).

Use of the operant paradigm is widespread. The most popular use of operant techniques is the token economy. In the token economy, groups of people are shown that reinforcement is specifically contingent upon their behaviors. By performing designated behaviors (generally socially desirable behaviors such as brushing one's teeth or paying attention in class) the person receives tokens, with which he can later buy rewards (e.g., candy, books, or privacy). Token economies have been used in many settings such as classrooms, mental hospitals, and day care centers. Recently, the operant conditioning paradigm has been used in more open systems such as the community. For example, several applied behavior analysts are using these techniques in Juniper Gardens, a large, black, urban housing project in the poorest section of Kansas City, with results that include better schooling for the children, new well-run preschool classes, a clean, well-managed recreation center, and a new tenants' association which uses behavioral techniques to solve neighborhood problems (cf. Goodall, 1972).

In therapy, operant conditioning is most often used in treating psychotic and "problem" (acting out) behavior.

Systematic desensitization. The systematic desensitizaton technique substitutes a favorable response to a stimulus (generally relaxation) which is incompatible with the unfavorable response (generally anxiety). Although elements of the technique has been introduced earlier, Wolpe is generally recognized as the developer of this technique for the treatment of neurosis. In desensitization therapy, a list of situations involving the patient's fear is ranked according to the amount of disturbance it produces. This ranking is called a hierarchy. The following illustrates a hierarchy for fear of "rejection" (from Wolpe, 1973, p. 3) (number 1 is the most anxiety provoking, number 8 is the least: that your hierarchy may differ demonstrates the individualization of the technique):

1. My apology for a blunder is not accepted by a friend.
2. My invitation to a friend to my apartment for dinner or drinks is refused.
3. I speak to a peer and he does not seem to hear.
4. A project important to me is criticized by peers.
5. I am left out of plans or not invited.
6. I am spoken to by a peer in a tone of voice sharper than the speaker uses for somebody else present.
7. Nobody remembers my birthday.
8. My greeting to an acquaintance in the street is not returned.

After the patient is taught how to relax, he is told to imagine the least anxiety-provoking item on the hierarchy. Eventually the anxiety response to the item is desensitized by having the patient relax while imagining the situation, then the next item is imagined until the person is able to imagine the strongest item in the hierarchy without any anxiety.

Wolpe discusses this technique in more detail in his paper in this book. Wolpe (1973) notes that what makes systematic desensitization worthwhile is the generalization of change of response from each imaginary situation in the hierarchy to the corresponding actual life situation. If this was not the case, the procedure would be worthless. This technique is occasionally supplemented by other behavioral techniques when necessary, e.g., assertion training. Systematic desensitization may be most appropriate in treating phobias and inhibitions.

Modeling. Bandura (1971b) states that social learning research in modeling and imitation indicates that practically all behavior that is learned through direct experience can be learned vicariously by observing other people's behavior and its consequences for them. Therefore, observation of a model can be used to achieve psychological changes in many areas.

Several major effects of modeling influences are reported by Bandura (1971b), each of which can have important therapeutic consequences:

1. In the *observational learning* effect, new responses can be learned through observation and reproduced later in similar form.
2. *Inhibition* of responses that are already present in the observer's repertoir of behaviors can be strengthened or weakened by observing the consequences of an act to the model.

Modeling may be most appropriate when the problem is due mainly to faulty or deviant behavior: the skills are not well developed (Bandura, 1971b). The technique of modeling in therapy is also suggested by Jourard (in this book) but with a different emphasis.

Aversion therapy. Although Skinner doubts that punishment can be used to achieve long term beneficial effects, several behavior therapists have used punishment to inhibit deviant or unwanted responses. For example, when an aversive stimulus (e.g., nausea-inducing drug) is paired with deviant behavior or thoughts (e.g., a fetish), the deviant behavior becomes unpleasant and is avoided by the patient (Raymond, 1956).

In a form of punishment, used in several token economies, called time-out, the person who behaved badly is put into seclusion for several minutes and several tokens may be taken away (Burchard, 1967).

Aversion therapy may be a preferred method of treatment when the target behavior is enjoyable to the patient, e.g., addictive behavior, such as alcoholism. It may be combined with operant conditioning or modeling to teach more appropriate behaviors which would replace the old ones.

HUMANISTIC THERAPY

Although Maslow proclaimed humanistic psychology as the Third Force in psychology—the other two being psychoanalysis and behaviorism—Maslow himself was not an originator or practitioner of a unique type of humanistic therapy. Many therapy techniques however, have developed in the humanistic school. A number of them are individual therapies, and we discuss some of these below. Also, there are now a considerable number of group "therapies" that are closely or loosely tied to humanistic psychology.

Which individual therapies are humanistic in the way we have been discussing the approach implied by this term? Clearly the therapies of Rogers and Jourard fit the description. After much thought we have decided to omit discussion of proponents of other related therapies, such as Frankl, Ellis, Perls, Schutz, and others. To include all those who merit some consideration as humanists would extend too far the scope of this discussion. Therefore, our focus will be principally upon what we view as the mainstream, nondirective or client-centered therapy.

Rogers' approach to therapy has been variously known as nondirective or client-centered. This therapy encouraged the establishment of a person-to-person relationship of mutual interaction, a relation of two equal persons, rather than a patient-to-therapist relationship of inequality. Early in his career Rogers advocated a nondirective approach in which the therapist would not explicitly advise or exhort the client. More recently, Rogers recommends a more active participation by the therapist, but still refers to the therapist as a "facilitator."

The specific problem or difficulty of a person who seeks help from a Rogerian therapist or counselor covers a wide range of possibilities. However, a Rogerian has a generalized conception of problems within which specific problems can be viewed. This generalized conception reflects the view of the primacy and importance of the inner nature and needs of the organism, that these needs are striving for actualization or expression, *and* that the specific maladjustment of the person results from a clash between these inner needs and the self which has been molded by external forces and pressures. This incongruence between the true nature of the organism and the self is subceived (that is, perceived below a conscious level) and ultimately leads to feelings of being threatened, anxiety, and defensive behavior.

What is necessary, of course, is increasing the congruence between the organismic tendencies and conscious self-strivings. Client-centered therapy is intended to provide an atmosphere where self-directed change can occur and bring about greater congruence. Client-centered therapy is predicated on the assumption that the individual has sufficient capacity to deal constructively with all those aspects of his life which can potentially come into conscious awareness (Rogers, 1961, p. 104). The client can reopen communication between organismic and self-evaluations.

More recently, there has been a greater emphasis by Rogers on the *interaction* between a therapist and client. In this way, Rogers' recent writings deal more with what is the relationship between good therapists and their clients than on the specific techniques therapists should employ. Therapists should express accurate empathy, nonpossessive warmth, and genuineness. These terms are defined by Truax and Mitchell (1971, p. 302):

1. An effective therapist is nonphony, nondefensive, and authentic or *genuine* in his therapeutic encounter.
2. An effective therapist is able to provide a nonthreatening, safe, trusting, or secure atmosphere through his own acceptance, positive regard, love, valuing, or *nonpossessive warmth*, for the client.
3. An effective therapist is able to understand, "be with," grasp the meaning of, or have a high degree of *accurate empathic understanding* of the client on a moment-by-moment basis.

Self-disclosure. In his self-disclosure therapy, Jourard retained the basic Rogerian goals of therapy of promoting psychological health, but differed somewhat from Rogers about the means of doing so. Since Jourard relates his position later in this book, we will mention only some of his emphases, those dealing with self-disclosure and modeling.

Jourard describes a person seeking therapeutic help as suffering from ways of being or living that are no longer "life-giving." The person is in a rut that is very limiting and debilitating. The person has reached an impasse in life.

The therapy that Jourard discusses attempts to reaffirm the patient's potency in determining his own life course, and in altering his ways of being. Jourard sees the role of the therapist as a "guru," as a model, as one who may have experienced a problem similar to a client and can be evidence of the possibility of resolving such problems. Even if the therapist's experience is quite different from the client's experience, the therapist may serve as a useful model. The therapist needs to show how he has coped with and transcended some aspects of "facticity." In short, if the therapist can show how he has coped with these problems, then perhaps the patient will attribute power to himself in his own struggles.

The therapist serves as a model by self-disclosure or by being transparent. The therapist is open to examination or scrutiny by the patient as an example or model of one who has liberated himself from dehumanizing forces. Jourard believes that self-disclosure creates a depth of experience when both therapist and client search for meaning together, and will assist in restructuring problems of experience.

Jourard also focuses on the behavior of the therapist and the therapist's relation to the client, rather than the particular theoretical orientation or technique employed by the therapist. In this way, a behavior therapist could be an exemplary therapist by Jourard's criteria.

Sensitivity and T Groups. In the last few years, there has been a proliferation of group "therapies", closely or loosely tied to humanistic psychology. Rogers has been instrumental in the popularization of these as well. An earlier impetus was the influence of Kurt Lewin. To many followers, these T groups and variants represent the core of "therapeutic" *methods* in humanistic psychology. There are many variations of these groups, however, both in terms of goals and methods. Some groups are intended to train participants in becoming sensitive to others' feelings and the impact of one's self on others, while other groups emphasize therapy. Regardless of the emphasis, these groups deal directly with techniques of fostering personality change.

These techniques are predicated on or related to many humanistic assumptions. These assumptions include the view that the locus of power for change is within the person, and the goal of congruence between expression and feeling. (The reader is referred to Gibb, in Bergin and Garfield (1971) for an excellent and more detailed discussion of these groups.)

These groups in many cases did not explicitly develop from principles of humanistic psychology. Humanistic therapists have recommended caution with regard to participation for certain persons. Humanists have been excited by the possibilities of these groups because of their emphasis on the basic encounter of persons in building relationships, sensitivities, and understanding of others and self.

II. CHARACTERIZATIONS

To highlight the behaviorist–humanist controversy in broader perspective, this section provides common characterizations of the theoretical, empirical, practical, and ethical differences between the approaches. Some of the characterizations may subsequently be exposed as myths, and many will be declared stereotypes of the positions rather than accurate descriptions.

We will begin by discussing these common reactions to and understandings of the two positions. As the articles in this book provide further discussion and evidence, the reader will be able to evaluate the veridicality and usefulness of these characterizations. The characterizations to be discussed are: (1) scientific vs. intuitive; (2) means vs. ends; (3) external behavior vs. internal emotion; (4) behavior change vs. insight; (5) manipulation vs. humanization; (6) active vs. passive therapist; and (7) direct vs. indirect control. The behaviorist position is listed on the left side and the humanist on the right side for each characterization. The characterizations are closely interrelated. Additional ones could have been added, but only some of the most pervasive ones have been included.

Scientific vs. Intuitive

Techniques of behavior therapy have some basis in laboratory research on learning theory (and social influence). To the behaviorists, humanistic techniques are derived from clinical experience "in which the observed data and the treatment given may be confounded and in which the therapist formulates his experiences as he treats" (Ullmann and Krasner, 1969, p. 246). Actually, there are differences among behavior therapists in the value they place on scientific rigor in treatment. Lazarus (1971) and Wolpe (1969) feel that the therapist should be flexible in treatment. While Lazarus goes so far as to advocate a form of eclecticism of tested and untested techniques, Wolpe (1969) argues that "the scientifically minded behavior therapist need not confine himself to methods derived from principles. For the welfare of his patients he employs, whenever necessary, methods that have been empirically shown to be effective" (p. vii).

Eysenck and Beech (1971) are behavior therapists who oppose this point of view and take the behaviorist ideal-type position (p. 602).

"We deplore this [eclectic] attitude in behavior therapists as we deplore it in psychotherapists; we believe that it results in a gigantic mishmash of theories, methods, and outcomes that is forever beyond the capacity of scientific research to resolve. Theoretical differences should be recognized and their practical and applied consequences differentiated as clearly as possible; only in this way can the good and bad points of each theory be disentangled."

To those with a "scientific" bent of mind, humanism occasionally seems quite vague and hence nonscientific and intuitive. About many particulars regarding theories of personality change or suggested modes of treatment, humanists' positions cannot be neatly organized within the behaviorists' tight scientific frameworks. Actually humanists do not seem themselves as less scientific than behaviorists. Rather, they see humanism as relying upon a different conception of science in which intuition, subjective experience, and active participation are more important methods of understanding than are experimentation and objectification. Rychlak (in this book, and 1968) argues that humanists employ a different mode of explanation than the physical science notion of cause–effect used by the behaviorists. Most psychologists are less accustomed to and comfortable with the humanistic mode of explanation and hence it appears nonscientific. Behaviorists appear much more precise in the use of terms, and employ a rigorous emphasis on empirical testing of organized theoretical assertions. In these ways, humanists rely more on intuition than behaviorists, but are not necessarily less scientific.

Means vs. Ends

It is often held that behaviorists emphasize the development of *means* of changing behavior and humanists emphasize the *ends* toward which change should be directed. For instance, behaviorists have developed a variety of therapeutic means for behavior change (e.g., systematic desensitization therapy, token economy, etc.) from principles of learning such as modeling, reinforcement, and others. But to what ends should these means be employed? Presumably for anything, although in fact most behaviorists personally are humanitarian and dedicated to the alleviation of human suffering. Behaviorists often argue that they use behavioral means for the ends desired by the patient, although sometimes behaviorists work for various institutional ends. The behaviorist position is one of developing (and understanding) means of changing behavior and not formulating the ends to which these techniques might be used.

Humanists, on the other hand, believe that specification of ends should precede the development of modes of treatment. Thus, humanists talk about self-responsibility, self-determination, congruence between internalized feelings and external expression, and compassion as ends to be pursued. Only after these initial values are chosen should techniques that will not contradict the value be discussed.

A belief in some form of this means–ends distinction is embodied in suggestions that humanism and behaviorism can be synthesized by combining behavioristic techniques with humanistic philosophy.

The extreme version of this characterization is that behaviorism is a science and that humanism is a social philosophy, or even religion. Behaviorists go about the business of science, working in laboratories, testing hypotheses in experiments, building theories, and developing means of behavior change. Humanists are less interested in these scientific activities but rather are engaged in discussion of social conditions and of how mankind *should* be treated in order to maximize human potential. An intermediate version of this characterization holds that behaviorists have developed (and are developing) techniques which can deal with behavior and personal problems, while humanists describe the ends to which those means (or some means) should be utilized.

But we must question if this is an accurate characterization. Are there any humanistic means or techniques for therapy or for inducing personality change? A common belief in this regard is that there *are* humanistic techniques, but they are less effective techniques (see the later sections on the manipulations vs. humanization characterization, and the Lambert and Bergin and the Harding articles in this book), and hence the usefulness of humanism (if any) is in its philosophy and ethical statement.

The means–ends controversy is further complicated in the debate between leading exponents of the behaviorist and humanist positions, Skinner and Rogers (see, e.g., 1956). To Rogers, the Skinnerian error is the specification and priority of means and ends. According to Rogers, the values or ends to which this technology will be used are not specifiable within the science of human behavior. Rogers and the humanists demand that the determination of value be prior in choice to the means. And, this determination must not be rigid. We must not choose static attributes, like honesty, but a changing process such as growth. Rogers describes these processes as open processes of "becoming," of developing human potential. After this admittedly subjective value choice, the question becomes what means can be invented to obtain or foster the desired processes? Rogers' answer, of course, includes his type of therapy as an example. In addition, the choice of ends requires that certain techniques of control *not* be employed, even if effective, since they would violate the freedom of humans.

External Behavior vs. Internal Emotion

This characterization holds that each position *is* a psychology, and possesses or implies a certain set of values, but that the two approaches are directed toward different kinds of problems. Behaviorists deal with *external behavior* problems, and humanists deal with *internal emotional* problems. Behavior therapy is useful in resolving certain problems, in particular behavior problems such as smoking, overeating, aggressiveness (i.e., it is useful in changing clearly identifiable and observable behaviors). Humanistic therapy is useful in resolving a different set of problems, such as problems of personal identity and meaning in life (i.e., it is useful in attempts to forward and give direction to one's life).

This characterization clearly implies the positions are *not* incompatible: they simply deal with different problems. Because of the basic trend of research undertaken by each approach—behaviorists into behavior problems, humanists into problems of life's meaning—the question could be alternatively asked: How would a humanist treat a schizophrenic? or How would a behaviorist treat an identity crisis?

While this characterization has intuitive appeal, it has its problems also. First, several humanists (e.g., Rogers, 1967) *are* attempting to deal with schizophrenics and several behaviorists *are* attempting to deal with identity crises (e.g., Krumboltz and Thoresen, 1969). Second, these descriptions of each domain can be reconceptualized into a different domain, as both humanists and behaviorists have occasionally done. Is a snake phobia a behavior problem or is it an internalized fear? Is an identity crisis an internalized problem, or a set of behaviors with associated affect?

This characterization is a popular one. It forces us to ask what elements of commonality there are in the domains of interest and in the domains of therapy, or to what extent they are arguing at cross-purposes.

Behavior Change vs. Insight

One major criticism made against behavior therapy is that it deals only with surface symptoms (overt behavior) and does not deal with the underlying causes (e.g., motives, intrapsychic dispositions) of behavior. This was discussed in the section on personality. Psychoanalysts, in particular, propose that if you remove a symptom (treat a behavior) without dealing with the underlying cause, symptom substitution will result—since you have removed only the symptom, another symptom will take its place. Behavior therapists have several answers to this charge. First, since behavior is often the problem, behavior is what should be treated. Several studies, e.g., Lazarus (1971), Wolpe (1969), have followed up patients treated by behavior therapy and have found that symptom substitution, if such a phenomenon exists, occurs in a maximum of 5% of the cases and these cases can often be explained in other terms. Second, to argue that behavior therapy is the removal of a specific symptom is a misconception, according to Ullmann and Krasner (1969). Rather, "behavior therapy replaces the maladaptive response with a socially more appropriate response. The former behavior is not removed—it is replaced" (p. 252).

Humanists are more concerned with achieving awareness or insight into the nature of a person's problems. There is also a realization among humanists that insight might not be effective in removing a problem. Nevertheless, insight may allow the person to cope with a problem in more effective ways. In fact, to some humanists, problems and distress are much of the basic stuff of life. To remove them completely would be absurd, *not* because other symptoms would appear, but because the problems may be instrumental in producing more effective modes of living and without problems, an essential part of life is being denied.

On the whole, however, humanists are willing to admit the change of behavior as an acceptable goal of therapy in certain instances. However, humanists certainly do not rely on that type of change as the only acceptable change, and in fact, believe that awareness or insight is usually the more appropriate goal.

Manipulation vs. Humanization

This characterization holds that behaviorists manipulate people (occasionally against their will) and that humanists attempt to sensitize people to their uniquely human characteristics and possibilities. Such a characterization attracts many students to humanism and repels them from behaviorism. That college students react in such a manner may be related to values to which they subscribe and the particular cultural context in which they live, or to the fact that many of the personal problems of college students are interpreted by themselves as being humanistic in the sense of relating and meaning in life. At another time, behaviorism might be seen as an effective technology and humanism as a therapeutic pretender.

The behaviorist Skinner sees the manipulation–humanization characterization as a way many people respond to behaviorism and humanism (Skinner, 1972). He believes that the philosophy of humanistic psychology is ultimately selfish—people are seeking their own, rather than societal fulfillment—and that such a philosophy perpetuates the myth of personal control and responsibility at the expense of initiating useful environmental controls that will solve the problems facing individuals and cultures. Behaviorists are frequently accused of being manipulative and cold-hearted because of their relative emphasis on techniques of change rather than values. But while many behaviorists believe values reside out of the scientific domain, the values many of them subscribe to reflect a concerted concern for the human condition. For Skinner, behaviorism *is* humanism (by which he means humanitarianism) and it has the advantage of being effective humanism. That is, behaviorists have the means to change behavior *and* in an humanitarian way, whereas humanists are merely discussing ends. Thus, Skinner recasts the humanization–manipulation characterization into a means–ends characterization.

The issue is important. Reaction to the humanistic and behavioristic therapies along value dimensions like those described here may determine adoption and usage of the various techniques more than "success" rates and indices of the effectiveness of the positions.

Active vs. Passive Therapist

Wolpe (1969) states that "the most distinctive feature of behavior therapy is the command it gives to the therapist both in planning the general strategy and controlling its details as it goes along" (p. 12). Rather than having the therapist passively hope for something constructive or "growth," he can use active techniques.

In Krasner's view (1971b) the nature, role, and function of the therapist has changed, especially for therapists using the operant paradigm.

"It has shifted from an individual in the social role of a healer, therapist, physician, psychiatrist, or psychologist to that of a natural member of the environment—a nurse, aide, teacher, parent, peer, or research experimenter. The latter individual is now behaving 'therapeutically' (with intent to change behaviors in a socially desired direction) towards the target individual" [p. 645].

The behavior takes place in natural settings rather than the therapist's office.

A humanistic therapist can be more adequately characterized as a passive catalyst. While Jourard believes that a therapist should be a model for a client, a therapist should be more concerned about maintaining certain styles of interaction than with explicitly providing advice or direction to the client. Implicit in this view is that a significant source of change is within the client himself, and this fact can be realized through relationships with the therapist.

Direct vs. Indirect Control

Another major criticism raised against behavior therapy is the issue of therapist control of behavior. Since behavior therapy seems to be so effective, it makes salient the ethical problems of whether the therapist should deliberately control or manipulate the behavior of the patient.

Skinner (see Rogers and Skinner, 1956) and Ullmann and Krasner (1969) and many other behavior therapists propose that all therapists control through the use of social influence. Patient behaviors or disclosures which confirm a psychotherapist's theory are often rewarded by increased interest and perhaps verbal reinforcement. Ullmann and Krasner cite several studies investigating various forms of therapy which show that "improved" or "successful" patients change their personality attributes or values in the direction of their therapist's theories or values. According to Ellis even the nondirective therapist takes a role because he thinks it will be effective in influencing the patient. "The real question is not whether the therapist is authoritarian and controlling but in what manner he exerts his authority and control" (Ellis, in Ullmann and Krasner, 1969, p. 252). Finally, even if the therapist tries to speak and act as if he is not an authority, the patient usually considers him one. Thus, behavior therapists argue that all therapists control, but in behavior therapy control is explicit and admitted while other therapists fail to acknowledge their control.

Humanists could respond that control is a complex concept, as Rychlak (1968) does, and that there are differences in types of control. Rychlak argues that there are three uses of the word control, two of which are directly relevant to this discussion. One definition of control is synonymous with "to have an effect on", e.g., positive reinforcement, persuasion. A second use of control is as a deliberate means of social influence. To control in this sense is to plan deliberately a set of procedures designed to have certain effects upon a person, often without his foreknowledge. Humanists believe that the form of control they exhibit is the former type of having an effect on—providing the client with a situation in which complete openness and awareness exist between client and therapist. Humanists also believe that behavior therapists exhibit the second type of control, in which techniques are applied to a compliant patient, thereby reducing the patient's dignity. Several behavior therapists reply with a medical analogy (e.g., Wolpe, 1969) that the amount of patient acquiescence is the same as in any other branch of medicine and the therapist uses the most effective techniques at his disposal to relieve the suffering of the patient.

It is interesting to note a relatively recent development in behavior therapy, in which several behavior therapists such as Meichenbaum and Cameron (1974), Gold (1973, also in this book), Thoresen and Mahoney (1974), and Kanfer and Karoly (1972), work with the patient to bring behavior under self-reinforcement. (Gold describes this procedure and the issue of locus of change in this book.) According to Bandura (1971b), ". . . in a comprehensive treatment program, after behavior has been brought under external reinforcement control, efforts should be made to establish self-reinforcing systems so that a person's actions become increasingly governed by the intrinsic and self-evaluative consequences they engender" (p. 703). This procedure does not completely solve the controversy of the ethics of control, since the therapist guides the patient in what to control and how to control it by first bringing it under external reinforcement control. The issue of ethics of control is a point of bitter argument, as is illustrated in the Jourard and Wolpe discussions that follow this article.

III. ARE HUMANISM AND BEHAVIORISM COMPATIBLE?

We will conclude this article by examining briefly various views on the present and eventual compatibility of the humanistic and behavioristic approaches. Yates (1970) has described four of these positions and we add two additional positions. The positions are:

1. Humanism and behaviorism are utterly irreconcilable.
2. Humanism and behaviorism are complementary.
3. Humanism and behaviorism are reconcilable, and humanism can be "reduced" to behaviorism.
4. Humanism and behaviorism are reconcilable, and behaviorism can be "reduced" to humanism.

5. Humanism and behaviorism are reconcilable by a fundamental and new synthesis of the positions.
6. Humanism and behaviorism must be viewed from a broader perspective, and from this view, a variety of syntheses are possible.

Position one: Humanism and behaviorism are utterly irreconcilable. There have been a variety of reviews from both the humanistic perspective (e.g., Barrett-Lennard, 1965; Murray, 1963) and the behavioristic perspective (e.g., Eysenck, 1959) which present the view of irreconcilable fundamental differences between the approaches in philosophy, technique, and theory. For proponents of this position, the humanistic and behavioristic approaches can each be seen as paradigms of personality change. The two approaches are addressed to largely the same set of issues, with similar domains, but the theories of both positions cannot be correct. Eventually, by scientific or nonscientific criteria, one paradigm must be discarded. This confrontation of positions is known as the paradigm clash.

The paradigm clash notion is the extreme version of this position. A more moderate position holds that the theories are utterly irreconcilable, but only at a few points, and crucial experiments will be done to determine the validity of the respective claims at those points. For example, behaviorists and psychoanalytic psychologists have argued about the issue of symptom substitution. Behaviorists have treated patients with behavior problems (e.g., "symptoms" such as enuresis) by unlearning the behavior or by rewarding alternative behavior incompatible with the symptom. Psychoanalysts have claimed that treating the symptom by such techniques leaves the underlying intrapsychic cause untouched, and hence other symptoms are apt to appear (Yates, 1958; Bookbinder, 1962; Cahoon, 1968). Behaviorists and psychoanalysts have claimed that the resolution of this issue will determine the adequacy of the respective formulations of treatment of behavior problems, although it will not determine the validity of the position with respect to other issues. Alker in this book presents a more detailed discussion of the paradigm clash issue.

Position two: Humanism and behaviorism are complementary. This position holds that, taken together, the approaches provide a rather comprehensive guide to theory and technique in psychotherapy. Those advocating this position usually cite the behaviorists' general focus on behavior problems (behavior deficits or inappropriate behavior) and humanists' focus on more philosophical problems such as how to deal with life's absurdities, lack of meaning, and depression. Thus, one school might productively apply to a certain set of problems while the other applies to another set. In fact, many clinical and counseling centers have a combination of humanists and behaviorists on their staff for this division of labor. Some therapists use a behavioristic or humanistic technique depending on the nature of the problem. It is commonly believed that certain types of problems are more amenable to some type of therapy than others, although there has not been much systematic research on this point.

In this book, Harding discusses compatibility based on this complementarity notion at length.

Position three: Humanism and behaviorism are reconcilable, and humanism can be "reduced" to behaviorism. This position holds that the two schools are reconcilable, and in fact, humanistic therapy can be reduced to behavior therapy. That is, the success that humanists enjoy, however meager, is in fact due to the unintentional application of principles derivable from the behaviorist position, rather than to the humanist position. If only these techniques were more commonly and systematically employed, success rates would be higher and less accidental.

Within this book, Harding discusses Rogerian therapy as rather systematically employing reinforcement contingencies and interprets therapeutic success as due to this application of learning techniques. Rogerians, of course, were not *intentionally* employing these principles in this manner, nor would they interpret their behaviors as demonstrating the principles of learning theory.

Position four: Humanism and behaviorism are reconcilable, and behaviorism can be "reduced" to humanism. This position is similar to the third, and holds that behavioristic therapy can be reduced to humanistic principles. Whatever success therapists have is actually attributable to humanistic principles.

Humanists such as Rogers and Jourard have maintained that the interpersonal relationship between therapist and client is crucial in producing therapeutic change. Jourard, in fact, believes Wolpe is an excellent therapist not because of the techniques Wolpe employs but because of the "fine man he is" and the rapport he develops with his patients.

Also within this volume Lambert and Bergin discuss "therapist variables" which, if systematically related to therapeutic outcome, would provide substantial support for the humanistic position.

Position five: Humanism and behaviorism are reconcilable by a fundamental and new synthesis of the positions. This position holds that the approaches will add to each other with a resulting new approach utilizing virtues of both behaviorism and humanism. For instance, in this book Gold describes one synthesis of the two approaches in the development of a program for children. Curtiss describes another form of synthesis in a mental hospital program. Thoresen (1973) and Mahoney (1974) see their approaches as a kind of synthesis. However, in their discussion of "behavioral humanism" (Thorsen and Mahoney, 1974) the particular type of synthesis seems to be an acceptance of cognitive variables into a behavioral framework. Humanists would certainly argue that their position contains more than a set of cognitive variables. The Thoresen and Mahoney positions are in many ways similar to some recent writings of Mischel and Bandura.

We are interested in the possibility of a fundamental synthesis. In this type of synthesis, major parts of the two approaches would be combined to form a new approach rather than simply picking a small number of elements from one approach and adding it to the basically intact other approach.

Position six: Humanism and behaviorism must be viewed from a broader perspective, and from this view, a variety of syntheses are possible. This position suggests that the most fruitful way to view humanism and behaviorism may be from a vantage point outside of either approach. Adopting this external perspective may suggest types of relationships and syntheses less apparent from simply the joint comparison of the two approaches.

This point will be elaborated at various stages of this book, especially in Part VII. Ricks and Fleming present a life history view; Devereux provides a sociological perspective; Alexander, Dreher, and Willems present an ecological approach; and Bandura provides a new social learning perspective. Each of these perspectives provides a different picture of humanism and behaviorism and types of compatibility.

Which of these six positions is the most viable? At this point, rather than attempting to resolve this controversy, we would like to temporarily leave it as an issue for the following papers. As additional facts are established and claims are made throughout this issue, what do they imply for the overall relationship of the two schools of thought and their theories? Is integration at certain points possible? The reader is encouraged to evaluate critically each approach in terms of the characterizations presented earlier and to ponder areas of compatibility which may benefit from integration and areas of incompatibility which may need to be dealt with by procedures of paradigm clash or value judgments.

PART II

II.A. A Symposium—Humanistic and Behavioristic Approaches to Personality Change

II.B. Therapy Sessions Led by Sidney Jourard and Joseph Wolpe

INTRODUCTION

II.A. A SYMPOSIUM—HUMANISTIC AND BEHAVIORISTIC APPROACHES TO PERSONALITY CHANGE

Part II.A presents the transcript of a two day symposium held at Cornell University. Sidney Jourard describes his approach in "Changing personal worlds: a humanistic perspective," and Joseph Wolpe describes his approach in "Behavior therapy: a humanitarian enterprise." Question and answer periods follow each talk. The symposium concludes in a discussion period with Jourard and Wolpe moderated by Harry Levin, chairman of the Department of Psychology at Cornell at the time.

The reader will note how issues discussed in Part I (e.g., direct vs. indirect control, external behavior vs. internal emotion) are raised and discussed throughout Part II. We will highlight several of the major issues that will be discussed.

What is to be changed? To Jourard personality change involves changing the ways one experiences and acts in the world, disengagement from the present ways, and re-entry into a freer, less restricting path. Wolpe discusses personality change in terms of stimulus–response relationships and the unlearning of maladaptive habits.

How is change to occur? Jourard explores the controversial possibilities of recognizing the psychotherapist as a model of how to transcend an aspect of "reality" which has blocked others—this involves liberating oneself from dehumanizing forces in society to lead a life one has chosen independent of others. Jourard focuses on the personal qualities of the therapist and the relationship between the patient and the client. Wolpe discusses the methods used by the behavior therapist. The diagnostic role of the therapist and the behavior therapy techniques used to treat neurotic behavior (such as systematic desensitization and assertion training) are described.

Closely related to the last question is what is the model of human nature each uses. Jourard presents a model that is based uniquely on human life rather than on monkeys or pigeons. He portrays the person as trying for freedom from environmental forces. This view of the relationship between the person and the environment is challenged by several authors in later articles (e.g., Ricks and Fleming; Devereux; Alexander, Dreher, and Willems). Wolpe discusses behavior in terms of the principles of learning theory, which may be common across species. He is less specific than Jourard about his model of human personality. Many of the audience's and Jourard's questions to Wolpe are addressed to this issue.

What is the role of empirical evidence in therapy? To Wolpe therapy results determine the type of therapy to use. He argues that all therapies except behavior therapy share a common rate of helping people and that this is probably not due to the techniques they use, but rather to common non-specific processes they share. Behavior therapy techniques add significantly to this common rate. This view raises many questions from Jourard and the audience. Jourard acknowledges a role for results but gives demonstrated results a lower priority.

II.B. THERAPY SESSIONS LED BY
SIDNEY JOURARD AND JOSEPH WOLPE

The therapy sessions are included to demonstrate the style and content of therapy sessions conducted from humanistic and from behavioristic perspectives. Not every humanist or every behaviorist would handle a session like Jourard or Wolpe, but the sessions may be considered representative of the type of approach a humanist or behaviorist might take. It may be valuable for the reader to contrast the style of the two therapists and evaluate the therapy sessions in light of some of the characterizations discussed in Part I. For example, to what degree is control direct vs. indirect for Wolpe and Jourard? To what degree does the accusation of manipulation fit Wolpe? Questions such as these regarding the characterizations of behavior change vs. insight, manipulation vs. humanization, active vs. passive therapist, direct vs. indirect control, scientific vs. intuitive should give the reader a greater understanding of the techniques and values discussed by Wolpe and Jourard in the symposium. Several comments by the editors regarding the therapy sessions and their correspondence to ideas expressed in the symposium follow the therapy transcripts.

Changing Personal Worlds:
A Humanistic Perspective[1]

SIDNEY JOURARD

Formerly of Department of Psychology, University of Florida
Gainesville, Florida 32601

Everything depends on what you believe man is like.[2] If you assume that man is something like a machine, that assumption is, in a way, not an assumption alone. It is sort of an invitation and a prescription to man to be in the world in ways that mimic a machine. Man seems to me to be a very peculiar creature: he can conform himself to all kinds of images, because he doesn't have any rigidly fixed nature or design to determine how he will be in the world, how he will act, and how the world will be for him. Now, if you assume that man is a being like a monkey or a pigeon, then that too is a kind of invitation that a person may accept.

I have been exploring with as much vigor and ingenuity as I know how the implications for living, for doing psychological research, and for applied psychology when I assume that man is *human*, and hence more like me than a machine, monkey, or pigeon.[3] One implication of this assumption is that, as I

---

[1] A version of this paper was presented at a Cornell University symposium on "Humanistic and Behavioristic Approaches to Personality Change," May 1972.

[2] It seems to be the case that we seek to understand the unknown by comparing it with aspects of the known world which it resembles. Psychologists since Wundt have compared aspects of man with chemical compounds, animals, machines, hydraulic systems, etc. I am proposing that we explore the resemblance between a person's experience of himself, which he knows directly, and other aspects of the world. In short, I am exploring a new kind of anthropomorphism.

[3] Several months after this talk was given, I obtained a copy of a recent book in which "an anthropomorphic model" of man is explored as a basis for explaining man's social behavior. See Harre and Secord (1972). This sophisticated essay in the philosophy of science made me see more clearly that the use of myself as a conceptual model guided my conception of psychology as I wrote it, especially in my book *Disclosing Man to Himself* (van Nostrand Reinhold, 1968).

learn something about myself, I will have learned a certain amount about you. When I assume that you are a being something like me, this will influence the way I interact with you when you are my friend, a member of my family, my student, my research subject, or when you're my patient. I'll probably address you truly in the second person, as "you," rather than speak to you in the pretense that you are indeed a "you," a being something like me, while in my imagination I'm really talking to my colleague who truly is "you" to me. He and I are talking about the "him" which is "you"; you exist for us in the third person from this perspective.

Now I will explore the theme of changing personality, which might also be called changing behavior, or changing experience. Actually, I prefer the title "Changing Personal Worlds: A Humanistic Perspective."

First, we'll concern ourselves with the theme of personality. From my point of view, the term "personality" simply means *one's ways of being a person.* To be a person refers to a way of experiencing the world and a way of acting upon the world.[4] You can turn that around, and say that to be a person is a way for the world to be experienced and acted upon. If you have two persons present, you have two ways for the world to be experienced, and two ways for it to be acted upon. When I say "experienced," I'm using the term experiencing in the phenomenological sense; that is, I am referring to the different modes of experiencing, which include perception, remembering, thinking, imagining fantasy, and dreaming. These are all ways for the world to be experienced by persons. Each one of us embodies a way for the world to be perceived, thought about, remembered, imagined, and so on.[5] But your experience is a determiner of your action. As you change your ways of experiencing the world you'll also be changing, to some extent, your ways of acting in the world.

The theme that I am addressing, then, is how does personality change occur? How might somebody foster it, or facilitate it, or make it happen, or help it happen, when we talk about man, not as a "him" or an "it" in the third person, but as a "you," as someone who exists for me in the second person, and for himself in the first person. Personality change, when viewed from the perspective of a humanistic perspective on man, entails some disengagement of a person from his present ways of experiencing and acting in the world, followed by an opening of his field of experience to new dimensions of experience that were always possible but were not yet realized, followed then by a reentry into one's situation in order to make it more livable. This is a view

[4] This definition is adapted from that provided in Laing (1967).
[5] Cf. Jourard, S. M., *Disclosing Man to Himself,* especially pp. 174–177.

of personal change that has gradually been emerging from my own thinking and my own research.[6]

Let me address the theme of *trying* to facilitate or invite change in another person. This is what a professional counselor and psychotherapist does.[7]

A psychotherapist can be seen as a repairman, as a trainer, as a doctor, as a guru, as a zaddik—each model or metaphor calls for him to do or be in some ways and proscribes some other ways. I refer you in this connection to Kopp's recent book (Kopp, 1971). Here I want to explore the image of a psychotherapist as a specialist at transcending, one who has displayed expertise at transcending some aspect of facticity to which men have hitherto adjusted. The master learns to liberate himself from dehumanizing forces, freeing himself thus to lead a life that he has chosen. He is then in a position to show others how he did it so that they might do it too. His technique, if he has any, is to serve as a model, to show off, to make himself transparent. This view of the therapist is not meant to replace other models, simply because it cannot. But I intend it, rather, to supplement prevailing images of therapy and to invite more psychotherapists to explore the therapeutic possibilities of modeling, of being a model.

Let me just make a digression at this point. We're talking about trying to foster or invite personal change, change in a person's way of being in the world. This presumably is what psychotherapists are supposed to be skilled at doing. There are two ways to approach this. If one experiences the other individual as "him," in the third person, then one's approach to personal change almost necessarily calls for techniques of manipulation, influence, hypnosis, shaping, doing something. From a broader perspective you can say that this is the exercise of power *over* another, when one experiences the other in the third person. When one is inviting change by example, then the other individual exists in the second person, as "you." Other metaphors make sense; one is seducing, one is showing off, one is inviting, one is challenging.

Let's just pursue this. Modeling (showing off) can be seen as a case of *the attribution of power and strength* to somebody. To attribute one's own capacity to cope to another person is what is implicit in the act of modeling, in letting another person see how you've done it. I'll develop this question in several ways here. We can just ask this question, "to whom do you attribute the power to change your situation: to another person? To yourself? To God?" This question is decisive. If we think of modeling as a special case of

---

[6] *Ibid.,* pp. 111–120, 152–172.

[7] Parts of the following remarks are from a forthcoming paper of mine; see Jourard (1972).

attributing power to others: power to cope, power to transcend, it brings therapy into the possibilities of research by techniques that already have been developed in social psychology by people like Fritz Heider (1958) and Ronald Laing (1967). One has to become interested in the whole logic and theory of attribution. How do I experience you? What power or capacity to cope or to grow do I attribute to you? Do I see you as a creature inhabited by forces over which you have no control, so that you need my power to help you control it? Or do I experience you as someone with the capacity to cope with damn near anything? If a person becomes a patient, it is because he has clung to a way of experiencing himself, others and the world, and he has clung to ways of acting in the world *which no longer are life-giving.*

When a person is suffering, it is almost *prima facie* evidence that his ways of being are no longer viable. They are no longer effective in sustaining wellbeing and growth, and it is time for him to change some aspect of his world.

Let us explore just what it is that we think needs to be changed. If one addresses a person with the resolve to alter his behavior, to extinguish or shape it (this terminology comes from a behavioristic approach to the study of man), this can alter that person's experience of power. But the question is, *whose* power is a person experiencing when he has altered his behavior at the instigation of some expert at behavior change? He may have his view confirmed, that *the other person's* theories and powers are very powerful indeed, but it may not enhance his own sense of his own powers, or his felt capacity to change his world and his situation at his own initiative. As for myself, I resolutely refuse to see another person as one who is condemned to weakness or as one whose existence and growth is dependent on drugs, doctors, or on charting his responses. I insist on seeing the other person *as a person* who has the capacity, when his life has reached a stalemate, and he is no longer living in viable ways—*I see him as one with the capacity to transcend that,* to cope with that, to withdraw, get a better picture of what is going on and charge right back into the situation and change it in some nondestructive way so that life is more possible. And I see the great psychotherapists (or psychotherapists whom I see great) as specialists in coping with some dimension of facticity that most people yield to or accommodate themselves to. The great therapists stand as living proof that that which has subjected most other men is to them a challenge that they have tamed or transcended. By so doing, they are living exemplars of the possibility that you and I and anybody else can do it.

Everything can be a metaphor for anything else. For instance, you can see me as a tiger or a monkey. Or a woman can be seen as an iceberg or an inferno.

Metaphor and simile and analogy are all tokens of a vital imagination and these release man from the hypnotic spells of perception and memory. Every metaphor is an invitation or a challenge to transmute what is perceived or remembered into the metaphor. As soon as one envisions a different self and a different world and begins to make them actual, then the present self and world become a kind of metaphor, a pale simile for the world to come.

A therapist can be seen as a metaphor for the patient. His way is a possibility for the patient if he shows how he did it, how he tamed some facticity, how he emancipated himself, healed himself, perfected himself. From this perspective, the patient is his therapist *manqué*.

The most obvious implication of this view is that it really doesn't matter in what theoretical school a therapist has been trained, nor do his techniques matter. What seems crucial to me is that he be a continually growing person, that he be continuously engaged in the struggle between his freedom and the facticity amidst which all of us live. The effective therapist is, perhaps, adequate at taming most of the facticity he encounters but he is magnificent at coping with some one dimension of it so that he is heroic and graceful in his victory. Such a person is proof that a mere human can do it, almost as if to say, "If I can do it, so can you" or "If he can do it, so can I and you."

My flying instructor—I take flying lessons—is a boring man outside of the airplane. He speaks in a monotone, his personal life and his political philosophy, as I know them, are unimaginative and stereotyped. To me, however, he is a hero, the master of flight, a tamer of gravity, a birdman. He holds a certain charisma for me. He's willing to show me how he does it and I'm learning and oddly enough he shows me how it's done by imitating a teaching machine. As we sit in the airplane, he gives me "frames." He offers frames from a program instruction booklet that change you from a groundling to a pilot. I don't, however, consult with my flight instructor for help in how to live my marriage, my professional life, or my life in the community in ways that would preserve my eccentricity and magnificence.

I invite you, now, to look with me at some psychotherapists whose careers seem to me to be evidence to support the hypothesis that I've been presenting, that the great psychotherapists are exemplars at taming and transcending some aspect of the factical world that subjugate most of us.

The hypothesis seems obvious to me. To assert that some other factor such as training, tricks, or techniques are the only effective agents in psychotherapy, teaching or influence seems to me to be stupidity, bad faith, or a futile quest for the means by which little men can pretend to be larger men in order to influence others out of proportion to their merit. I might add, be careful whose techniques you use, because you may not be person enough to use them properly. A corollary to this hypothesis is that a psychotherapist cannot himself lead a person to a freer and more enlightened existence than he himself has attained or can imagine for himself and is presently seeking. According to this view, he leads and influences his patients like the Israeli officers who do not say, "charge," they say "follow me."

Now let me turn to what I call the "exemplary magnificence of some psychotherapists." We'll start with Freud. We could actually start with Moses but Freud is a good place to begin.

Freud mastered some forces which could have prevented him from becoming the man who invented psychoanalysis. He suffered "Portnoy's complaint," as millions of people in the west have—a seductive, doting mother and a father who was both strong and weak, loved and feared. The result of struggling with such conflicting parental demands has been neurosis and diminished growth for many. Freud's courage lay in facing his recollections and fantasies, his sexuality, his anger, and discovering that one's past need not preclude fuller functioning, whether it was genital, intellectual, or physical functioning, in adult years. I believe he was most effective as a therapist with persons whose suffering grew out of antigrowth forces comparable to those which he himself had tamed. The therapeutic technique he taught others has not been notorious for its effectiveness. Freud showed in his very person that it's possible to marry, make love, raise children, and defy all kinds of social pressures in one's time and place in spite of having been raised as a middle class, minority group member with parents whose demands and expectations were not always compatible with the free flowering of individuality. I suspect he might have helped his patients more swiftly—he sometimes kept patients seven years or more—if he were not so shy and so reluctant to share his experience with his patients.[8] It's interesting that Freud apparently was never so effective with older people as Jung was, people who had already struggled through their childhood hangups but were finding life meaningless in their forties and fifties, not because of unresolved Oedipal problems but because life, as an adult, had reached the end of its tether. It was time to let go of those forms in order to go forward.

Now I'll discuss the magnificence of Hobart Mowrer. Mowrer was not helped with his incapacitating depressions by more than seven years of orthodox Freudian therapy. He lived into adult life plagued with guilt over

[8] There is something pernicious, to me, about viewing people with difficulties in living as sick and weak. This seems to be a case of the attribution of weakness to a person, who then experiences himself as weak and helpless.

some childhood peccadillos and adult transgressions against his own ethical and moral standards. Hobart Mowrer doesn't mind my presenting this information because he has already put it in the public domain. There are millions of people who have to try to live a meaningful and rewarding life though they are possessed, notice what I say, they are possessed, they don't possess, they are possessed by a powerful, puritanical conscience. What Mowrer found to be ultimately and recurrently therapeutic was absolute openness and transparency before all those with whom he dealt. For him to lie, even a little, was analogous to a heroin addict who in the process of trying to get rid of the habit decided to take just one little wee shot. And so Mowrer developed his integrity group psychotherapy. He participates continuously in an ongoing small group to help him stay on terms of authenticity with himself and others. Mowrer showed that the temptation to lie and to cheat, to misrepresent one's self can be tamed, thereby averting profound guilt and depression for those who are afflicted with a similarly puritanical conscience.

Now let me mention Carl Whittaker and R. D. Laing. I suspect that Ronald Laing and Carl Whittaker enjoy the kind of experience that many of their colleagues call schizophrenic. They can maneuver effectively in the conventional world despite or because of the fact that they are capable of such transcendental experience. If the average person is terrified by the experience of the dissolution of his world and his identity, then he must repress his capacity for enlarged experiencing, thereby limiting his capacities for growth and for functioning. (Whittaker is Professor of Psychiatry at Wisconsin; Ronald Laing is probably one of the best known writers on themes relating to living life and a very competent, practicing psychotherapist.) Both these men show that it's possible to be effective in personal and professional life and to live with one's possibilities for madness, which they see as an opportunity for either the destruction of one's world and letting it stay there or the beginnings of an enlarged world in which one can live more fully.

Let me mention Alfred Adler and Eric Berne. I believe that we can look at Adler as a person who in his lifetime suffered from other people's efforts to make him feel inferior, to put him down. Many people yield to others' suggestions that they are worthless and they live only half-lives because of such yielding; and everybody has been victimized to one extent or another by someone who can say, " Oh, you're looking very well *today*." Adler recognized the games that were being played with him, and the self-defeating counter-games he was playing, and so he became a *magister ludi*, a master of the game. He was able then to help others who grappled with the same dilemmas. He strongly influenced Eric Berne in the process. Now, because of the writings of

Adler and Eric Berne, millions are shown how people try subtly to gain control over one another's existence and how one can gracefully get on with life in spite of such games or, better, without them.

Now let me mention the founders of various self-help, nonprofessional groups. The alcoholics and drug addicts and obese people who "kick" their self-destructive addictions in order to live more effective and meaningful lives are living testimony that addictions can be tamed. The way of life which the founders of Synanon, Alcoholics Anonymous, and Weight Watchers developed is teachable or demonstrable. The way of life that they embody does tame the urge to engage in self-destructive behavior. I see a similar dynamic at work in women's liberation and in the various Black movements. Some one person understood and mastered the forces which were controlling people as a master controls his victim. The liberated woman and the self-respecting Black both attest that the forces which were diminishing the victims could be transcended.

Fritz Perls, the founder of gestalt therapy, discovered that there were many factors operative that could prevent a person from living fully in the immediate present with all senses and moods of experiencing fully active and with the freedom to act spontaneously. He identified these factors and spent his personal life taming them. He was himself, in person and beyond any of his writings, living testimony to man's determination, as well as his power, to struggle to transcend and prevail over forces that would diminish his sense of vitality. And he was able to show many people how it's done.

Victor Frankl impresses me, not so much by his therapeutic theories, but by the very fact of his survival as a magnificent human being, in spite of the Nazi effort to incinerate him. Frankl was able, daily, to find *raisons d'être*, reasons for living, when all about him in the death camp others were giving up, or permitting themselves to be killed by Nazis, or by weakness.

Now I would like to look at some behavioristic psychologists—Skinner, Ogden Lindsley, Professor Wolpe, Eysenck, and my colleague Pennypacker. They too are all exemplars of a certain kind of magnificence which I take to be the discovery of techniques for teaching others how to analyze large behavioral units into manageable bits, the better to control it. It's unclear to me yet how effective these men are at attributing power to patients. I think they believe power resides in the idea of behavior modification, or the various conditioning theories and techniques. What I found most fascinating about the whole field of behaviorism or behavior science is that its appeal is to those who are most fascinated with the problem of management and control of somebody's behavior.

Now I'm most familiar with the efforts of my colleagues at Florida where we have a very flourishing division of behavior management within our department. My colleague, Pennypacker, has hundreds of people "managing" reading-behavior. He trains one group of students as "managers" and they have questions on three-by-five cards; students read chunks of a book, and then chart the number of correct answers they get in five minute episodes. They all get straight A's because they can answer questions efficiently. It's still not clear yet what this kind of monitored studying does to the capacity of the student to tackle large challenges.

I have to share with you an amusing anecdote. Pennypacker and I are very good friends and colleagues and have been for the past ten years; we each were compulsive smokers. He and I both were smoking two ounces or more of pipe tobacco a day every day, inhaling every puff. We were totally addicted. About two years ago I decided to quit. But as an addict, I had withdrawal symptoms. I became terrified. I asked myself, "How can I quit? I know what, I'll do what Hank Pennypacker does, I'll count something. I'll count puffs, chart it, and establish a base rate."

I then said, "The hell with it, that's for children and animals, and I'm neither. I will trust in my own theories." I was interested in yoga, and I developed this technique for stopping my smoking out of a Hatha Yoga exercise. I kept my pipe in my hand at all times; every time I got an urge to smoke, I would take a slow yoga breath.[9] If the urge persisted, I would do another one. That first day I had to do about fifty cycles of that but then the second day it was cut to twenty-five, and the third day about a dozen, the fourth day about half-a-dozen and the fifth day two or three. That was it, there was no more. I have not smoked for two years now, and I have had no urge to resume.

Pennypacker believes in his own techniques and he keeps careful count. He has a wrist counter, and he's on to cigars now and he's trying to bring his urges and the cigar under stimulus control. It's hilarious. He has one of those little buzzers, a one hour buzzer. You can set it for an hour or half-an-hour. At executive committee meetings we'll be talking away about the policy of the department and all of a sudden buz-z-z-z. Pennypacker will whip out a cigar, but my colleagues all start drooling like Pavlov's dogs because you never know what's being conditioned with what.

I want to explore, briefly, some of the implications of this hypothesis for

---

[9] I would inhale slowly, to the count of 8, hold the breath for 8 counts, release it to the count of 8, and await the next inhalation for the count of 8. This constituted one breathing cycle.

psychotherapeutic practice. What I'm saying, incidentally, extends to some of the so-called humanistic growth-promoting techniques that you read about or involve yourself in—encounter groups, yoga, the various sensitivity training techniques—they all share something in common with the thesis that I'm presenting here: a refusal to yield to the path of least resistance which is one way of saying "being determined." They share a struggle, in other words, to disengage from that which was controlling you in order to discover new possibilities of one's self and of the world in order then to dive back in, as Odysseus returned to Ithaca, to make it fit for a grown man to live in. I think it's elegant that I'm here in Ithaca because the Odyssey myth looms large in my life.

I think its high time we stopped regarding people who aren't able to get on with life as sick because we may then feel it's essential to cure them. Better to regard them as sickened or, better, as unenlightened and subdued or misguided. In such cases, one can enlighten, encourage, and guide more appropriately. Clearly the sickened ones have not known how to transcend the forces which sicken people.

How elegant if those committed to healing and helping would themselves be exemplars of the ways to live that maintain vitality and foster growth. Now to whom do professional psychotherapists turn for help when they find themselves in some sickening or dispiriting impasse in their lives? Do they seek yet more analysis or client-centered therapy or behavior modification or gestalt psychotherapy? I don't. Instead, I pull back, I withdraw from the ways in which I'd been living up to that point and through meditation or conversation with an honest friend or travels to get away from the scene, try to get a perspective on my situation. I try to reinvent my situation and my ways of being in it in some enlightening ways. This takes time, so I need to be able to put up with depression and boredom and some anxieties. I'm glad to get all the forebearance from friends and family that I can get during this time of withdrawal in order to reinvent myself. I don't want to be healed. I just want to be left alone or talked to as a human being. If I turn to psychotherapists it's not because of their technical orientation but because I know them as persons, and I respect their prowess at coping graciously with dilemmas which presently overpower me.

I struggled with the realization that others see me as middle-aged. I've got bifocal lenses, I have gray hair, I'm in my forties, and my children are nearly grown. I arrived at a kind of impasse that Jung has described with considerable vividness. I and a lot of my colleagues and friends find ourselves in this particular bind, and as America becomes increasingly affluent, people will arrive at this bind at younger and younger ages—in fact, they already are.

Then the question is, how then do you cope in life-giving ways with an impasse of this sort? I turned not to psychotherapists but to one of my colleagues who happens to be a sleep researcher. He has handled this possibly devitalizing time of life very graciously and even with elegance. It was in conversation with him that I coined the statement of an immortal truth which might catch on: "Middle age is definitely not for children." But just as one does not send a student who wishes to learn dancing to a voice teacher, I think it's ridiculous to send someone who can't control his urge to drink to someone who's expert at overcoming his dead parents' influence on the way he lives his adult life.

If I were suffering because I had to spend my time struggling against an impulse to dissociate and hallucinate, I wouldn't seek the help of someone skilled in controlling anger: I would want to consult with an acknowledged madman who has proven his ability to pass in the straight world. I want him to show me how he did it and to supervise and challenge me as I try to find my way.

Here then is an argument for psychotherapists, and for that matter, counselors and encounter group leaders and teachers to examine themselves and answer the question, "In what ways am I magnificent, what aspects of facticity do I transcend with the greatest elegance?" If we can answer these questions then we might be able to help others in a more direct way once they came to trust us; and they would if we were trustworthy. This is an invitation to psychotherapists to share with their patients not just technical expertise— which is what one applies in the third person as one talks about it in the second person to one's true peers—but also their ways of staying alive and vital and growing when all about them others are devitalized. Sharing this when it becomes relevant is the dialogue that I call psychotherapy.

Perhaps a new system of classifying specialists is implicit here. Imagine a brochure which listed the names of all the therapists, not by their theoretical orientation but by the kinds of dilemmas, backgrounds and crises that they had faced and transcended. This actually does have some far-reaching implications. You know how they have computerized dating and mating. You fill out a card: you like chess, you like horseback riding and this music and that literature and you shuffle the cards together and the computer drops out the names of five or ten possible people. Well, I don't see why it wouldn't be possible in a neighborhood or a community to identify the people who are just superb at transcending some dimension of facticity so that when someone is overwhelmed or near suicidal from it, you call Aunt Molly, or the bartender or Uncle Willy who is good at it, and he comes over, just as in Alcoholics Anonymous when someone is ready to take a drink he calls a buddy and they sweat it out together. One could identify those people who had tamed the facticity that is subjugating somebody else and they might then avert the necessity of a great deal of professional care.

Let me conclude by saying that there is a sense in which I regard efforts to foster change in another by environmental control or by shaping techniques or by any means that are not part of an authentic dialogue as in some ways pernicious and mystifying, probably not good for the well-being and growth of the persons to whom these efforts are addressed; and probably not very ennobling for the people who practice them.

DR. JOURARD—QUESTIONS AND ANSWERS

Question: You mentioned that part of your effort is to invite people to avoid the path of least resistance. Since that tends to involve suffering, I was wondering if you could expand a little bit on the value of suffering that must be recognized?

Answer: I've been reading the Old Testament for the first time in my life and finding it fascinating. I have become enthralled with the difference between worship of the true God, which to me means "living in a life-giving way" as opposed to idolatry. Idolatry is, in a last analysis, living in devitalizing or killing ways. Suffering, it seems to me, is an indication among other things that you're not living right. But there are also times when in order to get from here to there—it's worth getting there—that there's hardly any way of avoiding suffering.

Now, there's some balance that calls for wisdom: to *seek* out suffering is a peculiar sort of idolatry or it's a very odd way to live one's life. To avoid suffering in a compulsive way, and to do everything in one's power not to experience effort and pain is in itself a kind of idolatry. Let's say that it is painful to experience anxiety, and it really is. An anxiety onslaught is devastating. But to struggle as a so-called neurotic does, to live an anxiety-less existence, he pays a tremendous price for it. He gives up damn near anything in order not to experience anxiety. The ability to hang in and to gird one's loins and grit one's teeth and endure pain and suffering in order to get at something worthwhile seems to me, among other things, to have the capacity to build strength.

Q: You were saying that we should categorize therapists according to what dilemmas they've overcome. What does a person who is thinking of going into therapy do? Should the person say, as a therapist, that I have been through something like this? (Sure) Would the therapist really turn around to a person and say, "No, I have not experienced something like that, I don't want to take the responsibility of helping you through this thing because I haven't been through it myself"? They sort of have this thing, you know, this overpowering god-like image at times that they can help a person.

A: I think honesty is what is essential on the part of the therapist. I've never experienced what it's like to menstruate; someone may have menstrual cramps and that may interfere with their life or something of the sort. But I've had diarrhea and belly cramps. That's a trivial example. I think I have been consulted by people who have had devastating tragedy in their life and it's incapacitated them and I have not experienced tragedy of such intensity, of such havoc-producing dimensions. I wouldn't pretend to, but I would let them know how much I had experienced and that I would struggle to try to understand them and to help them endure it and to grope, try to be helpful in groping with them for ways to live in spite of the tragedy. There are many professional people, however, who insist on a mask of professional anonymity. That's all right, too, because there are many people who attribute power almost in a magical way to the professional anonymity of the expert. Their experience of power residing in the therapist would be diminished if they discovered that he ate, drank, made love, went to the toilet, and so on.

Q: But you are saying that there are generalizing qualities to the ability that you have found to handle the problems in your own life, which you can generalize to other kinds of dilemmas which you haven't faced which someone else has?

A: There may be generalizing power such that if you coped with one kind of dilemma, that gives you the capacity to hang in there, to use your imagination, courage and resourcefulness to cope better with others. I believe that to be true. I believe it to be true to such an extent that I believe that efforts to make everything easy and effortless and in small manageable steps is training for flabbiness. I see this as interfering with the development of strong men and women.

Q: If I'm hung-up with one experience which you never experienced before and I wanted to come to you as a therapist depending on how different my hang-up is from any of those you've experienced, then you've got a judgment about whether you could relate to me or not relate to me?

A: Let's take the very term "hang-up." You see that implies that my world and my way of being in it are fine and splendid except for some one attitude, a way of experiencing or way of acting in a situation that gets in my way. If that is indeed the case, then I would think that the most appropriate way of coping with that obstruction to a more fully lived life is to seek out someone who is very good at breaking habits, someone in the behavior modification or conditioning tradition. There are many instances where some attitude or habit persists long past the point of serving any adaptive function; it is often difficult to get rid of such habits. If I couldn't break it myself, I wouldn't hesitate to ask someone to help me break it. But the peculiar thing there is that I cannot help but feel that there's a self-fulfilling prophecy there. I know very well that my habits, like smoking, can be broken in an instant. If you've got faith, it can be done. Pennypacker has no faith in breathing. He would say that it's through reciprocal inhibition, the inhibition of one habit by acquiring another. But you don't see me taking deep Yoga breaths all the time.

Q: I was very glad to hear you include the Black Nationalists in the category of psychotherapists and I was thinking particularly of Elijah Mohammed and Malcolm X, and I can see very clearly that they would not be effective psychotherapists for, let's say, middle class white college students who have struggled with different problems. My question is, is the effectiveness of that movement and those people in changing people's lives simply a function of the fact that the men who were prominent, who have been prominent in it, have struggled with the same problems as the people who they are trying to help or does it have something to do with the positive solutions which they're offering which tend to be rather highly structured and precise, especially if you take Elijah Mohammed? Do you see what I'm driving at? Is the effectiveness of the psychotherapist just a function of the problems with which he has struggled or does it have something to do with the solutions or the ideology which he offers?

A: That's a difficult question. Let's start off first by saying, I don't know. But then I'll talk for a minute, like a college professor. We can make the assumption that people want to live as groovy a life as it's possible for them to live with as much satisfaction and meaning and challenge and value in it. And when someone is being subdued or diminished by circumstances he may believe that that's what life is all about: to live a subdued, subjugated existence. Until he sees somebody with whom he can identify, somebody who's "like us," who has made it, who's gotten out, who's gotten on top. Once he sees that, he can no longer pretend that he is fated to remain where he was. If I were a dictator and I had managed to convince people that this is the way life is, and there is little we can do to escape, and then someone escaped, I would want to destroy him as swiftly as I could because others would see him and say, "If he can do it, I can do it." Now, the man who transcended it may not be able to show in any but a superstitious way how he went about doing it but at least he's living proof that it can be done.

Q: How do you know when the madman that you're consulting for your madness isn't back into a mad streak right then? What guarantee do you have that now he's out of his madness?

A: I think that there is a very basic factor of human trust and trustworthiness that develops out of dialogue between a person and the one he is consulting. And while people are vulnerable to being misled, in time they discover when they are not being helped by someone whom they were consulting for help. And if Ronald Laing's or Carl Whitaker's patients found that their capacity for living was radically destroyed by consulting them, they would probably stop consulting. I was a patient of Carl Whitaker for a while; I trust him, and I don't think my capacity to cope with existence was diminished for having seen him. And I don't know what that proves. Your question, I think, is a searching one.

Q: If you helped that man who had helped himself would you go down with him when he is reverting?

A: I certainly wouldn't go down with Laing or Whitaker.

Q: Because of the issue of authority, I was wondering if somehow you could have people that were actually magnificent heroes and yet wouldn't come down in such a way so that when the person gets some change occurring he can attribute it to himself?

A: I make this assumption for myself, that the other person has much more power than he ever dreamed he has. When he consults with me, he is arguing, "You are strong, I am weak." And I'll say, "You don't seem weak to me. You've got the strength of a horse." "No, I am sick," he might reply. "You don't seem sick to me. You seem bewildered or confused or befuddled or timid." He attributes characteristics to himself that I disagree with and I attribute characteristics to him that he disagrees with. And we have a kind of argument going. If he wins the argument, he loses a great deal indeed, because he is saying over and over again, "I cannot, I cannot." And I'm saying essentially, "You can, you can. I have done it. He has done it. We are human. You are human. You probably may be able to do it." And so on.

Q: But suppose afterwards, now he wins this argument with this magnificent figure and he comes across feeling, "Gosh, I really can do something." But suppose then, you know, a couple of months later he thinks, "Gee, that guy was clever." He didn't tell me about the sort of subtlety of what may really be manipulative in the sense that he may attribute it to a kind of game where you let him win this argument so that he would feel that he had this kind of personal control. But then he becomes aware of it a few months later, and what's he left with? (I don't know.) Isn't it better to come straight on with it like a behavior therapy kind of technique where you're saying, "Well, this is the game of life, these are the rules, this is what the change is going to be attributed to, and so forth." Then you'll not be left with this appendage where a person simply doesn't know at the end what produced the change or if *you* really produced the change and not himself?

A: I don't know. I think I can say this, that if someone is seeking the help of one who is competent and who has faith in behavioristic techniques and principles and that's the package that is being presented and sold, I have no quarrel with it. But for that person to pretend to be doing something other than what he's doing, I have some quarrel with that. I do think there is a way of looking at the human scene in the light of attribution; we'll call it attribution theory for want of a better name. How do we regard ourselves? How do other people regard us? To what extent does the other person's view of me effect my view of myself? If you want me to be diminished, then all the time I'm in your presence and if I spend a lot of time in your presence you need never say a single word but I probably will feel diminished. And if you want me dead, in due time I may find my zest for living diminished. If you want me impotent, I suspect....

I'll tell you an anecdote. I worked in a setting with a bunch of professional women once and I noticed that for months at work I never once felt remotely erotic. Some of these women, you know, had conventionally attractive appearances and I discovered as I came to know them better, that these were people who had some difficulties with men and could best deal with a man who was desexualized. And so there was a marked absence of all the little flutters, and wiggles, and twitches that remind a person of the difference between the sexes. It was not something that was actively being done; it was simply an incarnated expression of the wish that the other person be desexualized. I'll state as a hypothesis, that the view of the other person's possibilities that I truly hold and act upon is a very important factor in the transaction between him and me, whether I state it in words or whether it is a continuous non-verbal expression of this view that, "you can do it, you can do it, you can do it."

Q: I wonder if it's your intention to leave the audience with the idea that you can only help somebody with a problem if you've experienced it yourself? I think lots of times, in terms of one's experience of psychotherapeutic relationships with another person, no one does know what to do unless one lives through a situation with another person; and in this sense what grows is a laboratory of adaptive behaviors which you can help the other person model or develop for themselves.

A: No, it is not my intention to leave this audience with the impression that one can only help another person with problems that one has conquered oneself. I believe that it is true that the more experience that one has had oneself, and through watching other people struggle and learning from them and maybe intervening helpfully with them, the more one does develop a repertoire of commonsense knowledge—I'm not sure I would say expertise, although that may be involved. I introduced this paper on modeling by saying it's not meant to replace, but to invite therapists and others to discover just what is their magnificence and to share it. It may enlarge their capacity to be helpful. Incidentally, I am that committed as a therapist and teacher, that if I'm truly engaged with somebody and that which is standing in the way of wherever we think he's going to go is going to call for shaping or standing on one's head or doing Yoga, then by God that's what we'll do.

Q: A fault is that a patient comes to you and says, "I'm having a problem coping with this." You're saying to them, "Well, just follow me, watch my example. Yes, you can do it." I can think that my own response has to continue to be, "That's terribly threatening because here's a guy who can do it and I can't do it: I don't need to be reminded of the fact that it can be done but I can't do it." If I really believe I can't do it, then I'll believe the therapist doesn't understand me.

A: You were saying, suppose the seeker was intimidated by the chap who already has coped. Well, all right, if you've consulted with me and you're intimidated, let's talk about that. You see, there's a lot more to being helpful than modeling. There's discussion, there's argument, there's clarification. I spend a lot of time getting a person to stop kidding himself. I have an 18 year old girl consulting with me. She has a 36 year old lover who's married with three children, who lives on the West Coast. It's the romantic affair of a lifetime. He spends $1500 a month telephoning her, to control her life. And she's complaining about the control. And she also has a 35 year old man in love with her back home and she can't quite understand how these men get so involved with her. "You can't understand? What are you talking about?

You're having the time of your life. The only other men available to you are 19 year old pimple-faced lads." She began to say, "Well, yes."

Q: I don't know how applicable all you're saying is to young people, but I work with early adolescent kids, and I've seen a lot of evidence of developmental theories of moral growth and learning; and it seems to me that at certain stages of people's lives they aren't ready to follow models. That is, there needs to be some other kinds of motivating factors, some other kinds of interpersonal interactions which far overwhelm the effect the model will have. Wouldn't that leave the model looking terrible?

A: Let me put it this way, we really don't have a hell of a lot of choice in a model whom we follow. We are to follow available models who are right there from literature or from fiction or in our own imagination. The fact that I may not be a very good model to some teenager for something or other doesn't preclude the possibility of my being helpful to him in some way other than being a model. I repeat: I was presenting a hypothesis about how some therapists who are regarded as great, why they appear great to me. And I believe that there is some generalizable validity there, but it's not to say that the only way that one person can help another is by being an exemplar. But I'll state it the other way around. It's doubtful to me, if someone can for long inspire the confidence and trust of people as a source of help in living their lives, when he himself is totally inept and maladapted and lousy at coping with his life.

Q: Necessary but maybe not sufficient?
A: All right, necessary but not sufficient.

Q: Suppose you felt physically attracted to this type you mentioned who are twittery coy type women and not particularly physically attracted to, shall we say, a stronger woman, would you disclose this feeling you had to her and, if you felt beneficial would you have sexual relations with her?

A: To the last, no. No, it isn't worth the trouble and I'm not sure that it would be beneficial. But I would disclose the feelings that I was experiencing if it came up in the context of our ongoing dialogue. As with this little 18 year old, 19 year old girl. I'd say, "I feel attracted to you, too. I can see how you would be devastating for middle-aged men." But I'll be damned if I would follow along that path. The question that you're raising is, "Do I think that a professional psychotherapist can perform love therapy?" It's not licensed yet; and I'm fairly straight.

Q: I'd like to comment on your statement describing great psychothera-pists; and you mentioned Freud. Some of the research that has recently been done by the feminist movement is that his way of analysis was actually a violence against the mentality of women. I think it's rather dangerous to put him in that kind of light, if you knew what had happened when he saw women. The other comment I would like to make about psychotherapy is that perhaps we could interpret it as advocacy of a person's wish to express himself in a different way and to help that person actualize it regardless of the therapist's own feelings, opinions, leanings, repulsions. As for example, I think another violence that's practiced today is the whole area of working with people who are homosexuals in view of the taboos. And there are not enough people to help people who want to express themselves this way and want to feel good and whole and acceptable and marvelous?

A: You're making, I think, a very important point: to wit, what is the view of the good society, let's say, that a given therapist embodies, because that cannot help but affect what he regards as acceptable and unacceptable ways of being men and women, black and white, young and old. And I think the "radical" therapists as well as Ronald Laing and Fritz Perls are utopians of varying degrees of clarity of vision, either anarchists or socialists, but cer-tainly opposed to rigid definitions of social roles that may well be destructive to the person living them. I mean, in point of fact, if I were to claim a kind of magnificence for myself in this area, it's in stubborn refusal to limit myself to other people's definitions of what my age, sex, occupational, familial, and other kinds of roles ought to be. That's the response I'd like to make to you.

Behavior Therapy—A Humanitarian Enterprise[1]

JOSEPH WOLPE

Temple University Medical School and
Eastern Pennsylvania Psychiatric Institute,
Henry Avenue, Philadelphia, Pennsylvania 19129

What has to be realized about psychotherapy is that it is concerned with habitual behavior. There are all sorts of problems that people come to consult other people about. A lot of these are immediate situational problems: "What college should I go to; what courses should I take; shall I marry the girl?"; and other questions of that sort. All these problems call for guidance and help, but that help is not what we mean by psychotherapy. Psychotherapy is concerned with habitual behaviors that persist, are unpleasant, and lead to various disabilities, and that are undesirable to the individual, who does things that he would rather not be doing. It is necessary to realize that the activities of concern are not just motor or "doing" behaviors. There can also be undesirable emotional behaviors and thinking behaviors; and very often the problem consists of a combination of these. Actually, there is a sense in which all three are always involved. Dr. Jourard referred to this comprehensive involvement in rather an interesting fashion when he said that the patient feels that he is no longer living in viable ways. Perhaps that person never has lived in viable ways. In any case, it is a good way of epitomizing that which brings the patient to be treated.

Most of the habits which make life nonviable, and certainly those to which psychotherapists address themselves, have been acquired through experience. The behaviors within the psychotherapeutic purview have been learned, and it seems that the only way you can lastingly change learned behavior is to reverse the learning, to bring about unlearning. This is absolutely central to

[1] Lecture presented at Cornell Symposium—"Behavioristic and Humanistic Approaches to Personality Change."

the behavioristic approach. In fact, behavior therapy is defined as the application of experimentally established principles and paradigms of learning to the changing of unadaptive habits. Notice the word "unadaptive." If a person complains about a habit of his, it is presumably unadaptive in some sense: it is unpleasant like anxiety, or functionally inefficient like impotence or frigidity. There is always something about it to make him complain.

Now, the kind of definition of neurosis I have given you, referring to "the use of experimentally established principles," may lead some of you to feel that we are jumping straight out of the laboratory and not considering the person as a human being. This is a point that Dr. Jourard made this morning, but it is quite an inaccurate characterization of what goes on in behavior therapy. In the first place, you should have noticed that I alluded to the patient's suffering; and that is what we start from. What we are really concerned about is to do the most appropriate things—overcoming the habits that are disturbing and disabling to him. Once it is perceived that these habits are based upon learning, it makes sense to look to learning principles to overcome them because they are likely to generate the most direct and efficient means of relieving the patient's suffering. Since, as I have pointed out, the suffering can be of many kinds, the behavior therapist who is properly schooled will explore the whole person, or more correctly, all the person's behaviors and not be limited to the particular complaint that the patient has brought to the fore. So, although we make use of learning principles, we are very much concerned with the human being. We do not view him as a monkey or a pigeon in making use of common features among human beings, monkeys, and pigeons. But from observing what happens in the monkey, we can get clues regarding what to do about similar behavior in the human being. Our therapeutic repertoire thus has a source of supply—for the benefit of man—that is closed to those too "humanistic" to study the parallels between psychogenetically related organisms.

In this context, I would also dispute two more of Dr. Jourard's imputations. One is that behavior therapy is done by people who have an inner need to control other people. He did not quite put it that way, but I do not think I take a great liberty in paraphrasing it like this. We behavior therapists do have a desire for a kind of control. We want to control the suffering that our patients bring to us. It takes a pair of wild logical jumps to infer from this admission, first, that we want to dominate over them, and, second, that we have distinctive personalities. I do not know of any objective study that shows that people who do therapies other than behavior therapy are in some way nicer and more human than those who do behavior therapy.

The second and related imputation is that to use principles that come from the laboratory may not be good for the patient or ennobling for the therapist. I do not know what is more ennobling for a therapist than to be able to help his patients. To me the whole situation is precisely parallel to that which exists in the practice of medicine. When a patient comes to a doctor, the doctor will try to do whatever seems most likely to be effective. Sometimes the measures most likely to be effective are, in the present state of our knowledge, quite crude. They may involve such things as cutting out tumors or incising into abscesses. I suppose you could say that the doctor, in doing these things, is seizing control. He is; but what is ignoble about it?

Having vindicated our moral position, let me return to the substance of behavior therapy (Wolpe, 1958, 1969). Principles of learning would naturally be relevant to removing unadaptive habits based upon learning. What are the clinical conditions that are made up of learned habits? There are four main categories. First and foremost are the neuroses. We define a neurosis as a persistent unadaptive habit which has been acquired by learning in an anxiety-generating situation or a succession of anxiety-generating situations. It must be added that anxiety is almost always central to the manifestations of a neurosis. I'll come back to that. At this stage I am giving you the definition, but that also requires justification, which also I shall provide.

The second category of learned habits we call "other pure learned habits"—meaning purely learned unadaptive habits that do not have the anxiety feature. I refer to such problems as tantrum behavior, enuresis nocturna, thumb-sucking, nail-biting, and bad study habits. To a very great extent these are motor behaviors without anxiety and, therefore, as a rule, treated differently from the neuroses, in which anxiety is so nearly consistently central.

The third category is drug habits. There is something peculiar about a drug habit. Somehow, the taking of certain substances has the result that sooner or later the individual develops a craving for that substance. Some change has been wrought in his body, making him want to or need to compensate for it by further administration of the substance. The truth is that we know nothing about the processes involved in this. Since there are no experimentally established paradigms for drug habits, strictly speaking there is no behavior therapy of drug habits nor, by definition, can there be until we have the paradigms. But behavior therapists do try, like everybody else, to treat drug habits. The one truly behavioristic thing they do is aversion therapy, in which the craving is counteracted by means of a strong negative response, such as induced nausea.

Finally, we have the learned habits of schizophrenia. Today, there is really no doubt left, I think, that schizophrenia is a biological disease. There are at least a dozen chains of evidence in different areas which converge to that conclusion. Among the most important developments are the studies at the Lafayette Clinic in which it has been found that there are abnormal globulins in 100% of schizophrenics and that they all lack an enzyme which destroys these globulins and which is isolatable from animal brains and from nonschizophrenic human beings. It seems that some of the manifestations of schizophrenia are the direct result of the physiological state; but that physiological state also predisposes the individual to the acquisition through learning of some bizarre habits. Those habits which have been acquired by learning can be modified by the use of learning principles.

Of the classes of conditions I have mentioned, the first, the neuroses, are the most appropriate material for behavior therapy. It has been applied to them more than to anything else. I have given you a formal definition of neurosis. We need now to look at how neuroses present themselves in the clinic. The definition I gave you gave great prominence to anxiety as a persistent unadaptive habit. The anxiety is often immediately manifest in neuroses. Many patients are continually anxious or have anxieties aroused by other human beings. But there are other neuroses in which the anxiety is not at all obvious. Take, for example, impotence and frigidity, sexual deviations like homosexuality and transvestism, psychosomatic states like asthma or neurodermatitis, or reactive depression. Anxiety may not be evident when the patient comes to you, and yet if you do a behavioral analysis you will almost always find it. The only consistent exception is the classical hysteria with *la belle indifférence.*

Let me illustrate how anxiety comes into the picture by reference to a condition in which it shows up strikingly—the case of the stutterer. In the great majority of cases you find that he does not stutter at all under certain conditions, e.g., when he is with members of his own family. You then have to ask yourself what provokes the stutter; and almost invariably it turns out to be associated with certain social situations. The business of the therapist is to define these social situations. This is part of what we call behavioral analysis. Frequently, the social factor that determines the stutter is the strangeness of other people. The stuttering depends for its severity upon how strange another person is. It may also vary according to the number of strange people, their age, their sex, their demeanor, and their authority status. You have to find out what is relevant. With a little further looking, you discover that the factors that provoke the stutter are anxiety-evoking stimuli. Thus, the stutter depends upon social anxiety. It follows that if you can de-condition the anxiety aroused by these social situations, you will also remove the stutter. You need do nothing else in many cases. There are some in which you do need to do other things too because there are operant conditionings involved. But what I am pointing out here is the centrality of anxiety. It is equally relevant in all of the other conditions that I have mentioned—the sexual neuroses, the obsessions, the character disorders, and the others. The main task in the vast majority of neuroses is to remove anxiety.

Now when a person has unadaptive anxiety, it can be based on two kinds of learning, and what you need to do is very much determined by the habit structure of the case. Consider the diagram (Fig. 1). The rectangle represents a human being. At its right-hand side you see R_A which means that he is having an anxiety response; and at the left-hand side there is big S_1. That means there is outside him, or maybe inside, a stimulus to the anxiety. I want you to take it that the anxiety is unadaptive. The stimulus could be a harmless snake or an objectively innocent pain in the chest; but the man is very anxious about the harmless snake or the pain.

Let us look inside the organism and see what could be happening. The rs_1 inside the figure is the individual's percept (Russell, 1940) of the stimulus S_1. S_1 is outside and it cannot produce responses unless it is received and processed by the individual's nervous system so as to form the percept. Similarly, rs_2 is a percept, a consequent of rs_1. One possibility is that there is a direct line from s_1, the snake or the pain in the chest, to the anxiety response. The other possibility is that the image rs_1 evokes rs_2, the thought: "It may kill me." Now the harmless snake cannot kill him. Similarly, the pain in his chest is, *ex hypothesi*, due to an innocuous cause. If he is anxious because he thinks something will kill him that is really not going to do so, what is needed is information. A physician should examine him and assure him that there is no

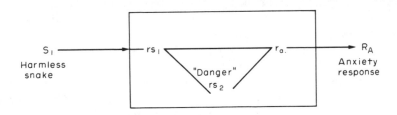

FIG. 1. The harmless snake S_1 causes the perceptual response rs_1 which may lead to the molecular responses for anxiety r_a either immediately or through the intermediary of the conditioned concept "danger," rs_2.

heart disease; and then the pain will no longer mean danger. That will be all that needs to be done.

But sometimes, even though a man is utterly convinced that there is nothing wrong with his heart, the pain will still evoke anxiety because there is also a direct connection $(rs_1 - r_A)$ between that sensory stimulus and the anxiety response. Where the unadaptive fear depends on the $rs_1 - rs_2$ chain, the task is to break a bond between percepts. You would not want to break the anxiety response habit subserved by the connection of rs_2 to r_A because you would not want the man not to be concerned when he is in real danger. By contrast, you do have to break an anxiety response habit when the operative sequence for the unadaptive fear is $rs_1 - r_A$. For example, the young man with the stutter I referred to who has an anxiety response habit to certain people knows that they will not actually harm him, but he has an automatic response of anxiety to them; and that is what we ahve to oercome.

Let me indicate to you the character of the experimental paradigm which has been most fruitful in generating methods of breaking these anxiety habits, and which has arisen in the context of experimental neuroses. When Dr. Liddell was here at Cornell these were a very active topic of research. You can produce a neurosis in an animal if in a confined space you can evoke high anxiety. You can evoke this high anxiety in two ways: by conflict or by noxious stimulation. Dr. Liddell's experiments were mainly based upon noxious stimulation, many weak noxious stimuli. I will now tell you about some experiments that I did using strong noxious stimulation. A cat is placed inside a cage which is forty inches long and twenty inches wide, and has on its floor an electrifiable grid. If you sound a buzzer and then administer through that grid on the floor a high-voltage low-amperage shock of two seconds' duration, it greatly disturbs but does not damage the animal. If you repeat the procedure a dozen times, you find that the responses elicited by the shock become a permanent feature of the animal's responding in the experimental cage, even though you never shock him again. Consistently thereafter he shows dilated pupils, hair standing on end, rapid respiration, and various other signs of anxiety. Whether you give him a break of six months or bring him back every day for a short period or a long time, there is no tendency for this anxiety response to diminish. In other words, there is no experimental extinction, which is, of course, in itself a very interesting fact. The important thing is that the anxiety response does not become weaker.

Like animals, human beings can be conditioned to be disturbed in all kinds of situations where it seems irrational. They know there is no reason to be petrified about being in a crowd, in an elevator, or on a plane—there is no real danger, and yet they have anxiety reactions. Inappropriate anxiety may similarly arise in social situations—anxiety stirred up by critism or implied disapproval from unimportant people, or even by positive behavior like praise. Whatever the details, all these are emotional habits, and they do not get extinguished by thinking. It doesn't matter what you think if you have the $rs_1 - r_A$ kind of habit. What goes on in the cortex—thinking as such—makes no difference to the emotional habit. The habit in the human, as in the animal, is very persistent.

It is also an unadaptive habit. To continue to be anxious in a situation in which, even though you have been harmed in the past, you no longer will be, is unadaptive. In the case of the experimental animal, there is an even more striking demonstration of the unadaptiveness of neurosis. If you starve a neurotic cat for 48 hours and put him into the experimental cage all over whose floor you then throw pieces of fresh meat, he will not touch any of that food, no matter how long you leave him there with it. For an animal not to eat available food when hungry is poignantly unadaptive.

The human parallel to the non-eating cat is anorexia nervosa. It is much more common to see other adaptive functions being interfered with by anxiety. Impotence is usually caused by anxiety about some aspect of the sexual situation. The same applies to most cases of frigidity. Anxiety in the social situation will lead to unadaptive responding there; and anxiety can interfere in the work situation in a whole host of ways. For example, if a person is disturbed by authority figures, by being enclosed, or merely by being looked at, he may be unable to work effectively at his job. In fact, there is no function, no activity, that cannot be impaired by anxiety.

Let me now mention one more feature of experimental neurosis that it shares with human neurosis. It is generalization. The experimental animal is not only disturbed in the experimental cage but also in the experimental room. That is not surprising because when he was shocked, stimuli from that room also acquired the power to disturb him. But in addition, he is disturbed in other rooms in a measure that depends upon their resemblance to the experimental room. That is generalization.

In order to overcome these neuroses, I made use of two of the facts I mentioned: first, that anxiety inhibits feeding, and second, the fact of stimulus generalization. You see that if anxiety inhibits feeding it must, in a sense, have a greater "voltage" at its disposal than feeding. So I figured that if we could reverse the relative "voltages," perhaps the feeding impulse would dominate and would inhibit the anxiety; and that that would result in weakening of the anxiety habit. This is precisely what happened. I offered the animal food in these various rooms to which anxiety was generalized, in descending order of their resemblance to the experimental room and always found one where the animal would eat, at first with hesitation and then more and more readily, so that at last he would be looking around for food. Then he would eat in a room more like the experimental room; and going through our succession of stages, he eventually ate in the experimental cage and finally lost all signs of anxiety there.

This finding led to the formulation of a general principle called the "reciprocal inhibition principle" which, briefly, is that any response that can compete with anxiety can weaken an anxiety habit to a given stimulus if it is evoked strongly enough to inhibit the anxiety evoked by that stimulus. There are many clinical techniques that have been based upon this. Although feeding has been used in children, it has not been successful in adults. Fortunately there is a horde of other responses that are capable of inhibiting anxiety. The most commonly used is relaxation, the autonomic effects of which are demonstrably opposite to those of anxiety. Other emotions can be induced through imagery, such as sexual emotions, or the pleasurable responses to scenes like lying on the beach or skiing. One may also use responses obtained by direct suggestion. Other media that have been used include transcendental meditation, oriental exercises and certain drugs that inhibit anxiety.

In order to illustrate how the reciprocal inhibition principle is used, let me describe briefly the standard systematic desensitization procedure that uses relaxation. The patient is trained to relax. The sources of disturbance are organized into what we call hierarchies. For example, if you take the stutterer I referred to, suppose that he is anxious according to the number of strange people that are around. There would be a sequence of numbers according to which anxiety significantly arises. This sequence would be his hierarchy. The sequence might go like this: one, two, three, five, seven, ten, thirteen, sixteen, twenty, twenty-five, thirty, and so on until an asymptote is reached. When the hierarchy is completed and the patient sufficiently trained in relaxation, he is ready for desensitization. He is made to relax in a comfortable chair and asked to imagine for a few seconds being exposed to just one strange person, the image being repeated every minute or so until it no longer evokes anxiety. This usually requires three or four repetitions. Then two strange people are imagined, and so on all the way up the numerical list. What matters is that there is a transfer of the nonanxiety from the imaginary situations to the real. This will not happen in about 15% of people in whom anxiety can not be aroused by imaginary situations to begin with. In these people, you have to use real stimuli, or pictorial representations, if you wish to effect desensitization.

It may very well seem to you at this point that there is something cursory about the conduct of behavior therapy—that the therapist finds out what scares a person and does desensitization. Well, it really is not that way. With any patient who comes for behavior therapy, a careful survey is made of all areas of unadaptive responding. This history of each response is taken and its quantitative aspects studied. A detailed account is taken of the patient's early home life, of his educational and occupational history, and of his love life from its very first beginnings right up to the present. Then he is given a number of questionnaires to throw further light upon his behavior. Only then does the therapist begin to plan therapy.

I would like to give you an illustration of what is involved in the behavior analysis and how it determines the content of behavior therapy. A woman of thirty-six was sent to me by a probation officer because for about sixteen years she had been shoplifting very, very often. She had been caught at least a hundred times and arrested four times, all of this in spite of the fact that her husband is a prosperous businessman. By going into the details of the circumstances surrounding the acts of stealing, I found that she had a lot of tension at giving up anything of value. The analysis pointed to two contexts for emotional desensitization. One was this: if she were to take her three children out to dinner at a coffee shop and if the bill were to come to more than five dollars she would become anxious. So, we had one desensitization series in which she imagined herself sitting in the coffee shop with the kids. In the first scene the bill was six dollars. This at first produced some anxiety, but with repetition it went away. Then we made the bill seven dollars and the same thing happened, and gradually it was raised to twenty dollars in the course of two sessions. She then reported to me that she was for the first time able to say to her kids when they went out to dinner, "You can have anything you like on the menu." And she was quite undisturbed by this.

The other context was more directly germane to the shoplifting problem. It was anxiety at having failed to appropriate an article she could easily have taken. She was asked to imagine the following: "You've just come out of a department store and you remember that you were in a remote corner of the store where you could easily have taken a jar of artichoke hearts for 69¢, but you didn't do it." Now, you see, the thought that she could have done it but did not evoked anxiety. This diminished to zero in a few repetitions. I gradually increased the value of the untaken item, and in two sessions its value was $65.00. It is now about four weeks since we did this, and she is very pleased with herself because she says she now goes into stores with a feeling of freedom. There is no longer any emotional compulsion to steal things.[2]

One thing I want to mention is that apart from desensitizing ways of treating anxiety (making one's way up a hierarchy), there is another important mode that has recently come into prominence, and that is called "flooding." Here the patient is exposed to a moderately strong anxiety stimulus continuously for prolonged periods. In quite a number of patients the first effect of this is ascending anxiety, and then, in ten to forty minutes, the anxiety level starts coming down. If it does come down substantially one finds that at the next session, anxiety does not go up quite so high. Sometimes rapid recovery ensues from this kind of method. While it is most correctly called "flooding," other names have also been attached to it emerging from other orientations—"implosive therapy" or "paradoxical intention."

All of these methods that I have so far spoken about relate to what you might call "phobia-like" anxiety of which the model is the classical phobia. It is certainly not a classical phobia to be excessively disturbed by criticism—but there is a basic similarity in being a passive respondent to a disturbing stimulus. In either case, there is nothing that the person can do about the object that produces anxiety. There are other stimuli to which anxiety can be conditioned towards which the person can and needs to take action. For example, there are people who are inhibited by anxiety from appropriate behavior towards those who take advantage of them. What is needed here is to teach them how to express their proper feelings, which are usually angry feelings. You can easily see that if a person is taken advantage of, one does not want to desensitize him to being taken advantage of. One wants him to be able to deal with the situation. The method we use is called "assertive training." To take an example that I frequently use, I say to the patient, "Suppose you are standing in line and somebody gets in front of you, what will you do?" He replies, "I feel all mad, I just boil up inside." I ask, "Why don't you do anything about it?" His answer is: "I don't want to hurt the other guy's feelings," or "I don't want to make a scene." "Why don't you want to make a scene?" "Because I would be disturbed if I made a scene." So I point out to him that it is proper for him to stand up for his reasonable rights and that he ought to say to the person, "This is a line and would you please get to the back of it" or something like that. In doing this, he would be expressing his feelings of annoyance. In expressing these feelings he will be pushing back the anxiety that he simultaneously feels. If he does this kind of thing constantly in suitable

---

[2] Recovery has now persisted for seventeen months.

circumstances, he will feel less and less anxiety. He will be breaking the anxiety habit and at the same time building up new motor habits for these situations. The motor habit is reinforced by its positive consequences—in the above example by the intruder going to the back of the line, and by the approbation of the other people standing there.

Another context into which a need for new motor behavior enters is where there is inhibition of sexual responses. In men who suffer from inadequate sexual performance the problem is generally associated with anxiety in the sexual situation. A built-in counter-anxiety agent is available. The sexual response itself is anxiety inhibiting. Anxiety can interfere with it, unless it is relatively strong, in which case it will inhibit the anxiety. What the therapist must do is find out at what point in the sexual approach anxiety begins and instruct the patient not to go beyond that point. For example, if he is anxious just lying in bed nude with his wife or girlfriend, he is told not to make any further approach. You can easily see that if he were suddenly to lie inert without explanation, his wife might think it odd. So she has got to be told that there is a therapeutic program afoot and asked to cooperate by not pushing him or ridiculing him. If she does, you will usually find that progressive approximations can be made, going eventually to partial intromission, increasing intromission, and increasing movement. Provided that there are frequent opportunities for interaction, about 70% of these subjects overcome this problem and 15% more improve substantially in an average of about eight weeks.

Now I come to one of the crucial things in this symposium—the matter of results. You get all kinds of new therapies appearing on the scene: reality therapy and encounter groups and marathon therapy—a thousand different things. The protagonists are very enthusiastic about their therapies. Each thinks that he has got the "open sesame" to neurotic problems. The fact is that all therapies produce substantial results. It seems not to matter what you do—outside of behavior therapy—you will get something like 40 or 40% of your patients substantially better. This is fortunate in one way. It means that some of the patients of all therapists get better. What is unfortunate is that this amount of success leads all the therapists to think that their specific procedures are effective. It is most unlikely that they are all effective to the same extent. The inference is that there must be some common factor which operates in the therapies leading to 40 or 50% of the results. The only therapy in which a systematic attempt has been made to measure whether the therapy itself adds anything to this common source of change is behavior therapy. It has been clearly established that systematic desensitization at least produces effects which are statistically superior to those attributable to the nonspecific common process. A study that is particularly significant in this context was done by Gordon Paul (1966b) at the University of Illinois, because the five therapists involved were all psychoanalytically oriented. Each treated severe public speaking fears with their own insight methods, systematic desensitization, and a procedure called "attention placebo." They got significantly the best results with systematic desensitization.

There have been a number of studies of this kind supporting the conclusion that behavior therapy adds something to the nonspecific effects. The question that Dr. Jourard must face, if he proposes that self-disclosure therapy is specifically effective, is whether in doing it he gets results that are measurably greater than those that he would get if he were doing something else, like Christian Science. It is quite evident to all of us who have been listening to Dr. Jourard that his personal impact on his patients must be very great indeed. Unless he has the evidence of controlled comparisons like those that behavior therapists have been putting forth, I can see no alternative but to put Dr. Jourard in the same boat as the reality therapists, the marathon therapists and the others.

The final thing that I would like to say is that when people of a psychoanalytic persuasion are told of behavior therapy they prognosticate that though it may produce results, these are subject to relapse and symptom substitution. The truth is that these things do not happen. Neither relapse nor substitution occurs in behaviorally treated patients whose cases have been analyzed and treated by trained therapists. It is of some interest to add that recently a controlled study was completed in our department by uncommitted psychiatrists, in which the effects of psychoanalytically oriented therapy were compared with those of behavior therapy. A result that surprised them was that behavior therapy produced more change in general adjustment than psychoanalytically oriented therapy did.

DR. WOLPE—QUESTIONS AND ANSWERS

Question: When a person comes complaining of suffering, doesn't behavior therapy mold him into the society rather than encourage change in the society?

Answer: The society, like the climate, is part of the general environment. A person says, "I get anxious when I go into a lecture theater," and he would like not to be anxious. The judgment about what is to be changed comes from him.

Similarly, this woman that I told you about, this kleptomaniac, would rather not steal but she goes on doing it. She is the one who sets the target. Our job is to provide the method for achieving the patient's target. Does that answer your question or not?

Q: Not really. It's a question of value between a different kind of society other than the society that bred the values.

A: I don't understand. In what way would the person who has kleptomania have a different goal in another society?

Q: Well, it depends how you look at the value of property. ("Oh, dear"— girl in audience.)

A: The point has to be faced that there are certain rules which make it possible for people to live in harmony. It seems reasonable that people should not steal what doesn't belong to them. This doesn't mean that there ought not to be a more equitable distribution of property in our society. But in any society you simply have to have rules. There are certain behavioral problems which would transcend society. Is there any society in which a person would, say, want to be anxious in elevators? But if he were content to be anxious in elevators, I would not forcibly try to treat him. I only treat people who dislike being anxious in elevators, or planes and cars or whatever it is.

Q: I'd be interested to hear why you think that in the Temple study those receiving behavior therapy made more personality change. I assume from that that you mean that successful treatment of the symptom sometimes generalizes to other aspects of a person's personality.

A: My answer is just an opinion based on what I know about how behavior therapy is conducted and what I presume to know about how insight therapy is conducted. The tendency would be for the behavior therapist to try to be aware of and plan reconditioning for everything that seems to be a difficulty for the patient. Time will be given to each problem. By contrast, the insight therapist will concentrate especially on insight related to the central target symptom.

Q: Could I ask you to address yourself to whether changes in a person's personality functioning occur through behavior therapy even though it is focused on a particular center?

A: That brings us to one of the widespread fallacies about behavior therapy. No therapist who is knowledgeable about behavior therapy would confine his attention to a single area. The behavior therapist makes a wide survey of the patient and may find several areas of unadaptiveness that the patient has not mentioned. Take, for example, this woman with kleptomania that I told you about. It looks as though she has recovered from the kleptomania. But my history elicited a very unsatisfactory marital situation. When she comes to see me now, we will be giving most of our attention to trying to set the marriage right. To this end, she and her husband are both coming next Tuesday. In other words, as long as a person is not functioning adaptively across the board, there is concern for the behavior therapist.

Q: Let's say you have desensitized a man to his anxiety and got him to the point where he is responsive sexually and satisfactorily happy, or you have relieved this woman of her kleptomania and she can comfortably take her children out for meals for the rest of her life. If these people later go to someone else for insight psychotherapy—if, for instance, they are experiencing some general dissatisfaction—and they want to dig deeper or somebody says that they ought to dig deeper does this ever reverse the achievements you've accomplished?

A: Well, first of all, I think this hardly ever happens. I suppose it can happen and when it does, the answer is "No." It does not reverse the achievements; but therapists can do things that are positively harmful to patients, and some therapists do. If you're interested in this topic, you ought to read a book by Richard Stuart called *Trick or Treatment* (1970), in which he quotes transcripts showing how therapists do increase the anxiety of patients. I myself have seen some shocking things done by therapists. When I was at the University of Virginia, a patient was brought to me for my opinion by the resident by whom she had been treated at the University hospital for a year. This resident had been supervised by an analytically oriented therapist who had on one occasion seen the patient and made a catastrophic remark to her. The patient had a kind of agoraphobia that was not getting better. The supervisor had said, "If you don't start improving, we'll send you to Western States Hospital." That produced another neurosis, a dread generalizing to all hospitals. I do not know whether or not psychoanalytic teaching can be blamed for that statement; but things like that are said and harm done not infrequently.

Q: If a lady steals a pair of stockings because she doesn't have the money to buy them, it might be considered unadaptive behavior in the legal context of our society. Yet it may be adaptive because she needs the stockings. How would behavior therapy treat that sort of case?

A: From the viewpoint of the lady who steals the stockings, if she succeeds and is not caught, she has performed an adaptive response. Society would frown on it, of course. If she were caught and sent to me, I might very well decide that there were no grounds for psychotherapy. What there would be grounds for would be an improvement in her economic position.

Q: In many of the papers I've read about behavior therapy, either the patient is in a controlled environment such as a hospital or the problem is under control because the stimulus isn't present. Do behavior therapists work in crisis intervention situations where one doesn't have environmental control over the patient and where the patient really isn't under a kind of control?

A: Certainly, many patients come in a state of crisis. In the December, 1971 issue of the *Journal of Behavior Therapy and Experimental Psychiatry*, there is an article on the use of behavior therapy in crisis intervention, by Paul Balson. I commend this journal to you. Among the journals devoted to behavior therapy, this one is especially geared to presenting the topic from a practical point of view.

Q: Let's say that it is May 13 and it is final exams and a student is on top of the gorge. Enter Dr. Wolpe. He's ready to jump. How does a behavior therapist approach a crisis situation such as that, and what kind of therapeutic technique would he use?

A: He would rush to the student and hold him back! There are all kinds of emergency problems. There are crises like failing examinations and losing all one's money at the stock exchange. These do not call for habit change operations—at least not primarily. A behavior therapist would try to comfort the person, give practical advice, or save his life, like anybody else.

Q: Would you address yourself to the question of the therapist variable? Is there a differentiation between the therapist's personality and your specific methods?

A: This is an important topic. The impact of the therapist can be very potent. As I mentioned in my lecture, it seems that a great part of the therapeutic effects that anybody obtains, including behavior therapists, is inadvertent and apparently depends upon the impact of the therapist as a person. The degree of impact must be to a great extent a personal matter. One patient may be positively attuned to a certain therapist and another to a second. The determining factors should be studied. What I would like to point out, though, is that it seems that when this interactive effect takes place it is also a matter of reciprocal inhibition. What happens, apparently, where benefit results, is that the patient reacts to the therapist with a complex of emotions which is variably made up but never predominantly anxious. This complex of emotions serves to inhibit the anxieties that would tend to be aroused verbally during the interview, because the patient will speak about things that disturb him, and if the anxiety is not too great it will be inhibited by the interpersonal emotional response.

DISCUSSION

Moderator (*Dr. Harry Levin*)*:* The first 10 minutes or so will be used to the two speakers to respond to each other's presentations and the rest of the time will be used for questions from the audience.

Dr. Jourard: I think the first thing that impresses me about Dr. Wolpe's presentation and Dr. Wolpe himself and what comes through over and beyond anything that he says is that he is a very nice and warm human being. And, I think, this is of the essence. If I were having difficulties, and I am having difficulties, as a matter of fact, in my life, I wouldn't find it repugnant to present myself to him because he inspires confidence and trust in me. (*Looking to Wolpe*) I want you to know that. I think also that you're a man of intelligence and judgment, so that if you saw that what you are doing is having consequences that you didn't want to happen, you would stop and take a fresh look, not just at what you are doing, but at your ways of thinking, and so on. In other words, I don't see you as a fanatic or a monk about your theory. I think your aim to foster life itself overrides your loyalty to any particular ideology, technique or theory.

Dr. Wolpe: I feel very reassured.

M: I would like as a speaker to hear all those nice things about me.

J: Now, these are reactions to you that I had had for one reason or another. I don't know what your original training as a psychiatrist was, but over the years it's evidently become increasingly meaningful and rewarding to you to think of the people who consult with you in the terms that have grown out of the study of behavior. This, it seems to me, has enabled you to do what you take to be your job as a physician and a psychiatrist more effectively, more ethically, and according to the dictum *primum non noscera*—the first thing must be you mustn't hurt the person consulting with you. And with all of this, I am in hearty agreement. I agree, for example, that whether a person is trained as a physician first or an academician first and then as a counselor or psychotherapist, there are persons in my acquaintance who share none of the characteristics that I attributed to you—a kind heart, common sense, and so on—they become fanatics. I think what I don't see acknowledged in your presentation or in the presentations of many of my colleagues who are very much into behavior analysis or behavior modification and so on is an explicit consideration of nonpsychological issues such as: In what kind of a society are we living? What is the connection between the life niche in which this person finds himself and the difficulties that he is seeking help for? For example, I wondered, as did our young friend here, about the klepto-maniac woman. The first kind of thought that occurred to me might be, "Is she bored? Is there a lack of excitement in her life?" Might it not be possible to look, not at a kleptomaniac, but instead to regard a kleptomania the way one regards a headache, boredom, or some other experience or action as an indication that all is not well? And one might look not at that symp-tom and not in the life history, either. I am no afficionado of the Oedipus complex. But I would look in the immediate life situation in which the person finds himself and see if there isn't something the changing of which might be, well, not easy as pie, but also not impossible. Then the so-called presenting symptom may vanish. This has happened in my experience many and many a time. The "symptomatic act or experience" is an indication that the person is not leveling with their spouse, or something of the sort; and when they start leveling with their spouse, the symptomatic happening vanishes. That's one qualification, or question, really, that I have. Is behavior therapy anything more or anything less than the alteration or suppression of what are taken to be symptomatic acts—which is not a bad thing, because to be able to get rid of unwanted emotional reactions or unwanted actions is groovy. The question always is, at what cost? Another comment I want to make is in response to your raising the question of what is the effectiveness of ways of doing or being a therapist. And I agree with a behavioral analysis, using that as a kind of metaphor, but you do what's rewarding and meaningful for you to do. And I have found that for myself, my ways of being with the people who consult with me are rewarded or reinforced by a swifter and more enduring report of competence where there was incompetence, hope where there was hopelessness, self-control where before there wasn't, and improvement of one's situation, not just one's behavior, but the garden in which one lives. I don't have data on it because I'm not particularly in a position yet to do systematic research or assessment, so I can only give a personal report. That's enough for an opener.

M: Thank you. Dr. Wolpe.

W: First, I would like to make some responses to the things that Dr. Jour-ard last said. First, with regard to the kind of patient that I described who came with, shall we say the "symptom" of kleptomania. There is something that needs to be remarked upon about the use of the word symptom. If you say that a certain behavior is a symptom, you are implying that there is something underlying. And that underlying thing, of course, most commonly is supposed to be a repressed complex. In other words, the behavior that you are seeing is presumed never to be the problem; it's always something else. In fact, some University of Chicago students long ago crystalized this into one sentence: Whatever it looks like, that's not it. Well, I don't know that you can say that, but, all the same, if you look at the way this particular case was treated, you will notice that we did not treat stealing as behavior. We tried to see what the chains of reaction were, and it became apparent that there was an emotional reaction that sort of compelled the stealing behavior, and the therapy was directed to changing the emotional reaction, with apparent success. Now, I don't say that this is all that was wrong with this patient, and I did mention that there are problems associated with her marriage to which we are directing attention. However, I would be quite dogmatic and prepared to say that she would not have stopped the kleptomania if her marriage was put right, for two reasons. Number one, the kleptomania began before she was married. Number two, there was a time, the first couple of years, in which the marriage was very satisfactory. So that, at least as far as I can tell, could not lie behind it. Again, the question has got to be raised, if there is something else, say in the marriage, is it a matter of not leveling? I don't know whether it is or not. I can tell you this, there is something wrong with the husband's approach to marriage. It's really quite bizarre. For example, one of the things that excites him most of all is for her to recount to him her experiences with other men. So there's quite a lot of openness, as you might say, inside that marriage as far as sexual behavior is concerned. You see, the point is still this—and I come now to Dr. Jourard's final remark. He says that he doesn't have data, but his impression is that he gets good things happening. Well, the fact is that this is what everybody says. And everybody attributes it to the specific interventions that he employs. I can very sincerely throw the softball back into Dr. Jourard's lap and say he's a very fine person, I'm sure. The non-specific interactions, the pleasant feelings that he arouses in many patients, must be very great indeed, and it may be those and not the other things that he did that are really proving effective. So until there is some kind of control data, we really don't know, and he doesn't know any more than you or I, whether or not his interventions *per se* are proving to be effective. Just one or two other things arise from his main presentation. I thought there was something rather interesting about Dr. Jourard's remarks about what Mowrer did to make himself feel better. Mowrer apparently found that he was very distressed by himself performing an act of dishonesty such as lying, and for that reason he made it a very strong principle to be absolutely open and disclose himself all the time, and so he felt better. Now, I would regard that as really a kind of defense behavior, an avoidance of something disturbing to the person's behavior, because I think that you can make no absolute, or almost no absolute, statements about human behavior. I think that a person ought to be able to lie under certain circumstances.

J: Me too.

W: Right. Well, I'm very happy to hear that. And if Mowrer is totally unable to lie, he's going to be very distressed whenever he does. He is incapacitated to an extent, and what he needs is to be desensitized so that he can lie to a reasonable degree.

J: It's not quite unfair, I think, to talk about Mowrer, because he is in the public domain and his matters are matters of his own writings and his own speeches. But Professor Mowrer, I think, is a very sound critic of certain kinds of therapy. His main whipping boy was psychoanalytic, orthodox psychoanalytic therapy, but he's also quite opposed to many of the encounter group techniques, and so on. And what he is saying is that for him and for many people like him, depression is an organic condition which is exacerbated by lying and duplicity, and can be helped by living truthfully and finding certain drugs that will help you. I have no quarrel with that. My quarrel with Mowrer, as it would be with you, and my behaviorist colleagues, is this: For whom is somebody good? How far can one assert that one's ways of trying to intervene helpfully in another person's life, while effective here, are going to be effective there and there and there? I know that for myself, in many instances—incidentally, I am not rigidly committed to any one way of being, including transparent—I concur that a person who is stuck on one way and only one way of being is a very deficient human being indeed. But I invented Jourard's rule: It's better to be able to do two things than one; it's better to be able to do three than two, and then to somehow get the wisdom to know when one, two, or three is appropriate. With children, for example, I certainly relate in ways that are an approximation of both desensitization and operant conditioning procedures because I'm not wholly unaware of that approach. And with other people, speaking to them in the context of dialogue where the nature of my intervention is to challenge them or to encourage them, there is nothing technical at all; and that turns out to be a way for them to take the initiative in changing their life. I think it good that there be a variety of approaches available both for someone who is a practitioner and for people who are seeking help. The problem is, what is the seeker to do when it's very expensive to shop around? How does one find the person and/or the school or theory of helping that is most likely to be the most helpful?

M : Dr. Jourard, let's go back to the audience and give them the last crack. It'd be most useful if you'd tell us to whom you're directing your question. Yes.

Q : This is mostly directed to Dr. Wolpe, about the majority of his work on inhibitions and things like that. In regard to the idea of a behavior model, which your behavior therapy does approach more than the humanistic approach, is there a danger in a sense of getting artifactual results which are due more to a supportive role? In specific, where you have gotten compliance of a woman in the therapy with a man, haven't you in a sense eliminated the negative stimulus of the woman's devalued role to the man's performance, which is what produced his anxiety in the first place? And, in a sense, you've eliminated the bed as the marriage battleground, and you produced results which, in my mind, would be more in a sense due to the supportiveness of the wife than to your behavioristic techniques. How can you qualify the effects?

W : Well, that's a good question and let me answer it. Where you treat a patient for a sexual disability in the way that I've described, by limiting the wife's behavior, you're quite right in saying that you're diminishing the impact of the wife's critical output in the sexual situation. But, you see, you are doing it in such a way that as you go along in the treatment, you're overcoming the little hurt. That amount of critical feeling which exists just lying next to her is removed by the counteracting effect of the sexual arousal, and then the patient gets a bit closer to intercourse, which reduces a little bit more criticism, and so on, and eventually he's actually having intercourse. He's having full intercourse and what happens is that he is feeling good about it, she is feeling good about it, and, insofar as his sexual performance is a major part of the grounds for her criticism, those grounds are removed. So you have changed not merely the physical act of sexual performance but all the consequences that originally emanated from failure.

J : I'd like to speak to this point because there's a great deal that Dr. Wolpe does, and some of my behavior modification colleagues do, which they describe in the terminology of that discipline but which can also be described—the same actions and interactions can be described—in another framework. So that when I talk about cases and I describe what I think has happened or what has been recorded, then one of my colleagues will say, "Well, clearly what that is, is a case of you eliciting this kind of behavior and then reinforcing it that way," to which I always reply, "Well, yes, it can be described that way, but here is how it was for me," and I'll mention a concrete instance of, let's say, a cured homosexual. I was barely 30 years old and just out of graduate school and training. And this young PhD around 27 or 28 had been, in his own words, "a flaming fag" since he was about 15 years of age. He was very troubled because it was going to get him into real difficulty. He was in danger of being betrayed, losing his job, reputation, and so on. And in the conversations that went on between us, he said he had been in therapy with a psychoanalyst for something like 300 hours, and with an orthodox Rogerian through the VA for another 250 hours, and, incidentally, he was collecting material for a dissertation on techniques of therapy. I knew that it was futile for me to be psychoanalytic or Rogerian with this chap. He was one of the people who helped me learn how to be a therapist beyond my training, as a matter of fact. And I found out about him from himself that he had grown up in a rural area, was very shy, had a very martyred mother, and they lived in a small house in the country. The father was a phys. ed. school teacher and a real brute of a man and the mother used to complain about what a burden she had to bear. He would hear them making love at night with loud noises. The father thought the boy was a sissy, why doesn't he go into town and play football with the other lads, because he listened to records and read, but if he did go into town and get involved with girls he should be careful, because you get the clap, and they might seize up on you like dogs. So he grew up thinking it hurt the women and it's dangerous for the men.

And he got seduced by a homosexual and it was kind of repugnant but meaningful for him, and I saw him as shy. And he was going with a girl who was interested in him, and he in her, but he could never get anywhere with her because he was afraid that something dangerous might happen to him if he got in, even though he knew better, and he would hurt her. He told me this story about when he was on the farm and all alone, he used to make it with a mare, a sheep, a turkey, and a cow. And when he told me about the cow, I burst out laughing and I asked him, "How, how do you make it with a cow?" He told me, "You stand up on the stool behind the cow and you place the tail to one side." I just burst out howling with laughter. He thought I was crazy, and he asked me why I was laughing and I told him when I was helping the Canadian War effort in about 1942 in Canada, we all worked on farms because everybody was at war. And the hired man had this city boy whose job it was to strip the cows after the milking machine had been on and that was my job so I said, "How do you do it?" He said, "You get on a stool behind the cow and you push its tail to one side and reach under it and grab hold of the teats and squeeze." Which is exactly what I did, and the cow kicked me in the belly and sent me sprawling into the manure. When I told this to this boy he started howling with laughter too and I said, "You mean you're afraid of a soft, gentle, lovely woman and yet you would get behind a cow, a highly dangerous beast?" And so he howled with laughter and about two days later he called me for an emergency meeting. I thought it was a homosexual panic because I still believed in that sort of thing, but it wasn't that at all. He had spent the night with his girlfriend and he had made it four times. He was like Ensign Pulver of *Mister Roberts*, and he was rejoicing that it not only didn't hurt, but it beat men all to hell.

M: Well, I'm sure this case Dr. Wolpe could handle very nicely in his framework, too, and I think instead, if I could take that urge away from Dr. Wolpe, we'll return to the audience. May we have further questions.

Q: I would like to address one question to each of our speakers. Dr. Jourard, I wonder whether you have any concern about humanity, transparency, openness, honesty as suitable or adequate coping devices for people who are going to be thrust back into the kind of world in which we find ourselves living. How appropriate, for example, is this value system for the bomber pilot, business executive, and so on down the line to perhaps even teachers, people whose position requires them in some ways to treat other people instrumentally, exercise control, and so on? Should I put the other question now, too? Dr. Wolpe, I'm very much impressed with your work and that of others in your field dealing with specific—I avoid the term symptoms—behaviors that are clearly aversive that the patient would like to get rid of. I'm curious to know how you might apply this approach to one of the most generic kinds of problems today: apathy, undermotivation, the kids who are alienated, don't give a damn, perhaps don't even see themselves as problems as much as their mothers do.

M: Take the second question first.

W: Okay. There are, of course, people who have a variety of what you might call chronic emotional states that don't seem to have relation to anything—apathy, depression, and anxiety which is sometimes what you would call free-floating anxiety. The fact is that in all these cases you have to do a behavioral analysis. It's the same thing that applies to anything else. First of all, there is such a thing as free-floating anxiety, which is anxiety that is there all the time and not attached to any clearly definable stimulus. We believe that this is, however, anxiety which is attached to basic aspects of experience such as the awareness of one's own body, or space and time, light and shade contrasts, things that are sort of persistently present. In fact, a free-floating anxiety can be temporarily washed away by a remarkably dramatic technique, giving the patient several single full capacity inhalations of about 60% carbon dioxide and 40% oxygen, just one breath at a time. If you do this three or four times, you will find that very persistent anxiety may be brought down to zero or close to zero and will stay like that until the patient is again exposed to a specific anxiety-evoking situation. Well, there are some depressions which really are anxiety equivalents, that you might call free-floating depressions, depressions in the same sense as there is free-floating anxiety. And, as in the case of the anxiety, what you find yourself needing to do is deconditioning the feed source of this ongoing depression which you have to identify. There is also a class of depressions which is related to frustration or to loss. There is now a very interesting experimental analog for the classical kind of depression that has been presented by Martin Seligman of the University Pennsylvania. I can't go into the details, but in essence if you persistently shock an animal so that he can do nothing about it, he develops a kind of habit of helplessness even in situations with shock from which he could escape; and this is closely analogous to the human development. He has worked out a treatment paradigm which can be applied to human patients of this sort. Now, as regards the apathy which you specifically mentioned, I think that has various sources. Sometimes I think it is a form of depression. It is in fact this experimental or conditioned helplessness to which Seligman refers. Sometimes it is a result of being in a true dead-end situation. Sometimes it turns out that your case is schizophrenic and there isn't anything very much behavioral that you can do about it.

M: If I may paraphrase Prof. Devereux's question, I think it is: Behavior therapy has an easier job with actual overt behavior that one can bring under control, but how about the lack of behavior? I'm talking about an operant situation in that case, where the apathetic person's behavior has to be shaped outward, as it were.

W: Well, if behavior therapy has to be instituted, your analysis must tell you what the person needs to know and, in fact, this kind of thing enters in a variety of ways. I have seen a person who was very unadaptive to a great extent because she simply didn't know how to do a variety of simple acts such as, incredible as it may sound, how to pour a cup of tea, and these behaviors had to be shown. There is a case that I'm just at this very time treating, in front of a group of Temple residents, of a young man with a kind of exhibitionism. It's not a real exhibitionism. Well, let me tell you very quickly what it's about. He's been arrested three or four times because what in essence he does is to go into a young woman's bedroom (once he climbed through a window and on a couple of other occasions made his way through the door), where he completely undresses and waits for her to come. I'm using the word in a special sense, I mean "arrive." Well, his thinking is that when she does arrive, she will just lie down on the bed and wait for him to have intercourse with her. Of course, she doesn't. Instead, she screams and calls her parents and the police and so he's been arrested. Now, it turns out that the trouble is that he simply does not know how to begin to make an approach to a girl. So the first thing that we did was to show him physically, using one young woman student as a model, what you are supposed to do and said: "Now go out and see if you can do it". Well, while I was away in Dallas, there was a two week gap which gave him time to try his behavior. Well he came back on Wednesday and he said that he hadn't been able to do it. Now, why hadn't he been able to do it? Because there was great anxiety at the idea of making this kind of approach. So there's an anxiety block for the behavior. What we started to do at this last session was desensitize him so that he no longer has anxiety to making the approach. I expect to take two or three sessions to do that and then I think he would be able to go ahead, make approaches, and make it.

M: Now, the first question: How about when transparency is unadaptive, in reference to modern jobs?

J: I have no difficulty conceptually or existentially. I think it's good to be able to be absolutely transparent in situations where it's appropriate, as in personal relationships, for example. And where it's going to be destructive, I think it's very important to be effective at acting, lying, subterfuge, cunning, and anything else that's called for. I do think, as Professor Wolpe and I agree, that it's better to be able to swing both ways than to be fixated in one particular mode.

Q: Prof. Wolpe, You mentioned several times about getting enough done on some of the things which Prof. Jourard mentions, such as transparency and openness, and I would like to refer you to work that started out with Eysenck's challenge to psychotherapy, which was in the mid-1950s; and that challenge was taken up by Rogers and his associates in Wisconsin. Much work was done with therapists who were psychoanalytically oriented, and Rogerian therapists, and other therapists who had been trained in various schools of thought; and they found that certain counselor variables—empathy, sex, congruence, and nondetrimental attitude—were very important in the counselor–client relationship. They developed a training program which has since moved to the University of Massachusetts, and Alan Ivy has recently put out a book on micro-counseling. I really think that the charge that systematic research has not been done is a very, very bad one, when it has.

W: Well, can I defend myself? It's quite true that certain therapist characteristics have been correlated with outcome in psychotherapy, but this relates to the nonspecific factors, the kinds of factors which belong to all kinds of therapy. What I was referring to was the specific interventions, the kinds of things the therapist makes the patient do, even if it's standing on the head, which is one of the things Dr. Jourard mentioned as a possibility. That kind of thing has not been systematically studied except when the interventions have been behavioristic.

Q: The challenge to psychotherapy by Eysenck was on the basis that psychotherapy had not been systematically studied; and what actually came out of the work of Rogers was that it does not matter as far as your intervention is concerned. What really matters is your counselor variables, and that is the most important thing. One of the more important things in the counselor–client relationship related to the extent that clients will get well is if the counselor has very high empathy and congruence, which is similar to transparency, and accepts the client, whereas the client will not get well if these variables are not found. And work was also done toward the personality theory of adjustment–maladjustment on the variables in the client–counselor experience.

W: Okay. In fact you really are agreeing with me. You see, the thing is that there are those factors that are relevant to the nonspecific interaction. Now, it seems to me at this moment, all therapies other than behavior therapy depend almost exclusively upon those factors. What you're saying must be true of them but it does not seem to be true of behavior therapy because there is evidence that behavior therapy achieves effects over and above those that you can attribute to these personality variables.

J: I'll agree with him in principle if not in data, because I don't have as much experience with that as he has, but the introduction of some kind of a change needs to be made when someone is not living effectively. Any approach to a person that is successful in getting him to begin to change his action is an intervention, and it need not take very long. And I can say from my own experience that the more I embody what he's calling these nonspecific factors, the more likely it is that the person will accept an invitation to change something. And, as I say, I don't hesitate to invite a person to try something. And if he tries it and fails, I'll say, "Well, I'm glad that you tried." And you can state that in behavioristic terms, and I don't care how you state it, but I certainly am concerned with trying to help a person break out of an impasse in a nonharmful way by changing something.

M : These characteristics of the successful therapist remind me very much of what we hear about as the characteristics of the successful teacher. It doesn't matter what the teacher does so long as she's understanding, warm, empathetic, and so on, and that seems to me really not the answer to Eysenck's question, because something must happen in interaction between the therapist and the client. What does this warm person do? Simply having these personality characteristics locked in a box so that the other person, the client, doesn't see them obviously isn't going to make any change. So I would say that every time we come out with a series of studies of this sort, and we do in a variety of fields, saying it has to do with the characteristics of the person is only the first step. It really isn't the answer to the question; it's making the question a little more difficult.

J : You're talking really about effectiveness as a kind of leader or seducer or someone in whom one can place confidence, so that when he suggests something or leads or points, you'll pay attention to it. I think the specific factors beyond the nonspecific, I don't know what to call it, faith or confidence that is inspired is probably a factor of common sense. I know a lot of teachers who are empathetic and warm and congruent, but they don't challenge their students to read or to write things. I have a reaction to, I guess it's not your work Professor Wolpe, so much as my colleague who has all these students reading textbooks in programmed ways; and they all get A's on the final exam. The question is, will these people then get on and read on their own, or have they been trained to expect to be able to speed-read through or get through swiftly to answer some functional questions? There's no answer to that question yet, I'm sorry.

M : There's a question here though. Yes.

Q : Dr. Wolpe, you seem to be talking a lot about conditioning of the human organism. That is, if I wish to learn to read, I can learn to read efficiently. Or if I wish to reduce my anxiety, you have ways of helping me to reduce my anxiety. That's fine, in fact I think it's essential that we know ways of doing this, but do you think that your psychology really addresses itself to a full study of man? I mean, does it include motivation? That is, will I go out and read more, will I determine what I want to read, can I get that from you? Does behaviorism help me in any way towards that? Are you willing to say that there are other areas that are essential to the human being, such as empathy, love for the child? The child needs a lot more than just reinforcement, unless you're going to say love is reinforcement.

W : It is, isn't it?

Q: Well, it can serve that, it can be that, but it can be a lot more. What are the essential needs of the human being? Further to Dr. Jourard: You don't seem to be willing to say that there are human beings who want to go out and read something, and should know how to read efficiently. If it can only read very, very slowly, and can't read when it wants to, then it's going to make it feel terrible. It may not even do well. You don't seem to be willing to say, if you have a patient who claims he has just a bad habit or isn't functioning well, "You don't need my empathy, my warmth, and the kinds of things I am very good at giving. Go and see my friend, Dr. Wolpe." Do you do that, or do you. . . .

J: Or, better still, I have tried to learn how to be effective at getting a person to begin a program of changes, something very specific like that.

Q: Would you say you do it in a way of encouraging them to take on the burden? And it's, I think, a lot more than that. You know, they have to be directed to the right ways of taking on that burden. It's more than just that, they want to take it on.

J: I have sent my colleagues, Malgody and Pennypacker and some of their students, students and patients who are finding it difficult to make it in school because they couldn't efficiently prepare for exams, rather than have them dither with me about their mother doesn't like them or something.

M: And there was a part of the question for you, Dr. Wolpe.

W: Well, the question seemed to me to be: Apart from trying to overcome people's unadaptive habits, can I do something more, give people motivation, make them receptive to love and things like that? I'm not terribly clear about the question; I would like some more specification, because the way it stands, it really seems as if to ask: Can I create a human being? I mean, here's a person who's functioning well enough but, well, he doesn't perhaps show warmth as much as some other people. Well, you know, there are great variations in human beings, and I think some degree of that has got to be accepted.

Q: I wasn't clear. Does a human being need reinforcement, shall we say, but does he need specifically love, does he need empathy, does he need. . . . What constitutes a human being in terms of his needs, in terms of his experiences, more than just how efficiently he's able to handle things in the world and not have anxiety get in the way?

W: Are you asking: Should the individual find love, should he find someone to love him? I would say on the whole, yes, because to most people this sort of thing is rewarding, and therefore he ought to have the techniques, the behaviors that will lead him to finding love. That, I suppose, is one of the things we are trying to do to this young man who undresses in ladies' bedrooms. Is that the kind of thing you mean or not?

Q: I'd say, yes, he should have the ability to do what he wants, and that's what you've addressed yourself to. And if he wants love, he should know the proper ways to go out and effectively get it. I'm saying, can your psychology of man begin to address itself to really what the needs of human beings are? That is, do they just want any reinforcement they can get, and do you just tell people how to get all those reinforcements?

W: I'm going to tell you that I don't set myself up, nor do I know any behaviorist or probably—I'm not quite sure that this is correct—but certainly I think it's true of most psychotherapists, they do not set out just to change people in society. They really treat the people who come to them because their function is in some sense below standard or they're having some positive suffering. They try to remove what is disabling. You say to me, "Can I make a person capable of responding with love to a wider range of women than, say, he does?" Maybe. I'm not quite sure.

II.B

Existential Quest

SIDNEY JOURARD

American Academy of Psychotherapists Tape Library

The tape is of the second interview with the client. The interview actually took place at the television studio at the university. The client wanted to produce an authentic example of therapy for students in counselor education. He feels it is not necessary to mention this, because, as he puts it, "I could not have been with you [Jourard] as I was, if I hadn't had some legitimate needs to take to the therapy hour."

In my view, he was quite courageous in letting himself be seen (on video tape) as the troubled person he was. Our interchange, as recorded on the tape, is real.

He and I did not have any further sessions, but I know that the encounters which occurred in our two sessions were instrumental in helping him firm up his resolve and courage to make some changes in his life, abandon some compromises that weren't working for him any more, and to take some public stands on controversial issues that made him much more of himself.

Patient: Now, I've been thinking, ah, since we talked last week. One of the things we talked about, ah, that's been kind of ratting around in my head— and I, I feel as if I kind of glossed over it—was this business about, well, I don't remember just in what words, but about my attitude toward my work, and toward, ah, the feeling that, I think that I said that I have more or less come to terms with, a kind of balance in which, I, invest myself in a lot of activities— and not, know myself out on the job to the exclusion of other things. I was part of it. I was sort of dealing with some of my mixed feelings about not being as productive and successful in conventional terms, or usual criteria as sometimes I think I ought to be. But I, I manage somehow to not realize til after the session was over, and sometime later, that there is more to it than

83

that, really. I think what bothers me is, a kind of recurring feeling that I'm just not as vitally interested in my professional field, as I sometimes would like to be, or I don't know whether I would like or think I ought to be. I, a lot of the time, feel as if this whole business of counseling and guidance in the schools and colleges is not a very exciting thing. It's kind of overrated. It's somewhat stagnant. It has a place, but I can't get—amount of great deal of enthusiasm about striding forward with great pioneering efforts and innovative efforts to, to make it the great crusade of the 20th century.

Therapist: You're talking so low and flat. It makes me wonder why. You seem hardly with it here.

P: Yeah, well, I think it's partly that the lights and the cameras, although I usually get over that pretty quick. (*Pause—lights a cigarette.*) I think that it is partly this, this is difficult and distasteful for me to talk to you about it. You know, maybe it's easier for me to talk about this with somebody who is not a big-shot fellow professional, and some of it, of that—but I go through these feelings of ah, well, in the last year or so, I have fantasied from time to time about retirement. And, I'm fifty years old and it seems to me that this is awful young to start spending much time thinking about retirement. (*laughs*) But, the freedom of having a modest but adequate income to do a little traveling and things of this kind and just sort of spend your time not loafing but doing things that you want to do, doing things I want to do, is—has a powerful appeal to me. Now, I've even done some, some calculating as to, if I retired x number of years earlier than 65, ah, how much would my retirement income be. Would it be enough? You know, I guess once you've been on the payroll of the university for ten years, you are in the retirement system—

T: From what you've been saying, it's almost as if you retired—from your career before you really got into it. I hear you saying that—you are not really gung-ho about being a professor or counselor or whatever. There's something else you'd rather be doing. What would you rather be doing?

P: Well, I think that part of the problem is, there isn't any one thing I would rather be doing. There isn't any one—there isn't another career I would rather have. The thing I think I would rather be doing is a kind of collection of hobbies rather than a single career. Ah, hobbies. Hobbies sounds kind of, sort of a mosaic, a constellation, not a grabbag but, a sort of constellation of small things, I guess in which none of, not one of which do I invest my whole self. (*T:* Well, then, what's been stopping you from doing this, all along?) Well, I approximate it, but you have to have one—you have to have an income. And, I don't have, I don't have a whole bunch of marketable talents out of which I can make an income, without any one of them being a full-time job. Besides,

I haven't always seen it this way. I mean, I think, I'm not sure I always see it this way now. I get very enthusiastic from time to time about some particular thing I'm doing in my work. It's just that it's not sustained. It's not consistent. It frequently wanes.

T: I hear you saying—that your life's gone stale. There's nothing, there's nothing in it, to turn you on, for any long period of time. You're casting about for something to do with yourself.

P: Well, it seems to me that what I'm saying is, that my—what'd you say?—You hear me saying my life's gone stale. This sounds to me much more conclusive, and negative than I feel. I don't feel that my life's gone stale. I feel that it ought to have a kind of continuing thrust that centers around a main activity. A job, a career. Whereas, instead it has a kind of faltering, sputtering—the career, certain things about it, about my work, I enjoy and get satisfaction out of, but I don't have, I don't have this feeling that there is a big, significant contribution that I, that I have to make to the field, and that everything is kind of woven around that. I feel more like a hack or a technician than a creative person in my field. But, I don't feel that my life's gone stale because I'm—there are a lot of things I do that do turn me on. They just don't all seem to have a, they aren't all—or mainly—they aren't mainly built into a job (*pause*).

T: You strike me—just in the way you are, right here and now, as sort of flat, turned off, depressed, all those things. I think you came to life for a minute; you were waving your hands. But, most time, you were sitting like this and talking in a very low flat tone. My voi—my work; I'm sort of a hack technician in it, and I don't feel that I'm making a contribution there, and I'd like a mosaic, of things.

P: Yeah, well I think that's the way I feel. I feel sort of depressed. I also feel a little bit, as if I'm—I want to talk to you and that, I—I find myself just slightly feeling as if I'm justifying myself to you or arguing with you instead of talking to you. As if, when you said, that I sounded as if I were saying my life had gone stale, you know—it wasn't just now. I want to be clear in what I'm saying, but, a little bit as if I'm being—you're accusing me. And, also, I had the feeling that, and I don't know whether you meant it this way, but that when you tell me I'm, ah, my voice is low and flat, that this too, is an accusation. I should—a good counselee is more lively (*laughs, as does T*). I guess, you were just saying this is what, you were perceiving. And not, that it shouldn't necessarily be that way. (*T:* Well, I'm wondering, why?) Yeah.

T: And how I can be helpful if you don't like being that way. I myself am just coming out of a kind of slump. It's lasted almost a year from—I work best when I have a big project going. And it keeps me jumping and vital and alive and when I finish it, I go a little bit crazy. I don't quite know what to do with myself; I do get depressed; and I make a whole bunch of false starts. Ah, which gets me into a lot of trouble. I implicate other people in them and then I drop them, and it's only in the past couple of months that I've begun to get—the dim view of some new, new projects that are turning me on. And I wonder if something like that isn't going on with you. You're about ten years older than I am. You may well have reached the end of one tether (*pause*).

P: Yeah, well of course, I mean part of the problem—part of the problem I was talking about last time is that (*lights cigarette*) the guilty feelings that I sometimes have about the size of the projects that I do get involved in. I guess, this is what I mean by being a hack. I don't write books; I don't invent theories—I—by certain standards, the projects I get involved in are rather modest. And also, I sometimes—sometimes feel like avoiding getting involved in them. For instance, ah, when I wrote a proposal for an NDEA grant, Guidance Institute. I enjoyed this and I got a sense of satisfaction and accomplishment of, of its being, out of its being successful. And then I did another one. (*T:* Now, I fail grants.) Yeah, well, you know I fe—Immediately I catch myself starting to, ah, with my usual style, to, to give the demurrs, you know, and it won't, it wasn't no great big thing and all that—and, there was a certain amount of model to go by and so forth, but anyway, all right, so this was something. But after two of these, instead of saying, well, now by golly, let's look around for something even more imaginative, even bigger and so on, my feeling is, well, let's quit while we're even. OK, I don't want to do anymore of these, now. I'd like to ah, sort of get back into the, into the crowd for awhile and just, do little things.

T: You don't say it very joyously—and I can't help wondering, what's wrong with that? (*P:* Ah, what do you mean?) What's wrong with wanting to be in the crowd for awhile and doing little things?

P: (*pause*): Well, partly, the same old business of, its wrong because that's the way it is defined. (*T:* By who?) By the, by the people who control the rewards in professional life. Promotions and pay raises. And it, you know, I mean, I was talking about this last time—in a sense, I feel that if I don't agree with them, then—I'm sort of in a half-assed position—because I stay in the system; I accept, because I'm forced to, their evaluation of me by their criteria, sort of meekly. Now I say, well, I'm not interested in doing research and publishing. I'll do these other things, which seem good to me, but which are not as highly valued by the valuers, so I'll take their results, which is more meager pay and less frequent promotion, and maybe not as high a promotion in the long run. I don't know. I guess I have the feeling, sometimes, that if I had the courage of my conviction, if this is a matter of conviction rather than just an inertia or fear, that I would get into some other system, where the rewards were more related to my criteria.

T: I'm a bit confused here. Ah, you say that the evaluators, whoever they are, put a little value on you. You don't get promoted; you don't get the raises and so on, and because you don't meet their criteria. But, I also hear you saying that the way they value you is the way you value yourself. And that puts you into a kind of a bind. Do you share their values?

P: Well, I think what I was saying was that, I think this is a point on which I'm confused. I think that I have my own values—and that I don't share theirs, for me. I have a certain amount of understanding—

T: Well, no. I almost hear you saying of yourself, ah, I'm a nebbish. I'm not really worth very much. I'm a hack. My contribution isn't worth much and the proof of it is, I don't get paid. I don't get promoted. Is this really how you feel about yourself?

P: NO, NO! I'm saying I am perceived as something of a nebbish and this is the proof, cause these are the, these are the rewards of—but I, the way in which I see myself as a nebbish, in-so-far as I do, is that I stay here, and let myself be evaluated this way, not that I evaluate myself this way—unless that is what it winds up amounting to. But that—I'm raising the question, if I really think that I'm a valid person, that my way of being me is a good way and is right for me, and that I don't have to do these things that some others expect of me, then why do I stay in a place where that's what they expect of you—and where the things that I think are right for me are—well, I started to say, are not officially rewarded. Yet, see I'm also, I think of myself as somebody who doesn't, who I don't need to get rewarded for everything I do. I really, I mean, ideally I'd like to live a life in which what I do is intrinsically rewarding because I enjoy it. I'm kind of going around in a circle on myself, I think.

T: I'm trying to figure out, what kind of a conscience you've got and could I live with it. Cause you seem, you do sound to be berating the daylights out of yourself, but in a kind of confused way. It's almost like, I'm worthless, because I don't produce, and I should feel guilty. But on the other hand, I'm told that it's all right to be the way you are—so I shouldn't feel guilty, or worthless. You're sort of caught in that—ah—confused bind.

P: Well, I don't, the only thing that sounds wrong to me in that is the, I am told—because that implies that all of my—that I see all of—all of the bases for self-evaluation as coming from outside, and I don't. I think part of my sense of being nonproductive is my own feeling, of lack of commitment, that I st—that

I mentioned earlier, that I started out with. In other words, there are a lot of things that interest me, but I see myself not as a nebbish, but as a kind of a dilettante. As a person who refrains from immersing himself very, very thoroughly in one thing.

T: Well, that's a way to be. But you don't like it. I hear you saying you should be gung-ho, great producer. And, and since you're not, you don't feel right about it.

P: (*laughs*): Yeah, it's the trouble is, it's not, I guess what I'm seeking for is a, is not an absolutely, stagnant thing, but a kind of consistent feeling. Some of the time I do feel very right about it. Some of the time I feel kind of rebelliously right about it because I feel other people don't but I do approve of it. Some of the time I feel sort of comfortable with it. I suppose, particularly when I'm enjoying, ah, certain amount of, sense of achievement in one of these activities. Whether it's the job, or something recreational. If I feel that I'm doing it, that I'm doing it, using myself in it, doing it well and enjoying it—But it, I go through periods, such as the one I've been going through lately, of a just kind of feeling that it all adds up to less than I want. Now, you say, what's wrong with a, being I mean there are various ways of being, and that's the way you could be, and I don't know. My reaction is fine, sure. There's nothing wrong in the abstract with being a person who does a lot of things and doesn't commit himself completely to one of them.

T: Just a sec, ah, it's possible, I think to do work that earns your salary and it doesn't completely turn you on, but its meaningful and you do it, and you do it well. But you throw your passion into some other part of your life. What's the rest of your life like? Family—leisure—what have you got going there?

P: Well, I think that's what I'm saying. It's, oh, well, I have a lot going for me there. I also have some going for me in my job. I mean there, it's almost as if there are certain segments of my job which are like some of my extracurricular activities. My work in the theatre—my wife and I work with a drama group extracurricularly and, associated with a church. This takes up a, only a small amount of time but it's something that, I get a great deal of satisfaction out of. And I occasionally act in the plays in the community theater, and I'm a member of a Great Books group and these things are, all very satisfying to me. I think there was a time in my life when I sort of reached out to certain activities like this for, ah, excitement.

T: Something doesn't fit. You're talking about all these satisfactions, and I experience you as half dead. (*T:* Well (*long pause*) M-m-m.) No, let me give it to you. My extracurricular life is, has a lot of satisfaction in it. I take part in this. It doesn't take much time, but there's a lot of satisfaction in it. And in my work, there's a lot of satisfaction—granted you're not involved now in all these things. You're involved right here and now with me. Maybe that's depressing (*laughs*) but, the whole impact of the way you are with me just now, is like I said. I suppose that's why you're here.

P: I don't know. I guess, maybe the—I have two reactions to this term, halfdead. On one, I guess, in one sense, I took it almost literally; not, not literally, but spiritually literally, and in this sense—ah, I partly I wanted to reject it very strongly, and God damn it, no I'm half dead—and—

T: Well, I'm not saying it to put you down. I'm giving you my experience of you as I experience it.

P: Well, I don't think it matters—Well, I suppose it would matter. I mean the fact that you're not saying it to put me down—doesn't make it any less difficult for me to handle it. If it's true, it's far more devastating to me that it's true, than what your motive was in saying it. And I didn't feel you were trying to put me down. I felt you were saying, this is the way I come through to you, as half dead. And I, that kind of stopped me, because well, you know, you asked me, all right, what do you do with the rest of your life and I started telling you and all right—it sounded like a kind of maybe the enthusiasm that, maybe, I experience in doing some of those things didn't come through in the reciting of them. I felt a little bit, I'm trying, I'm being asked here to kind of drag out my little goodies and justify myself. If you don't live fully on the job, then do you live fully in some of these other things, and prove it, you know. Well, I could say, come watch me sometime, you know. Watch me at work in a rehearsal, or something, and judge for yourself. But then, you're not saying that, you know, at first, I thought you were saying your life sounds half dead, to me but what you're saying—(*T:* You make it sound half dead to me) (*pause*) I guess the other thing about the half dead that stopped me and made me, I'm trying to deal with is, whether there's any hope of revival of the half dead part or whether it's dead in the literal sense of, you know, unrevivable.

T: No, I don't think it's a hopeless proposition. I think, from what you've told me so far anyway, that you can't find something to get enthusiastic about—a relationship, a project—

P: Well, the way I see it is, I'm afraid to get enthusiastic about a big major project. Because I don't know, I don't know if I feel this way, but—(*T:* Maybe you're afraid of enthusiasm?). No—no, I'm not afraid of enthusiasm.

T: It's just—there's something that's nagging at me—and I'll tell you how it occurs to me. I'm repeating myself from last week, too. I get the image of you, ah, in a boat and it's got to stay dead level. And man, you're afraid to shake it.

There's something about the way you're living your life that makes me get the idea that you're afraid to make, to let go of anything or make any change that you've got a life that's more or less liveable but you're suffering from it one way or another because you're looking for help, of some kind. But you don't want to rock the boat too much—which is fair enough.

P: I think this is true. I think the way I've been thinking about it is—that there isn't any, well, I have to depart from the boat analogy—there isn't any direction in which I feel attracted to depart. I feel as if I would be happy to make a change, if there were, if I could find a direction in which I wanted to go, that I felt enthusiastic about. And then, I say to myself almost in the same breath, are you sure that it is a matter of not finding something you want, or is it just being afraid—afraid to rock the boat—afraid, as you said, to alter this nice balance. And the fear sort of prevents me from even taking the first step of finding something. For example, you mentioned the, at one, perhaps, acceptable pattern for life, is to have a job that's useful but not particularly, extraordinarily exciting, and then invest oneself in some other ways. I feel as if I'm in the kind of occupation in which you can't do that. You can't just kind of rock along. You're supposed to—not supposed to—the job demands the, the job demands a creative kind of commitment. There are jobs that don't. There are what Harry Hurst calls a society-maintaining jobs in contrast to the ego-involving jobs. The sort of caretaker jobs. And I sometimes fantasy about getting one of those—being a postal clerk or a proof reader, or some damn thing, where you go to work forty hours a week, eight hours a day and you don't take anything home with you mentally. And you go back and open up the office the next morning and start again. And you lock that part of your life off, and you have the rest of it, and then I wonder why? Why, why do I fantasy about that? What the hell kind of satisfaction would this give me? It would be deadly. It would be being half dead. And the things that I do enjoy, about my work, are not the—really the safe little predictable, non-risk things (*pause*). I think it's interesting that I come through as a—not wanting to rock the boat—

T: It's not just what you said today. It's what you said last time, too.

P: Yeah, right. Yeah, it's this feeling if I, if I can't or since I can't get involved in some major project that really sort of—uses up all my energies over a period of time, that maybe I can justify my existence to myself and the world by kind of carefully balanced group of little projects, that are all the time going along and ah—(*T:* Ah, ways to pass the time—?) No, no, no. Not just ways to pass the time, no (*laughs*). (*T:* No?) No, if it were ways to pass the time, it would be crossword puzzles and bridge, rather than staging a production of

McBurd, for Christsake—or something like this. (*T:* Or booze, which you've kicked?) That's the way to pass time.

T: You know, for what it's worth, I've taken my life from time to time, and just shaken it up, when it's gone stale. When I went, for example, on that sabbatical—it was a boat-rocking kind of thing. I was just feeling stagnant as could be. And, I could sit and coast along for a long time, and I couldn't see any new ways to go, or any new parts of myself that would come out. So I got out of the country. Ah, I was lucky. But, I know other people who do something comparable to it. Ah, take a year off—you know, in situations like ours, even if it costs them some money. Go to a new part of the world; take on some radically new challenges, and they come back renewed, changed, one way or another. I haven't heard you talk about this kind of thing. Does it ever occur to you?

P: Yeah, it does, it does. I think I get in certain, dead ends, when I think about it, and I don't know if this is just another business of being afraid. I've thought about—well, several years ago, I applied for a, through a number of channels, of some way of getting abroad for a year. AID, and I almost had one. It turned out they wanted somebody whose main interest was in developing tests. This was in India. Developing—they were very much on a kick of developing Civil Service exams, and they wanted somebody who had actually developed tests independently, and ah, so that fell through. But I worked pretty hard at trying to get this. This was partly, when I was kind of going stale in the counseling center, during the period when, ah, after Justin Harlow died. And then, another kind of thing I've thought about is—getting completely out of—my present profession, except in some way that I may be able to preserve some of the skills I've acquired. And it's because, hell, you—I'm a, I feel a little old to learn some totally new profession, like law or medicine, from scratch. But, doing something like, something that call—that cries out to be done. (*T:* Yes?) Like, ah, like the population explosion. Going to India, to help with the public relations aspect of birthcontrol, or something of this kind.

T: It was never clear why you were consulting me in the first place, but try this out for sound. I don't think you're consulting me because you want radically to—to change or uncover some neurotic process, or other. I think, what we're up to here, we can call it existential counseling. Your life the way you've been living it, is becoming somewhat stale. And you're groping, and looking for help in your groping, for some ways to change your life, in ways that may open you up again, and renew some sense of zest, or meaning, or direction, or contribution. Does that, how does that sit with you?

P: Well, that sits so well with me, that I'm a little suspicious that, I mean, that sounds awful nice. That, that's kind of admirable, positive—I think it's true, to a large extent, but I think it may not be the en, the whole truth. Because it—it's such a more comfortable way of looking at it all.

T: Yeah, but this breaks me up, though. Ah, the way I've gotten to know you, you're most comfortable if, ah, whatever comes out of your counselor, your therapist is punishing in some way. So that if I were to make some piercing interpretations that would make you wince, ah—that somehow you feel sounder; whereas, when I say you're looking for a way to live your life, that seems to be letting you off easy.

P: Ah—Yeah, Well, in other words, I'm most uncomfortable, when I'm comfortable. (*T:* Yeah (*laughs*).) I'm uncomfortable as hell when I'm uncomfortable, but I'm even more uncomfortable—yeah, I think this is true. Although, I wasn't feeling uncomfortable then, although I was protesting. No, but—well, what I was thinking when you were saying that was—ah, when I quit drinking, which was about, almost eight years ago, this, almost by itself was—this was such a tremendously therapeutic thing, you know. I mean it was like stopping beating your head against the wall—and your head begins to clear and the throbbing stops, and all kinds of possibilities open up.

T: I picked up my pipe to smoke, as soon as you said when you stopped drinking (*laughs*).

P: And, I went, I mean, I think for a long time, I felt as if this was all the motive I needed now, see? Ah, I was going to sail, ah—it was clear sailing—if I may mix my metaphors, ah, and a lot of creative powers and powers for zestful living that had been mired down were released. And then the, finally, well there came a period when I decided well, that's not enough, you see. It, you can't grow forever, on just having quit drinking. This releases certain powers to grow, but those powers need nourishment themselves. You have to stay alive. You have to find new excitements, new interests, new projects.

T: If booze was a harbor for you, and I guess it was, it took some guts to let go of the harbor, and see how you can, get on, out, you might say, out in the open sea. (*P:* Yeah.) And, I think, from what you've been telling me, your life has settled into a pattern. It's more or less successful, more or less satisfying, but it's kind of stale. Ah, but it's a harbor, and the question comes up, what, what's worth getting out of the harbor for? (*P:* Yeah.) It gets kind of suffocating in port—when you were a kid, did you have any dreams, ah, about what you might do with your life?

P: Yeah, well, I wanted to be an actor. This was on and off, and I don't know what I wanted to be when this was off. There were times when I felt, ah, discouraged about that, but I didn't really have any viable alternatives from, oh, I don't know, from really quite young, all the way up through my junior year at college when I decided that, that you really had to be tall and handsome or else you had to be extraordinarily talented and lucky. You know, like some little guy like Victor Moore or something. And, I decided I wasn't—I didn't know about the luck, but I wasn't that talented, and so I cast around for something else. But that was the—dream. But you know, I've decided a long time ago that an awful large part of the motivation for that was that—was the dissatisfaction of being me. I mean it sounds—corny—like a sort of a cliche about the motivation of actors, but I really believe this because I felt it. I remember vividly feeling the release of getting away from my grubby little self and being somebody else on the stage and in rehearsals, and wondering as a sophomore in college how the hell were all these other people, who weren't in the theatre, how they lived? I thought they were all sort of dead. What did they do? I mean there is really only one source of kicks, I thought, you know? I mean I knew this wasn't true, but I felt that it was true. And, when I got over this, or got sufficiently over it so that I had at least some willingness to be me, and live as me, then the need to be an actor—well, I got so I could enjoy being an amateur actor instead of, instead of having to do it, instead of being compulsive about it. And so I'm not sure. You asked me, you know, didn't I have a dream as a kid with the assumption that this might lead to a possibility for taking that ship out to sea. Now, I used to fantasy about having something happen to me such as happened to, ah, I forget his name, but there's some successful Hollywood actor who, I think he's dead now, who was—he became an actor at age 35 or 40. He was a business man. And I used to fantasy when I was still the other side of 35, and the other side of 40, that you know, I might get discovered and change careers. But I haven't needed that for many, many years now. I wouldn't, I don't think I'd take that—if it were offered me. Now not necessarily because I wouldn't like it, but because I don't think it would be offered me in any form that would be secure enough and that I would feel confident would really fulfill me. I would like nothing less than to be a performer in soap-operas and grade B movies.

T: Well, I still see you in this bind. Here I am. I'm 50 years old. I've raised a family—gotten somewhere professionally in the world. It's not everything I might have hoped for, but it's something. And in another, say 30 years, I'm going to be dead. How am I going to pass the time?

P: Well, I guess that's what it boils down to. And yet, you know, I feel—I don't have misgivings about how to spend the time after retirement. I may be kidding myself, and I realize that a lot of people go into retirement with a lot of anticipations, and then go stale as hell and it all turns sour on them. But I've got all kinds of ideas for retirement. It's the years between here and retirement that—(*T:* All right. 15 years.) Yes. (*T:* How are you going to pass the time?) Yeah. (*T:* And who are you going to pass it with?) You mean besides my wife? Yeah, that's a, that's part of it, too. Because this, this kind of halfway, and waxing and waning commitment to my work I think is also true of my relationship with my colleagues. I hesitate to go all the way in disclosing myself and sharing myself and getting involved with my colleagues (*pause*).

   T: I fit the fantasy for me—but I may do it. I don't know. Ah, when my kids are grown, I don't really need a certain level of money—if I find myself getting restless, I'm going to stick a pack on my back, and go—either with my wife or without. It would be more meaningful without my wife, and if she were an adequate person, I'd just take off. But, that's my fantasy.

   P: (*laughs*): I've had that one, too. I, I have the Anthony Adverse fantasy—I don't know if you remember the novel, but he went at one point in his life, after tragedy, he went into the jungle for three years—completely alone (*both laugh*). (*T:* Well, that will test you.) I could see if I could really grow a beard (*lights cigarette*). I keep thinking though, that I, and I think this is partly why, even though maybe it's my style to, to prefer to be punished than praised by my counselor, I think part of what I was thinking when you said, this was kind of an existential quest for—part of what I was thinking was that, yeah, all right! I haven't got any, I didn't come to you with a feeling of a need to uncover a lot of hidden, neurotic mess, but I do have the feeling that some of my, the things I'm afraid of, which I—I think I've gotten over an awful lot of, of the fears that have bedeviled me through my childhood and adolescence and early adulthood, but there are some of them that are still lurking. And I think part of it's the fear of, of criticism, of hostility, of the opinion of my peers and superiors. I notice in myself an attitude toward the authority, that is kind of, well, it makes me feel sometimes, kind of disgusted with myself cause I seem to be rebelling and fawning almost simultaneously. Not fawning, that's too strong. I had, I had a dream last night, which I told about it—tennis match that I had seen about 30 years ago, or so, in a room. There was a visiting dignitary of some kind, and I was telling about this, and I knew, while I was doing it, that this guy was a tennis buff, and I was trying to impress him—and I didn't know who he was or anything. And I woke up, and I remembered it vividly, because I had dreamed it just before the alarm clock rang, and later in the day, it suddenly—it suddenly flashed in my mind, what this dream was about. I think it was an analogy with something that had happened yesterday in a staff meeting, in which the dean of the college came. We had a special meeting of our department, counselor education staff, with the dean. And part of what was happening was the dean was kind of challenging us. What the hell are we doing about the culturally deprived? (*T:* A-huh.) Ah, are we, are we teaching our counselors to deal with them? And some of the staff were a little defensive. (*T:* Yes.) Sure we are. We're doing this, and we're doing that, and we're doing the other thing, you know. And I found myself saying two things. One, yeah, we're doing some things; but, also there's some things that we aren't doing that we ought to be doing, you know. And there are a lot of things we don't know, that we ought to look into, and—then I said to myself, what the hell am I doing here? Am I trying to placate the, the big boss man? And, am I trying to say, ah, yeah! You're right to criticize us?—

T: Is this any kind of hang-over from kid days? Like, between you and your father? Is this what you're saying?

P: Well, it never seems to me to come out that way when I think about it. I don't have—recollections of ah, much—I would, I was af—occasionally got afraid of my father, but by and large, I don't have memories of—(*T:* Yeah) any particular difficulty there. And yet, I can point to any number of examples of—in my adulthood of when I have—been afraid of, and resentful of, and kind of rebellious toward a boss. Even when I'm on good terms with him (*laughs*). Some feelings—(*T:* Yes—) of rebellion, and—ah—I—

T: You know, I almost hear you plaintively saying that you would like to be rid of these fears. I honestly don't know anybody who doesn't have one set of fears or another—including me. And, there's a choice: to yield to it, or to forge ahead anyway, by guess and by God, and do whatever it is you're going to do, or planning to do.

P: Yeah, well, I guess, partly I'm, I'm thinking kind of logically. I've had certain fears, that I have been able to overcome. Some of them as a result of, or, and in the context of, and I think unquestionably partly as a result of counseling, on previous occasions. And some of them, kind of, as a result of, therapy of life, and so it occurs to me, maybe some of these that I'm still beset by, and kind of vaguely, not very sure just what they are, maybe, if I could get a clearer picture of them, and work on them in similar way—I could get the same treatment.

T: Do you want to spend some time talking about your fears?

P: Yeah, I think it might be—it might be a profitable direction to go. Not necessarily right now, since I think we're probably out of time.

Initial Interview in a Hypochondriacal Neurosis

JOSEPH WOLPE

*Temple University Medical School and Eastern Pennsylvania Psychiatric Institute,
Henry Avenue, Philadelphia, Pennsylvania 19129*

Dr: What is your complaint?

Patient: I feel nervous all the time. I have pains across my chest and in my arms practically all the time. I feel that I'm going to die because of my heart.

Dr: When did your nervousness begin?

P: It started in 1937—when my mother passed away.

Dr: 1937?

P: 1937. My mother was 37 when she died and I was at that time 13 years old.

Dr: Can you remember the exact circumstances?

P: Yes, I can. She had a burst appendix and peritonitis set in and she died. The doctor had said she had locked bowels and he gave her a big laxative which they said really caused her death when the appendix burst. I can remember how mad I was at the doctor because I felt that he killed her. Then, about fifteen months after that, I began to have attacks of pain in my right side. I fell on the floor holding my side thinking I had appendicitis. The first few times my dad took me to the doctor. The doctor checked me and said there was nothing wrong with my appendix and to go about my business and play. That lasted a few months.

Dr: The attacks of pain?

P: The whole works, the feeling I had appendicitis. My mother died when I was in the 7th grade and I went all through high school without any problems. I was active in sports and acting and school activities. Then I married at 18 and we moved from the little town where I lived. My dad had remarried in the meantime. It was in 1941, the day Pearl Harbor started, that I was married.

Dr: Let me get one thing clear. After your mother died, when you had this pain in your side you thought it might be your appendix: that made you feel quite nervous?

P: I don't know whether you could call it nervous.

Dr: Scared?

P: Scared. Scared I was having an appendicitis attack.

Dr: Yes. And you went on being scared for the next few months.

P: I'd say several months—but it wasn't every day—it might have happened to me two or three times a week—it would always be at home—it would never be out anywhere. One day, after I had done it a few times, I can remember my little brother kicking me—I was on the floor and he told me to get up—there wasn't anything wrong with me.

Dr: When you didn't have the pain, you felt OK. You didn't feel scared?

P: I don't know whether it was the pain or just the fact that I thought I had the pain.

Dr: But you felt something—

P: Yes.

Dr: Did the doctor tell you it was not an appendix?

P: Yes.

Dr: That didn't make any difference?

P: It did at first—I mean, I wouldn't have another appendicitis attack for a few days.

Dr: In a lasting way, did the doctor's reassurance help you?

P: I believe it did, because I didn't have any more of this problem forever.

Dr: So there was a later stage when you would have these feelings and they wouldn't worry you?

P: Right.

Dr: I see. Well, eventually these particular feelings stopped and you were quite happy again?

P: Yes.

Dr: When was the next episode?

P: The next episode was after I got out of the Marine Corps. I was married in '41 and went into the Marine Corps. I had them set my draft number up so I could go in because so many people wondered why I wasn't in the service. I had a son who was born 8 months after we were married. I went into the service the latter part of '43, and was in combat in Guam and Iwo Jima. I got a "Dear John" letter when I came back to Guam. My wife wanted a divorce— said she fell in love with somebody else.

Dr: What year was that?

P: In '45 I guess it was—and so later on in '45, while I was still overseas just before the war ended, I started going to the sick bay with headaches.

Dr: Well, do you think this had something to do with your wife?

P: It must have, because I didn't go to the sick bay to get the all-purpose compound pills or whatever they gave me until after I got the letter.

Dr: I see—it started at that time.

P: I wrote her and told her if she wanted a divorce to get it, but that I would probably get our son. After going to the sick bay several times on Guam, they sent me to a divisional psychiatrist one day. When I saw the sign that said "Psychiatrist," boy, it scared the hell out of me. I went in this big tent where people were sitting around staring at walls—this scared me—scared the heck out of me. I finally talked to a psychiatrist and I said "If I'm crazy, well shoot me; and if I'm not, let me go back to duty because I don't want to be in with any of these people." Of course that was my first experience with psychiatry. I went back to duty and never had any more headaches.

Dr: OK.

P: Then when I came back from overseas, I tried to live with my wife for a while. I had a spell hit me in a bank one day.

Dr: What hit you?

P: "Spell" I call it. I got the sweats. I was going to cash my check and I got real nervous and I thought I was going to faint before I got to the teller's window and I thought I had indigestion or something—I don't know what it was. I was just shaking when the lady was going to cash my check; and when I walked outside, I fell in the street.

Dr: What year was that?

P: That was in 1946—after the war was over.

Dr: What do you think caused that spell?

P: I think it was built up of feelings that I had because I was still worrying about my wife—that she'd been running around during the war.

Dr: Were you worried about it?

P: Yes.

Dr: It was on your mind all the time?

P: Quite a bit, because I wondered who she'd been with maybe last year, and I tried to live with her, due to the fact that I had a son and didn't want to leave him, and although I thought if I had been in the States and she had been in Guam, I might have done the same thing she had done. I thought I'd try to live with it, but it just didn't work that way, and I kept getting progressively worse after that spell in the bank.

Dr: Was there anything special on that day...?

P: The only thing I can remember is that I had been eating a ham sandwich and after that I went to cash my check and that happened to me, and it scared the hell out of me and from that time on I had nervous problems.

Dr: Now just one second—I want to know more about that spell in the bank—You felt nauseous?

P: No, I tried to get my breath and couldn't and thought I was going to pass out.

Dr: Well, how did that affect you afterwards. You had the spell and the spell was done.

P: Right: and then when the guy picked me up—the people were crowded around on the sidewalk and some guy asked somebody to take me to a doctor and the doctor said it was probably a nervous condition that caused it—but it still worried me.

Dr: How did it worry you?

P: I was afraid it would happen again.

Dr: I see. Well, how long did you go on being worried about that?

P: I'd say quite a while—because I got so worried I was afraid to ride in the streetcar or anything else—I was afraid I was going to have some kind of a fainting spell and die or....

Dr: So, you were afraid to go in streetcars—what else?

P: I wasn't going to go around in crowds or anything like that. Finally I got to where I was actually shutting myself off.

Dr: What about elevators?

P: Well, it doesn't bother me too much in elevators.

Dr: What about riding in a car alone?

P: Right now it bothers me.

Dr: But at that time?

P: At that time—same thing. I was afraid to go anywhere. The best way to put it, I was afraid of being afraid.

Dr: Yes.

P: And this was pretty new to me, because when I went to combat I never was afraid—that is I was afraid, but I was careful, but I wasn't to the point of panic. It never entered my mind that I was going to get shot.

Dr: Well, this got worse and worse at that time?

P: Yes—and then I finally started calling my father who lived in Kansas City, Missouri, and told him that I was getting real bad and I needed some darn help somewhere and I didn't know what to do and so he asked me if I wanted to come back to Kansas City and he'd see if he couldn't help and get some help and this was probably in the early part of '46 and so I did, and I went into the hospital at Menninger's in Topeka, Kansas. I was in there just a few months and I got feeling real good again—in other words I didn't do anything except I had a little therapy—talk therapy—they didn't do anything else while I was there.

Dr: Was it a lot of talk therapy or just a little?

P: Quite a bit.

Dr: Every day?

P: Yes.

Dr: Did you lie on a couch?

P: No.

Dr: Just face to face.

P: Yes—and it wasn't with aides, it was with doctors.

Dr: Well, what do you think made you better?

P: Well, I met a woman I married (and am still married to).

Dr: You met her there in Kansas?

P: In the hospital. She lived in that town and she would come out on Thursday nights when they'd have dances and I'd dance with her—I like to dance and that's where I met her. Later on, about a year later, I married her.

Dr: You didn't tell me that you divorced your first wife.

P: Oh, yes, I divorced her after I got back. While I was in Menninger Hospital, I divorced her.

Dr: Oh, I see—so life opened up for you again?

P: Seemed like it to me.

Dr: Having met her and feeling optimistic and so on, you stopped being concerned about fainting and all that?

P: Yes, yes. I knew I was successful in my business venture—I had opened up a fruit and vegetable outfit and did real well at it and then my wife's folks. who were retired people who had raised fruit and vegetables—her mother and dad came down here to Dallas and helped.

Dr: I see.

P: And I did pretty well until my father died—had a heart attack.

Dr: When was that?

P: My father had his first heart attack in 1954.

Dr: So you were perfectly OK and unscared from 1946 to 1954?

P: I think in 1952 I got a little scared. There was a job I had taken on with an insurance company when I first went into the insurance business. I was man of the year in my first year with this company—then I had a nervous breakdown and I lost a lot of weight and started drinking.

Dr: What upset you in that business?

P: I don't know except that I always wanted to be on top all the time—I wanted to be the highest salesman—I still am in that business.

Dr: What was special about the situation at that time.

P: Well, I don't know—I can't say what was so special about it. I think I just burned both ends of the candle—I wasn't getting any sleep—I wasn't eating right and lost a lot of weight, and so I went to a psychiatric hospital and took shock treatments.

Dr: Did that help you?

P: It helped me—I'd say it scared the hell out of me, but I think it helped a little. I don't think it cures anybody—it got about thirty pounds on me that I needed real bad. They said it would put weight on me, which it did—then when my dad had his heart attack in '54, the first one, I started to get nervous again. I wasn't too bad in '53 to '54.

Dr: Did you have your scare after his first heart attack or earlier than that?

P: No I wasn't too scared after his first heart attack—it was shocking to me but I wasn't real scared—they called us that they didn't think he was going to live and I flew to Memphis where he was in the hospital. I can remember seeing him in the hospital—tubes in him and everything else which I can remember wasn't a very happy experience. Then he had five or six coronaries after that.

Dr: When was the last one?

P: He died in 1960.

Dr: Well, did you become more scared after each attack or—

P: I'd say I did—but I was taking medication, I think because I started going to the doctor and he started giving me the seconal capsules in 1954.

Dr: When you say you were scared, you mean you walked around—

P: I wasn't scared all the time, no—not like I am now. I'm more scared now—

Dr: I want to know what happened then.

P: Then I think I was relieved by taking the pills.

Dr: Were you constantly thinking about having a heart attack?

P: No. I played golf—

Dr: When would you be scared?

P: There wouldn't be any certain pattern.

Dr: Every now and then you would think you would have a heart attack?

P: Yes: and so I had a cardiogram made.

Dr: After each coronary attack that your father had, did you think of this more and more.

P: I think so, yes sir. I think I was worrying more about when he was going to die than I was worrying about myself.

Dr: Well, finally he died in 1960.

P: Right.

Dr: What happened then as far as you were concerned?

P: As far as I was concerned, 1962 is when I started taking the seconal capsules.

Dr: After your father died in 1960 did you stop thinking about coronary attacks?

P: I don't think it bothered me for a couple of years.

Dr: Then what brought the concern back in 1962?

P: I don't know whether it was the heart attack so much as the fact that I thought I was going crazy or something in 1962.

Dr: What exactly happened in '62?

P: I just started getting very nervous and scared and was afraid of facing the public again—in other words—it was another failure—I went into another stage of regression—just quit talking to anybody, quit seeing anybody, quit selling insurance, quit everything.

Dr: What was behind it?

P: I can't tell you.

Dr: This was just something that happened to you without cause?

P: I had a cause evidently, but I don't know why it happened—I don't know why I just was getting worse.

Dr: This happened without any external cause—there was nothing in your situation—nothing happened that was negative.

P: No. You mean, as far as...

Dr: Your wife, your family, your business.

P: No—my business was good and...

Dr: Everything was good.

P: Seemed like it was. Then in 1962 I started going to a psychiatrist and he's the one who put me on seconal and I did real well until ten months ago.

Dr: Did you take seconal all these years?

P: Yes—eight years.

Dr: How much did you take?

P: Well—the doctor told me to take five or six during the day. I didn't take them at night—I didn't need them at night. Then I cut them down to about three a day myself for I'd say several years. I was taking five or six during the last year and a half.

Dr: Did you have anxiety about heart attacks or anything at all during these years?

P: Yes, a little bit. I'd say I've been scared all the time a little bit.

Dr: All the time—you never stop being scared?

P: Not 24 hours a day, but when I went to Honolulu a couple of times—I went to Mexico—even there I'd be scared—afraid I might have a heart attack. Even when I'd go out and play golf I thought I might drop dead—a little bit of anxiety—but not like it has been since I've been here. I think now all the time I'm awake, when's the next one going to hit—when am I going to have a real one?

Dr: What happened eight months ago?

P: Eight months ago I was regional director of this life insurance company—I started ten months ago, not eight—I was regional director and would travel all over the state of Texas hiring insurance men for my insurance company and the vice president of the company asked me if I would move to Austin from Dallas and take this job to move through the country hiring these people and I said this was a pretty good advance for me and I said "sure" and so I did travel all over the state—I'd fly most of the time.

Dr: You moved to Austin?

P: Moved to Austin and we were up there—I sold my home in Dallas because I felt, "Well, Austin's going to be my home from now on." I was making real good money, and then about three months later the company decided they didn't want to hire anybody else. They got into a little bit of trouble with the insurance commission and they told me that as far as my job was concerned they would give me a fancy office as divisional director in Austin. I could just sell insurance and hire anybody in Austin if I wanted to for myself but they didn't want any more people hired throughout the state of Texas. I thought this was a demotion, and, as time went on, I started having these attacks—felt like I was going to have a heart attack and then it kept building up and building up. I had that office about four months, I guess after I moved out of the home office and then they wanted me to move back to Dallas which I did, and when I moved back I didn't hardly get out of my house from that time until I came to this hospital, except to go to the doctor for a cardiogram.

Dr: Are you telling me that when they told you to confine your activities to Austin—you felt it a demotion and that you brooded about?

P: Yes.

Dr: You really felt very upset about it?

P: Yes sir.

Dr: Did this move involve much financial loss to you?

P: No—I was still making the same amount of money.

Dr: I see. So it was really a prestige matter?

P: Yes sir. They always thought that I had high ego and all that kind of stuff.

Dr: Well, in actual fact I suppose the firm really didn't need any other people.

P: Well, they might not have, but after the first of the year they started hiring a lot of people so I thought maybe I wasn't cutting the mustard. After I got sick when I came back to Dallas I didn't do anything; I called a former president of this company and he told me not to quit—just don't answer any letters. So they terminated me from my job.

Dr: Why did they do that?

P: Well they thought they would scare me into action—they didn't think I was sick.

Dr: Oh, I see. This is when you were back here?

P: Back in Dallas, yes.

Dr: Well how do you feel about this now?

P: Well now I feel that as far as the job is concerned I'm damn glad I don't have it because there is a lot of pressure involved in it and I've since signed a contract with the owner of another insurance company. I've got a lawsuit against them now which they want to settle out of court. I'm too darned nervous to even sit in a courtroom but my wife can take care of it if I can't but that don't even enter my mind—the only thing that's in my mind most of the time is these pains I have in my arms and my chest and the scared feeling I get, that I'm going to die. Here I am lingering with this mental illness—a word which I don't like to use.

Dr: Well, it's not a mental illness; it's an over-reaction.

P: To me it is taking the pattern of some kind a failure or some kind of death in the family every time.

Dr: When did you begin to have these pains?

P: In Austin, Texas.

Dr: But only after the job was changed.

P: Yes.

Dr: Only after you began being upset?

P: Yes.

Dr: Where exactly are these pains?

P: This arm hurts practically all the time and I have pain across the chest.

Dr: Do you realize intellectually that there is nothing wrong with your heart?

P: Intellectually I know that there wasn't the last time they took a cardiogram; they don't know now.

Dr: But at any rate do you know that the symptoms that you were having up to the last cardiogram couldn't have been caused by the heart—so that in order to have any reason to suspect there is anything wrong with your heart, you would need to have new symptoms? Do you have any new symptoms?

P: The only new symptom I have is a numbness in my fingers.

Dr: But you had that before?

P: Only since I've been in the hospital.

Dr: So are you suggesting that it is caused by the heart?

P: No—I think it is caused by the medication I've been taking.

Dr: That's more like it.

Dr: It is clear that the symptoms that you suspected as being heart symptoms couldn't have been heart symptoms because there was nothing wrong with your heart the last time you were tested. There are no new symptoms. Now, the question is—Do you realize intellectually that there is nothing wrong with your heart?

P: I can't make myself believe that there isn't.

Dr: I am trying to distinguish between two things—one is intellectual...

P: Yes, I believe it intellectually.

Dr: Are you saying that although you know and believe that—yet when you get the pain you just get a fear reaction?

P: Yes, I fear that it might be one coming on.

Dr: So whenever you think, you have a fear.

P: Yes.

Dr: These fears can be overcome. It would be nice to have a pain in your chest and not care, wouldn't it?

P: It sure would.

Dr: One other thing which could be done would be to try and establish what does cause the pain. Sometimes it is caused by rheumatism, or by winds in the intestines that may be produced by anxiety.

P: There are times when I feel that I can't breathe or I'm choking.

Dr: Very often, feeling unable to breathe causes over-breathing which can produce exactly these kinds of pains.

P: When my heart beats real loud and fast it worries me too.

Dr: That is part of nervousness too. Let me ask you one more thing—how do you feel now about this idea that you had before that confining you to Austin was a demotion? Do you still think it was?

P: No I don't think so at all. One day I was speaking to some student doctors and they asked me if I had the pain at that time. I said, " No." Now I haven't had one pain since I've been sitting here. Now when I get out of here. I'll have some.

Dr: In a very general way, do you regard yourself as a sensitive man?

P: Yes—very sensitive.

Dr: If anyone says anything nasty to you or criticizes you, it upsets you a lot?

P: Yes. I've not been one to criticize other people—except lately I've been very irritable here in the hospital because I feel like what's the use of me staying around here?

Dr: If you were standing in a line and someone got in front of you ... ?

P: I don't like it—I won't stand in line. It makes me too nervous to stand in line.

Dr: What makes you nervous?

P: I don't want to be a slow-stepper in a crowd.

Dr: Since you've been in the service?

P: Yes—same way with going to a movie—I want to sit on the outside seat near the back or even in church the same way.

Dr: What would you do in the following situation. You go into a shop to buy some socks and you've selected your socks and the assistant is busy with someone else. You wait and while you're waiting another customer comes in to get some socks. The assistant finished with the original customer and he turns to the one who came in after you and waits on him.

P: It irritates me. I would put the socks down and leave the store. I probably wouldn't say anything though.

Dr: Yes—but don't you think you should.

P: Yes—and at times I have but this is not a regular way that I would act. To me it would be rude to say this; it also depends on whether the client knew that I was there before he was.

Dr: Well, if he didn't know, what is wrong with telling him?

P: There wouldn't be anything wrong with it except it would embarrass both of us.

Dr: Why would you be embarrassed?

P: I don't know; I don't like to hurt people's feelings.

Dr: It isn't good for you to keep feelings pent up inside of you. It is hard at first to change, but it would become easier and easier. I don't think we can get much further right now. I'll discuss it with your doctors and see if we can set up anything that will help you; I think that we ought to be able to. Is there anything you'd like to ask me?

P: Have you ever seen anybody cured of this?

Dr: Yes—it is unusual for people not to be cured.

P: Thank you very much, doctor.

A Desensitization Session

JOSEPH WOLPE

Temple University Medical School and Eastern Pennsylvania Psychiatric Institute,
Henry Avenue, Philadelphia, Pennsylvania, 19129

The following transcript consists of two excerpts from the fourteenth session with a patient whose treatment, consisting of the correcting of misconceptions, assertive training, and, most of all, systematic desensitization, was drawing to a close. In common with the case figuring in the previous transcript, she had hypochondriacal fears, although in other ways she was markedly different.

The patient was a forty-year-old married woman who, since the age of seventeen, had had a fear of "passing out" in public places. She had never actually lost consciousness. In churches, restaurants, and other public places, she had become anxious in anticipation of passing out. A particular disability was that she could not go shopping or take her children swimming or elsewhere without anxiety. Her anxiety syndrome was characterized by knees shaking, hands perspiring, and a slight feeling of rotation. As these became worse, dizziness would appear, which she interpreted as foreshadowing unconsciousness, which, naturally, exacerbated the anxiety. She also had inappropriate anxiety in situations involving illness or injury of other people, and when exposed to funerals and burials. These were manifestly intertwined. Another neurotic reaction unrelated to them was a moderate degree of social timidity.

During earlier sessions, the patient had received assertive training, and the fears associated with illness and death had been treated by systematic desensitization. As preliminaries to the latter, she had been trained in deep muscle relaxation and instructed in the reporting of anxiety on a 0–100 subjective scale (Wolpe, 1973, p. 120). The numbers she refers to in the interview relate to this scale. The transcript includes, in full, the final major desensitization period. A letter written four months later is appended.

109

TRANSCRIPT

Dr.: How do you do today?

Patient: Wonderful! I got up at zero[1] and maintained it the whole way down—that's a first.

Dr.: What did you do yesterday?

P: Lots and lots of shopping. When I left here, I did a number of small errands.

Dr.: And how were they?

P: Fine—no problem. And then I took the children to the pool for an hour and then went to some department stores with my daughter after that. I felt a trifle apprehensive when we started out but it really didn't last very long.

Dr.: How much?

P: Fifteen, which is less than usual.

Dr.: Let me see . . . if we go back a month, how much would you have been starting out?

P: Forty—if not more.

Dr.: And you say it didn't last long. How long did it last?

P: Until we got in the store and began shopping and then I was comfortable again.

Dr.: Now in the old days when it was forty, how long would it last?

P: Until I got home.

Dr.: Did you have any other anxiety at all since I saw you?

P: No.

Dr.: Now as far as one of the first areas that we dealt with is concerned—the hearses and things of that sort—I wonder if you've noticed anything about your responses to going past cemeteries and things like that?

P: I haven't even noticed. I've been driving by but have had no reaction.

Dr.: Well, in the past, did you notice them?

P: Yes. I'd always look to see if there was something going on.

Dr: As you know, there are two different sources of fears. [*A long discussion emphasizing the distinction (which had already previously been made) between fears due to misconceptions and directly conditioned fears intervened between the foregoing initial conversation and the desensitization that follows.*]

Dr.: Well, I think we ought to get back to work. Now, relax all the muscles of your face, jaws and tongue. [*Pause—15 seconds.*] Relax your neck, shoul-

---

[1] This and subsequent figures are on the 0 to 100 scale referred to above.

ders and arms. [*Pause—15 seconds.*] Now, while you are so calm, I'm going to ask you to imagine some scenes. First, imagine that you're driving past a cemetery and you can see about 150 yards away a mourners' procession. (*Pause²—5 seconds.*) Stop. How much?

P: None. (*Pause—10 seconds.*)

Dr.: Now, imagine that you are *walking* past the cemetery and you see a mourners' procession 150 yards away. (*Pause—5 seconds.*) Stop. How much?

P: None. (*Pause—10 seconds.*)

Dr.: Imagine that you can see a mourners' procession 75 yards away. (*Pause—5 seconds.*) Stop. How much?

P: None. (*Pause—10 seconds.*)

Dr.: Imagine that you can see a mourners' procession 40 yards away and, of course, you notice the pall bearers carrying the coffin. (*Pause—5 seconds.*) Stop. How much?

P: None. (*Pause—10 seconds.*)

Dr.: Imagine the same thing from a distance of 20 yards. (*Pause—5 seconds.*) Stop. How much?

P: None. (*Pause—10 seconds.*)

Dr.: Now, suppose that the person who has died is an old man whom you knew but not very well and imagine that you are 20 yards behind as a member of this procession. (*Pause—5 seconds.*) Stop. How much?

P: Five.³

Dr.: Now, just relax. (*Pause—15 seconds.*) Keep on letting go, and now again imagine that you are in this procession about 20 yards behind the pallbearers. (*Pause—5 seconds.*) Stop. How much?

P: None. (*Pause—10 seconds.*)

Dr.: Just relax. (*Pause—10 seconds.*) Now, we'll change the context. I want you to imagine that once again you are on the sixth floor at Wanamakers, standing in line for the cashier and feeling somewhat dizzy. There are two friends with you whom you tell that you're feeling a bit dizzy. (*Pause—8 seconds.*) Stop. How much?

P: Five.

Dr.: Just relax. (*Pause—10 seconds.*) Imagine that same scene again. (*Pause—8 seconds.*) Stop. How much?

² The patient always raised her finger at the end of the description of the scene to indicate that she was visualizing it; and it was visualization that went on for 5 seconds.

³ Note that in response to desensitization scenes, anxiety never goes up by more than five at this stage of treatment, and goes down to zero at the second presentation. During earlier sessions, the initial level was often much higher and three to five presentations would then be needed to bring it down to zero.

P: None. (*Pause—10 seconds.*)

Dr.: Now imagine that you are heard to say, "I feel dizzy," by two friends and a stranger. (*Pause—5 seconds.*) Stop. How much?

P: Five.

Dr.: Relax. (*Pause—20 seconds.*) Imagine the same again. (*Pause—5 seconds.*) Stop. How much?

P: None. (*Pause—10 seconds.*)

Dr.: Now imagine that a total of four people hear you say, "I feel a bit dizzy." (*Pause—5 seconds.*) Stop. How much?

P: Five.

Dr.: Just relax. (*Pause—20 seconds.*) Imagine the same scene again. (*Pause—5 seconds.*) Stop. How much?

P: None. (*Pause—10 seconds.*)

Dr.: Now, imagine that a total of six people overhear you say, "I feel a bit dizzy." (*Pause—5 seconds.*) Stop. How much?

P: None.

Dr.: Relax now. (*Pause—10 seconds.*) Imagine that there are nine people who overhear you say, "I'm feeling a bit dizzy." (*Pause—5 seconds.*) Stop. How much?

P: None. (*Pause—10 seconds.*)

Dr.: Imagine that thirteen people overhear you say that. (*Pause—10 seconds.*) Stop. How much?

P: None.

Dr.: Relax. (*Pause—10 seconds.*) Now, let's go back to another area where we've been before. I want you to imagine that you're in a hospital ward and you see that there are four people who are receiving transfusions. (*Pause—5 seconds.*) Stop. How much?

P: Five.

Dr.: Relax. (*Pause—20 seconds.*) Imagine the same again. (*Pause—5 seconds.*) Stop. How much?

P: None. (*Pause—10 seconds.*)

Dr. Imagine that you are in a hospital ward and there is a patient with an abdominal drain. (*Pause—5 seconds.*) Stop. How much?

P: Five. (*Pause—20 seconds.*)

Dr.: Imagine the same. (*Pause—5 seconds.*) Stop. How much?

P: None. (*Pause—10 seconds.*)

Dr.: Imagine that you see a young man in an intensive care unit with quite a bit of his body wrapped in bandages, some of which have a good deal of blood on them. (*Pause—5 seconds.*) Stop. How much?

P: Five.

Dr.: Relax. (*Pause—20 seconds.*) Imagine the same again. (*Pause—5 seconds.*) Stop. How much?

P: None. (*Pause—10 seconds.*)

Dr.: I want you to imagine that you're at home and you're thinking of the fact that you're going to be shopping at Korvettes in King of Prussia. (*Pause—5 seconds.*) Stop. How much?

P: Five.

Dr.: Relax. (*Pause—20 seconds.*) Imagine it again. (*Pause—5 seconds.*) Stop. How much?

P: None. (*Pause—10 seconds.*)

Dr.: Now, imagine that you're at home and you're thinking of the fact that you're going to do shopping at King of Prussia and that you're going not only to Korvettes but also to Gimbels and Wanamakers. (*Pause—12 seconds.*) Stop. How much?

P: Five.

Dr.: Now, just relax. (*Pause—20 seconds.*) Imagine it again. (*Pause—5 seconds.*) Stop. How much?

P: None. (*Pause—10 seconds.*)

Dr.: Now, I would like you to imagine that you are reading minutes to a crowd of 300. (*Pause—12 seconds.*) Stop. How much?

P: None.

Dr.: All right. Now I'll count to five and you'll open your eyes and feel calm and refreshed. One, two, three, four, five. (*Patient opens eyes.*) How are you?

P: Very calm.

Dr.: Is there anything you want to say about today's session.

P: Well, in envisioning the things . . . I just don't seem to feel very upset about it anymore.

Dr.: That's clear. You've certainly done very well, and tomorrow will be our final session in this series. It may not be the last session that you're ever going to need. We may have one or two after that.

The following is a follow up report received from the patient four months after the termination of treatment.

"Dear Dr. Wolpe:

In contrast to feelings I had before meeting with you, I wake up in the morning and experience little or no fear when thinking of the day's activities.

Activities which for the first time cause absolutely no second thoughts are:

> Driving children to and from their many activities regardless of the amount of traffic or delays at traffic lights;
> Food shopping which I am now doing without my husband for the first time in years;
> Shopping and doing errands in small local centers—again alone;
> Walking instead of using the car to visit nearby stores;
> Going out to dinner, ball games, plays, etc.

I still experience a slight fear—maybe a 7 in terms of the scale we used—in the following:

> Shopping in large department stores;
> Large meetings at the schools my children attend;
> Going to bridge clubs;
> Attending church.

Even then, in contrast with the past, once I get involved in the activity, I relax and enjoy what I am doing. For instance, instead of just rushing into a department store to purchase what is necessary and then leaving, I now stop and browse with the children.

There has been only one incident involving the sight of blood. My son received a cut on the thigh which required stitches, and I was able to clean it initially without any problem. However, I must admit I was relieved when my husband stated he would drive him to the hospital.

As regards the fear of seeing others faint, I have twice been in the company of friends who complained of being dizzy without fearing I would experience the same sensation.

> Sincerely,
> L.S."

Comments on Therapy Transcripts

THE EDITORS

The transcripts of the Jourard and Wolpe therapy sessions provide insights into the techniques these two persons use. They also raise some questions. Of course we do not know how representative of Jourard and Wolpe therapy sessions these transcripts actually are. Also, the fact of taping the sessions may affect both the therapist and the patient. In addition, the transcripts contain merely the linguistic reports of the sessions. Other paralinguistic information—posture, eye contact, gestures—are not available here. Many have argued these latter modes of communication reveal as much as the meaning of the words used. Specifically, Jourard states that his client strikes him as being "stale" and "half dead." This is to some degree revealed in the verbal material, but actually to be in the session (or to have an audio-visual presentation of it) would be far superior. In short, we have available the skeleton of the session, and much of the flesh is missing. Nonetheless, the transcripts are valuable and worth further scrutiny.

What do the transcripts reveal about the styles of Jourard and Wolpe? There are several major contrasts in the roles their comments play in the sessions. First, Wolpe is actively in control of his session. He steers the conversation along specific pathways. Wolpe uses much of this session to determine the range of symptoms and their linkages to specific environmental events. While using the systematic desensitization procedure Wolpe is still explicitly directing the client's thoughts and responses. Jourard does not use this type of active control of the session. Jourard and his client are having a discussion, and begin on several paths, sometimes retreat, and then return. But Jourard is also, although in a much less direct fashion, determining the range and specificity of his client's problems.

A second contrast between the styles of Jourard and Wolpe is the amount of time talking in the session. Wolpe's questions and comments are generally short and to the point. Jourard occasionally has lengthy contributions to the discussions, sometimes engages in digressions, and even reports on his own fantasies.

A third contrast is the greater apparent affective involvement of Jourard in the session. Jourard and his client occasionally laugh together. Wolpe and his client are involved in a more official, business-like affair. (It is important to note here that this contrast may be more apparent than real. If one actually observed the session, Jourard and his client might be in what would then seem a boring, lifeless discussion as contrasted to the apparent vitality reflected by laughter in the transcripts.)

The second and third contrasts suggest that Jourard and his client are co-equals in a joint venture, whereas Wolpe and his client are not co-equals. Friends laugh together, and each contributes to the discussion, as perhaps is occurring with Jourard. On the other hand, those with power and respect can ask the questions and control the session, as is occurring with Wolpe.

A fourth contrast is the reflective style of Jourard as opposed to the direct style of Wolpe. Jourard frequently describes how he is experiencing his client, not in a normative but in a reflective way. His client then usually elaborates or qualifies Jourard's remarks. Wolpe infrequently uses this reflective style. When he does, it is used to gain specific clarification on a comment made by his client rather than to stimulate new thought.

A major issue is the correspondence between the actual therapy session and the putative theory supporting the therapy. Let us first examine the Jourard transcript. Jourard has emphasized the importance of mutual self-disclosure and of modeling. We cannot ascertain from these protocols whether mutual self-disclosure has had any beneficial effects, yet it is apparent that there are major instances of self-disclosure. Jourard is nearly as apt to reveal his fantasies and problems as is the "real" client. There do not appear to be many instances of Jourard's attempting to be a model for his client. One brief example that does appear is Jourard's discussion of his sabbatic as a "boat-rocking kind of thing" which he used as a way to get rid of feeling stagnant. Another example is Jourard's mention of his current "coming out of a slump" after working on a big project.

Thus, there are observable instances of the elements Jourard emphasizes as being crucial to growth in therapy. We do not get a chance to observe the relationship between the techniques and the growth, however. Also, it is difficult to determine from the available protocol the appropriateness of the self-disclosure and the modeling styles over a range of clients. In this case, Jourard's client is a counselor and an academician, and hence similar in many ways to Jourard. It is easy to have a discussion with one whose experiences are similar to your own. And Jourard can conveniently be a model, that is, one who has experienced problems similar to his client's precisely because they are in many ways similar. We are forced to wonder what the rapport would be, and specifically what the modeling would be, if the client were quite different from Jourard.

With respect to Wolpe, the protocol demonstrates the systematic probing on the part of Wolpe to identify the range of symptoms, and how they occur in rather regularly identifiable circumstances. The effort is to establish stimulus-response connections involved in unadaptive habits. The theoretical structure underlying the interview is apparent and the mode of treatment that is employed seems to derive from the theory. The material of the interview is rich and vivid, however, and there will be those who argue for alternative interpretations, as well as different treatment modalities.

An interesting note is Wolpe's extreme confidence at the end of the interview. In response to a client's question of whether he will be cured (in a different protocol) Wolpe replied that it is unusual for people not to be cured. This suggests the possible importance of the relation of the client and the therapist, particularly the confidence of the client in the therapist, as important moderating variables in the ultimate outcome of the therapy. Wolpe's theoretical system emphasizes the importance of the treatment itself, while saying little about relationship elements such as trust in the therapist.

The last issue is the appropriateness of the treatment for the client. There is a naturalness about each therapy session, and we are struck with the feeling that if the clients were to switch therapists there would be an awkwardness. Wolpe's client, incapacitated by anxieties, might well feel Jourard is not really able to bring about any changes. She might believe that Jourard does not have the practical suggestions or treatment that will cure her. Jourard's client, the co-counselor, might feel that Wolpe would be missing the subtleties of his experience. Wolpe would probably attempt, more than Jourard, to determine the specific feelings of the counselor and the situation in which they occurred. But this counselor is articulate and requires various subtle distinctions in the statements Jourard reflects back to him. This might well complicate the process for Wolpe and impose major constraints in the therapy session. In any case, the proposed "switch" would provide additional useful information in this comparison.

PART III

Self and Personality— Humanistic and Behavioristic Viewpoints

INTRODUCTION

Is a concept of self necessary, or even useful, for psychology? This issue has troubled psychologists for decades. Historically, those with roots in experimental psychology have tended to dismiss the "self" as mystical and perhaps religious at worst, and a mere epiphenomenon at best. Those with roots in personality psychology ("personologists" as Henry Murray called them) have usually found a use for some variant of the self concept. Without a self, how can we account for the central organizing aspect of a person's perceptions, motives, and values?

In this historical dichotomy between experimental psychology and personality psychology, the behaviorists were with the experimentalists and the humanists sided with the personologists. The debate in this book shows some rapprochement between humanists and behaviorists, but the concept of self is still an issue on which there is dissension.

In this section Walter Mischel and Joseph Rychlak debate the use of the concept of self in personality psychology. Rychlak, the humanist, argues unequivocally that a self concept is necessary and Mischel, the behaviorist, expresses ambivalence at the self concept. In many ways these are the expected answers by a humanist and a behaviorist, but the forms of the arguments are very different than they have been historically.

Mischel is classified here as taking a behaviorist viewpoint, but he (as well as others, like Bandura, Thoresen, and Mahoney) have departed from the

119

radical behaviorists (Skinner). The radical behaviorists would have no part of a self: Mischel is only "ambivalent" about it. Mischel titles his approach "A cognitive social learning view" rather than a behavioristic one. Some consider Mischel (and Bandura) to hold a compromise position between the radical behaviorists and the humanists. In a sense, then, Mischel represents a type of synthesis of humanism and behaviorism.

The self Mischel accepts is one which is equivalent to the whole person, not a distinctive internal agent. This self (or, according to Mischel, person) reciprocally interacts with the environment, with each producing alterations in the other. The person has certain capacities which enable him to alter the environment much as the environment coerces change in the person.

The self Mischel rejects is one which is a causal agent distinct from the person. This he equates with a pseudoexplanation of behavior. But it is precisely at this point that Rychlak argues that a self *is* necessary.

Rychlak bases his humanism on a mode of explanation which requires a self as a causal agent. Rychlak discusses the distinctions between various types of causal explanations, namely, final, formal, efficient, and material. Psychology in general has relied upon efficient and material causes whereas his humanist position is predicated on the belief in final and formal causes.

Rychlak's arguments present a view of philosophy of science that he has propounded for several years but to which many psychologists have not been systematically exposed. He requires a self for his view of human teleology. Rychlak also describes some of his own research based on assumptions related to this mode of causal explanation.

It is important to note how Rychlak's humanism differs from other types of humanism. Some humanists have based their humanism on humanitarianism (in this respect, Skinner is also a humanist) or on the necessity of human models for human behavior (Jourard is this type, and Child, 1973, identifies this as the major aspect of humanism). Rychlak, however, bases his humanism on a mode of causal explanation. And Rychlak requires a self concept for this explanation. The self is an important concept for many humanists— frequently humanistic theories are labeled self theories—but their definition of self usually is different than Rychlak's.

Mischel and Rychlak conclude by discussing their views on the possible compatibility between their positions. They tend to emphasize their differences.

Is a Concept of "Self" Necessary in Psychological Theory, and if so Why? A Humanistic Perspective

JOSEPH F. RYCHLAK

*Department of Psychological Sciences, Purdue University,
West Lafayette, Indiana 47907*

The editors of this volume have asked me to address the question, "Is a concept of 'Self' necessary in psychological theory, and if so why?" As a psychologist who considers himself to be humanistic in orientation, they can count on my answer being "yes." Of course, I have a certain position on what humanistic psychology amounts to. As the various papers in this collection make clear, there is really no single approach to humanistic psychology. Quite frankly, I am not confident that the view I will present is even faintly representative of most humanistic positions in psychology. In trying to answer the "and if so why" portion of the question we will have to proceed as follows. First we will review what it means to be a mechanist or a humanist in the way that I employ these terms. Next, we will frame a definition of the self as a necessary corollary to the taking of a humanistic position in psychology. We will then try to show why mechanistic efforts to capture the teleology of self-theories must always fall short. Finally, we will give a quick overview of a fifteen year research program in which I have tried to study a humanistic conception of learning in a rigorous fashion.

WHAT HUMANISM AND MECHANISM MEAN

I have tried to show in various contexts just what this distinction between humanism and mechanism in psychological theory means (Rychlak, 1968, 1969, 1970, 1972, 1973a,b; Rychlak and Barna, 1971). In developing my argument over the years, it has been refined to three essential "areas" of what might be termed metatheoretical consideration. These three areas which each theorist *must of necessity* take a position on include: the presumed causes of behavior, dialectical versus demonstrative meanings, and Lockean versus Kantian models of mind or behavior. In the present section we will survey each of these areas before attempting to define humanism and mechanism.

Causation Theory

All theorists (thinkers, philosophers, scientists, etc.) explain the objects of their interest by relating these to other referents, which is a way of saying that meanings inevitably reach for "something else" to which they relate, point to, suggest, etc.—literally, "[to] mean!" Our survey of theory construction issues begins with a consideration of *four* such reference points which were first brought together into a theory of knowledge by Aristotle, though at least three of these metaconceptions were reflected in amn's thought before Aristotle came on the historical scene.

Based on reference points which stressed a universal *substance* that made up everything, such as water (Thales) or the "boundless" (Anaximander), Aristotle named his first cause the "material cause." One can say that he knows something about an item of experience if he can name the substance of which it is constituted, and there are various substances in the make-up of our world that "cause" it to be (existence is substantial). Another factor in knowledge which had fascinated earlier thinkers was the question of motion, impetus, flux, or change (Parmenides, Heraclitus), and Aristotle captured this aspect of knowledge in his "efficient cause" construct. How does an event or a "thing" come about? What forces work to construct or arrange things, and how are events moved along over the face of time?

Earlier philosophers (Heraclitus, Plato, Socrates) had pondered the fact that nature takes on various patterns (logos, eidos), as in the stable outlines of a mountain, the changing yet recognizable figure of a human being, or the fleeting yet identifiable form of a cloud. Aristotle called this a "formal cause," and one need not limit this metaconception to patterns in visual space. For example, Aristotelian logic takes on rigid, definite "rules" of syllogistic deduction which can be diagrammed figuratively or stated vocally as in the sense of "voicing a line of argument." A major premise is often such a formal cause, in that some predicated factor is said to bear a rigid and inflexible relation (i.e., pattern) to some stipulated or inferred consequent, as when "All men are mortal" predicates what any "man" will be said to be when he is later confronted.

If we now look at some object like a chair, and try to explicate what we know about it in Aristotelian terms, what can we say? We might argue that we know it to be a chair because it is made of wood (metal, marble, etc., i.e., a material cause); not many chairs are made of cotton or of ice cream. We also surmise it to be a chair because it is clear that it is a manufactured product (efficient cause). Some person or machine made the chair, constructed it, or put it together. This construction resulted in an identifiable form, for it "looks" like a chair made to conform to the structural needs of a human body (formal cause). Do these three causal conceptions circumscribe the full "nature" of the chair-object standing before us? Aristotle did not think so, and thus he added a fourth cause to his array of descriptive meanings, having to do with the possibility of a *purpose* in events or objects.

Aristotle was to hold that a "final cause" must be added, which takes into account the meaning of "that, for the sake of which" events or objects come about. Aristotle would say that there is a purpose in the chair's existence, as to serve the end or goal of human comfort and utility. In accounting for leaves on the limbs of trees Aristotle suggested that they were there "for the sake of" providing shade for the fruit borne by the tree and he concluded thereby "that nature is a cause, a cause that operates for a purpose" (Aristotle, 1952, pp. 276–277). This employment of final causes in a theory makes it a teleology (*telos* from the Greek meaning end, or goal, i.e., the "point" or "reason" for existence, action, and so on). The unique feature of a teleological formulation is that it thrusts our explanatory perspective to the "first person" expression, because in order to fiave a purpose "that thing, over there" becomes "if I were that thing over there, or, if I made that thing over there, what would I do, or why would I have made it?" You cannot speak about forces acting (efficient causes) on an object in an intentional fashion, unless you *also* get over "into" that object and see how *it* acts to direct forces toward some end. I call this first-person theoretical formulation the *introspective* perspective, and contrast it to the third-person type of statement which is *extraspective* in theoretical perspective (i.e., refers exclusively to "that, over there" as if set off and standing apart from the observer).

Keep in mind that Aristotle was not saying that leaves *themselves* have purposes, anymore than he would hold that the chair has "a" purpose. It is nature or the designer and constructor of chairs that can be said to have a purpose. But the point of importance is: Can we fully explicate the nature of leaves and chairs *without* some such purposeful meaning permeating our theoretical mix? Aristotle would say "no" and thus infused his account of physical nature with teleology. The churchmen to follow emulated Aristotle and employed formal and final cause arguments to account for God's hand in nature. A Supreme Being had formulated a Divine Plan (formal cause) "for the sake of which" (final cause, framed introspectively as God's willful intention) he then constructed a world. Though they do not presume to speak for God, much of the theologian's efforts are devoted to assessing just what this deity has intended in bringing to bear the Divine Plan. As we know from history, the "physics" which was to issue from such armchair speculations resulted in a tragic confrontation with Galileo and others around the turn of the 17th century—which is the period from which we usually date the beginnings of modern "natural" science.

It was Sir Francis Bacon (1952, pp. 44–45) who led a scathing attack on the formal and final causes as proper scientific descriptive terms. He denied that bringing more causes to bear resulted in better, more fuller accounting of events (a thesis which Aristotle had defended). Saying that leaves protect fruit by design merely "anthropomorphizes" natural events when in fact we should be describing what we—standing here as observers—can see and hence measure in "that," over there, *and nothing more*! This calls for only material and efficient cause usage in science. Bacon relegated formal and final cause description to esthetics (art) and ethics (morality), and helped fix the so-called rule of parsimony (drawn from the earlier razor of Ockham) in scientific description. From his time onward, we find natural scientists taking as a "cause" *only* the material and efficient cause meanings. This has the effect of confining description in natural science to an extraspective perspective, so that the very suggestion that we might as rigorous thinkers begin to consider an object under observation from "its" (first person) perspective now strikes the natural scientist as improper theoretical usage. The language of observation must ever be about "that" (see Stevens, 1935, p. 517, for the origins of this attitude in laboratory psychology).

Dialectical versus Demonstrative Meanings   The next issue we must consider builds on our recognition (see above) that meanings always reach for "something else" to relate or point to. The very word "meaning" has Anglo-Saxon roots stemming from "to intend, purport, or convey a significance." We might think of this relating "something else" to which a term points as its *polar* reference. The term polar here suggests a guiding reference point, to which a symbol (word, image, etc.) relates and therefore "signifies." Meaning is obviously a final-cause conception, but putting this aside for now the question we can ask is: Are meanings *always unipolar* significations (point-ings), or are they sometimes (even most of the time) *bipolar* in that to which they point?

In the ancient Grecian world it was presumed that all meanings interlaced by way of oppositional ties, and thus in effect, added up to a single totality (one in many, or many in one thesis). One could begin his examination of a phenomenon in error, basing his argument (unknowingly) on fallacious grounds, but thanks to what Socrates and Plato called the *dialectical* method of reasoning (i.e., by opposites), in time come to know truth. Why? Because "truth" and "error" were essentially opposite sides of the same coin. Since all meanings interlaced oppositionally, one could through dialectical examination in discourse (Socrates) or internal dialogue (Plato) come to separate what was truth and what was error.

Aristotle was our first toughminded thinker, for he challenged the view that one can begin in error and come to know truth. If a major premise is fallacious in reasoning, then all conclusions flowing from this erroneous meaning complex will *also* be fallacious. One must begin a line of inquiry from premises which are "primary and true," which means they signify a unipolarity! These premises are either tautologically true (X is X), or, they constitute empirical facts. Aristotle is the father of biology because he wished to base his knowledge on propositions which were *not* open to an either–or, bipolar examination. This style of reasoning from unipolar "givens" to iron-clad deductions Aristotle called demonstrative, opposing it to what he considered the less rigorous dialectical reasoning which was based ultimately on opinion (which is correct, X or Y?). Even so, Aristotle, did not deny that human beings could and often did reason dialectically. Indeed, there are times when a rigorous thinker *must* resort to dialectical strategies. This arises when two or more premises (hypotheses, propositions, etc.) are being contested, and we are unable to tell from a careful study of the definitions being used, or from an examination of the empirical facts, which of the two (or more) alternatives is the most sound presumption (formal cause) "for the sake of which" (final cause) our scientific theory should be furthered. In this circumstance all humans fall back on dialectical defense (adversary procedures).

Throughout medieval history a role for dialectical theory—and even "proof"—was recognized and accepted. St. Augustine based his theology on dialectic, and his Holy Trinity conception is properly seen as one such "model" (Jaspers, 1962, pp. 196–197). Centuries later, though he was to be just as distrustful of the dialectic as Aristotle, St. Thomas Aquinas held that at times one has no alternative but to fall back on dialectical reasoning or a dialectical model in order to make one's case. The dialectic is very compatible to the introspective theoretical perspective, although in time Marx was to take the Hegelian introspective dialectic (of a God, coming to consciousness) and freeze it extraspectively into the impersonal, very "substance" (material cause) of empirically observable material-reality (dialectical materialism). But most dialecticians in Western *and* Eastern thought (e.g., Zen Buddhism) are prone to express their theories from the introspective theoretical perspective.

With the onset of natural science, and the rise of British empiricism as epitomized in the philosophy of Francis Bacon, Thomas Hobbes, and especially John Locke, we witness a pre-emption of the field of explanation by demonstrative concepts and reasoning strategies. It is impossible *by definition* for an organism to reason dialectically in this school of thought. British empiricism holds all meanings to be unipolar "building blocks," which summate in quasi-mathematical fashion to make up more and more complex meanings. Since this is the model or paradigm (Kuhn, 1970) on which modern science has proceeded, it is an unfortunate but true fact that dialectical conceptions of human behavior have *never* been properly named, even though psychology and psychiatry are shot through with such conceptualizations.

Lockean versus Kantian Models   We come now to the third issue to be reviewed, which crystallizes the points we have already been considering into two general *models* which recur in the theories of modern psychology (see Rychlak, 1968, 1973a, for more detailed presentation of these models). The first, Lockean model, we have begun considering in the previous subsection. This is a constitutive model of "little things, adding up to bigger, more complex things." It is an extraspective and demonstrative model. We can see reflections of this model in the Darwinian theory of evolution, the Newtonian conception of scientific laws, as totaling up to higher and higher levels of efficient causality, and in the stimulus–response conception of inputs from the environment which presumably combine and recombine (mediate) to form the hierarchical array of "habits" that are said to form the behavior of the individual.

In contrast, we can speak of the Kantian model of theory construction, which is a more active, conceptualizing view of events. Unlike Locke, who thought of the mind as working solely *after* experience had etched meanings onto its *tabula rasa* beginnings at birth, Kant held that mind brings meaning-framing "premises" (categories of the understanding) to experience in a *pro forma* sense—also, from birth! These *precedent* categories of the understanding (cause–effect, unity–polarity, etc.) *sequaciously* determine what "can be known." Knowledge is conceptual and not only or primarily constituted. The mental idea for Locke is an atomic building block, or, it begins in such simple *unipolar* units of information. There is no implicit bipolarity in meaning— ever!—and hence *in principle* no such thing as dialectic or dialectical reasoning. Whatever is "in" the idea-receptacle has been put there "all of one piece[s]" by reality (simple idea) and only subsequently combined into the more abstract totalities (complex ideas) of abstract thought. Opposite meanings are therefore separate and distinct inputs, albeit frequently associated together contiguously in actual practice.

The mental idea for Kant, on the other hand, is like a conceptualizing frame or series of frames which are implicitly bipolar; i.e., they are framed by way of opposite meanings. This makes it possible for free-thought to concoct meaningful constructs entirely at variance with "reality," thanks to the functioning of a *transcendental dialectic* in this most abstract level of reason. This results in a certain modicum of *arbitrariness* in the meanings one takes as "true" or as "possible," since what is input from reality suggests alternatives from the very fact that ideas have implicit opposites to which they point as polar referents (see above). Because it was possible to concoct fanciful ideas completely devoid of factual existence in speculative reason, Kant was just as cautious about resting with dialectical reasoning as Aristotle and Aquinas had been before him. He emphasized in his methodological approach to science that we must bring things in mind down to empirical test. But, his model of mind *does* allow for a contribution from mind, which in turn draws us more to the introspective perspective as we must ask ourselves "what is in in the person's premises that precedently determines what he can sequaciously know?" We must slip on the other person's intellectual spectacles and look at the world the way he looks at it before we fully understand what factors enter into his behavior (see Rychlak, 1973a, pp. 10–11 for schematization of the Kantian and Lockean models).

Humanism versus Mechanism We can now identify in a technical sense what it means to be either a mechanist or a humanist in theoretical orientation. So far as I am concerned, a humanist in psychology is someone who describes behavior—knowingly or unknowingly—by way of formal and final as well as by way of efficient and material causes. The mechanist, on the other hand, strives to remain within the Baconian restrictions and sticks to material- and efficient-cause description. The mechanist is almost always a

Lockean and his conception of meaning is demonstrative. He keeps his descriptions extraspective, so that the reason we call him "mechanical" is the resultant lock-step rigidity and impersonalism of his third-person formulations. It is as if he is describing an efficiently-caused machine, moving unidirectionally "over there." The humanist, on the other hand, makes his commentary from the introspective perspective, trying to see things the way the conceptualizing intellect sees them. What are the authentic, genuine, self-disclosed, congruent, etc., attitudes, feelings, world-designs, personal constructs, etc., through which the person "comes at" his world? The tie binding all humanists is this assumption that the individual "makes a difference" or contributes to the flow of events. Not all humanists are aware of the dialectic, but many employ it as rationale and some (Jung, Binswanger) have even named it.

In the present exchange between Sidney Jourard and Joseph Wolpe we witness an almost classic confrontation between a Kantian and a Lockean theorist. Jourard views psychotherapy as a transcending activity, one in which the individual can bring his personal "power" to bear in effecting changes that *he desires* (introspective perspective) to bring about. In curing himself of the smoking addiction, Jourard rejected extraindividual manipulations (extraspectively conceived) in preference to his own theories (precedent assumptions). Jourard always speaks of mental illness and therapy—or mental health—in telic terms (see Jourard, 1974, for a recent example), as helping to enlighten, encourage, and guide patients, thereby fostering their personal growth. Critics are wont to call such statements "arty" or "mystical," but what Jourard is saying is that he wishes to provide a better "that" (system of open attitudes and beliefs) "for the sake of which" life can be enriched (i.e., teleologically furthered). Consciousness or self-direction is *central* to this conception of humanity.

Wolpe, on the other hand, has used the analogy of consciousness versus behavior as being entirely separate events, in the sense of two electrical circuits which are wired *in parallel* rather than *in series* (see Wolpe, 1958, p. 16). This alignment of two strings of efficient cause–effects, removing one (consciousness) from any direct control over the other (behavior) is the quintessence of extraspective theorizing. Human beings may have illusions of self-direction, and possibly some kind of self-stimulating feedback capacity exists (see our comments below on the mediation model), but the essential point is that behavior is 100% under the control of environmental influences, which are efficient-cause inputs cemented into habit by material-cause drive-reductions. Mind, consciousness, or self-direction of *any* sort is simply an archaic, nonscientific formulation. Though the Skinnerian operant theorist has dropped this reference to drive-reductions, the essential frame of behavior as tantamount to a string of efficient cause-effects over time without recourse to formal–final cause notions is the hallmark of all behavioristic theories. It comes down, really, to the humanists trying to reintroduce final causes and the mechanists trying to keep them out!

Psychotherapy for the behaviorist is thus purely a question of how to rearrange the course of (efficient) cause–effects over time. Although developments in recent times seem to be bringing more of the introspective perspective back into behavior therapy, and there are a few efforts in the present volume to combine behavioral with humanistic formulations, the *crux* of what separates our two camps remains this question of "how much responsibility are we going to assign to the person *qua* person for his behavior?" As a humanistic psychologist, I feel it is essential that we acknowledge *at least* as much of a role for the person in determining his behavior as we allow for the environment. This in no way detracts from the brilliance of the theorizing done by men like Wolpe or Skinner, nor does it deny the efficacy of the cures behavioral therapy has to offer. I speak more to the focal issue of "what is human nature or human behavior like?" and draw my polar references from the teleological, dialectical, and Kantian lines of descent. I do so because it seems to me more instructive in the long run, and that in the final analysis is the only reason anyone "theorizes.." What, then, do we mean by "self" and why is it an essential humanistic formulation?

A CONCEPT OF SELF

The word "self" has Anglo Saxon roots meaning the "same" or "identical," and when we say something is self-induced or self-motivated we usually imply that the "same" organism did something today along the lines of what it did yesterday. The action may have varied a bit across time (the "many" events) but there was a recognizable continuity nevertheless (the "one"). Walter Mischel (1968, 1973b) has wrestled with the behavioristic account of what is changing and what is constant over time in personality description, and Kenneth Bowers (1973) has added a more humanistic commentary as well.

I think we have erred in trying to construe "selves" as total organisms (persons), employing thereby all four causes to this description. Very likely this is the heritage of Gordon Allport (1937), whose distinguished trait theory fixed things in the neural substance so that now we feel that a "self" must also be constituted of something or other. Another problem with the self-construct is that we feel it is necessary to account for it in efficient-cause terms—which are, of course, *not* well suited to the description of continuity in events, but rather to the change in events. Modern psychology is saturated with the concept of change thanks to the bias we have for efficient-cause description. Drop the term "self" into a conversation among psychologists, and you are likely to get questions like "What antecedent factors *caused* this 'self'" to form in the first place?"

Well, you simply cannot speak of *identity* by saying *change*! You cannot say "that which brings to bear an effect" by saying "that which is shaped by efficient causes." If you want to look at the organism as behaving from a *given* premise, one which precedently determines what will sequaciously follow, based on the meanings intended in the premise, then it is just impossible to say this in other than a formal–final cause way. I therefore hold that what we *should* mean by this term "self" is a fixed, unchanging contribution which a reasoning organism makes to the efficiently caused sequence of events within which it behaves. The content of a premise might change over time, but insofar as we can isolate "a" behavioral event "for now," the contribution which a *self* makes to this behavioral event is a fixed one.

I therefore view the self as a kind of "logical thrust" from the side of conceptualizations which organisms under my observation bring to bear as they "come at" the world in that sense of the Kantian model. Their conceptualizations, which precedently determine to some extent what will sequaciously follow in their behavior, may be thought of as one of George Kelly's (1955) "personal constructs," or Thomas Kuhn's (1970) more institutionalized "paradigms." When these premises are put into a series of events by an "identity" i.e., the individual applying them in his behavior—they are so far as I am concerned, being expressed by a "self." In fact, I would view the assumptions which the statistician makes preliminary to reasoning through a data problem in some research project as self-induced. There can be no logical reasoning without a premising reasoner, a *self* who brings the fixed parameters to bear across a series of events to lend them order and thereby concoct something meaningful. The gestaltists, existentialists, and related phenomenological positions are quick to fall back on self-theories because of their great sensitivity to the requirement of a stable framework in the course of human events.

This "bringing to bear" of a construct, paradigm, or statistical assumption combines both a formal- and a final-cause meaning. Let us take a more mundane example, of the "game plan" a football coach might sketch onto the strategy board for his athletes to study preliminary to a contest. It obviously required chalk, a board, and a moving arm uniting the two to get this game plan sketched into recognizability; so, to this extent it can be said that a material and an efficient cause were involved in the observable behavior of the coach. But surely, the *self*-expressed strategy here, reflecting the coach's game mentality, is the *formal* cause aspect of the game plan. This strategy remains consistent enough across situations to be recognized by a fan as the coach's "style." In what sense does the final-cause meaning enter here? I would say that there is a self-expressed "that for the sake of which" in the coach's intention to put his meaning on the board and thereby to get it across to his players. The plan as sketched on the board is nothing but a pattern of chalk (formal cause). The plan *qua* plan *lacks* purpose, or "a" purpose. It merely reflects the coach's purpose, but when eventually put into play on the field of competition we again have a final-cause meaning entering our theoretical account. The players acquire an intention as they execute the plan. Each player reflects a self-induced behavior in the precedent assumptions he makes about how to style his play, which in turn sequaciously determines the actions to follow (i.e., at least as much as anything else in the circumstance which develops will influence this behavior).

I call this beginning, fixed point from which the self takes a premise the *protopoint*. Behavior is thus seen to move, not only in an efficient cause–effect fashion, but mentally considered it moves also—or additionally—in precedent-to-sequacious cause–effects. Granting *this* (for the sake of this) that follows. But it takes an identity to conceptualize the precedent-to-sequacious form of final causality, and this is where we need a concept of self. Organisms which bring meaningful premises to bear are usefully designated as contributing a self-influence to the course of events, and particularly so when they recognize that they *are* doing so. With these provisos I can now offer a definition of the "self."

> The self may be defined as a construct enabling the theorist to conceptualize the contribution made to behavior by an organism which brings meaningful premises to bear from a protopoint. The term self captures the impact or "logical weight" of a precedent meaning (premise) conveying sequacious implications (inductions, deductions, etc.) for the sake of which behavior to follow is at least partially determined. To the extent that a behaving organism does (1) precedently and arbitrarily formulate meaningful premises at a protopoint "for the sake of which" it sequaciously behaves, (2) is conscious of

doing so, and (3) seeks to improve on the advantages gained from the use of such premises, to that extent can it be said to be self-enhancing in behavior, or, to be promoting "self-realization."

There is nothing in this definition to suggest that a "something" exists to be called the "self" in the sense that an organ called the "liver" exists. Nor is it held that the self "acts" according to principles which are emergent, irreducible, or otherwise mystical and not open to description. The self-concept is presented as an introspective formulation, reflecting that sense of orientation and identity in behavior which mechanists are prone to consider illusory experience (Immergluck, 1964; Lefcourt, 1973). Just as motion (efficient causality) is not required for the successions of logical or mathematical responding to "follow," so too do we now claim that the effects of self-implications on behavior are free of impetus considerations, drawing their rationale from the patterns and intentions (formal and final causes) of psychic life. These self-induced features of behavior have a *logical* impact on events, and this involves both dialectical and demonstrative forms of logical reasoning.

If the organism reasons dialectically, then it is clear that the self (identity at the protopoint) has a range of arbitrariness in the particular premise it does affirm "for this unit of time" (see Rychlak, 1973b, for a more thorough discussion of the role of arbitrariness in behavior). Much of what we call the unreliability of traits or self-concepts to predict across situations is due to this fact that more than one "fixed premise" is implied as the organism "comes at" any one life situation. The "next time" it comes at this same situation, the organism could easily switch premises. The taking of a premise is therefore more akin to *conformity* than it is to a compelling sense of "no alternatives but this one" to entertain. When one conforms he realizes that he *could* be taking another position on the matter. Since this multiplicity of premises is psychologically uncomfortable (confusing, illogical, irrational, etc.), I think the usual course is to affirm a certain premise and to ignore or argue away the others. The unconscious features of behavior probably stem from the fact that unconfirmed premises do not simply "go away." As C. G. Jung (1954) made so clear, these "shadow" premises can be entertained in dreams and complexes, particularly if the self-definition is poorly articulated and therefore overlooked (self-control) by the individual.

Note that a certain "level" of self-development is implied in the definition, since it *is* possible to have a greater or lesser awareness of one's function as a premising organism. There is no claim made here that all behavior is equally self-induced. The nonteleological formulations of a learning theorist might hold for much of behavior. I would say that as we ascend the phylogenetic scale a greater probability for self-induced behavior takes place. I think this is true because there seems a greater potential for dialectical reasoning among higher organisms than lower organisms. Stimulus–response psychology seems to fit lower organisms quite nicely, with their more demonstrative behavior patterns. It seems a bit foolish, in the light of our history concerning the anthropomorphizing of lower animals, to speak of self-induced factors in subhuman behavior. But it is not excessive, and we should not be too intimidated by our history to say that the self aspects of behavior could extend below the human level. It is difficult to talk about this aspect of behavior because we lack proper terminology. We presume that "a behavior" is "a response or series of such responses." This makes it sound impossible to "do" anything as an organism which transcends motion (impetus, efficient causality). Recently, I have been experimenting with the term *telosponse*, to capture what we have been discussing here as self-induced behavior. I think telosponsive behavior—behaving "for the sake of" fixed premises—increases as we ascend the phylogenetic scale.

Alfred Adler's (1964) conception of the self emphasized the working-toward-a-goal feature that we have included in the definition. This idea of self-enhancement or self-realization has been central to the ethical theories of history. As scientists we need not let this tie of self to ethics disturb us, since it follows that a mentality which becomes aware of its own influence on the course of events should in time consider the likelihood of improving the relative standing it enjoys among events. Concepts of "perfection" no doubt stem from this capacity for human beings to see how their aspirations and directed efforts can improve the quality of life. Of course, this does not mean that selves must *always* seek the "higher" aims in life.

One of the attitudes I personally dislike about many humanistic positions today is their seeming commitment to a goody-goody, "life is beautiful" concept of civilization. I am no pessimist, and think that it is marvelous for any one individual to have such a pink-cheeked view of humanity. But, as a scientist who must strive to retain objectivity, it seems to me a decided mistake to begin precedently with this *single* assumption about the data under study. I prefer to say that self-enhancement is surely one aspect of human nature. But whether or not all people do in fact work to become "whole," self-consistent (Lecky, 1969), or congruent (Rogers, 1961) is an open—which means empirical—question. Improving one's relative standing among an environment full of possible advantages is hardly limited to "brotherly love" behaviors. Surely sometimes this self-enhancement *also* takes on a truly "selfish" quality, which means the individual is out purposively to injure or otherwise demean a fellow human being.

I like to draw a distinction between a humanist and a humanitarian. If you are out to help humanity in some way—either literally, by improving their lot, or conceptually, by describing people in an uplifting fashion—then I would consider you a humanitarian. In this sense, many mechanists are humanitarians and I would place Dr. Wolpe and Dr. Skinner under this designation. These are the "nice guys" of our profession, and we should never want to equate the humanistic stance with a commitment to humanitarianism. But this is what I see taking place today and I do not like it anymore than I like the mechanistic mask which some of my humanitarian friends are trying to stretch over the face of mankind. My own motivation to further psychology is not as a humanitarian, though naturally I hope that my theories prove helpful. In that sense, every scholar is also a humanitarian. But my teleology is conceived strictly as a statement of empirical fact—one which must be discounted by evidence and not dismissed by innuendo. There are no gods (deity teleology) or a benign march of natural selection (natural teleology) lurking in the wings of my presentation of teleology as there so often are among humanists and even mechanists. I am strictly a humanistic (human teleology) theorist, using certain technical devices to express my meanings because I find them instructive and consistent with my personal sense of reality, and my observation of other organisms who come at life much as I do.

MEDIATION THEORY AND THE SELF

Frequently, when I talk on this question of humanism, someone in the audience comes up with a supposed resolution of the humanism–mechanism controversy as follows: "Let us simply acknowledge that the living organism *does* mediate between the inputs and the outputs of experience, and that thanks to a feedback mechanism of some kind, there *is* an influence being brought to bear on the new input as the human being begins to acquire earlier environmental inputs in memory, and so forth. Is this not a 'self-induced' line of behavior in your sense? Old inputs are the 'that' for the sake of which newer outputs are mediated. Why not say things this way and end all of this divisiveness in psychology by making it appear humanism and mechanism are so incompatible when they are not!"

Much as I would like to play the role of arbiter and resolver of psychological disputes, in point of fact mediation theory just does not get at what is separating the Kantian from the Lockean theorist. There has always been a recognition by the Lockean theorist that individuals influence their behavior in this mediational sense. Locke himself discusses many ways in which the mind makes use of past information to influence the processing of new information (see Locke, 1952, pp. 178–200). In psychology, we tend to trace mediation theory to Tolman's sign gestalts, or to Woodworth's S–O–R ideas (Goss, 1961; Rychlak, 1973a, pp. 283–290). However, even our so-called "founding fathers" had conceptions which recognized an influence from yesterday's learning on today's behavior: Helmholtz in his "unconscious inference" construct and Wundt in his "apperception" construct (Boring, 1950, pp. 308–311 and 338–339 respectively). What then is the crux of our Lockean–Kantian distinction?

The fundamental issue is, does the organism *from birth*—or even possibly a bit before literal birth—"do anything" in a *pro forma* sense to the inputs of experience? Or, is the organism exclusively *tabula rasa* at this initial proto-point? Mediation theory prejudices the case in favor of Lockean models, since it puts this conceptualizing ability at the organism's disposal only *after* an initial input has been etched upon the *tabula rasa* intellect. Sign gestalts and related constructs such as the cue-producing response (Dollard and Miller, 1950) are efficient causes *first* (inputs), formal causes *second* (patterned manipulators), and *never* final causes! Kantian formulations aim to stress the formal and final causes *first*, and then recognize the efficient cause features of how a brain "works" *second*. This is why it is so reckless to gloss over the differences between our two models, and to seek ways of saying one thing when you are trying to express the meaning of another. It is impossible to say "teleology" in efficient-cause language.

Mediation theory therefore falls short of a genuinely telic commentary in at least three ways: (1) mediators (signs, rules, models, etc.) are input and hence "past" responses rather than "present" telosponses, which means that (2) a true "that for the sake of which" decision in the sequence of motion is never achieved (i.e., there is no arbitrariness in behavior), resulting in exclusively a (3) demonstrative way of describing the course of behavioral events since no possibility for dialectical reasoning is left open. We can never speak of "transcendence" on the mediation model and mean by this what Kant meant when he coined the term (Kant, 1952, p. 115).

When I begin speaking about some influence which mind brings to bear at birth—an influence which, as it is nurtured and furthered, constitutes a "self-realization"—I leave myself open to the charge of believing in "innate ideas." Thanks to the supremacy of the Lockean model in experimental psychology, it is often hard to make clear that an innate Kantian idea is something quite different from an innate Lockean idea. Locke looked at ideas as receptacles, as if some information that had flowed in now occupied the idea as a unipolar designation (a "bit" of information unto itself)—the way water fills a glass. The idea was not a conceptualizing (organizing, lending-meaning to, etc.) process in mind. It was an "effect" in the efficient-cause sequence. What was "in" the idea, as a meaning, was put there by the environment, just as the water is put into the glass.

Kant's categories of the understanding as so-called "innate ideas" are something much different from this receptacle notion. These were more akin to conceptualizing "formal causes" for the sake of which perceived (phenomenal) reality was organized. What was innate about the idea was the ability to *lend meaning* to life experience as well as the dimensions along which such meaning could be induced; e.g., unity—plurality, possibility–impossibility, and so forth. Kant was not saying that individuals were born with the meaning of the words "unity" and "plurality" pocketed in little receptacles. As a neo-Kantian, I can claim that not until the child "knows" the meaning of left, will he know the meaning of right. Not until he grasps up will he grasp down, or the same for good and evil, long and short, and so forth. Coming to know one side he knows the other because meanings are bipolar and not only unipolar designations. I do not have to claim—as Locke forces me to claim—that the child has an innate capacity to know what left, up, good, and long means—much less their opposites. The specific content of an idea waits on experience. But, at least *some* meanings as input from experience in the Lockean simple-idea sense are not so simple! They will be oppositionally complex from the very point of input, calling for an active affirmation by the organism (in time, as a "self") to affirm "this" meaning or "that" in the situation which continually arises before it.

In therapy, the humanist tries as best he can to encourage his patient to re-examine the life premises on which he (the patient) proceeds. This is what he means by "insight." When he says that he is *not* controlling his client the humanistic therapist is himself (precedently) presuming that the client has a dialectical intelligence, and that the course he will eventually affirm (and follow) *can* be self-induced "to some extent." No one can work miracles, walk through walls, achieve an intelligence he is incapable of by the strictures of physical nature, and so forth. But since the humanist presumes the client has gotten to this point in life thanks to affirmations of premises that were in many ways arbitrary presumptions, he asks for a re-examination of these protopoint decisions and hopes in time that the client can align a more satisfactory precedent–sequacious course of behavioral events. Mechanists confine their commentary to an exclusively extraspective perspective (see Bakan, 1965, for an excellent discussion of this phenomenon). They do not view the mediators as in any way self-initiated, even though as many of the papers in this volume suggest, there does seem to be a sentiment among certain behaviorists to bring in more of this commentary recently. Whether a complete rapproachement is possible between the two views is debatable. I am pessimistic on this point, if we mean a rapprochement at the level of "mind." I sometimes think the only resolution possible is to take a demonstrative view of the "body" and bring in dialectical constructs at the level of "mind." This seems to violate parsimony in the thought of many of my mechanistic friends, but this is about as close as I am able to come on this question of resolving the Kantian–Lockean schism.

A PROGRAM OF RESEARCH ON A DIALECTICAL, HUMANISTIC CONSTRUCT

How would a humanist, who believes that individuals (selves) influence their course of learning at least as much as does the environment shape their learning proceed to prove this? If we are to be rigorous humanists we need to have an approach to science which stands up to laboratory test, but also tells us something about our humanistic conceptions. I have always believed that there were mountains of evidence in the laboratory to support humanism. But if an experimental hypothesis is not framed as having a humanistic intent from the outset, it is impossible for "rigorous experimental evidence" to be presented in its support—ever! Most rigorous laboratory psychologists *never* frame such hypotheses. They never look for dialectical features in behavior *knowingly*. I say "knowingly" because Osgood has most surely stumbled onto the dialectical side of meaning in his excellent series of researches *unknowingly* (lacking the proper hypotheses to study) (Snider and Osgood, 1969). Operant conditioners were dismayed by the findings on awareness (DeNike and Spielberger, 1963; Dulany, 1962) because it had never occurred to them to look for the more introspective features of behavior. I think they have offered lame excuses for the fact that they are not so much controlling their subjects as making it possible for the subject to conform to the experimental hypothesis *or not* (e.g., Page, 1969, 1970).

About fifteen years ago I initiated a research program which precedently began with the assumption that individuals could and did influence their course of learning independently—to an extent—of the environmental circumstances which also were shaping their learning. I took a view of learning *a la* logic, and now call this "logical learning theory" but include here dialectical as well as the classical demonstrative (Aristotelian) logic. We begin from the Kantian assumption that humans *at birth* have the capacity to judge, evaluate or assess environmental circumstances (inputs, stimuli, etc.). Judgment is an *active* process of bringing mentality to bear. This notion of assessing one's environmental circumstance is my "Kantian category," we might say. I do not think human beings are simply "responding," in behavior. A response comes *after* stimulation, or, if we deny this as the Skinnerians seem to do, then a response is still nontelic—it "happens" or does not happen in relation to something else and then gets tied to something else by way of reinforcements (or it does not). I reject this efficient-cause account as insufficient to handle what we know about human behavior. It is not a wrong theory; it is just incomplete and simplistic. We need better, more sophisticated accounts of learning than we now have to supplement the classical efficient-cause theories of behaviorism.

I believe that, in addition to "responding" to environmental factors, human beings are also continually assessing their life circumstances. One of the clearest definitions of final causation is precisely this ability to judge (evaluate, assess, etc.). When we judge something we assess its status *in terms of* or *for the sake of* something else. We align the fish we have just caught with a ruler, and announce that it is 21 inches long. The rules is a "that" for the sake of which we can make our judgment; it is a patterned sequence of steps in distance that helps us to organize our thinking about experience.

But there are other kinds of judgments we continually make in coming at life by way of our protopoint premises about life. These are not demonstratively derived metrics of the ruler variety, but dialectical judgments of a like–dislike, good–bad, adient–abient, etc., variety. They are purely idiographic assessments, Kantian-like projections meeting stimuli at their point of contact with "mind" and framing things according to the meaning contained in the premises (precedent–sequacious influences). I call the judgment of "like–dislike" an affective assessment, and the technical measure which we take from such judgments proffered by subjects is called *reinforcement value* (Rychlak, 1966). Thus, we argue that reinforcements are not *only* in the environment, or in the tissue needs of the body, as modern learning theories imply. Reinforcements are positive or negative thanks *also* to a contribution made by the affectively assessing human organism who must come at life each day.

Are people "born" with preferences? Is the child who dislikes turnips and likes pudding reflecting an inborn preference? This question is a rephrase of the inborn ideas discussion, above. In holding that people are born with the capacity to dialectically assess "like–dislike" as they come at life in maturation we are *not* claiming that what is liked or disliked—the specific content of preferences—is innate. Do not a person's preferences stem from past experience? If a mother pricks a child with a pin and the child cries out in pain, coming to dislike (be fearful of) pins or other sharp objects over time, is this not proof that the child's preferences are "effects" and not true "that for the sake of which" judgments? This kind of argument strikes me as illogical. It seems to suggest that because the grounds for a decision today are based on past experience, by definition a true judgment cannot be made today. The logical error arises from a confusion between the passage of time, antecedent–consequent, and cause–effect. Time seems to flow from antecedents (befores) to consequents (afters), and the efficient-cause concept of cause–effect slips in nicely here as well. But we must keep in mind that an antecedent–consequent conception can *also* be a formal-cause designation, as in the case of antecedents and consequents in "If, then . . ." propositions. Such designations have nothing whatever to do with time, and you cannot pre-empt their meaning by efficient causality because in a logical sequence time is irrelevant! Hence, it is important to appreciate that just because something is earlier in time does not make it *ipso facto* the efficient cause of something that comes later. Earlier factors can be acting as formal-cause grounds "for the sake of which" (final cause) a reasoning intellect functions in the present.

Returning to the mother who accidently pricks her child with a pin, I would argue that the child *does* affectively assess the pinprick even as he feels the entirely physical pain as an emotion. Affects are more on the side of formal–final causes, whereas emotions are more on the side of material–efficient causes. Emotions are often said to be assessments or appraisals (see Arnold, 1970, for a thorough discussion of the emotion construct). But I claim that emotions are never arbitrary. When you have an emotional feeling, it is—phenomenally speaking—always "having you." There is a judgment of your circumstance in this emotion all right, but—as the James–Lange theory suggested generations past—this assessment is entirely automatic and after-the-fact. Emotions are truely "effects" in that efficient-cause sense, rooted in our organic structure and occurring reflexively. But in the psychological realm we have our affective states and these depend on our unique judgments, which in turn of course, reflect the grounds we have worked out over a lifetime of making such judgments.

It is always easy to show how the environment influences us by choosing the right examples. Positive and negative reinforcements " in " the environment are easy to point to by looking at the extremes. Getting hurt is negative, so think about the times in the past when you were injured, or spanked, or you failed a test, or got fired from a job. Being pleased is positive, so think about the times in the past when you were shown love, or scored an academic triumph, or ate a marvelous meal. But now, what of all the other times? What of all those " inbetween " times when the high and low points are not so easy to delineate? This is where you usually " live." Do you think your environmental circumstances in the past as you went to school, met some new people, spent an evening alone at home, woke up one morning, took a day off, had a lot to do, etc., were *clearly* positive or negative as to reinforcement quality? And do you suppose that in those cases where the meaning of the environment was not clearly positive or negative, that the way in which you began to formulate this upcoming " environment " had anything to do with the positive or negative reinforcements that you were to receive "as inputs" from this environment?

I think so. As Alfred Adler (1964) has suggested, there is always a modicum of arbitrariness in just what sort of position we are going to take on life. We do have something to say about what is furthered meaningfully and what is not furthered meaningfully as we walk along life's way—no matter how irrationally and inconsistently this influence might be. We arrange circumstances to come out as we would prefer for them to come out—at least, we do this to the fullest extent possible. Now, when I say " we " do this, my theory is clearly written from an introspective perspective and the first-person designation which I need to fill in the account is this thing we have called the " self." It takes a conceptualizing organism to round-out my theory because I am an introspective theorist. So, I *need* a self-concept—or, more accurately, concepts of the self are germane to the conception of mankind as a precedently-sequaciously behaving organism. Since human beings have always sensed this quality, of a continuing actor, a constant evaluator, a fixed point of view from which behavior emanates, I think it is essential to retain this concept. Actions, evaluations, and points of view are all " functions " of that organism we in science are trying to describe—the one which also digests, bleeds, sleeps, and dies. None of our terms need be reified, but as we all look at the same human organism we need to employ constructs to make clear what it is we are trying to say. And, I think the self-construct is necessary even as I have said that we should stop trying to capture the "whole organism" in this conception. What we want to capture here is more the formal–final cause designation in behavior.

I have found in my researches that what the individual thinks of himself—as generally positive or negative in reinforcement value—is an important feature of the kinds of meanings he will be seen to further in his learning style. This self-evaluation seems to act as a grounds, or a "that," against which the rest of life's meanings are aligned and furthered or not. Although most people further meanings which they take to be positive very readily, abnormals (schizophrenics) or normals with negative self-concepts actually diminish this "positive reinforcement-value effect" or reverse it entirely and further negative meanings more readily than positive meanings (Rychlak *et al.*, 1971; 1974). These studies are done in a verbal learning format, using paired-associates, free-recall, or recognition-learning procedures. We have found positive reinforcement-value effects in the learning of consonant–vowel–consonant trigrams (Rychlak, 1966), words (Andrews, 1972), abstract designs (McFarland, 1969), and names-to-faces (Galster, 1972).

Critics were quick to suggest that the reinforcement-value measure was actually due to the association value (familiarity, recognition-value) or the frequency of word-appearance in the standing language structure and not due to the act of evaluation *per se*. Frequency conceptions stem from the classical principle of contiguity, and they are central to the Lockean model. Judgments are "input" by contiguity and not "expressed" from birth, so we must reduce the reinforcement-value construct to the frequency of past inputs which "obviously" must determine it. We spent considerable time disproving this Lockean counter, establishing so far as I am concerned beyond doubt that reinforcement value is entirely independent of such frequency or contiguity factors as the Archer (1960) lists (trigrams) or the Thorndike–Lorge (1944) tables (words) (Abramson *et al.*, 1969; Rychlak *et al.*, 1973b; and Tenbrunsel *et al.*, 1968). We have even done cross-validating factor analyses to prove that reinforcement value cannot be reduced to a frequency dimension of meaningfulness (Rychlak *et al.*, in preparation). Even so, there is not a submission I make to a journal in which the Lockean-oriented reviewer fails to come up with something like "but couldn't these likability ratings be due to the frequency of past associations with a word or quasi-word?" He invariably wants to force my findings for a teleological theory into *his* efficient-cause theory.

In addition to the work on abnormals and normals with weak self-concepts, we have found that underachievers are especially sensitive to the affective factor in their learning styles. Overachievers seem to rise above this factor and learn what they dislike almost as readily as what they like, but the underachiever learns what he likes dramatically better than what he dislikes (Rychlak and Tobin, 1971). This finding leads me to suspect that reinforcement value is not a simple "motivational construct" in the classical meaning of that term. If we can assume that overachievers are highly motivated, then this finding suggests their motivation works *against* the positive reinforcement-value effect. Tachistoscopic recognition of faces in the style of the old "perceptual defense" thesis is seen to be facilitated by positive reinforcement value in certain cases and inhibited by negative reinforcement value in others (Rychlak *et al.*, 1972).

We have found that when dominant subjects learn dominant word-meanings they show a positive reinforcement-value effect (i.e., acquire their liked dominant word-meanings more rapidly than their disliked) but that no such affective distinction can be shown for their learning of submissive words (Rychlak *et al.*, 1973b). We have found that learning disliked verbal materials previous to liked materials results in significant (nonspecific) positive transfer taking place across tasks, but that reversing the procedure and moving from a liked to a disliked task results in little positive or actual negative (nonspecific) transfer taking place (Rychlak and Tobin, 1971; Rychlak *et al.*, 1974).

I have wondered whether the discounted theories of formal discipline which held that learning classical studies such as Greek facilitated the learning of other courses such as mathematics, were not arrived at thanks to a misinterpretation of a reinforcement-value phenomenon. Assuming that the study of Greek was generally more disliked by students than mathematics, if a teacher had begun the school half-day (a.m. or p.m.) with a class devoted to the former subject (negative reinforcement value) an improvement in the latter subject (positive reinforcement value) might have been pronounced enough in the class to make a lasting didactic impression. Finally, in what is probably the most exciting finding to date, black females have been shown to learn-more along reinforcement-value lines than do white females, who focus relatively more on the word quality (association value) of trigrams than on the reinforcement value of these materials (Rychlak *et al.*, 1973a). Could it be that much of the so-called black inferiority to whites on academic tasks and tests of intelligence is due to some such affective factor? What if we were to find that blacks are predominantly "inferior" on their *disliked* tasks and IQ items? How could this finding be dealt with *vis-à-vis* the typical genetic explanations proffered to account for such racial differentials?

My principle of explanation in accounting for such findings is the "tautology," although I use this term more in a *psycho*logical sense than in the more familiar logical sense. Logical learning theory holds that affective assessments are dialectical in nature. A person cannot really be neutral and also be affectively assessing something. He would simply be "not" judging in a neutral situation (off the dimension of judgment altogether). The tautological principle suggests that once people have sorted out their existence into this affective bipolarity, they align meanings (inductions, deductions, implications, convictions, etc.) according to the identity achieved from the judgment (like, dislike) and the material aligned (as liked or disliked). The individual thus "knows" what he "knows," what he judges to be "one" (same, identical, etc.) with that which is precedently judged either positive or negative. There is a kind of thrust in learning, a "weight of [psycho-] logical" meaning-enhancement taking place by way of tautological identity. This power to influence events may be called the "self" and I hold that a concept like this is sufficiently instructive and consistent with the experimental data to be retained in psychology.

The Self as the Person: A Cognitive Social Learning View[1]

WALTER MISCHEL

*Department of Psychology, Stanford University,
Stanford, California 94305*

I have been asked to discuss in this paper the "self and personality." Although the invitation was for a "behavioristic position" on this topic, I have always been uncomfortable about applying that label to myself; perhaps a phrase like "cognitive social learning" fits my position better (Mischel, 1973a). But rather than fuss about proper labels, let me try to make explicit what I think about the self.

AMBIVALENCE ABOUT THE "SELF"

Most psychologists (myself included) are ambivalent about the concept of the "self." The positive side of this ambivalence seems rooted in the subjective reality of the experienced "self;" beyond infancy, each person seems "aware of himself," at least some of the time. Each mature individual discriminates between self and the rest of the world; each has a sense of himself or herself as a distinct entity. In spite of the fact that every cell of the body changes in the course of life, this perceived identity, this self-consciousness, appears to be a basic human experience and its loss is interpreted as no less than a loss of "reality" itself.

On the negative side, this ambivalence seems based on the reluctance to create a self as an extracausal agent that resides in the person and somehow is responsible for (generates, causes, regulates) behavior in ways that are separable from the organisms in which "it" dwells. Consider, for example, this excerpt from Carl Rogers: ". . . when the self is free from any threat of attack

[1] The writing of this paper was facilitated by research grant MH-6830 to Walter Mischel from the National Institute of Mental Health, United States Public Health Services.

or likelihood of attack, then it is possible for the self to consider these hitherto rejected perceptions, to make new differentiations, and to reintegrate the self in such a way as to include them" (Rogers, 1947, p. 365).

For Rogers the self seems to be not a synonym for the "me" or "I" or "ego;" it is a self apparently distinct from the total person and from what he or she does—indeed it is a self that even can "reintegrate the self."

Many psychologists (including Gordon Allport who, in 1937 and 1961, wrote so persuasively on this topic) are unwilling to give the self such extraordinary causal powers: "To say that the self does this or that, wants this or that, wills this or that, is to beg a series of difficult questions. The psychologist does not like to pass the buck to a self-agent . . . It is unwise to assign our problems to an inner agent who pulls the strings" (Allport, 1961, pp. 129–130).

THE SELF *IS* THE PERSON

To resolve ambivalence about the concept of self, one wants to avoid the pitfalls of pseudoexplanations (into which the concept of a self as causal agent quickly leads) without throwing out the subjective reality of self-experience (self-awareness) and without neglecting the person who does the experiencing. A first step might be to fully equate such terms as the "self," the "I," and the "ego," and to treat each as a synonym for the total individual. This equivalence should be least reduce the chance of being beguiled by "explanations" in which the "self" is used to account for the individual's behavior, or in which a person's problems are seen as due to his "weak ego." Behavior is generated by the person, not by a self, ego, or other agent distinct from the individual.

The suggestion to equate self and person is hardly unique. Indeed, it seems to be shared by such diverse theorists as Skinner (1974) and Royce (1973). As the latter put it:

"The 'self' here is not a mental construct, but a living organism, a person. When I say that I cut myself shaving this morning, I do not mean that I cut a mental construct. Likewise, if you hit *me*, that 'I' who got hit is not some 'ego' of Freudian theory. We are talking here not about one's self-concept or self-image but about the existing reality. And this reality is the same referent when we say, 'I understand,' or 'I choose' or 'I run'. . . ."

"The person or self, then, *is* the behaving organism." [Royce, 1973, p. 885.]

LOOKING FOR THE LOCUS OF CAUSATION

The radical behaviorists, most notably B. F. Skinner (1974), quickly dispatch "pseudoexplanations" by refusing to invoke either the self or the person as a causal agent. Instead, they attribute the "control" (cause) of behavior to the individual's environmental and genetic history. While the extreme emphasis on the environment successfully avoids animism and "ghosts" it does so at the cost of neglecting two crucial points (Mischel, 1973a). It ignores the ways in which the individual *transforms* the environment psychologically, processing information about events selectively and constructively in light of his or her own psychological state. It also ignores the fact that behavior reflects a continuous *interaction* between person and conditions rather than a one-way influence process in which the environment molds the person. (For an elaboration of the limitations of simplistic behavior theories, see Bandura, 1974.)

Skinner argues cogently for the significance of the environment, and specifically the "contingencies of reinforcement" as determinants of human behavior. But the credibility of his position seems undermined by extreme neglect of the interaction between person and environment, revealed in glaring oversimplifications like this: "Whatever we do, and hence however we perceive it, the fact remains that it is the environment which acts upon the perceiving person, not the perceiving person who acts upon the environment" (Skinner, 1971, p. 188).

Such curious assertions reinforce the stereotype that behaviorally oriented psychologists lose the person in a one-sided focus on the environment. In Skinner's case the stereotype may fit: the charge of "situationism in psychology" (Bowers, 1973) seems justified when the environment is depicted as molding man without recognition that man acts on the environment; indeed, much of the effective human environment consists of people, not of things or of a contingency-generating apparatus. Skinner's occasional claim for the one-way impact of the environment on the person creates a bizarre schism in which the individual's capacity to change the environment (which, curiously, seems a fundamental feature of his original concept of "operant" behavior) is somehow denied.

Such environmental extremism encourages critics to charge that in recent years psychology has been overemphasizing the importance of the environment and the situation while underemphasizing—or even "losing"—the person (e.g., Bowers, 1973; Carlson, 1971). Bowers (1973, p. 307) attacks a "situationism" that emphasizes situations as the causes of behavior while "being inattentive to the importance of the person." Situationism is defined as an explanatory bias that tends "either to ignore organismic factors or to regard them as . . . subsidiary to the primary impact of the external stimulus" (Harré and Secord, 1972, p. 27).

Closely paralleling the charge of "situationism" is the humanistic protest against the behavioral (experimental?) approach in general. The essence of the humanistic protest is that behaviorally oriented psychologists (i.e., "situationists") treat and manipulate man as if he were externally controlled rather than a free, self-determining being responsible for his own actions and growth. Some of these criticisms and charges seem justified objections against a simplistic environmentalism (e.g., Skinner, 1974). The characteristics of the environment interact with the people in it, and it would be hazardous to ignore either side of this interaction.

But the extreme of the humanistic view on causality is as untenable as Skinner's. Alker, for example, unequivocally asserts (in this volume, page 210): "Man, rather than the manipulation of environmental change, is the locus of causation." Such grand declarations imply an unreal dichotomy between man and environment, ignore the fact that much of the human environment consists of people interacting with each other, and fails to realize that each man also "manipulates" and changes the environment (indeed, with every breath he draws and every act he performs).

It is essential to recognize the importance of environmental determinants, but unreasonably pre-emptive to make the environment *the* determinant; similarly, it is essential to recognize each individual as an active determinant of behavior, part of nature's endless causal chains, but unreasonably pre-emptive to make the individual *the* determinant. To look for *the* locus of control in either person *or* environment risks obscuring their continuous dynamic interaction. To pre-empt causal powers either for the person or for the environment exclusively also seems to guarantee incomplete explanations. Research cannot fully examine when and how and why individuals do what they do without linking human activities to the psychological conditions in which they occur. For me, the analysis of covariations between behavior and conditions remains an essential method if incomplete explanations are to be avoided. It can of course also be argued (quite rightly) that explanations based on "environmental contingencies" are equally incomplete unless they include the determinants of those environmental contingencies—which, in the case of human societies, often turn out to be human beings. Moreover, contingencies do not exert their effects independently of the interpretations and psychological transformations imposed by the individuals who perceive them.

The fact that both the environment and the individual are basic for human behavior seems to be increasingly accepted by personality psychologists. But a psychological approach requires that we move from descriptions of the environment—of the climate, buildings, social settings, etc., in which we live—to the psychological mechanisms through which environmental conditions and people influence each other reciprocally. For this purpose, it is necessary to consider how the environment influences the individual whose behavior, in turn, shapes the environment in an endless interaction. To understand the interaction of person and environment we must consider person variables as well as environmental variables, and we must analyze the nature of person–situation interactions, as considered next.

PSYCHOLOGICAL ACTIVITIES
AND PERSON VARIABLES

A reluctance to create homunculi, and a full equating of self and person, does not relieve us of the need to examine the psychological activities of the individual and their products. These psychological activities subsume such cognitive work as information processing with all its many ramifications. They include selective attention and encoding, rehearsal and storage processes, cognitive transformations, and the active construction of cognitions and actions (Bandura, 1971a; Mischel, 1973a); Neisser, 1967).

Obviously, the individual's psychological activities, as well as his total genetic and environmental history, do not result in an empty brain; they generate a set of complex psychological products or "person variables" (Mischel, 1973b). Such person variables may be notoriously difficult to infer in useful ways, but their role in human functioning requires recognition by any comprehensive psychological theory.

I have elsewhere proposed a synthesis of seemingly promising constructs about persons developed in the areas of cognition and social learning (Mischel, 1973a). Such person variables may be notoriously difficult to infer variables." The selections were intended as suggestive and constantly open to progressive revision. These variables were not expected to provide ways to predict accurately broad cross-situational behavioral differences between persons. In my view, the discriminativeness of behavior and its unique organization within each person are facts of nature, not limitations specific to particular theories. But these variables should suggest useful ways of conceptualizing and studying specifically how the qualities of the person influence the impact of stimuli ("environments," "situations," "treatments") and how each person generates distinctive complex behavior patterns in interaction with the conditions of his or her life.

SUMMARY OF PERSON. VARIABLES

To summarize very briefly, individual differences in behavior may be due to differences in each of the person variables summarized in Table 1 and in their interactions. First, individuals differ in their cognitive and behavioral *construction competencies*, i.e., in their competence or ability to generate desired

TABLE 1. SUMMARY OF COGNITIVE SOCIAL LEARNING PERSON VARIABLES (Mischel, 1973a)

---

1. Construction competencies: ability to construct (generate) particular cognitions and behaviors. Related to measures of IQ, social, and cognitive (mental) maturity and competence, ego development, social-intellectual achievements, and skills. Refers to what S knows and *can* do.
2. Encoding strategies and personal constructs: units for categorizing events and for self-descriptions.
3. Behavior-outcome and stimulus-outcome expectancies in particular situations.
4. Subjective stimulus values: motivating and arousing stimuli, incentives and aversions.
5. Self-regulatory systems and plans: rules and self-reactions for performance and for the organization of complex behavior sequences.

---

cognitions and response patterns. For example, because of differences in skill and earlier learning, individual differences may arise in cognitive–intellective achievements. Differences in behavior also may reflect differences in how individuals *categorize* a particular situation. That is, people differ in how they encode, group, and label events and in how they construe themselves and others. Performance differences in any situation depend on differences in *expectancies* and specifically on differences in the expected outcomes associated with particular response patterns and stimulus configurations. Differences in performance also may be due to differences in the subjective *values* of the expected outcomes in the situation.

Finally, individual differences may reflect differences in the *self-regulatory systems and plans* that each individual brings to the situation. These latter person variables require amplification here because they are central to the issues under discussion in the present volume.

While behavior depends to a considerable extent on externally administered consequences for actions, everyone regulates his own behavior by self-imposed goals (standards) and self-produced consequences (Mischel, 1974). Even in the absence of external constraints and social monitors, we set performance goals for ourselves and react with self-criticism or self-satisfaction to our behavior depending on how well it matches our expectations and standards. The sprinter who falls below his past record may condemn himself bitterly, while the same performance by a less-experienced runner who has lower standards may produce self-congratulation and joy.

Another feature of self-regulatory systems is the person's adoption of *contingency rules* and *plans* that guide his behavior in the absence of, and sometimes in spite of, immediate external situational pressures. Such rules specify the kinds of behavior appropriate (expected) under particular conditions, the performance levels (standards, goals) which the behavior must achieve and the consequences (positive and negative) of attaining or failing to reach those standards (Bandura, 1971a). Plans also specify the sequence and organization of behavior patterns (e.g., Miller *et al.*, 1960). Individuals differ with respect to each of the components of self-regulation, depending on their unique earlier histories or on more recent situational information.

Self-regulation provides a route through which we can influence our environment substantially, overcoming "stimulus control" (the power of the situation). We can actively *select* (choose) the situations to which we expose ourselves, in a sense creating our own environment, entering some settings but not others, making decisions about what to do and what not to do. Such active choice, rather than automatic responding, may be facilitated by thinking and planning and by rearranging the environment itself to make it more favorable for one's objectives (e.g., Thoresen and Mahoney, 1974). Even when the environment cannot be changed physically (by rearranging it or by leaving it altogether and entering another setting), it may be possible to *transform* it psychologically by self-instructions and ideation (Mischel, 1974).

While the proposed person variables obviously overlap and interact, each may provide distinctive information about the individual and each may be measured objectively and studied systematically. But it would be both easy and inappropriate to transform these person variables into generalized trait-like dispositions by endowing them with broad cross-situational consistency or removing them from the context of the specific conditions on which they depend. Consider, for example, the variable of "generalized expectancies" (Rotter, 1954). In fact, "generalized expectancies" tend to be generalized only within relatively narrow, restricted limits (e.g., Mischel and Staub, 1965; Mischel *et al.,* 1973). The generality of "locus of control," for instance, is limited, with distinct, unrelated expectancies found for different kinds of outcomes (Mischel *et al.,* 1974). If the above person variables are converted into global trait-like dispositions and removed from their close interaction with situational conditions they are likely to have limited usefulness.

The purpose of relisting these variables here is merely to record once more the fact that my theoretical position does not omit the person, nor does it relegate him or her to a passive, reactive role; the persistence of such a stereotype puzzles me greatly.

CONCEPTUALIZING INTERACTION

The conditions or "situational variables" of the psychological environment may be conceptualized as providing the individual with information; this information influences person variables, thereby affecting how the individual thinks and acts under those conditions. "Situations" (environments) thus influence our behavior by affecting such person variables as how we encode the situation, the outcomes we expect, their subjective value for us, and our ability to generate response patterns.

Recognizing that the question "Are persons or situations more important?" is misleading and unanswerable, one can now turn to the more interesting issue: When are situations most likely to exert powerful effects and, conversely, when are person variables likely to be most influential?

Psychological "situations" ("stimuli," "treatments") are powerful to the degree that they lead everyone to construe the particular events the same way, induce *uniform* expectancies regarding the most appropriate response pattern, provide adequate incentives for the performance of that response pattern, and require skills that everyone has to the same extent. A good example of a powerful stimulus is a red traffic light; it exerts powerful effects on the behavior of most motorists because they all know what it means, are motivated to obey it, and are capable of stopping when they see it. Therefore it would be easier to predict drivers' behavior at stop lights from knowing the color of the light than from making inferences about the "conformity," "cautiousness," or other traits of the drivers.

Conversely, situations are weak to the degree that they are not uniformly encoded, do not generate uniform expectancies concerning the desired behavior, do not offer sufficient incentives for its performance, or fail to provide the learning conditions required for successful genesis of the behavior. An example of such a weak stimulus is the blank card on the TAT projective test with the instructions to create a story about what might be happening; clearly the answers will depend more on the storytellers than on the card.

In sum, individual differences can determine behavior in a given situation most strongly when the situation is ambiguously structured (as in projective testing) so that each person is uncertain about how to categorize it, has to structure it in his own terms, and has no clear expectations about the behaviors most likely to be appropriate (normative, reinforced) in that situation. To the degree that the situation is " unstructured " and the person expects that virtually *any* response from him is equally likely to be equally appropriate (i.e., will lead to similar consequences), the significance of individual differences will be greatest. Conversely, when everyone expects that only *one* response will be appropriate (e.g., only one " right " answer on an achievement test, only one correct response for the driver when the traffic light turns red) and that no other responses are equally good, and all people are motivated and capable of making the appropriate response, then individual differences become minimal and situational effects prepotent. To the degree that people are exposed to powerful treatments, the role of the individual differences among them will be minimized. Conversely, when treatments are weak, ambiguous, or trivial, individual differences in person variables should have the most significant effects.

So far we have considered "treatments" like those in laboratory studies or therapy programs. But the complex social settings of everyday life also vary in the degree to which they prescribe and limit the range of expected and acceptable behavior for persons in particular roles and settings and hence permit the expression of individual differences (e.g., Barker, 1968; Price, 1974). In some settings the rules and prescriptions for enacting specific role behaviors greatly limit the range of possible behaviors (e.g., in church, at school, in a theater, at a conference), while in others the range of possible behaviors is broad and often the individual can select, structure, and reorganize situations with few external constraints (e.g., Ricks, 1972). Because in particular settings certain response patterns are rewarded while others are not, different settings become the occasion for particular behaviors in different degrees (e.g., Raush *et al.*, 1974; Price and Bouffard, 1974).

SPECIFIC INTERACTIONS BETWEEN BEHAVIOR AND CONDITIONS: ACTIVE ORGANISMS IN ACTIVE ENVIRONMENTS

Traditionally, trait-oriented personality research has studied individual differences in response to the "same" situation. But some of the most striking differences between persons may be found not by studying their responses to the same situation but by analyzing their *selection* and construction of stimulus conditions. In the conditions of life outside the laboratory the psychological "stimuli" that people encounter are neither questionnaire items, nor experimental instructions, nor inanimate events, but involve people and reciprocal relationships (e.g., with spouse, with boss, with children). We continuously influence the "situations" of our lives as well as being affected by them in a mutual, organic interaction (e.g., Raush *et al.*, 1974). Such interactions reflect not only our reactions to conditions but also our active selection and modification of conditions through our own choices, cognitions, and actions (Wachtel, 1973). Different people select different settings for themselves; conversely, the settings that people select to be in may provide clues about their personal qualities (Eddy and Sinnett, 1973).

The mutual interaction between person and conditions cannot be ignored when behavior is studied in the interpersonal contexts in which it is evoked, maintained, and modified. The study of social interactions vividly reveals how each person continuously selects, changes, and generates conditions just as much as he is affected by them. If you change your behavior toward another person he or she generally shows reciprocal changes in behavior toward you (Raush *et al.*, 1959a,b). In Raush's (1965, p. 492) studies of naturalistic interactions, for example, "the major determinant of an act was the immediately preceding act. Thus if you want to know what child B will do, the best single predictor is what child A did to B the moment before." Construed from the viewpoint of child A, this means that A's own behavior determines B's reactions to him; if A provokes B, B will reciprocate aggressively. In that sense, the person is generating his own conditions. The other side of the interaction is the fact that B's behavior is always constrained by what A did the moment before, as illustrated by studies of the interactions between husbands and wives (Raush *et al.*, 1974).

TOWARD A RESEARCH-BASED IMAGE OF MAN?

Traditionally most theorists of personality have invoked a few concepts and stretched them to encompass all the phenomena of human individuality, including thought, feeling, and behavior. As a result, we have theories of personality built on a few body types, or on a handful of factors, or on simple conditioning and environmental contingencies, or on the vicissitudes of one or more favorite motives—sex, aggression, competence, achievement, dissonance, self-realization, or on a humanism that correctly emphasizes man's humanity but too easily loses sight of (or perhaps interest in?) its antecedents—the list is long but the strategy is the same; take a few concepts and stretch them as far as possible. This may be a valuable exercise for the theorist interested in defending his favorite concepts. For the teacher it may provide a handy set of controversies in which any one set of obviously incomplete, fragmentary ideas may be sharply contrasted against any other, with each sure to be found sorely lacking in at least some crucial ways. But for the psychologist who seeks a cumulative science of psychology based on the incremental empirical discoveries of the field, rather than on the biases of theoreticians committed to defending their viewpoints, it leaves dreadful voids.

To help overcome these voids will require a conception of personality that, at the least, is nourished broadly by the research of the field. The massiveness of available data, and their frequent flaws, of course make it possible to read them in many different ways. In my reading, however, a distinctive image of man does begin to emerge from empirical work on cognition and social behavior.

One strand of this research suggests that the individual generally is capable of being his own best assessor; that the person's own self-statements and self-predictions tend to be at least as good as the more indirect and costly appraisals of sophisticated tests and clinicians (e.g., reviewed in Mischel, 1968, 1972). A related theme is that the individual's awareness of the contingencies in the situation—his (or her) understanding (not the experimenter's) of what behavior leads to what outcome—is a crucial determinant of the resulting actions and choices, including behavior in the classical and instrumental conditioning paradigms (as discussed in Mischel, 1973a). In the same vein, any given objective stimulus condition may have a variety of effects, depending on how the individual construes and transforms it (e.g., Mischel, 1974).

While these research themes focus on the centrality of each individual's interpretations, there is also much evidence for the potency and regularity of the effects that may be achieved when the rules of behavior are applied—with the individual's full cooperation and by the individual—to achieve desired outcomes (e.g., Bandura, 1969). There is also considerable support, in my view, that while consistencies surely exist within each person, they tend to be idiosyncratically organized (e.g., Bem and Allen, 1974), making nomothetic comparisons on common traits difficult and highlighting the uniqueness which Gordon Allport has so long emphasized.

Taken collectively, these and related research themes suggest an emerging image of man that seems to reflect a growing synthesis of several theoretical influences in current personality psychology. It is an image that seems compatible with many qualities of both the behavioral and the cognitive phenomenological approaches to personality and yet one that departs from each in some respects.

This image is one of the human being as an active, aware problem-solver, capable of profiting from an enormous range of experiences and cognitive capacities, possessed of great potential for good or ill, actively constructing his or her psychological world, influencing the environment but also being influenced by it in lawful ways—even if the laws are difficult to discover and hard to generalize. It views the person as so complex and multifaceted as to defy easy classifications and comparisons on any single or simple common dimensions, as multiply influenced by a host of determinants, as uniquely organized on the basis of prior experiences and future expectations, and yet as open to study by the methods of science, and continuously responsive to stimulus conditions in meaningful ways. It is an image that has moved a long way from the instinctual drive-reduction models, the static global traits, and the automatic stimulus–response bonds of traditional personality theories. It is an image that highlights the shortcomings of all simplistic theories that view behavior as the exclusive result of any narrow set of determinants, whether these are habits, traits, drives, constructs, instincts, genes, and whether these are exclusively inside or outside the person. It will be exciting to watch this image change as new research alters our understanding of what it is to be a human being—and how our humanness changes or maintains itself in relation to the psychological conditions of our lives.

Comments on "The Self as the Person"

JOSEPH F. RYCHLAK

Department of Psychological Sciences, Purdue University,
West Lafayette, Indiana 47907

After having completed my reading of Professor Mischel's paper for the first time, I had the following reaction: The reader must surely wonder what we two have to be arguing about! We *both* seem to be saying that some kind of identity across situational events takes place, whether we call this a "person variable(s)" (Mischel) or the "weight of logical telosponsiveness" (Rychlak). Is this debate just a terminological quibble?

No, I cannot accept this characterization. I not only know and respect Professor Mischel as a personal friend, but was a classmate of his at Ohio State University back in the 1950s. The intellectual climate in the clinical program at Ohio State at that time was a test-tube example of the Lockean–Kantian confrontation. Both Mischel and I took degrees under Julian B. Rotter, a neo-Hullian and therefore basically Lockean thinker. But we also attended classes with George A. Kelly, who was a foremost Kantian theorist. It is clear that since our graduate days I have moved more toward Kelly and Mischel has retained his identity with Social Learning Theory—to which he now appends the term "cognitive." So, though the reader may be wondering what Rychlak and Mischel *really* can be disagreeing about, the differences are not difficult to find if we keep the theory–construction issues discussed in my paper before us. Our differences are *not* based on anything personal, but simply reflect the divergences in how a theorist can think about his data which already had separated our professors and, indeed, all those individuals in the history of psychology who have purported to capture the human condition.

I would like to document this by reviewing with the reader Professor Mischel's statement on the self, pointing out what I take to be clear examples of the theorizing which my paper (written before Mischel's) claimed was typical of mechanistic accounts. It seems clear that Mischel is sensitive to being called a 100% mechanist, or a "non-self" theorist. He feels it is a misperception to claim that his theoretical position does not admit the person to the succession of lived events we call human behavior, and it puzzles him why people go on believing this "stereotype" even though he constantly says things to the contrary. I hope to show why this "misunderstanding" may arise, and to suggest that it is not so stereotypically incorrect after all.

To begin with, I think it is important to return to that word "cognitive" which Mischel attaches to his social learning theory. This is quite a popular term today, and so I have tried to track down its origin in the history of thought. The modern usage seems to date from William of Ockham (*c.* 1280–1350), who distinguished in his theory (theology) between the "intuitive cognition" and the "abstractive cognition." To cognize is to know, to deal in notions or conceptions, to have an understanding of, etc., and the distinction drawn here is an effort to say where the *source* of such knowledge is. Ockham was reacting to the Scholastic theologians like St. Thomas Aquinas (*c.* 1225–1274), who tried to prove the existence of God based upon supposedly self-evident, "intellectual" (Mischel would say "mentalistic") proofs. Ockham held that all such arguments were essentially hogwash, since knowledge is always dependent upon sensory input (intuitive cognition) and hence to play with thoughts (abstractive cognition) is to *add nothing* to what we now know, or ever can know. Knowledge is an input affair, dependent upon the senses alone, so the only acceptable proof of God's existence is some act of revelation (miracles) which He makes known to man's intuitive cognition.

This empirical attitude was then brought into the philosophy of British empiricism (see my paper), out of which evolved what we have called the Lockean model. When Mischel uses the term "cognitive," he means intuitive cognition since he basically holds that knowledge originates in the *situation* and not in the mentalistic realm of some kind of abstractive cognition. Mind is not really conceptual, but abstractive. The direction of knowledge in coming to know is from "outside to inside." This is quite at variance with the continental tradition in philosophy, which has the mind acting in a *pro forma* sense, to lend structural order to the "sensory noise" (noumenal reality) of intuitive cognition. This is how Kant viewed his categories of the understanding, and his general style of explanation now provides the theoretical rationale for modern phenomenological views (neo-gestalt, existential, etc.). My conception of affective assessment as something which the human intellect assigns to—rather than receives from—incoming sensory experience is decidedly in this continental line of thought. The meaning of "cognitive" here is quite different, and though Mischel may proclaim that his is an "active" view of mind, one can never quite capture the activity of a *pro forma* mind in a *tabula rasa* conception. Here is a basic difference between Mischel and myself, from which flow of necessity many differences in the theoretical styles we employ. Let us now turn to his paper.

Over the first few pages, Mischel is reviving the old bug-a-boo in psychology of the person *qua* substantial (and observable) being versus the self *qua* chimerical fancy, mentalism, or homunculus. When he says in the second paragraph that he does not wish to "create a self as an extra causal agent that resides in the person" he is telling us in a nontechnical sense that he does not want to introduce final-cause meanings into his theory. He wants to retain the time-honored descriptive style of Newtonian science. In taking this position, Mischel effectively drops the introspective perspective from his account since it is literally impossible to express "that for the sake of which" in extraspective terms. For example, to say that a pencil "has a purpose, for the sake of which it is used," is to comment on the intentions of the user and *not* on those of the pencil. The user's intentions here are being framed introspectively, even as the pencil remains a completely third-person "descriptive object." When Mischel now goes on to contrast Rogers (introspective) with Allport (extraspective) he confuses us on this question of self theory because he makes it appear these two theorists were expressing things from the same slant. We therefore begin on a note of confusion.

His section on the "Locus of Causation" draws out the confounded theoretical usage, because the effort here is to say "If I can (extraspectively) show that events in the situation (environment) are relevant to how the person behaves in the situation, then there is no necessity for me to postulate (introspectively) a 'self' as a little homunculus, running the person from within. In fact, the person is a *function* of the intuitive-cognition inputs afforded by the environment (outside to inside)." As Mischel points out, many (I think most) modern psychologists find this argument plausible and Skinner takes it to the extreme. This is psychology written from the convenience of a third-person observer, who, as spokesman for what an experimental finding is supposed to mean, has the option open to him to say "what is going on, over there—in the data."

But what if the person being observed over there "comes at" life with a (*pro-forma*) capacity to align premises just as the experimenter does, in his use of experimental design, assumptions made in statistics, and judgments made on the evidence which must be ordered in the creation of knowledge? And what if this premising capacity is *not* learned, even though it must take as contentual "givens" the demands of life as they appear environmentally in what Mischel calls "a situation(s)?" There is nothing in our observation of the facts which can determine which of these positions we take when we come to explain the facts. As theorists, this explanatory style is up to us. But it will lead to a totally different approach if we pitch our accounts from one perspective or the other, even as we deal with the *same* facts.

For example, consider the prisoner or the mental patient in one of the Skinnerian operant-conditioning environments now being put into practice. The person learns through living in this environment something like the following: "If you want to get a pass to the movie tonight you darn well better make up your bed." These are the contingencies of the situation. But does this in any way *prove* that the person is not reasoning "for the sake of" some such premising insight, or, recognition of the game plan being put into operation by the prison or hospital authorities? As Mischel himself tells us in his concluding observations, the evidence is preponderantly on the side of our now believing that only when the individual (self?) perceives the *pattern* (not "the stimulus," as so many express it today) of the response–reinforcement contingent relationship does "behavioral manipulation" of this sort take place. It has always seemed to me that such evidence supports a Kantian (introspective) account of things more than it supports a Lockean (extraspective) account. There seems to be a theoretical necessity here for acknowledging a logical reasoner, who sees the pattern, and makes the inference of "If I do that [behave for the sake of that], then such and thus will follow." But Mischel accepts the homunculus polemic at this point, feeling we would be in violation of parsimony to suggest that the organism under observation really does behave telosponsively in addition to simply responsively.

The reader may be thinking at this point: "But Mischel specifically says that there are *both* person variables (self-like, maybe?) *and* situation variables in any course of behavior to be observed in 'nature's endless causal chains.'" It behooves us therefore to look closely at what Mischel means by a "person variable." However, before we do this I would like to point to another one of those questionable practices which psychologists have fallen into in their thinking about the study of behavior. Mischel has raised this practice to a total outlook. I refer here to the universal tendency of psychologists to confound what is their *theory* with what is their *method* (of proving theoretical statements). A theory is the stipulated (suggested, analogized, "hunched," etc.) tie of two or more constructs into some kind of meaningful whole. A method, on the other hand, refers to the means or manner of proving a theoretical proposition. If we fall back on a coherence theory of truth, employing ultimately "common sense" (i.e., what seems to hang together and make sense), we rely on *procedural* evidence. On the other hand, if we design an experiment which "controls and predicts" circumstances in order to match observed outcomes, falling back on a correspondence theory of truth (i.e., hypotheses corresponding to observed facts), we rely on *validating* evidence (see Rychlak, 1968, for a more thorough treatment of these methods).

Now, to my way of thinking the term "variable" is best reserved for use as a *methodological* construct. It makes no sense to me to say that we search for variables in psychology. The reader can gaze about the room and fix his eye on literally *anything* he sees and take it as "given" beforehand that this—whatever it is—can be treated as a variable. We can play around with its color, possibly alter its shape, change the substance of which it is made, or, vary the values of its brightness or loudness, and so forth, *ad infinitum*. But why have we settled on "this" particular variable to play around with? Well, it could be a mere accident, convenience, or, a host of other factors which relate to our interests that accounted for the selection actually made. But note: these are *not* methodological factors but have to do rather with questions of theoretical predilections. Even the belief in "accident" can be challenged as a theoretical bias—as Freud was to do, in psychoanalysis. But our point is, scientific disagreements never stem from a question such as Do you or do you not favor the use of variables in scientific study? *All* scientists employ variables in their validational efforts; i.e., in their research designs. But it is our *theories* which define which variables we will put into the experimental hopper to see if they can stand up to a rigorous test. Mischel's theory breaks things up into person and situation variables, but H. S. Sullivan would have taken issue with this dichotomy since he did not see how *any* situation could exist without a "self" putting meaning into the equation.

The great danger of confounding our theories with our methods is that this leads to a naive acceptance of "experimental evidence" as supporting only one kind of theory (an efficient-cause theory, at that!). In other contexts, I have called this the S–R bind or the efficient-cause bind (see Rychlak, 1968). I think this is one of the most serious theory-construction problems we face in psychology. It means that when I do a study in which I lay out my teleological (final-cause) construct as an "independent variable" and conduct my experiment according to the ground rules of science (control and prediction), the journal referee in a typical "toughminded" journal can "see" in my data quite another form of theoretical verification. The journal referee sees *only* an efficient-cause sequence taking place here, rejecting as nonparsimonious all talk of self-directed purpose in the course of events under observation.

He can do this because it is easy to pair the independent–dependent variable (IV–DV) tandem of "seeing" a cause–effect over time with the stimulus–response (S–R) tandem of seeing cause–effects over time. The former, the IV–DV tandem, is a *methodological* succession of events and the latter, the S–R tandem, is a *theoretical* formulation of this succession of events. But thanks to the confusion between method and theory which has been propounded in psychology, this journal referee can sincerely believe that he "finds" or "sees" before his very eyes the Lockean paradigm of efficient causes all lawfully tying, one into another as "variables" (antecedents, consequents, etc.). I think Mischel has accepted this world view as a precedent assumption to his career work. Once he "sees" (i.e., defines ground rules for identifying) his two kinds of variables, the next step is to "see" which antecedents are the efficient-cause determinants of which consequents.

I think it is right here that we find Mischel's reputation as a mechanist or a situational determinist taking seed. His readers can put two and two together, and conclude as I have that Mischel's theory of variables is predicated on an exclusively efficient-cause account in which one variable efficiently causes a second to happen. This permits no teleology in his theory, even though it does allow Mischel to speak on the side of *method*, again and again. Toughminded theorists are wont to take a "let scientific observations in nature rather than theoretical speculations decide the issue" as they put forward—really arbitrary!—theories of nature. Mischel does this when he states: "In my view, the discriminativeness of behavior and its unique organization within each person are facts of nature, not limitations unique to particular theories." Though he speaks for "the facts" here, what this comes down to is a theory about people, as being constituted of variables ordered *in nature*, and subject to delineation by a sagacious observer. The upshot of this conviction about a natural order is that Mischel has turned his method (variables, ordered into "people" and "situations") into a metaphysics! This kind of faith in nature has provided behaviorists since Watson with an evangelical conviction that is at once admirable and frightening to behold. Humanists have been made to look the fool when they have, from time to time, questioned what was being seen "in the facts." Their theoretical points of order have been distorted into supposed attacks on scientific method itself.

Yet, the question of "variables" and the "functions of variables" stretching across time in nature's immutable course (to paraphrase Mischel's allusion) is not one that relates only or even primarily to efficient causality. The terms independent and dependent variable(s) were coined by Leibniz (1646–1716) and subsequently refined by Dirichlet (1805–1859) as entirely *formal-cause* designations. That is, these were held to be values stated in ratio form, so that in *arbitrarily* fixing one value (independent variable) the mathematician would have determined the other value (dependent variable) *by definition.* The latter was therefore said to be "a function" of the former. Now, the strategy of Gilbert's (1540–1603) scientific method was to observe what were presumed to be efficient-cause effects on some event that had been preceded by some other event. This empirical test of cause–effect became the foundation stone of Newtonian natural scientific method. Then gradually, as experimental conditions were put to test through statistical probability theories, the practice was adopted of calling the manipulation of an antecedent event the independent variable, and the observed outcome measure a dependent variable.

In the Newtonian world view the course of efficient causality was believed to obey a Godlike, mathematical precision (indeed, Newton believed that natural laws literally functioned "within God."). Hence, it was made easy to take the observed regularities of the experimental variables as efficient causes, subsuming and essentially eclipsing the meaning of a formal-cause patterning on which these terms actually are based. The resultant impact here is to remove the experimenter as arbitrary designator of variables from the scene and to give the *fallacious* impression that everything seen to bear a functional relationship with everything else is tied together by efficient causation! There was no harm done so long as the sciences remained exclusively extraspective, but now with the rise of an introspective science in psychology we humanists must call a halt to this confounding of theory and method. We do so because it is our wish to name independent and dependent variables in our experiments which will bear a functional relationship that we specifically deny is one of efficient cause–effect.

Mischel's definition of a "person variable" seems to be contained in the following: ". . . the individual's psychological activities, as well as his total genetic and environmental history, do not result in an empty brain; they generate a set of complex psychological products or 'person variables.'" The person has "variables" generated into his brain by the environment. In deciding how to think of Mischel—as a self theorist or a situational theorist, or both—we are as conscientious readers called on to get clear in our minds what he can mean by "psychological activities" in this definition. This is so vague as to mean almost anything, but the succeeding statements help to clarify things. We are told that "people differ in how they encode, group, and label events and in how they construe themselves and others." People also differ in their valuations of situations, and in their "*self-regulatory systems and plans.*" It is this "sound" of self-directedness in his theory that beguiles the uncritical listener into thinking that there is a teleological account under description (or, one that can suffice for a teleological account). But when we press down more firmly on the ideas being advanced, we find squeezing out at critical rupture points a very common sort of mediation model. We have to press down and infer because, in truth, Mischel has a way of seeming to say certain things by *not* saying them.

For example, Mischel can speak of people creating their own environments as follows: "Individuals differ with respect to each of the components of self-regulation, depending on their unique earlier histories or more recent situational information (p. 151)." Stated "as is," both a dialectical teleologist and a cybernetic or operant determinist could agree with this statement. But what does a "unique earlier history" mean? Does this mean a kind of cybernetic input memory bank of efficiently caused "events," summating today as output-behavior on the basis of some frequency or contiguity principle? Or, does this refer to a continuing framing of Kantian premises, uniquely arrived at thanks to the functioning of a dialectical intelligence which permitted the individual to reason to the opposite of his intuitive cognition and frame alternatives from "inside to out" rather than the reverse?

As we focus more closely on the usual emphasis given by Mischel, I think it is fair to say that he invariably places this on the side of the situation, as the ultimate determiner of intuitive cognition. A good example is this quote: "'Situations' (environments) thus influence our behavior by affecting such person variables as how we encode the situation, the outcomes we expect, their subjective value for us, and our ability to generate response patterns." Can we really be faulted if we think we see in such statements a theorist who must ultimately be relying upon situational determinism *exclusively*? What is an "encoding?" Is this a formal-cause construct, a stylized or structured frame "for the sake of which" behavior is carried out or, is this some kind of efficiently caused cue or "chit" which functions between the input and output to direct behavioral movements much as an IBM card moves along the mechanical processes of a computer? Do we evaluate situations independently of their unidirectional influence on us, or are our current values "a function of" input variables from out of our past? Can we in "generating a response pattern" think to the opposite of an input from intuitive cognition, and, at the level of abstractive cognition, reason to the opposite of an opposite, etc., until we "generate" a creative alternative not now "in" the memory bank of variables input from yesterday?

Though I may be in error on his position here, I do not think so and feel that if Mischel were to answer such questions as we have been raising in detail the mediational-model thinking at the base of his outlook would be made plain. The example he cites of a "strong" and a "weak" stimulus situation is a perfect case in point. To a Kantian, holding that red lights efficiently cause us (via mediating habits) to behave one way rather than another because of their propellant strength is simply off the mark entirely. There is no need to distinguish between the red-light and the blank-TAT-card situations in the first place, because it is not the "external stimulus" but the "introspectively held meaning" that each situation holds for the individual which is the behavioral determinant. It is only the unquestioned Lockean paradigm that guides Mischel's thinking here which permits him to see people as "responding to" rather than as "behaving for the sake of " red-light and blank-TAT-card stimuli in their environments.

Mischel speaks critically of those who invoke merely one or two constructs to explain all that there is in behavior, but we could easily fault him for erring in the other direction. As we noted above, since "anything" can be said to represent a variable, and since "people" can relate situationally to all of these potential variables, Mischel has effectively covered all possibilities imaginable in drawing out his case by way of the variable construct. His global usage is actually a kind of reaffirmation of the methodology of science. It says "Behavior is a function of everything!" And, as we have already documented, the resultant effort is actually a continuation of the mediation conceptions which presently are the most popular theories in psychology. Only the Skinnerians really vary from this general strategy of saying that yesterday's inputs, mediated by variables in the brain called "people" variables or whatever, efficiently cause the behaviors of people today. This is not the place to go into Skinnerian theory, but it is my thesis that Skinner is a true albeit hidden teleologist. I think of his operant response as *not* a response in the classical behavioristic sense, but actually as a telosponse, in my meaning of the term. In the Middle Ages, to speak of contingent causes was to speak of purpose and free will, and though Skinner thinks he has avoided this in his reformulations I do not.

But surely Mischel's theory is not a teleology, and this is why in a technical sense there is really no need for the concept of " self " in it at all. That is, there is no more need for the word " self " than there is for other words, such as " sun " or " food " or "sleep." We use words as mediators. Some words are about us "as people;" some words are about other things. To be a humanism we need much more concern here with options in life, with what a choice can mean, and so forth. In particular, we need some conception of arbitrariness to complement the determinism implied. Without some such notion the "person" can never cut himself free from what George Kelly used to call "the tail-end of his reinforcement history." This is why Kelly put his emphasis on man's (Kantian) capacity to construe events. Mischel uses the term "construing" in his paper, but can he mean what is meant in the Psychology of Personal Constructs? I think not. Kelly based his conception on a dialectical rationale, so that man's arbitrariness was made possible through reasoning to either side of a construct pole, or, reconstruing through opposition altogether (i.e., formulate a new construct). I have no doubt but that Mischel *wants* to think about human behavior teleologically, and he is working hard to bring this side of behavior into play even as he tries to stay within the strictures of a demonstrative, neo-Lockean image of behavior. But these latter, theory-construction issues *must* continue to trip him up. You cannot say one thing (efficient cause) and mean another (final cause)!

Furthermore, we are not going to find "selves" in empirical studies by beginning with an extraspective theoretical orientation. The "facts" as observed can never add up to selves unless we *begin* with a Kuhnian assumption that there is something like this taking place in the sequencing of events, "over there, in the apparatus." If we could only be more honest about *our* roles as scientists, then I think this kind of conception would have more ready acceptance among the rigorous thinkers in our specialty. We cannot in good conscience go on saying that we make assumptions (about statistics, about our paradigms, etc.), and then test them via judgmental acts which are open to alternative formulations (competing paradigms), without holding to the possibility that the subject under observation is *also* doing something of this sort. In addition, by discussing how we do our work as scientists we manifest the very characteristics which the humanist is trying to apply to the subjects under his study. What irony there is in the fact that we psychologists feel somehow a lesser scientist by the simple act of attributing these same behaviors to our subjects.

Descartes (1596–1650) was a mathematician as well as a philosopher, and, though he did appreciate that humans reasoned dialectically as well as demonstratively, he like most mathematicians of history was especially distrustful of this style of "sophistical" thought. It is therefore not surprising that when he finally found a basis for proving through self-evidence that he as a person (I, me, self, etc.) really existed, it was framed as a demonstrative proof. As the reader doubtless recalls, he said "I think, therefore I am" (*cogito ergo sum*). The reason I feel this is a demonstrative proof is because, although there is the suggestion of transcendence in the self-reflexivity of knowing that one thinks, the emphasis is still exclusively on the *act* of thinking rather than on the multiplicity of the things that might be thought about (i.e., meanings). Some have noted that all this statement can really prove is that thinking exists. Even as a mediating animal, man could be made aware of his thinking processes without having the ability to challenge the assumptions of what he is thinking about.

But, had he argued dialectically "I think, and realize that I could [arbitrarily] be *thinking otherwise*, therefore *I* exist," Descartes would have made a more convincing case for self-identity. For it is the logical weight of a self which chooses what it is that will be thought about in the face of other alternatives (this holds for unconscious identities as well). I hope that we all go on "thinking otherwise" in psychology. No one should be duped into believing that experimental variables provide us with "the" theory explaining "the" facts of nature. There is no better way of coming to know your "self," dear reader, than to focus on the "other" viewpoints open to you. When you find that you prefer one "style" (model, paradigm, school, etc.) of explaining things over an other(s), I think you can safely conclude that you have located your self!

Comments on "Is a Concept of 'Self' Necessary?"

WALTER MISCHEL

Department of Psychology, Stanford University,
Stanford, California 94305

Dr. Rychlak traps himself in a conceptual corner, pressing for his favorite dichotomies even when they do not fit. For Rychlak, psychology seems divided into humanism versus mechanism; its theorists are split into Kantians versus Lockeans; they argue such "either—or" questions as whether or not "the individual 'makes a difference' or contributes to the flow of events" (p. 128); whether or not "the organism *from birth*—or even possibly a bit before literal birth—(can) 'do anything' in a *pro forma* sense to the inputs of experience?" (p. 135, italics in original) and whether the direction of knowledge is from "inside to outside" or vice versa.

While such dichotomies may fit many bygone theories, they miss what I (not at all uniquely) see as perhaps the most fundamental conclusion emerging from our field now. Whether we focus on the study of complex human change and stability, or on interpersonal relationships, or on child development, or on cognition in information processing—regardless of content area—there appears to be a continuous mutual interaction between the individual and the conditions of his or her life (Mischel, 1973a). A comprehensive conceptualization of something even as relatively simple as how we identify a number or a face must have room both for the construer and for the construed. To make full sense of information processing, we must consider both the processor and the information. Knowledge, in my view, does not come from "outside to inside" any more than it does from "inside to outside"; it involves a reciprocal process, an accommodation as much as an adaptation. We inform and influence our world and are informed and influenced by it. You or I or our clients or students may focus on *any* aspect of that process at *any* point; hopefully we choose the focus that is most convenient for a particular purpose. But to cleave the process into stable halves, to

169

draw a line in the middle, and to align everyone either on one side or on the other—humanists versus mechanists, Kantians versus Lockeans—can produce an unfortunate hardening of the categories.

In sum, I believe that it is not fruitful to structure a "humanistic–mechanistic" debate in terms of a set of incompatible dichotomies in "either–or" form. It is unfruitful at a psychological level because it obscures the interacting nature of person–environment relations. It misleads us into thinking that we must take a committed stand on one side or the other of the hyphen in person–environment interaction. While Rychlak hails the virtues of George Kelly's contributions, his dichotomies miss Kelly's most important point: "constructive alternativism," the realization that any phenomena may be interpreted from many perspectives and in diverse ways. Depending on one's specific goal at the moment, it sometimes may be appropriate to focus more on the viewpoint of the construer (as in phenomenological analyses), sometimes more on the stimulus conditions (as when rearranging the environment therapeutically to make it more "convenient" or livable). The focus of convenience can and should shift freely back and forth. Finally, at a philosophical level, Rychlak's insistence on a fundamental incompatibility between teleological and mechanistic explanations of behavior—the essence of his dichotomies—ignores formal philosophical arguments that show these two types of explanations are *not* necessarily incompatible (N. J. Block, 1971).

I must reiterate that debates about the relative importance of person versus situation (or the innate versus the acquired) may distract attention from the specific mutual influence processes whose complexities wait to be studied in greater depth. I cannot prevent Rychlak from sticking my efforts into a slot called Lockean mechanist. But as I review my paper in this volume and its earlier version (Mischel, 1973a), I must underline (again) that my objective is a theoretical framework that recognizes the constructive (generative) nature of information processing, the active cognitive operations through which stimulus meanings may be transformed, the goal-directed, self-regulation and planning through which the individual may avoid "stimulus control," and the anticipatory quality of human expectations. Such a framework also holds that each person is potentially his or her own best assessor, engaged in the evaluation and interpretation of behavior as well as in its enactment. But it also insists on attention to the intimate links between the qualities of the person and the specific psychological conditions in which they develop, are maintained, and change. I cannot fit this framework into Rychlak's dichotomies. Rather than stretch to force a fit, might it be time to reconstrue—or even abandon—those dichotomies?

PART IV

Viability of the Two Approaches

INTRODUCTION

In debates between humanists and behaviorists the question of outcomes (Which therapy is more successful?) is often raised, as it was in the Jourard and Wolpe debate. Wolpe, in particular, emphasized that systematic research on the outcomes of therapy is crucial and should be the sole criterion for deciding which therapy to use for which type of problem. In their article, Lambert and Bergin deal with the question of which therapy is more successful as well as the more general question, What *are* the effects of psychotherapy?

Over the past two decades, many people have been involved in studying the effects of various types of psychotherapy. Eysenck (1952) fueled the controversy of whether therapy was helpful when he suggested that the same number of neurotics improved whether they were treated in therapy or not. Lambert and Bergin re-evaluate Eysenck's figures on spontaneous remission and summarize the present status of therapy evaluation.

In recent years, reports in the literature indicate impressive results using behavior therapy techniques. Lambert and Bergin raise the issue of whether the behavior therapies have been as successful as we've been led to believe. Similarly, are the psychoanalytic and humanistic therapies really so ineffective as Wolpe says they are?

What criteria are employed in determining the effectiveness of the therapies? In Part I it was emphasized that behaviorists tend to focus on external behavior problems and attempt to achieve behavior change, while humanists tend to focus on internal emotional problems and attempt to help the client achieve insight. Later in this book Alker emphasizes that humanists and behaviorists differ in terms of what is to be changed in therapy. Lambert and Bergin address this issue in their attempt to compare the effectiveness of the two types of therapy.

Lambert and Bergin go beyond the question of effectiveness to raise the issue of the process of change. Even when a particular therapeutic technique is generally effective in producing improvement, questions remain. Why was this intervention effective? Was it the technique? Or the person employing the technique? Or other incidental factors?

Lambert and Bergin are particularly helpful in the types of questions they ask of the therapies and for the suggestions they make to provide more effective interventions.

Psychotherapeutic Outcome and Issues Related to Behavioral and Humanistic Approaches

MICHAEL J. LAMBERT AND ALLEN E. BERGIN

Department of Psychology, Brigham Young University, Provo, Utah 84601

The application of the scientific method to questions of therapeutic change is indeed complex and most researchers are not yet convinced that our methods are equal to the task (Bergin and Strupp, 1972). Neither the description and measurement of therapeutic ingredients nor the estimation of outcomes can be achieved with anything like the precision we are accustomed to in other applied sciences. Consequently, the extremely optimistic conclusion adopted by the ardent enthusiasts for some therapeutic methods should be tempered by a realism that takes into account the complexity of the task and the primitiveness of the field. It is too easy to assume that we are going to obtain clear findings and solid implications for practice merely by applying "flashy" experimental and statistical methods. It is not even obvious any longer that our standard assumptions about science apply unaltered to human behavior (Coulson and Rogers, 1968).

It is not surprising that dialogue turns towards research and the cloak of scientific rigor when behavioral and humanistic approaches to psychotherapy are compared, and even less surprising that the first mention of research evidence is usually made by the behavioral therapist. So it is that Wolpe suggests behavioral therapies are more effective at alleviating human misery than other methods (including humanistic ones), and B. F. Skinner suggests in a dialogue with humanist spokesman Floyd W. Matson (1973) that ". . . behaviorism is humanism. It has the distinction of being effective humanism." In fact, it would seem that the behaviorist claim to being humanistic is based on its purported efficacy as demonstrated by empirical research.

Despite our intuitive feeling that new paradigms may be in the offing for this field, we will review and evaluate the traditional empirical evidence as it

173

relates to psychotherapeutic outcomes and issues related to the dialogue between behavioral and humanistic approaches. The general question, Is psychotherapy effective? will be dealt with and put into its historical perspective. In addition, the contributions of research to particular questions raised in the preceding discussion will be analyzed.

TRADITIONAL PSYCHOTHERAPY
(A BRIEF APPRAISAL)

Historically, Eysenck's (1952) review has been quoted frequently and is viewed by some as the catalyst for empirical research in the area of outcome. Certainly it has been in the center of controversy over the effectiveness of the therapeutic encounter. His literature review and the following polarization of workers in the area of psychotherapy is well known.

Briefly summarizing, its content is as follows: after reviewing 24 outcome studies, he suggested that within two years, two-thirds of the neurotics who enter psychotherapy improve substantially and that an equal number of neurotics who never enter therapy improve within a similar time period. Eysenck (1966) again reviewed this material along with six other outcome studies (involving adult neurotics) and again was very pessimistic about the effects of traditional psychotherapy. These results were given in the context of reports which were favorable to behavior therapy.

Truax and Carkhuff (1967) and Truax and Mitchell (1971) have also reviewed the research literature on psychotherapy outcome, concluding that on the average psychotherapy is ineffective, a conclusion in agreement with Eysenck except to clarify that this is an average change and not uniformly true.

Other reviewers have not been so pessimistic. Kellner (1965, 1967) found that results seemed more positive as more homogeneous samples and methods were used; but concluded that, because of heterogeneity, most studies yielded ambiguous findings. Cross (1964) and Dittman (1966) reviewed a limited number of studies suggesting basically positive results. Meltzoff and Kornriech (1970) are also more optimistic and suggest in their recent book that psychotherapy research has indicated a significant positive relationship between therapy and outcome.

Bergin (1971) has evaluated the outcome research and previous reviews, including those by Eysenck, and has tried to put the issue of efficacy to rest by demonstrating that the ambiguity of the original data makes divergencies of opinion inevitable and that, therefore, the issue cannot be fully resolved without new data. His own conclusions, based on a reanalysis of those studies reviewed by Eysenck, several additional studies reported during that period, and 52 investigations published between 1952 and 1969, can be presented quite briefly. He states: "While the methodological sophistication and precision of studies have improved markedly, the evidence continues to yield the general conclusion that psychotherapy, on the average, has modestly positive effects" (p. 229). He further attempted to reduce the ambiguity in the traditional data and demonstrate high efficacy of some percentage of psychotherapy by showing that (a) average therapy outcomes were depressed by the harmful effects of some therapists, and (b) spontaneous change rates for untreated cases are lower than assumed.

Deterioration Effect

One of the most powerful consequences of studying psychotherapy has been the growing awareness that it is not just ineffective or beneficial but that it has had, on occasion, harmful effects on patients. Both Wolpe and Jourard explicitly acknowledge this in their comments. The so-called deterioration effect has been documented elsewhere (Bergin, 1963, 1966, 1967a,b, 1971; Truax, 1963; Eysenck, 1967; Frank, 1967; Truax and Carkhuff, 1967; Truax and Mitchell, 1971). This finding is exciting for a number of reasons. It has made clinicians more cautious and determined to make certain therapy is not harmful. It has stimulated discussion and research in this regard. Secondly, it suggests the presence of something potent in therapy and leads to the conclusion that at least some therapy is quite effective, and that when these good effects are merged with the bad in outcome studies, the average effects seem limited compared to no treatment. A unique "improvement effect" may thus be considered as a corollary of deterioration effects. It has also helped researchers to discover possible behaviors and attitudes which may lead to deterioration, and has thereby lead research away from the general question of "the effects of psychotherapy" into the direction of greater specificity. Although some have questioned the evidence for the presence of a deterioration effect (Frank, 1967), Bergin (1971) has recently listed 30 studies which he feels substantiate the assertion that deterioration exists among patient populations. Bergin concludes: "In only four of the studies where I found it possible to assess the presence or absence of deterioration, was there little or no evidence of the phenomenon" (p. 248). It also appears that deterioration is more frequent among therapy than control samples, although it does occur among untreated cases as well.

There is a growing body of correlational data which associates deterioration with low therapist interpersonal skills (facilitative conditions). For example, in the Wisconsin project dealing with hospitalized patients (Rogers *et al.*, 1967) treated with client-centered therapy, therapists were divided into those providing high conditions and those who provided low conditions to their patients. There was a significant difference in the linear trend of getting out of the hospital across time between patients exposed to control conditions versus those exposed to high therapeutic conditions. Low conditions subjects tended not to get out of the hospital, or to come back to the hospital sooner (Truax and Mitchell, 1971).

This line of inquiry parallels the growing interest in specifying those therapist relationship skills and other personal attributes that induce strong improvement effects. Since Rogers (1957) suggested the necessary and sufficient conditions for personality change, there have been numerous attempts to support the importance of these conditions through research and empirical analysis. The subsequently measured therapist qualities of empathy, nonpossessive warmth, and genuineness are gaining in their demonstrated importance. Much of the work in this area has been summarized by Truax and Carkhuff (1967) and Truax and Mitchell (1971). Although there is still room for skepticism (Meltzoff and Kornreich, 1970), this research would seem to have considerable promise and has to date demonstrated that counselors who vary on these dimensions have differential success. Carkhuff (1969) writes:

"Thus there is substantive support for a solid core of the helping process, a body of primary facilitative interpersonal dimensions that account for much of the variability in a variety of the outcome criteria which we may employ to assess our helping. While, for example, the weight of these dimensions may vary with therapist, client and contextual variables, preliminary evidence suggests that in the general case we may be able to account for between one-third and one-half of the variability in our change indices at this point in time" [p. 80].

There are some equivocal results, however, which temper the enthusiasm of these conclusions. Garfield and Bergin (1969), for example, studied the relationship of therapeutic conditions and outcome. Using multiple criteria, they observed changes in outpatients treated by a sample of predominantly non client-centered therapists. Outcome criterion change scores were not correlated with the three therapeutic conditions. The authors raise questions about the applicability of the measuring scales for non client-centered therapists and question the generalizability of previous findings.

Despite such difficulties, it is our view that therapeutic encounters which are highly loaded with these positive relationship factors produce much higher outcome rates than are normally found in studies that lump together therapists of high and low ability to form such contacts. This implies that good relationship therapy has uniquely positive effects with respect to relevant criteria and patient population that are probably comparable to the effects of behavioral methods on specific target symptoms.

A related point is that when these so-called nonspecific relationship factors are specified, measured, and highlighted in a therapeutic method, they become technique-like in themselves and can produce large and predictable changes in clients. This, of course, does not answer the question of whether other technical skills can be added to them to further enhance outcome, but it does suggest that what Wolpe refers to as "common factors" in all therapies are not that common, but that when they are present in high degree the results are, in fact, uncommon!

Spontaneous Remission Effect

Another significant contribution of outcome research has been the elucidation, clarification, and substantiation of the phenomenon of spontaneous remission. The data when pieced together have some rather dramatic implications. The commonly observed tendency for no therapy control subjects to change positively as a group over time has been labeled spontaneous remission. Frequently quoted rates in adult neurotics have been around 70%, (Landis, 1937; Denker, 1946; Eysenck, 1952). It has been argued by Eysenck and others that the rates of improvement in psychotherapy should exceed this base rate in order to demonstrate their efficacy. Thus, spontaneous remission has been an important topic in the center of the controversy over the effects of therapy.

At present three conclusions seem reasonable based on the available evidence: (1) The suggested spontaneous remission rate of 70% is spuriously high and not justified. In this regard Bergin (1971) refers to 14 separate studies that have a median spontaneous remission rate of approximately 30%! (2) Spontaneous remission is not uniform and varies with the type of disorder being evaluated. (3) In the absence of formal therapy, control clients seek and obtain help from informal sources such as clergy, teachers, peers, parents, etc., or even from other professional sources (Frank, 1961; Bergin, 1971).

Aside from the obvious relationship this has to forming a real no-treatment control group, Bergin (1971) summarizes its other possible implications:

> "Thus, we have found that not only is the spontaneous remission rate lower than expected, but also that it is probably caused to a considerable degree by actual therapy or therapy like procedures. This certainly casts psychotherapy into a more promising position than has heretofore been considered, even though formal therapy still should do better than informal therapy, which it does. It still does not mean that the general cross-section of professional therapy is uniformly dramatic in its effects, but it does suggest once again that there are some important variables at work somewhere in the process" [p. 246].

The spontaneous remission phenomenon has also demonstrated to us that psychotherapy is just a special case of more general therapeutic conditions which occur naturally in society. It remains for future research to identify these variables more precisely and attempt to direct them more efficiently to relieve human misery.

With respect to the debate at issue in this symposium, the spontaneous remission data, like the deterioration–improvement effect data, underscore the existence of stronger therapeutic effects among the evocative therapies (e.g., humanistic therapy) than had previously been possible to deduce from empirical findings. This suggests that the comparative position of such approaches is not as weak as some behavior therapists imply.

BEHAVIORAL THERAPY (A BRIEF APPRAISAL)

Bandura (1969) and Franks (1969) have published the most comprehensive reviews of behavior therapy research. More recently, Eysenck and Beech (1971b) have reviewed the literature on desensitization and aversive methods, Krasner (1971) has reviewed operant approaches, and Bandura (1971d) has summarized work in the area of modeling principles. Less recent but more comprehensive and specific reviews of systematic desensitization have been published by Paul (1966, 1969a,b).

It is Paul who was responsible for one of the few methodologically sound comparative studies. This study, briefly alluded to by Wolpe in his presentation, is probably the most frequently referred to (by behavioral therapists) because it seems to demonstrate so effectively that systematic desensitization is superior to insight therapy. In addition to this already quoted study, Paul (1969a) reviewed all available uncontrolled reports of the individual application of systematic desensitization. Of the 55 studies reviewed, he suggests all but nine gave positive correlational results with only three reports in the negative direction.

He also reviewed ten additional reports (Paul, 1969b) which were methodologically sound enough to allow for cause–effect conclusions with the exception that systematic desensitization was confounded with other variables. Of these, all ten found treatments including systematic desensitization to be more effective. Finally, of an additional ten reports which could establish cause–effect relationships, two had methodological problems and eight found, according to Paul, solid evidence for the specific effectiveness of systematic desensitization. Generally speaking, this would tend to support Wolpe's enthusiasm for systematic desensitization; however, there are some reservations which might be expressed. First, in Paul's (1966a) comparative study, it should be noted that his subjects (patients) may not be considered representative of a clinical population nor was the therapy (5 sessions) a fair test of insight therapy. While Paul does consider the subjects to be representative, Eysenck and Beech (1971) do not. This is a somewhat important distinction to make since, to date, (as Paul admits, 1969b) systematic desensitization is more effective when the treated person is less severely disturbed or when his disturbance is limited in scope. Indeed, a large number of the purportedly positive results are based on analog studies using normal college volunteers who feared snakes or spiders! Also, another reviewer (Luborsky, 1973) found that in 17 comparative studies, behavioral methods excelled in only five instances. In addition, systematic desensitization has not proven effective with free-floating anxiety, or with a large number of other patient symptoms. In general, Eysenck and Beech (1971) are not as positive in their evaluation of behavior therapies in general, and systematic desensitization in particular, as is Paul. For example, they respond to several criticisms regarding the evidence for the efficacy of behavior therapy in the following way: "But on the whole we would agree that behavior therapists have not done conspicuously better than psychotherapists and psychoanalysts in demonstrating the clinical effectiveness of their methods as compared to other methods, or even to spontaneous remission" (p. 600).

Another note of caution with respect to the early dramatic results is sounded by new evidence indicating that the behavioral avoidance tests used in the outcome studies were loaded with artifacts, such as subjects' tendency to voluntarily comply with what they perceived as social influence attempts rather than therapy *per se* (Bernstein, 1973).

A related point is that even where desensitization (or other methods) are effective, they are probably effective for reasons that have little or nothing to do with "behavior therapy" or "laboratory experimentation." Wolpe's assertion that: ". . . behavior therapy is . . . the application of experimentally established principles and paradigms of learning to the changing of unadaptive habits" is open to serious questions. Human beings apparently do not function in terms of the so-called "laws of learning" in any way approximating extant behavioral theory (Bandura, 1969; Murray and Jacobson, 1971; Wilkins, 1971); and the term "behavior therapy" is misleading (Bergin, 1970) in light of the influence of social, cognitive, and emotional factors in the treatment. This semantic issue cannot be resolved by Wolpe's *ad hoc* adoption of terms like "emotional behaviors" and "thinking behaviors" because it leaves too many unresolved theoretical problems that are implied by the semantics.

The research evidence as it relates to other behavioral approaches is to date less impressive than that achieved through the use of systematic desensitization although there are areas of promise.

Bandura (1971d), as a result of extensive experimental work, argues that modeling procedures provide powerful conditions for the acquisition of new responses and the modification of old ones. It has also, along with systematic desensitization, been useful in reducing "conditioned" emotionality. His work has not been related to adult psychotherapy to a great degree and depends primarily on laboratory studies. Rigorously controlled clinical studies are virtually nonexistent.

Aversive procedures have enjoyed some success. Rachman and Teasdale (1969) have summed up the findings in this area and they can be stated briefly. Although the evidence is scanty and rarely meets the standards applied to other therapeutic effects with most types of disorders, the success rate found is a great improvement over existing conditions despite tendencies to relapse.

Davison (1969) has appraised the reports of operant behavioral therapy with institutionalized adults. He is to be applauded for his critical review of both his own and others work in this area. Specifically he chastises his cohorts for being less than scientific in their claims of success. He writes: "Perhaps because of the effectiveness of various conditioning procedures in changing behaviors that had hitherto been recalcitrant to other therapeutic intervention, there are discernible in the behavior modification literature certain tendencies to go further than is warranted either by data or by logic" (p. 270).

It would appear that behavior therapy has now passed through the stage of "miracle cures" and is presently facing the realistic limitations of applied science. Certainly, the growing number of publications devoted to behavioral therapy (at least four new journals to date) and the increasing space allotted to behavior therapy in established journals is evidence that enthusiasm in this area is very high at present. Continued research, however, is leading toward two significant changes: (a) a steady reduction in the claims for the methods, and (b) increasing attempts to either merge these methods with traditional ones or to more consciously manipulate traditional variables (such as cognitive processes) within the behavioral context.

RELATED ISSUES

The Selection of Outcome Criteria in Research

Here, as with other topics, one finds controversies, the roots of which run through the general philosophical and theoretical differences between humanistic and behavioral approaches. The choice of outcome criteria is a reflection of the orientation, values, and focus of the therapeutic endeavor; and they also determine the kinds of results that are obtained.

The most obvious issue is whether to choose criteria that reflect changes in behavior or changes in internal states of experience. Very little has been gained through global ratings of improvement. Likewise, changes in "experiencing" have been hard to specify and measure with much accuracy. Our efforts here are certainly limited by scientific advances in other areas of psychology such as personality assessment. To date, overt behavioral criteria, which require a minimal amount of interpretation, have been most reliable and easiest to implement. Meltzoff and Kornreich (1970), for example, note that studies which were well controlled also more often used observed behavior for at least one criterion. Outcomes were more often significant when observable behavior was used as an outcome measure. On the other hand, Malan (1973) has shown that specific symptomatic criteria tend to inflate outcome rates when compared to psychodynamic criteria; therefore, Jourard's and related types of therapy are perhaps victimized by the status of the research enterprise in that the kinds of change they produce are far more difficult to measure.

It is becoming more and more apparent that change is multidimensional and that different measures give different kinds of evidence about changes that are taking place. To be adequate, future studies must employ a variety of outcome measures. Lang (1968) for example, suggests that multiple measures of fear with good face validity do not change uniformly (at the same time to the same degree). The intercorrelations among measures of fear are consistently low and often insignificant. Paul (1966a,b) also included multiple measures to assess change in the relatively uncomplicated area of "speech phobias." In this regard, Davison (1967) and Cooke (1966) indicate that overt approach behaviors changed while reported fear was not affected. It seems clear that multiple measures are necessary, not only when a number of complaints or a concept such as personality is being modified but also when a single set of behaviors is the focus of study.

The possibility of tailoring change criteria to each individual in keeping with the therapeutic goals is mentioned with increasing frequency. This would have at least two positive effects because it would get us away from global improvement indices and it would likely make research of more practical value to practitioners by providing a closer link between therapist behavior and change criterion. It is obvious that we favor the use of outcome measures which attempt to identify specific changes relevant to the kind of problem and the kind of therapy. It is interesting to note in this regard that there is a growing attempt to assess outcome from diverse vantage points (Garfield, *et al.*, 1971; Luborsky, 1973; etc.). The behavioral approach has been to date more successful in the specification of outcome measures. It has, however, failed to assess sufficiently the more internal kinds of changes and broad personality changes. While they argue that these are not significant, we favor the position that changes in internal states are meaningful and should not be ignored.

These points highlight the fact that Wolpe and Jourard (and persons of related persuasion) are operating from highly divergent cognitive sets and value commitments. To the extent that their values do not permit agreement on criteria, the effects of their methods simply cannot be compared to their respective satisfactions. The outside observer or the consumer can, however, note which kinds of change each promotes and can then elect which system he or she prefers. This makes it all the more imperative for therapists to openly disclose their goals and the nature of their methods for attaining them.

Manipulation Versus Self-actualization

The issue of manipulation versus self-actualization is apparent in the polarization or humanistic and behavioral approaches to change. This distinction is commonly made by humanistic approaches and in the present discussion it is the essence of much of what Jourard finds objectionable in the behavior therapies. His concluding paragraph states this objection succinctly: "... there is a sense in which I regard efforts to foster change in another by environmental control or by shaping techniques or by any means that are not part of an authentic dialogue as in some ways pernicious and mystifying and probably not good for the well-being and growth of the persons to whom these efforts are addressed; and probably not very ennobling for the people who practice them."

It was this same issue which brought Skinner and Rogers into dialogue many years ago (Rogers and Skinner, 1956). It appears to be a philosophical (or moral) one and does not lend itself well to study. Bergin and Strupp (1972) have suggested, however, that the evidence favors the view proposed by the behavior therapists. They state in this regard, "Our reading of the accumulating evidence strongly suggests that all forms of psychotherapy exert planful psychological influence and are therefore manipulative in the sense of utilizing principles of social control."

Since Jourard (1971b) has committed considerable energy to the experimental study of self-disclosure and its effects on people in a variety of contexts it is surprising that he does not see it as a "controlling" behavior. Of course it is easy to agree with both the behavioral and humanistic positions to the effect that whatever control is initially instituted is in the service of the ultimate self-control and independence of the client. It remains to be demonstrated whether either or both are correct in this assumption.

Specific and Nonspecific Effects

In the present discussion it is Wolpe who mentions the specific and nonspecific effects of treatment by suggesting that all therapies have nonspecific ingredients which prove beneficial for patients, but that systematic desensitization produces effects that are superior to those produced by nonspecific processes. Wolpe does not mention what he means by nonspecific (except that Jourard has something which produces a lot of it) but evidently attributes changes that *other* therapies get to nonspecific interpersonal factors. Nonspecific effects may include such things as the effects of being treated, faith and hope of patient and therapist, interest and enthusiasm, etc.

Wolpe may not be on solid ground when he attributes the changes he gets by and large to his technique. In regard to placebo effects it has been historically true that they are attributed more commonly and in greater quantity to colleagues' treatments rather than one's own techniques. Shapiro (1971) has treated the topic of placebo effects extensively and concluded that the practitioner's attitudes toward the treatment (like faith, conviction, positive, and negative expectations, etc.) are a nonspecific factor in most therapies. The evidence here is broad and comprehensive including many varied treatment modalities and patient disorders and expands even into the laboratory with subhuman subjects (Rosenthal, 1966). Wolpe, it is obvious, has a strong belief in the utility of his methods. Such a belief is probably a powerful influence even though he would prefer to attribute change solely to his therapeutic methods. A comment by Strupp (Bergin and Strupp, 1972) is interesting in this regard: "It is my personal observation that all great therapists I have known have a profound faith in the utility of their therapeutic operations, to the point of fanaticism" (p. 414). Listening to both Jourard and Wolpe, it is easy to imagine that so-called nonspecific effects are not only in operation but of primary importance.

This statement bears a striking resemblance to Jourard's hypothesis that it is the triumph of the therapist in using his technique to overcome his own problems which make the therapist effective. Certainly, this would be a difficult hypothesis to test and it still assumes change is a function of technique although it seems to add the dimension of the therapist's personal experience to the technique. The therapist's belief in methods (for whatever reason) may be an easier hypothesis to test and, to date, it has more empirical evidence to support it. It certainly is going to be a difficult chore to separate the effects of specific from nonspecific variables. It would seem fruitful to question the assumption that specific effects are more powerful (because they are assumed to be scientific), and focus greater attention on all factors influencing therapeutic outcome.

Technique versus Personality

Closely related to the issue of specific and nonspecific effects is the issue of the relative importance of techniques to the personality of the therapist or the so-called therapeutic relationship.

On the one hand, behavioral therapists seem to be quite proud of producing results which have little dependence on the person of the therapist. In systematic desensitization, for example, there is great enthusiasm for advances which might be technical enough to automate the entire procedure. Lang (1968) discussed the development of DAD (Device for Automated Desensitization) which stores hierarchies and relaxation instructions on magnetic tape. Lang suggests that it is about as effective as a live therapist for reducing fear. At the very least, there is a strong tendency to deny or devalue the importance of the therapist and the therapeutic relationship. Eysenck and Beech (1971) even suggest that we may now exclude the hypothesis that the patient–therapist relationship is the vital point and they argue that when client–therapist contact is controlled and experimentally varied, no difference in effectiveness is evident.

Paul (1969b) suggests a similar finding although he has found that less experienced therapists are likely to have more negative results. He takes a more moderate position by stating that no evidence, either way, exists in the literature concerning the interaction of therapist characteristics (such as sex, age, prestige, expectation) with outcome in systematic desensitization. It would be interesting to apply content analysis methods in an examination of therapist personality in behavior therapy studies as has already been done with other methods.

On the other side of the issue are those theorists and practitioners who emphasize the potency of the relationship as the key to positive client outcome. Client-centered research strongly suggests the importance of a healthy personality in addition to attitudes of warmth, empathy and respect. Influence here is seen as being personal and much more than the simple application of techniques by an expert. Truax and Mitchell (1971) write: " We do, however, want to change the priorities. We want to emphasize the therapist-as-person before therapist-as-expert or therapist-as-technician. We want to emphasize the therapist as a viable human being engaged in a terribly human endeavor " (p. 341).

Resolution of this issue may not be as far off as would first appear. At present, research results suggest that it is necessary for the therapist to establish a relationship or create conditions that make the patient amenable to influence at the same time he gives technical procedures which influence the patient (systematic desensitization, self-disclosure, etc.). In many behavioral therapies, and specifically with systematic desensitization, it would seem fair to say that the technique is a dominant source of change but that its effects (contrary to Lang) are mediated via the therapeutic relationship and that therapist characteristics may add or detract from these effects. In therapeutic endeavors which rely mainly upon the interpersonal influence process, the personality of the therapist accounts for much more of the variance in outcome. It therefore makes less and less sense to attribute all changes produced by different approaches to the same mechanisms. The personality of the therapist is always a factor, but is more important in situations where the relationship is a prime mediator of therapeutic influence.

Research and Clinical Practice

One very important issue which must be dealt with in an analysis of empirical findings is the impact such findings have on the practices of behavioral and humanistic therapists. It is undeniable that to date the practice of behavior therapy is influenced far more by research evidence. This may not be due only to reluctance on the part of humanistic therapists but also to the type of research that has been done on their therapeutic modes. Research, it seems, has too often tested the effects of general (unspecified) procedures yielding results that are "significant" at the 0.05 level. Too often experimenters have failed to provide useful information—information about the specific procedures that work best with a particular type of problem under a particular set of circumstances.

Besides the lack of impact resulting from the inadequacies of research, there are several other probable reasons. Certainly beliefs and attitudes about the desirability of doing research (i.e., it is perceived as menacing and of little value) have played a part. It is, of course, an area of enormous complexity and results are sometimes difficult to generalize from well-designed but narrow or limited findings. There seems to be a parallel between the evaluation of psychotherapy and the evaluation of psychological assessment methods as they affect the users of such methods. To end this section, a quote from Paul Meehl (1960) seems appropriate: "Personally, I find the cultural lag between what the published research shows and what clinicians persist in claiming to do with their favorite devices even more disheartening than the adverse evidence itself." Certainly, we feel research does have something to offer even to the most confirmed antiscience practitioner. This position, of course, would be stated more strongly by Wolpe. It is fair to say that he believes all practice should be derived from empirical evidence or be continually tested in rigorous manner and that this is the only responsible position for the practitioner. Humanistic therapists might well take heed, particularly those contemporaries who are presenting dramatic (and sometimes bizarre) new methods without validation and for which high fees are charged.

SUMMARY

Our past attempts to evaluate the outcome of therapeutic processes have not been equal to the task. The traditional question "Is psychotherapy effective"? is no longer meaningful or appropriate. In this regard, researchers would do well to ask a different question: What specific therapeutic interventions produce change, in which particular clients, under what specific conditions?

Recognition needs to be given to the fact that therapists are not interchangeable units nor do clients react uniformly to therapists or therapeutic influence. Technique variables must take the first two classes of variables into consideration.

Progress will occur more rapidly, we believe, if the discovery of truth takes precedence over theoretical disagreements and the split between the clinician and the researcher. We believe strongly in the value of a nonschool approach and believe the trend to be in that direction. The collection of knowledge will proceed at a faster rate when more complex and theoretically diversified studies employ a more representative sample of criterion measures which cut across theoretical predispositions. This would mean that we would try more to let the facts speak for themselves and spend less time probing the efficacy of a broad theoretical system. Goldstein (1971) has tried to set forth rational reasons for greater cooperation between researchers and practitioners although he doubts the issues are just factual. We, too, feel that greater cooperation and communication is important at this time, that it is reasonable to call for the breakdown of barriers between ideologies, and that the adoption of a multidimensional approach will prove increasingly fruitful.

Outcome research has, we feel, provided a renewed awareness of empirical data. It is obvious that we are committed to a systematic and empirical analysis of psychotherapy and its results. This is related to the view that gains in this area will be continually limited without such a systematic approach. This means objectivity which in turn requires responsibility for stating findings in context with proper limitations and in meaningful terms. It means also being realistically tentative and remaining open to experience (the data). Our frame of reference might be called "accumulative fragmentism," which holds that truth is collected piece by piece. We must live with the anxiety that what Kelly (1970) has called constructive alternativism, i.e., the assumption that all facts are wholly subject to alternative constructions, is true. Of this point of view, Kelly has remarked: "Indeed it leads one to regard a large accumulation of facts as an open invitation to some far-reaching reconstruction which will reduce them to a mass of trivialities" (p. 27).

PART V

Questions of Compatibility and Synthesis of the Two Approaches

INTRODUCTION

In the previous section, Lambert and Bergin concluded that we need new approaches to psychotherapy if therapy is to progress and become more fruitful. They call for greater cooperation and communication, breaking barriers between ideologies, and the adoption of a multidimensional approach to promote more effective interventions. All of these require consideration of compatibility between the humanistic and behavioristic approaches.

The papers in this Part—by John Harding and by Henry Alker—directly address the issue of the present and eventual compatibility of the humanistic and behavioristic approaches. This of course is a recurring theme of this book, but Alker and Harding each approach the issue in a unique way.

Harding first examines some of the possible meanings of compatibility of humanism and behaviorism. An important issue is how humanism and behaviorism are to be defined. Harding chooses the behavior of the therapist in the therapy situation as the focal point rather than the theory of ideology to which the therapist subscribes. Thus, the question becomes, how do humanists and how do behaviorists conduct themselves in therapy sessions, and on this level is there a compatibility? (The reader may want to re-read therapy transcripts of Sidney Jourard and Joseph Wolpe on pages 83–114 after he has read Harding.)

Harding then traces historically some of the developments in the humanistic and behavioristic camps. He attempts to identify what these fields have encompassed and what is distinctive about them. The major thrust of the behaviorists—identifying a patient's problem in terms of the occurrence or lack of occurrence of some undesired or desired behavior—Harding finds easy to define. The humanists pose a harder problem in this classification. Harding suggests that a focus on subjective experience of the client and the attempt to develop " human " relationships with the client are the distinctive features. Harding then raises the issue of whether psychoanalysis is humanistic, since it appears to meet the aforementioned criteria.

Notice how Harding structures the issue of compatibility. By focusing on the therapist's behavior in the therapy session Harding describes several variants and degrees of compatibility. He then produces several examples to show that in fact these types of compatibility do exist.

Harding's discussion can extend the discussion of compatibility raised in the introductory chapter. Harding's mild form of compatibility—either the same therapist using behaviorist techniques at one time and humanist techniques at another time on different patients *or* therapists using both techniques on the same patient at different but relatively circumscribed time periods appears to fit into position two: Complementarity. Approach " one " may work best with "problem *x* ".

Harding's strong form of compatibility—the simultaneous use by a single therapist of humanist and behaviorist techniques on the same client—is difficult to classify in the earlier schema. This strong form of compatibility either belongs with position two (complementarity), position five (synthesis), or some position not previously described. This strong form of compatibility suggests that humanism and behaviorism could be jointly used, but it is not clear if this compatibility is a total synthesis of the two approaches (position five) or merely a joining of some portions of the two approaches (position two) or something different.

Alker takes a very different approach. His discussion suggests that humanism and behaviorism are two paradigms of personality theory and research, but the paradigms are largely arguing at cross-purposes and hence the discussions are irrelevant to the question of ultimate compatibility.

For instance, the paradigms differ in the stipulation of what is to be changed in therapy. Given this difference it becomes difficult (or impossible) to argue for the greater effectiveness of one therapy or the other since they are not really attempting to produce the same changes. On the basis of this analysis, Alker argues that crucial experiments wherein the approaches are pitted against each other are not really possible. Rather, the ultimate utility of either approach will depend on other factors.

When paradigms clash as humanism and behaviorism appear to be doing, it is possible that nonscientific criteria will determine which will be accepted by the scientific community. Alker hopes that some scientific criteria will enter into this decision, however, and suggests that the fruitfulness of either paradigm depends on the new discoveries it generates.

The behaviorists appear to be furthering their approach by the systematic accumulation of new knowledge by programs of research. There do not appear to be as many systematic programs within the humanistic camp. Alker therefore describes audio-visual self-confrontation as a potential program of research relevant to the humanistic approach. He discusses a research project using audio-visual self-confrontation and suggests that additional research on this (and other) humanistic topics will determine how far the humanistic approach can go.

In short, rather than directly confronting each other, Alker suggests that each approach attempt to advance its own research paradigms, and perhaps develop new ones.

Thus, Alker does not take a direct stance on compatibility as related to our earlier discussion. In some ways, he is arguing for position one (irreconcilable differences) although he does not rule out other possibilities. He suggests, however, that attempts at synthesis and rapprochement may not give the respective paradigms adequate chance to develop and to illuminate basic issues of personality change.

Behavioristic and Humanistic Approaches: Compatible or Incompatible?

JOHN HARDING

Department of Human Development and Family Studies,
Cornell University, Ithaca, NY 14850

I

The majority of behaviorists and the majority of humanists have assumed that their approaches are incompatible. This was certainly true of Carl Rogers and B. F. Skinner in their symposium in *Science* (Rogers and Skinner, 1956). A typical stance for a behavior therapist has been to attack Freudian psychoanalysis as the major rival whose claims must be exposed and to ignore the claims of humanistic theorists (Wolpe, 1958). Humanistic writers have usually taken more explicit notice of their behavioristic rivals. A common position has been to describe the humanistic approach as a "third force" challenging both the behavioristic approach and the approach of classical psychoanalysis (Maslow, 1968). Other writers feel their approach has more in common with Freud than with Skinner; thus Arthur Burton begins a recent book with the statement: "Modern-day psychotherapies are becoming polarized along two broad axes: the behavioristic and the humanistic" (Burton, 1967, p. xi).

Is there a basic incompatibility between these two orientations? A great deal depends on the terms in which the approaches are defined. The most widely read writers have been strong adherents of particular personality theories (or theories of behavior). They have usually *defined* their preferred approach to therapy as being essentially the application to personality change (or behavior modification) of the theoretical principles of their particular type of psychology. Joseph Wolpe defines behavior therapy as "the application of experimentally established principles and paradigms of learning to the changing of unadaptive habits" (Wolpe, in this book). He is willing to include procedures based on Skinnerian as well as Pavlovian paradigms, but his definition rules out *a priori* the activities of the therapist who derives his rationale from some other psychological or philosophical source than the learning laboratory. On the other side of the fence Burton defines humanistic psychotherapy basically as an approach that gives explicit attention to the characteristic concerns of existentialist philosophy: "The history of the humanistic movement in psychotherapy shows a progression from Freud to Sullivan to Rogers to Binswanger.... *Modern Humanistic Psychotherapy* was in fact written to place the humanistic–existential conceptions of philosophy into a proper framework of psychotherapeutic science" (Burton, 1967, pp. xi-xiii).

Definitions of the kind quoted give the practitioner the impression that in adopting a particular therapeutic approach he is making a basic commitment to some specific scientific or philosophical world view. If this is the case, the two approaches are indeed incompatible. A behavior therapist could not decide with a particular patient to abandon his customary approach and proceed in terms of empathic understanding and existential encounter without betraying his basic commitment to use in his work only procedures based on the positive findings of behavioral science. And a humanistic therapist could not decide with a particular patient to use systematic desensitization procedures without betraying his basic commitment to treat each patient as a free and responsible individual with whom he must deal on an I–Thou basis.

The thesis of this paper is that the behavioristic and humanistic approaches are much more compatible than they are usually thought to be. In particular, I believe that a fully trained therapist in the 1970s should be able—on appropriate occasions—to use either approach, and that such switches can be made without violating either scientific principles or ethical values. This thesis implies that the two approaches (as well as other possible approaches) should be defined in terms of *how the therapist conducts himself* rather than in terms of what the therapist takes to be the rationale for his conduct. In the next section of the paper I shall discuss the most widely used procedures employed by behavior therapists and the circumstances under which they are used. In the following two sections I shall try to characterize the "therapeutic stance" of the humanistic psychotherapist and of Freudian psychoanalysis. Finally, I will deal directly with the question of compatibility of the behavioristic and humanistic approaches.

II

The most characteristic feature of the behavior therapies is the way in which the problem of the patient is defined. It is viewed as either: (a) the occurrence (or too frequent occurrence) of some kind of undesired behavior, or (b) the lack of occurrence (or too rare occurrence) of some kind of desired behavior. Affective problems are dealt with by the behavior therapist as involving either the occurrence or nonoccurrence of certain emotional responses; in other words, feelings and emotions are treated as internal behavior whose frequency of occurrence one wishes to increase or decrease.

Virtually all of the procedures used by behavior therapists can be grouped under four broad headings:

1. Positive reinforcement and shaping procedures.
2. Modeling.
3. Desensitization.
4. Aversive procedures.

The first two are aimed primarily at increasing the frequency of desired responses; the last two at reducing the frequency of undesired responses. (This classification has been adapted from a somewhat more elaborate one presented by W. Stewart Agras; cf. Agras, 1972) I do not want to give the impression that in actual practice the behavior therapist typically makes a choice of one or another of these procedural strategies and then proceeds to confine his therapeutic activity to this procedure. This often seems to happen, but it is quite possible for a behavior therapist to use several of these strategies with the same patient—especially if the patient has a number of different significant complaints. It is also possible to develop a "mixed strategy" including procedures of several different types, and I have the impression from Dr. Wolpe's paper that he would be ready to do exactly this if he felt that it would be a promising approach to the problems of a particular patient.

One interesting characteristic of these approaches is that (2) and (3) in general require the cooperation of the patient (or "client"), while (1) and (4) do not.

The most widely used approach in behavior therapy seems to be (1) positive reinforcement of desired behavior (or approximations thereto), with nonreinforcement of undesired behavior. This approach has had many striking successes with subjects (or clients) who were not in a position to give informed consent to any therapeutic effort, or even to understand it. It has been used by

Ayllon and his associates with a wide variety of psychotic patients in a mental hospital (Ayllon and Azrin, 1968) and by Thompson and his associates with a variety of mentally deficient patients in a similar institution (Thompson and Grabowski, 1972). In the last few years this approach has been applied in an increasingly wide variety of school settings (O'Leary and O'Leary, 1972).

The earliest behavior therapy approach to be systematically described was (3) in a textbook on medical psychology by the German psychiatrist Ernst Kretschmer (1922). The approach was later elaborated by Joseph Wolpe in his book *Psychotherapy by Reciprocal Inhibition* (Wolpe, 1958). Wolpe's method requires the complete cooperation of the patient or client. In its original form it involved three steps: (a) training in thorough muscular relaxation; (b) construction of a hierarchy of anxiety provoking situations; and (c) exposure to these situations one by one while in a relaxed state. Wolpe has successfully treated hundreds of phobic patients with this method, and the approach has also been applied with considerable success to the treatment of a wide variety of conditions in which anxiety seems to play a key role. Some examples are bronchial asthma, frigidity, impotence, obsessional thoughts, and stuttering (Wolpe, 1969; Agras, 1972).

A number of authors have reported successful use of the desensitization approach without any training in progressive relaxation. Some have used drugs to inhibit anxiety, especially Brevital (Brady, 1972). Others have per-suaded patients to confront a feared situation either in imagination or in real life; anxiety is aroused, but extinguishes quickly. All these desensitization procedures require a high degree of confidence by the patient in both the knowledge and good intentions of the therapist. They are not suitable for patients who are psychotic or mentally deficient.

The major ethical problems in behavior therapy occur with the use of aversive procedures. In the majority of cases discussed in the literature the subjects of these procedures have been voluntary patients who have given informed consent to the procedures employed. In another group of cases aversive procedures have been used to eliminate chronic self-destructive behavior in children or institutionalized adults, with the informed consent of the individuals legally responsible for the patients. In a third group of cases short periods of "time out" from positive reinforcement have been made contingent on the occurrence of undesired behavior, i.e., used as punishment. This approach is very commonly used by teachers, with or without the consent of parents. There are two reasons why it has not seemed objectionable from an ethical stand-point: (a) the aversiveness of the punishment seems mild in comparison with the administration of noxious physical stimuli such as emetic drugs or electric shock, and (b) the procedure has traditionally been used in classrooms (and homes) as a punishment for disruptive behavior.

This brief survey of the behavior therapies indicates both the range of procedures used and the range of problems for which they have been used. The first systematic applications were in medical settings, but in recent years this approach has become more widely used in psychological clinics and public school classrooms. It seems fairly clear that at least the majority of practitioners have been responsible people, deeply concerned with the welfare of their patients or clients.

III

There is no general agreement on just what is and is not a humanistic approach to personality change. It seems to me that the most satisfactory definition is one that calls an approach "humanistic" if it meets two criteria: (1) the therapeutic effort is directed extensively (though not necessarily exclusively) to the subjective experience of the patient or client, and (2) the therapist makes a major effort to establish a particular kind of human relationship with the client or patient through such procedures as expressions of sympathy, acceptance, or warmth and communications demonstrating that he understands the feelings and experiences of the patient. It is assumed that the patient is a *person*, i.e., that he has feelings and experiences, that he has an interest in communicating at least some of these experiences to another person (the therapist), and that it is possible for the therapist to understand the feelings and experiences of the patient with reasonable accuracy and communicate this understanding to the patient.

With this definition there are many psychotherapists and many "schools" of psychotherapy that are clearly humanistic. I think the most important step in the development of a "humanistic movement" in psychotherapy was taken with the publication by Carl Rogers of an extremely challenging paper with the title "The necessary and sufficient conditions of therapeutic personality change" (Rogers, 1957). The basic thesis of this paper is that what really makes the difference in psychotherapy is not what the therapist does or does not do—in the sense of asking questions, giving advice, reflecting feelings, or interpreting dreams—but instead what the therapist *experiences* and *communicates* to the client in the therapeutic relationship. In this paper—and in his subsequent writings—Rogers abandons his previous claims for the superiority of the method of client-centered counseling and focuses instead on the therapist–client relationship.

What are the essential characteristics of a beneficial therapist—client relationship? In his 1957 article Rogers listed six, of which three are characteristics of the experience or behavior of the therapist. These three characteristics were subsequently discussed, and to some extent reformulated, by Rogers and Truax (1967), Truax and Carkhuff (1967), and Truax and Mitchell (1971). I shall quote the Truax and Mitchell formulation, because it seems to me to have benefited from ten or twelve years' experience with efforts to get these three characteristics reliably rated by judges working from tape recordings of therapeutic interviews.

The decisive characteristics of the therapist are said to be *genuineness, nonpossessive warmth*, and *accurate empathy*. "What do we mean when we say that a person is acting himself, is integrated, authentic, nondefensive, or genuine? We mean that he is a real person in an encounter presenting himself without defensive phoniness, without hiding behind a professional facade or other role" (Truax and Mitchell, 1971, p. 315). Truax and Mitchell believe that the evidence on the relationship of genuineness to therapeutic outcome indicates that what is important is a basic honesty and sincerity on the part of the therapist, an absence of defensiveness and phoniness. Jourard, on the other hand, argues that it is important for the therapist to go beyond this level of "genuineness" to a level at which he is entirely "open" to the client—ready to disclose unreservedly his own feelings in the therapeutic relationship (Jourard, 1971a, pp. 133–174).

Truax and Mitchell include among the components of nonpossessive warmth the commitment of the therapist to the welfare of the client, his effort to understand, his spontaneity, and the intensity and intimacy with which he relates to the client. "This does not mean a namby-pamby or sentimental acceptance of undesirable behavior, since the other person himself does not value all of his actions. Thus, in working with college underachievers, a good counselor can communicate very high levels of warmth and at the same time be able to confront the underachiever with the fact of his own laziness—not as a socially desirable or socially undesirable trait, but simply as what is " (Truax and Mitchell, 1971, pp. 316–317).

Finally, accurate empathy involves " the ability to *perceive* and *communicate* accurately and with sensitivity both the feelings and experiences of another person and their meaning and significance" (Truax and Mitchell, 1971, p. 317). The authors go on to discuss approximately 18 different studies with a wide variety of therapists, clients, and treatment settings in which these three characteristics of the therapist were associated with various indices of favorable personality change. In all but one or two studies the overall findings were favorable to the hypothesis that this triad of characteristics was beneficial for the client. No one of the three characteristics seemed to be more important than the other two.

IV

One of the questions most vigorously discussed by humanistic psychotherapists is whether classical Freudian psychoanalysis is or is not a humanistic approach. In his 1956 lecture on the 100th anniversary of Freud's birth, Erik Erikson claimed that Freudian psychoanalysis was from the beginning an approach of the type we have called humanistic; he argues that the most important feature in Freud's progress from the cathartic and suggestive methods of psychoanalytic treatment was his development of the notion of the "therapeutic partnership":

"Perhaps, if he treated them [his patients] like whole people, they would learn to realize the wholeness which was theirs. He now offered them a conscious and direct partnership: he made the patient's healthy, if submerged, part his partner in understanding the unhealthy part. Thus was established one basic principle of psychoanalysis, namely, that one can study the human mind only by engaging the fully motivated partnership of the observed individual, and by entering into a sincere contract with him." [Erikson, 1964, pp. 28–29.]

Some writers feel that Erikson idealizes Freud's therapeutic approach and underrates Freud's dogmatism and impersonality in therapy. However, almost everyone would agree that Erikson's own approach is humanistic in terms of his relationship to his patients and his interest in their subjective experience. This is especially evident in the case study he presented at a symposium in which he was asked to respond to the question: How does a good clinician really work? (Erikson, 1964, pp. 49–80). Many other case reports from Freudian and neo-Freudian analysts illustrate a similar conception of the "therapeutic partnership"; an extremely detailed example has recently been published by Dewald (1972).

Probably the two most influential theorists in the humanistic camp have been Carl Rogers and Abraham Maslow. Rogers has always stood aloof from Freudian psychoanalysis; before 1957 he maintained that the procedures of psychoanalysis were detrimental to therapeutic progress, while since 1957 he has argued that these procedures (like other procedures) make little difference one way or the other. Maslow's theories, on the other hand, developed out of a psychoanalytic background; and he has always expressed a high opinion of the value of conventional psychoanalytic therapy.

Maslow's conception of psychotherapy is a conception of two rather different enterprises—a narrower and a broader one. The narrower enterprise is called "insight therapy" and is conducted according to traditional Freudian principles. This kind of psychotherapy is required to achieve any lasting results in individuals with chronic, stabilized neuroses. "It is at this point that professional (insight) therapy becomes not only necessary but irreplaceable. No other therapy will do, neither suggestion, nor catharsis, nor symptom cure, nor need-gratification" (Maslow, 1970, p. 259). In this therapy there is a personal, human relationship of psychotherapist to client—very much like the traditional doctor–patient relationship—but the most important requirements for success are the training, the techniques, and the intelligence of the therapist.

Maslow also uses the term psychotherapy in a much broader sense to refer to almost any kind of helping human relationship. "Any ultimate analysis of human, interpersonal relationships, e.g., friendship, marriage, etc., will show (1) that basic needs can be satisfied only interpersonally, and (2) that the satisfactions of these needs are precisely those we have already spoken of as the basic therapeutic medicines, namely, the giving of safety, love, belongingness, feeling of worth, and self-esteem" (Maslow, 1970, p. 248). The Rogerian psychotherapist is doing for his clients exactly the same sort of thing that good ministers, teachers, friends, and helpful relatives have done since time immemorial. For everyone except the psychotic and the person with a chronic, stabilized neurosis this kind of psychotherapy is both necessary and sufficient. "A wholly proper part of the study of psychotherapy is examination of the everyday miracles produced by good marriages, good friendships, good parents, good jobs, good teachers, etc." (Maslow, 1970, p. 254).

Maslow's emphasis on psychotherapy as a good human relationship does not mean that he accepts Rogers' contention that the effective therapist must treat his client with unconditional positive regard. Maslow feels that a significant proportion of clients will be most benefited by a therapeutic relationship *different* from the one recommended by Rogers and Truax:

"While it follows from what has been presented above that the average patient would thrive best in a warm, friendly, democratic partnership relation, there are too many for whom it will *not* be the best atmosphere to allow us to make it into a rule. This is particularly true for more serious cases of chronic stabilized neurosis....

"Others, who have learned to regard affection as a snare and a trap, will recoil with anxiety to anything but aloofness. The deeply guilty may *demand* punishment. The rash and the self-destructive may need positive orders to keep them from harming themselves irreparably." [Maslow, 1970, p. 251.]

I hope that this exposition has been sufficient to indicate what is meant by a humanistic approach to personality change, and to establish the fact that there are a variety of humanistic approaches, just as there are a variety of behavioristic approaches. Every humanistic approach centers on the personal relationship between client and therapist, and every approach tries to supply through this relationship something important that the client did not find in previous personal relationships. But humanistic therapists with a psycho-analytic orientation, such as Erikson and Maslow, recognize that there is no simple formula of the kind Rogers and Truax tried to develop that will be ideally suited to the situation of every client. These writers emphasize *diagnosis* and *interpretation* as very important parts of the therapeutic enterprise even though they are carried out mainly in an ongoing dialogue with the client. They would agree emphatically with Bruno Bettelheim that "Love is not enough."

V

Let us now return to the central question of this paper: To what extent are behavioristic and humanistic approaches compatible with one another? I believe that we must distinguish two mild forms and one strong form of compatibility. The first mild form of the compatibility thesis asserts that the *same therapist* could appropriately use each approach, but on different occasions and with different clients or patients. The basic foundation for this thesis is the recognition that there is only a modest degree of overlap between the goals of the behavioristic and humanistic approaches. For the behavior therapist the goal of treatment is always a measurable increase or decrease in some type of behavior. For some humanistic therapists, such as Rogers, the fundamental goal of treatment is a change in the client's self-awareness— more specifically, an increased degree of self-understanding, a greater feeling of self-confidence and self-worth, and a greater willingness to accept responsibility for making decisions. These therapists assume that such changes in self-awareness will ordinarily lead directly to some changes in behavior, but these changes are byproducts of therapeutic success, not criteria against which therapeutic success should be evaluated. Other humanistic therapists, such as Erikson, accept cases in which the primary goal of treatment is some kind of behavioral change as well as cases in which the primary goal is a reduction of anxiety or some other form of subjective experience. (See especially the case reports in *Childhood and Society*, Erikson, 1963).

One extreme type of case is the severely mentally retarded patient for whom any type of insight therapy is obviously impossible. I think it would be hard to find a humanistic therapist who would not endorse the kind of behavior modification procedures described by Thompson and Grabowski (1972) with such patients. At the opposite extreme is the kind of young, intelligent patient often described by Erikson who comes for help after a breakdown during a course of professional training (e.g., Erikson, 1964, pp. 49–80). Behavior therapists who maintain that concepts such as feelings, experiences, doubt, and trust cannot legitimately be used by scientific psychologists would of course reject as meaningless Erikson's characterization of such patients as suffering from an "identity crisis," and would also reject any therapeutic approach based on interpretation of feelings and experiences. But there are less dogmatic behavior therapists who might say that for *this* type of patient a humanistic approach is not only legitimate but perhaps the most appropriate therapeutic strategy.

The second mild form of the compatibility thesis asserts that the *same client or patient* can appropriately be treated during a given time period by behavior therapy for one set of symptoms and a humanistic approach for another problem or set of problems. This possibility is most easily realized if different therapists are assumed.

Such a combination of behavior modification and humanistic psychotherapy was actually developed by Charles Slack and his associates in the Harvard street-corner research (Schwitzgebel, 1964). Delinquent boys were offered jobs as research subjects and paid from one to two dollars an hour for talking about themselves into a tape recorder in a street-corner laboratory in Cambridge. Verbal persuasion was used initially to recruit subjects. When a boy came to the laboratory, his arrival was immediately rewarded with soft drinks, fruit, or sandwiches. At the end of an hour's recording he was paid in cash for his work. The initial requirement for reward was merely that the boy arrive at the laboratory at some time on the day set for his appointment. Later the schedule of reinforcements was modified so that the amount of time a boy was allowed to work (and consequently the amount of money he earned) depended on how closely his time of arrival corresponded to the time of his appointment: "Typically, the boy's initial attendance at the laboratory fluctuated widely—from several hours early to several hours late—and during the first few weeks he might completely miss three or four meetings. Then, attendance would gradually become more dependable until, at the end of thirteen to twenty meetings, the boy would arrive regularly and on time" (Schwitzgebel, 1964, pp. 20–21).

The tape-recorded comments for which the boys were paid were guided by an interviewer whose intentions were those of a humanistic psychotherapist. The different interviewer–therapists had different theoretical orientations, and there was some variation in the kinds of relationships they established with their clients; however, the style of Schwitzgebel's own interviews is very much like that of early Rogerian nondirective counseling. Somehow the cumulative emotional impact of these sessions on the boys was tremendous. Schwitzgebel describes his interviewing approach as "philosophical discussion" and reports that "subjects interviewed on the basis of this philosophical perspective typically moved through a sequence of clearly noticeable stages that may be characterized as apathy, anger, despair, insight, and philosophical transformation" (Schwitzgebel, 1964, p. 26).

The strong form of the compatibility thesis asserts that it is possible for a *single therapist* to be using simultaneously a behavioristic and humanistic approach with *the same client or patient*. I believe this thesis is correct, assuming that the behavioristic and humanistic approaches are defined in the manner suggested earlier in this article. If the thesis is correct, it is extremely important to investigate therapeutic encounters using the combined approach, because the objectives of the behavioristic and humanistic approaches are to a large extent complementary. It is possible that a program of behavior modification which is also a venture in humanistic psychotherapy might do "more" for the patient than a program which is not; it is also possible that a combined program might simply result in behavior changes that were more enduring than those resulting from a "nonhumanistic" program of behavior modification.

My plan in this final section is to present four examples of therapeutic undertakings which seem to me to be simultaneously behavioristic and humanistic. My purpose is not to hold these up as models of therapeutic effectiveness—they do seem to have been quite effective, but so also do most other forms of psychotherapy when described by the therapists conducting them. The basic importance of these examples is similar to the importance of teaching a chimpanzee to talk in the sign language used by a great many of the human deaf. The demonstration is important because it shows that two characteristics often thought to be incompatible can, in fact, coexist. The fact of coexistence on one or more occasions, and the investigation of the circumstances under which coexistence is possible, seem likely to throw a great deal of light on the basic nature of the coexisting characteristics.

The first two examples involve therapists whose basic orientation is humanistic. The prime mover of the Harvard Streetcorner Research Project was Charles W. Slack. Before the project was formally organized he treated a number of delinquent boys in his office and laboratory, using the combination of approaches previously described (Slack, 1960). For Slack at this time the major purpose of the reinforcement procedures was to develop in hostile and nonintrospective subjects the behavior of reporting regularly to talk about their dreams and fantasies. Only gradually did he come to recognize the therapeutic potential of the situation and direct his interviewing procedure toward the attainment by subjects of insight into their own motivation and that of other people. Slack reports that a regular feature of the situation was the development of an extremely strong attachment to the experimenter–therapist:

> "The subject discovers that, perhaps for the first time in his life, another individual has taken a sincere interest in him and proved it in concrete ways. Just the mere fact that the experimenter can be counted on to be on time and to devote time and money to the subject—to really deliver the promised goods—starts to work some change in the attitudes and behavior of the subject. He begins to skip hours less and less frequently and only with more reasonable excuses. The hour starts to become a very important part of the subject's day; he moves other events around in order to show up on time. Furthermore, the subject is very likely to start giving indications of the development of that phenomenon *which is perhaps the single most outstanding feature of E-S psychotherapy—an extremely powerful, almost overwhelming positive 'transference, or rapport with almost no negative manifestation.*" [Slack, 1960, p. 253.]

My second example of behavior modification used within the framework of humanistic psychotherapy comes from the work of Carl Rogers himself. Charles Truax (1966) published a detailed analysis of 40 representative excerpts from a series of interviews with a young man successfully treated by Rogers at the University of Chicago Counseling Center in 1955. The client's statements were rated by five experienced psychotherapists on nine different characteristics, and Rogers' comments were rated on three: empathic understanding, acceptance or unconditional positive regard (referred to as "non-possessive warmth" in Truax's later writings), and directiveness. The last characteristic was considered a negative reinforcer.

Truax showed that there was a consistent tendency for client statements high in insight, problem orientation, learning of discriminations, and similarity to the therapist's style of expression to be accompanied or followed by therapist statements rated high in empathy and acceptance and low in directiveness. The reverse was true for client statements high in ambiguity. Most of the correlations involving these variables were statistically reliable, and some were as high as 0.46 or 0.48. Associations were strongest with the degree of empathy expressed by the therapist. All four of the characteristics that received consistent positive reinforcement increased significantly over the course of the treatment. The only nonreinforced characteristic to show a similar change was catharsis. Although at the time of these interviews Rogers was opposed in principle to differential reinforcement as a technique in client-centered therapy, he seems in practice to have been using it, and using it quite effectively.

One of the most creative theorists and practitioners of behavior therapy is Arnold Lazarus. In his book *Behavior Therapy and Beyond* (1971) Lazarus argues that a well-trained therapist should be able to employ a great variety of techniques and procedures; should use in a given case only those procedures which are compatible with this particular client's personality and expectations; and should regard his relationship with the client as an integral part of the therapeutic situation. An example of this behavioristic–humanistic approach is the technique of "rehearsal desensitization" developed by Piaget and Lazarus (1969). This technique combines the procedures of desensitization and assertiveness training previously described by Wolpe (1958), and is suitable for clients who are both extremely timid and extremely submissive. An excerpt from a case history illustrates the crucial role played by the client's relationship with the therapist:

"When the therapist suggested assertive training as a possible starting point, Mrs. T. smiled sadly and said that such a method had been attempted by a previous behavior therapist. She explained that she was simply unable to carry out her previous therapist's instructions....

"The next four sessions were used to complete the behavior analysis and to build an appropriate hierarchy. During this time, the therapist was extremely supportive and gentle with Mrs. T. in order to gain her trust and confidence and to establish a relationship between them conducive to optimal rehearsal desensitization. A twenty-four item hierarchy was constructed along a continuum of progressively more assertive behavior in the presence of one other person....

"Mrs. T. had considerable difficulty with several of the items, but the hierarchy was completed to the mutual satisfaction of patient and therapist after fourteen sessions." [Lazarus, 1971, p. 129.]

A final example of behavioristic–humanistic psychotherapy can be found in the work of a contributor to this book, Gilda Gold. The setting is a class for emotionally disturbed children. The main goal of the program is to increase the children's capacity for self-control. The basic orientation is that of behavior modification, with heavy reliance on a token economy, time out procedures, shaping, fading, modeling, and role playing. But there is also a strong emphasis on the emotional relationship between child and teacher and the development, over time, of a "therapeutic partnership."

"Initially, the teacher maintains control over child behavior as the children do not have the control themselves. She also teaches the children to trust that she will be reasonable and always carry through on her promises. In this way relationship factors are an integral part of the program. When the children develop faith in the teacher and start to feel comfortable, i.e. when the teacher becomes a positive reinforcer, she then begins to label the impulses that accompany behavior. At the next stage she helps the children to label the impulses by themselves. Finally, she teaches the children how to take action to control the impulses that stir the maladaptive actions." [Gold, p. 260.]

These four examples seem to me sufficient to demonstrate the compatibility of the behavioristic and humanistic approaches under even a strong interpretation of "compatibility." So far, so good. The demonstration has been made, and its theoretical significance is clear; nevertheless the practical significance of compatibility may be no greater than the practical significance of Washoe's linguistic accomplishments. I do not think that this is actually the case. There are many clients—perhaps a majority—whose problems are not tailor made for either the conventional humanistic or the conventional behavioristic psychotherapist. It seems to me highly probable that these clients would be best served by some variety of behavioristic–humanistic approach. At any rate, the promise of these combined approaches seems great enough to call for major attempts at evaluation during the next decade.

The Incommensurability of Humanistic and Behavioristic Approaches to Behavior Change: An Empirical Response

HENRY A. ALKER[1]

Cornell University

In an earlier paper (Alker, 1972) it was argued that behavioristic critiques of the personality theories of Erikson, Maslow, Murray, and even Freud were arguing at cross-purposes. Specifically, in the behavioristic critiques of personality research pressed by Mischel (1968), evidence that personality in situationally specific was regarded as incompatible with constructs in dynamic or humanistic personality theory. Those theories purportedly made an assumption about intrapsychic consistency of personality that was largely disproved by the evidence or situational specificity. This critique was rejected as an example of a pseudocontroversy. The logic of the argument, which compared the size of behavior change due to situation changes with the smaller amounts of behavioral differences due to difference between individuals, made no room for interactions between personality and situation. In other words what people do cannot be explained without considering the relation between what kind of individual and what kind of situation was at hand. Such interactions are logically fundamental for identifying purposively organized behavior across situations. An argument whose terms prevent the identification of purposeful interaction and consequently prevent also identification by contrast of purposively disorganized or irrational patterns, simply robs classical personality theories of a fair chance to win. It was argued, furthermore, that some individuals were more responsive than others to small changes in situational cues. These individuals could be considered to have somewhat greater adaptive capabilities in contrast to

[1] Appreciation must be expressed at this point for the assistance of Roger Tourangeau. Without his assistance in conducting this experiment, this report would not have been possible.

those who were simply oblivious and consequently unresponsive to such cues. Consequently, the behavioristic advocacy of situational specificity as a general proposition was less likely to be true for the kinds of individuals encountered in the clinical settings who have served to generate much of the classical dynamic and humanistic personality theories. This previous argument was largely formulated in terms of problems of prediction. The argument under consideration in this paper deals primarily with the manipulative control of personality change.

In the controversy between Wolpe and Jourard as well as in the larger controversy between humanistic and behavioristic approaches to personality change, the incommensurability of the relevant phenomena is apparent right at the start. The definition of what is to be changed differs from the different perspectives. Consequently a sustained empirical examination of the comparative manipulative efficacy of the two approaches is, again, at least partially a pseudoproblem. The definitional problem classically has been formulated in terms of curing a symptom vs. curing a disease. Without reviewing here the controversy about the applicability of the disease model to either mental or behavioral problems (see Alker, 1965, for a discussion of problems in conceptualizing mental illness), it can simply be asserted that behavior modification approaches are concerned with changing specific behavioral responses while humanists are more interested in changing peoples' personalities.

This issue has often been stated in terms of the existence vs. the nonexistence of symptom substitution. In Eysenck's writings (1969), in the writings of other behavior modifiers (Krasner, 1971a), and in the current symposium, there is dispute on this matter. The behavioral modifiers typically take the nonexistence of symptom substitution to be a crucial fact supporting the model of man which attributes causal determination largely to the manipulation of variation of situational contingencies. The nonexistence of symptom substitution supposedly falsifies psychodynamic models placing stress on the causal determination of behavior by intrapsychic forces. This problem has even been considered by Eysenck, on Krasner's (1971a) interpretation, as the crucial experiment between the two views in question. On the psychodynamic side, however, this claim has been rejected (Weitzman, 1967). The grounds for this response are that symptom removal, for symptoms that have been genuinely cathected with psychic energy, may by itself change the psychic energy equilibrium in an individual and thus not require the necessary generation of new symptoms.

Stating the issue as Eysenck does can easily mislead researchers into believing that there is some question of empirical fact that will ultimately settle the issue between these two different causal models of the nature of man. The evidence to date is apparently mixed. Jourard in this symposium reports frequent observation of symptom substitution. Baker (1969), on the other hand, in a thorough follow-up of enuresis sufferers treated by behavior modification finds no evidence at all for symptom substitution. Indeed, Baker found widely generalized adaptive responses following enuresis treatment. These empirical results further support our belief that new evidence will finally resolve this matter, if available evidence has not already done so in favor of behavior modification. The premise that we have a crucial experiment itself is, however, questionable given Weitzman's contentions.

The incommensurability of relevant outcome is apparent at several points in the discussion between Jourard and Wolpe. Firstly, there is a radical difference between the formulations of what the two therapists have as goals for personality change. In what appears to be, but is not, a *pro hominum* argument, Jourard congratulates Wolpe on what a fine person he is. It is being such a fine person or, better, becoming such a fine person that is salient in his conception of what kind of change Jourard, as a therapist, would like to facilitate. Wolpe, on the other hand, is more focally concerned with the unlearning of maladaptive habits. More specifically he mentions relieving patients' suffering "which means to overcome these habits that are disabling to the patient." This difference leads naturally to the related difference in what are considered to be the dependent variables in therapy conceived of as a manipulative scientific experiment. The reduction of an anxiety habit or other rather specifically described outcomes are preferred by behavior modifiers. Outcomes from the humanistic side, even if therapy is considered to be a form of natural experiment, are far more global. From the standpoint of a behavior modifier they appear vague, even mythical. But concepts like identity achievement, the attainment of meaning, becoming a productive personality, or minimizing discrepancies between actual and ideal self-concepts, and empathicly relating to oneself and others, are all constructs in various humanistic or psychodynamic personality theories. And none of these theories derive from the principles of learning theory developed by academic, experimental psychologists. This point does not mean, of course, that these theorists deny the vast contribution of what might be called learning to these forms of personality development. Outcomes are simply conceptualized in different and nonequivalent terms.

It does not follow from the presence of incommensurability of therapy outcomes that no scientific-based resolution of this controversy is possible. What does follow is that no single crucial experiment or set of crucial experiments is possible. Instead of assuming that paradigm clashes must be resolved exclusively by political, cultural, moral, or even irrational considerations, we may assume that dialogue within the context of science, that is dialogue regulated by attention to the concerns of explanation, prediction, and control, is still possible and relevant. As George Miller points out in his APA presidential address, cultural and even moral concerns may influence us to give greater priority to the scientific attainment of explanation and prediction than it does to the attainment of manipulate behavior control. Each of these criteria, nonetheless, is still a scientific criterion. And meeting or failing to meet these criteria is a matter of being consistent with empirical facts that we know or can discover. In philosophical terms this problem has been stated nicely by Popper's student Watkins (1960) in his paper on confirmable metaphysics. What we need are procedures whereby the outcome of the argument between alternative paradigms is adjudicated in a rational manner.

The thesis of this paper is that this outcome can be, at least partially, adjudicated by scientific discoveries. These discoveries will not be the outcomes of crucial experiments. Instead they will originate from the application of new research paradigms. Such paradigms already exist in work on behavior modification. Token economics in hospital wards and desensitization procedures for snake phobias are some examples. Such paradigms are rather scarce in the humanistic camp. One such emerging paradigm—self-confrontation—will be discussed at length below.

It is at this point that a basic issue concerning the locus of causation in competing paradigms must be identified. Is it what the psychologist does or is it what the person himself does that ultimately explains in the most satisfactory manner what we observe as personality change? Harré and Secord (1972) have eloquently argued in favor of an anthropomorphic as opposed to a mechanistic model of man. But their arguments have been substantially philosophical arguments. What will be developed in this paper are empirical approaches to this issue. One point ought to be clear, however, at this point. The empirical arguments develop here within the framework of a basic assumption made by the anthropomorphic model. Man, rather than the manipulation of environmental change, is the locus of causation. Naturally with this starting premise different approaches to research design can be expected. Different independent variables will be appropriate and different dependent variables will be used in a humanistic paradigm than would be appropriate within a behavior modification paradigm. These facts do not preclude empirical examination of the competing paradigms as will be considered below.

The criteria for adjudicating a paradigm clash between humanistic and behavior modification approaches are not the same as the rather popular criterion of research productivity. That criterion lends itself to facile quantification. And that criterion is easily confounded by political factors such as who edits the available professional journals. And that criterion also would be heavily susceptible to explanation in terms of what kind of research is currently fashionable and fundable by governmental and other institutions. Judgments about competing paradigms turn on different issues. How surprising and how relevant, for instance, is work within a given paradigm with respect to questions of enduring historical importance in the area of personality psychology? This criterion is neither conservative nor radical, or, more precisely, it is both a conservative and a radical criterion. The novelty of the questions asked as well as the novelty of answers provided support a given paradigm. New connections between phenomena are discovered where they previously were unexpected. But ultimately these novel questions and answers are integrated into the historical development of a field. Einstein's relativity theory, for instance, suggested the observation of a planet during an eclipse of the sun would reveal the curvature of light. Darwin's theory, to take an example from the life sciences, suggested relations between fossil remains of the ancestors of the horse. Neither of the resulting discoveries would have been made without radically new hypotheses having been formulated. But in each case the strength of these paradigms was ultimately established because their discoveries and concepts provided illuminating *vis-à-vis* basic issues that were being asked, respectively about the nature of energy and evolution. From this perspective we will now consider an emerging new paradigm for research within humanistic and psychodynamic psychology: self-confrontation.

AN APPROACH TO STUDYING HUMANISTIC PERSONALITY CHANGE IN THE LABORATORY

A promising procedure for laboratory investigation of humanistic personality change is audio-visual self confrontation (Bailey and Sowder, 1970). This procedure invites special attention in the context of our preceding discussion because (1) the procedure deals directly with increasing the person's capacity for self-directed change by increasing his awareness of his own personality. In this respect the procedure is more consistent with the anthropomorphic rather than a mechanistic model of man (Harré and Secord, 1972). (2) This procedure leaves no doubt that the person involved is the locus of causation. (3) This procedure also relates to one formulation of the general contrast under discussion, viz., a contrast between "insight" and behavior modification approaches to personality change (London, 1969). This relation results from the plausibility of considering audio-visual self-confrontation as a laboratory simulation of "insight."

The particular study to be presented here proceeds within the framework of Tomkins' theory of personality (1963b, 1965). This choice is made because of the relation between this theory and a clearly specified conception of what humanistic ideology is. This conception emphasizes a person's experience as the ultimate justification for what that person values. In contradistinction to the humanist, the normative individual regards his own experience as an inherently flawed basis for the discovery of value. Reliance should instead be placed on external standards. These may include the sacred dictates of superior others, e.g., the Pope, Chairman Mao, God, or be impersonal, e.g., the canons of rigorous science. Change in persons occurs through the operation of basic affects, such as love, guilt, surprise and shame. This change often involves a process labeled " ideo-affected resonance." A person's idea and his affects amplify each other when they are congruent.

No claim is made that audio-visual self-confrontation, in which a person confronts his own affective reactions, while discussing his values, uniquely operationalized this process. Nor is a claim made that audio-visual confrontation can not equally well be interpreted in terms of other processes of personality change. For Rogerians, for instance, a perceived discrepancy of actual self and ideal self serves to motivate change. This process in turn, may or may not adequately be explicated in terms of some form of consistency theory. What is being claimed is that audio-visual self-confrontation offers a means of exploring personality change in a context that is sufficiently relevant to humanistic personality theories so that results will bear on the merits and inadequacies of these theories and invite competing points of view. It is simply impossible to argue, for instance, that the desensitization of snake phobias is theoretically appropriate as a central arena for demonstrating the superiority of behavior modification to more humanistic approaches. That paradigm, while relevant to certain features of Freud's theory, is peripheral to a broad range of concepts in later ego psychology and humanistic psychology.

The hypotheses of the study to be presented are as follows. (1) Audio-visual self-confrontation facilitates the integration of one's personality. The dependent variable in this hypothesis is not a single specific response in a specific situation. Instead a more highly aggregated measure is deliberately employed. (2) Audio-visual self-confrontation will promote a more humanistic orientation in individuals participating in this experience. This certainly would not be chosen as an outcome measure in a behavior modification study but it nonetheless is considered relevant to the intention of humanistic personality theories. Despite these hypotheses, this study must be considered exploratory. That conclusion is necessary because self-confrontation research is still in an early stage of paradigm development.

Method

Subjects The subjects were 45 undergraduates at Cornell University. They were drawn from a volunteer subject pool in a large introductory psychology course.

Experimental Procedure In the experimental condition each individual was interviewed for approximately 15 to 30 minutes. The interview covered three topics; the interviewee's personal morality, his occupational aspirations, and his preferred way of relating to other people. On each topic the interviewee first was asked to state his values and then was asked to state a particular personal experience related to his views. The interviewer prompted the interviewee to cover both what he considered desirable and undesirable on the various topics. The interview was conducted in a generally nondirective manner with the general demeanor being one of interest and nonspecific approval of what the person was saying.

Following the interview, which was videotaped with the interviewee's knowledge, the videotape was played back for the interviewee's scrutiny. The interviewee was instructed to watch the playback and stop the playback machine at least three times. This intervention by the interviewee was to take place at times when he saw himself expressing any kind of positive affect. The purpose of these combined procedural requirements was twofold. Firstly, the interviewee's control over when the tape was stopped allowed him some protection against the procedure being too obtrusive. Secondly, the focus on positive affect was designed to enhance the acquisition of a humanist orientation as this orientation is, according to Tomkins (1963b) primarily though not exclusively grounded in positive affects. At each point that the interviewee stopped the videotape playback unit by depressing the appropriate lever, he was asked to identify what affect he was expressing. He was then asked why he thought that he felt that particular affect at that particular time.

The first control condition involved the same initial filmed interview without any subsequent playback.

The second control condition involved simply the scores on the dependent variable measures for a population recruited in the same manner as the first two conditions.

Dependent Variables   The major dependent variable in this experiment was the subject's score on the Tomkins' Polarity Scale (1964). This test is a 59 item measure of personality and ideology designed to indicate endorsement of humanist or normative orientations. The items employ a rather atypical format. Each item is bipolar in that a humanistic and a normative view on a given topic are paired. For example, one item pairs the view that "To every lover, his beloved is the most beautiful person in the world" with the view that "Love is blind. Otherwise no one would ever fall in love." The respondent may endorse the humanistic alternative (in this item, the first member of the pairing), the normative alternative, both alternatives, or neither alternative. There results from this arrangement of items four different interdependent scores for each respondent: total humanist score, total normative score, total "both" score, and total "neither" score.

A second measure employed in this study was Cottle's (1967) projective measure of temporal relatedness. Instructions for this test are: "Think of the past, present, and future as being in the shape of circles. Now arrange these circles in any way you want that best shows how you feel about the relationship of the past, present, and future. You may use different size circles." Completed circles may demonstrate either: (1) Atomicity. In this case circles fail to touch and by demonstrating no spatial relatedness earn zero points on the dimension. (2) Continuity. By touching at the periphery only, circles depict a flow of units with each unit occupying its own finite space. Two points are earned for each peripheral touch. (3) Integration. When circles overlap one another so that a particular space is shared by at least two zones, four points are earned. (4) Projection. Circles may be drawn within one another or be perfectly contiguous. Either configuration received a maximum of six points.

This measure is selected as an index of personality integration following the suggestion of Melges and Fourgerousse (1966) that "if an individual has no plans or cannot deal with the present in terms of the past, then behavioral disorganization will result (p. 138)." Present–future connections represent an extension of the relatedness into the future. Validity data available on this measure (Cottle, 1967, 1969) give promising support to such an interpretation. The measure correlates positively with intelligence, valuing achievement, and negatively with anxiety (Cottle, 1969).

A variety of other measures of temporal orientation from Cottle's study (1969) were also used in this study but as they play no role in relation to the hypotheses advanced here, they will not receive further discussion.

Results

The means for the four scores from Tomkins' polarity scale are presented in Table 1. A one-way analysis of variance was performed on each of these scores though they are not necessarily independent on each other. The "both" score showed a statistically significant increase following the audio-visual self-confrontation. ($F = 3.60$, $df = 2, 42$, $p < 0.05$, two-tailed.)

TABLE 1. TOMKINS' POLARITY SCORE MEANS

	AVSC	Interview	Test Only
Humanistic	35.0	38.9	39.9
Normative	4.1	3.3	3.6
Both	8.1	6.3	4.7
Neither	10.8	10.9	10.3
Circles test means			
	12.13	8.66	9.19

Inspection of the mean scores in Table 1 might suggest that there is an effect with humanist scores in the opposite direction from that predicted. This conjecture proves illusory as $F = 1.50$, $df = 2, 42$, n.s. Inspection of the differences between means in order to find out what contributes to the overall significant F value for the both score yields some clarification. The audio-visual self-confrontation group differs from the noninterview control,

$t = 2.24$, $p < 0.05$; while the experimental group differs from the interview only control marginally, $t = 1.73$, $p < 0.10$.

Turning to the circles test, we find a clear picture. The overall F test yields an F value of 2.50, $df = 2$, 42, $p < 0.05$, one-tailed test. The internal comparisons are quite determinant. The self-confrontation group compared with the interview only control yields a $t = 2.49$, $p < 0.01$. The comparison of the experimental group with the test only control is nonsignificant, $t = 1.64$, $p < 0.10$. The means for these groups are also included in Table 1.

Discussion

Surprisingly enough the second hypothesis of the study was not confirmed for the apparent reason that the first hypothesis was. The "both" score seems to have improved largely at the expense of the humanist score. It is the latter score that typically characterizes college students of the day. The "both" score is relatively unfamiliar in discussions of research with Tomkins' polarity scale, cf. Alker and Poppen (1973). Tomkins (1963) does comment, when introducing the concepts of normative and humanistic ideology, that historical advances and creative accomplishments in the history of thought typically embody syntheses of these opposing orientations. He mentions Kant and Freud, for example, as individuals who reintegrated humanistic and normative points of view in the respective fields of metaphysics and psychology. It hitherto has not been considered whether or not a "both" score on the polarity scale can have a similar implication regarding individual personality change. Certainly one can imagine individuals who endorse both alternatives to a bipolar item such as "numbers were invented vs. numbers were discovered" for the reason that they simply can not make up their minds.[2]

It is in this connection that the results with the circles test, although itself not a fully understood entity, are rather gratifying. For the weaker of the experimental vs. control comparisons, self-confrontation vs. interview,

---

[2] The reader troubled by the *post hoc* nature of this explanation may find consolation that subsequent studies have resolved this ambiguity in a manner consistent with the proposed interpretation. One study (Alker *et al.,* in press) using a less speculative index of personality integration, viz. an interview assessment of Eriksonian identity achievement, found positive results for the AVSC manipulation. And another subsequent study using parallel forms of Tomkins measure with a pre-post design found the apparent anagonistic relation between "left" and "both" scores disappeared. A "left" plus "both" score showed significant increase with AVSC. Apparently the after only design overwhelms the reorientation produced by AVSC with surprise at the novel format of Tomkins instrument.

this measure clearly identifies an effect. And this measure has very relevant conceptual relations to what Cottle (1969, p. 549) calls " the synthesizing force inherent in the spread of the temporal horizon." This concept undoubtedly will produce instant disenchantment for many behavior modifiers. But its relation to the writings of continental psychologists such as Fraisse (1963) and philosophers such as Heidegger (1962) suggest that such disenchantment can be put into an ameliorating perspective.

Furthermore, there is no compelling reason to deduce that the self-confrontation experience generated by the procedures described here would particularly motivate a Hamlet-like indecisiveness. In the light of other effects produced by various forms of self-confrontation, e.g. Boyd and Sisney (1967), this alternative interpretation is less plausible. These researchers found a reduction of actual self-ideal self discrepancies following audio-visual self-confrontation. Possibly the effects leading to an increase in "both" scores could be an instance of something like Eriksonian identity moratorium. Identity moratorium occurs when a person confronts major choices and temporarily delays resolving the issues. Results from a study by Alker *et al.* (in press) support this interpretation. High both scorers on the Tomkins' instrument tend to be identified as in a stage of Eriksonian identity moratorium. But this relation occurs in the context of an overall movement towards identity achievement also produced by a similar audio-visual self-confrontation procedure.

At this point comment must be made concerning the invitation of alternative explanations from perspectives in behavior modification. In spite of the fact that the dependent variables in this study are alien to such perspectives, the procedure itself is not.[3] Kanfer and Phillips (1970), for instance, include training in self-observation as part of their behavior modification program. Self-reactions and self-control and self-reinforcement are becoming increasingly popular concepts in the theory and research of persons considering themselves behavior modifiers (Goldfried and Merbaum, 1973). This author doubts that theoretical interpretation of the phenomena demonstrated in this

---

[3] Incidentally, in spite of the fact that the dependent variables in this study may be uninteresting to behavior modifiers, these variables still can be considered as behaviors. No assumptions are made that these behaviors are intrapsychic mythic entities or mere self-reports based on the subject's implicit personality theories. The dependent variables more plausibly can be considered samples of the kinds of behavior that occurs in various situations that humanistic and psychodynamic personality theorists consider relevant. Much of recent philosophical analysis, particularly of the Oxford–Cambridge variety, has questioned the claim made by earlier logical positivists that there is only one basic descriptive language that provides information from which any theoretical account must proceed.

and related studies will find satisfactory explanation when considered from some behavior modification perspectives. Speaking of "coverants," for example (Homme, 1965), a class of operant responses defined by their relative inaccessibility to observation, is unlikely to lead to convincing explanation of the processes involved in self-confrontation. Nonetheless, there is a convergence of sorts that appears to be developing. Self-observation and self-confrontation are being emphasized as crucial processes by numerous researchers with widely varying theoretical predilections. Specifications and investigations of different forms of self-confrontation using varying dependent variables can narrow the gulf between humanistic and behavior modification approaches. It might soon be discovered, for instance, that self-confrontation procedures promoting Eriksonian identity also change the class of reinforcers that is most significant for a given individual.

In broader perspective the results of this study together with the results of the other studies cited provide a gratifying confirmation of the hypothesis that self-confrontation will prove to be an attractive vehicle for refining and validating humanistic and insight-oriented approaches to personality change. It is not assumed that the procedures of self-confrontation that have been used in this and related studies are new "techniques" for wonderously successful personality change. The exposure is so brief and relatively simple that that would be a very optimistic assumption even though Boyd and Sisney (1967) and Tourangeau (1973) have found changes over periods of one or two weeks. What is nonetheless encouraging is that this approach has demonstrated relevance to central concepts in humanistic and modern psychodynamic psychology. There is no confirmation in this data of the widely held view that "insight" has little to do with personality change.

This author clearly does not conclude that the incommensurability of outcomes in humanistic and behavior modification research requires abandonment of all the values of science in favor of simple ethical or political dicta. Nor is it appropriate to claim that behavior modification approaches have any kind of exclusive monopoly on the exercise of scientific discipline or scientific imagination. This conclusion is not to be interpreted as yet another verse in the litany of science *über alles*. The values of a scientific adjudication of an ideological dispute are themselves beyond purely scientific appraisal. It is hoped that the appeal to evidence, when coupled with the potential for genuine surprise that characterizes good empirical research, will make the dispute more rational.

PART VI

Applications of Complementary Ideas and Syntheses of Humanism and Behaviorism

INTRODUCTION

A basic question which has permeated the book is whether new and fundamental syntheses between humanism and behaviorism are possible (position 5 in Part I to the book). In Part V Harding discussed the potential usefulness of combining the strengths of humanism and behaviorism. He separated types of compatibility between humanism and behaviorism into weak and strong types. Several authors (e.g. Thoresen and Mahoney, 1974; Staats, 1972) have recently proposed that there be a synthesis of humanism and behaviorism, but little has been done to clarify the types of syntheses possible. In this Part there are three demonstrations of syntheses of humanism and behaviorism in practice.

Humanists have given persuasive descriptions of the goals and ideals they are seeking. The behavior therapists, on the other hand, have focused on developing and validating techniques. The type of synthesis most often proposed has been the use of behavior therapy techniques to accomplish humanistic goals. Both Goldstein and Curtiss, in this Part, claim that this is the type of synthesis they have created. A major goal in humanism is to bring one's feelings and behaviors into congruence. Goldstein, a behavior therapist who has worked with Wolpe, describes appropriate expression training: "expression because the emphasis is on letting other people know how one truly feels and appropriate in the sense that it is an expression which has the highest probability of getting a person the most out of the situation." Goldstein describes the appropriate expression training techniques he uses with college students and with neurotic patients in individual and group therapy.

Curtiss, who has a humanistic background, describes her work as part of a consulting team to improve treatment procedures with chronic patients in a large state mental hospital. She describes the effects of using humanistic or behavioristic approaches alone and the attempts by the consulting team to break through the problems caused by the strict, albeit " successful " technical uses of a token economy system. The goals of the token economy unit included openness, sharing, responsibility, participation, and the need for constant effort to change behavior (these are very similar to the goals of therapy proposed by Jourard). Curtiss presents a vivid description of the promise and struggles involved in developing an open, humanistically oriented therapeutic community with a behavioristic technology. While reading the Goldstein and Curtiss chapters, the reader may ask whether these syntheses are limited to the use of behavioristic technology and humanistic goals or whether their techniques also are humanistic as well as behavioristic.

A more fundamental type of synthesis than behavioristic techniques and humanistic goals would be a synthesis which incorporates goals or techniques from both approaches. In their book on self-control, Thoresen and Mahoney (1974) review therapy programs which use self-control techniques to change behavior. The self-control programs use internal and external reinforcement (humanistic and behavioristic techniques) to accomplish behavioral goals (e.g., decrease maladaptive behaviors).

In the conceptualization of types of syntheses we have created, the most fundamental type of synthesis would use both humanistic and behavioristic techniques toward both humanistic and behavioristic goals. Gold's affective behavioral program is an example of this type of synthesis.

Gold discusses three dimensions which are useful in describing issues that have divided humanism and behaviorism: (1) locus of change—the humanistic focus of change is internal (i.e., self-concept) and the behavioristic focus is external (i.e., behavior); (2) mechanism of change—the humanistic method of change focuses on the relationship between patient and therapist and the behavioristic focus is on specific techniques; (3) source of change—the humanistic focus is on the client as the active source of change and the behavioristic focus is on the therapist as active intervener. The reader may want to think of locus of change as goals of therapy and mechanism of change and source of change as techniques of therapy. Gold has developed an exciting approach called affective behaviorism which uses an arousal–cognition–

behavior linkage. It is an integration of elements from the social psychology of attribution and emotion, from humanism and from behaviorism. Gold describes her promising theoretical and empirical work and demonstrates the viability and potential of the affective behavioral approach. Her affective behavioral remedial program for emotionally disturbed, behavior problem children includes labeling and control of arousal, relationship factors between teacher and child, play, child as an active source of change and positive reinforcement. She uses both humanistic and behavioristic techniques (e.g., relationship factors and positive reinforcement, internal and external sources of change) and humanistic and behavioristic goals (e.g., change in affect and decrease in disruptive behavior).

The reader should note the attention given to emotion in Part VI. Mischel (in this book), Bandura (in this book) and others have recently integrated cognition into behavioral frameworks. There has been no comparable theoretical and empirical integration with emotion and behavioral frameworks. The first and third articles in this Part begin this integration.

Appropriate Expression Training: Humanistic Behavior Therapy

ALAN GOLDSTEIN

Department of Psychiatry, Temple University Medical School

"Assertive training" (Wolpe, 1958, 1973; Alberti and Emmons, 1970) defines a series of powerful techniques used in behavior therapy. The use of these techniques is indicated by an inability of the client to appropriately express himself or herself in some area of life.

The use of the word "assertive" implies that the person is taught only to be aggressive; this notion needs to be dispelled. If someone has difficulty exhibiting *appropriate* aggressiveness, this can be one aspect of training; however, equal importance is assigned to all other affective modes as well. Often it is more difficult to express and respond to affection (and this is as important, if not more important, than having the ability to express anger). I would prefer that these operations be described as *appropriate expression training*, because this more accurately defines what is actually done. It is expression because the emphasis is on letting other people know how one truly feels and appropriate in the sense that it is an expression which has the highest probability of a positive outcome in terms of resolution of interpersonal conflict, and in terms of having the "expressor" come away feeling good about himself or herself.

The concept of "assertive training" has long been appreciated by all schools of psychotherapy. In the humanistic branches of psychology the concepts of self-image, level of self-esteem, etc., are indicative that self-assertion is an approved and viable goal. Client-centered therapy, gestalt therapy, and others associated with the humanistic movement encourage getting in touch with and expression of feelings. In the behavioral systems, assertion training has been operationally defined by Wolpe (1958) and popularized by Alberti and Emmons (1970). Thus, both the humanistic and behavioral schools recognize the effectiveness of teaching people to express themselves.

Early in the clinical application of behaviorism there was a tendency in assertive training to place a premium on teaching effective manipulation of

223

the environment with little emphasis on the genuine expression of feelings. When taught, expressiveness was limited almost exclusively to aggressiveness. Recently, however, assertive training has been extended beyond an aggressive approach with emphasis on genuine self-expression.

This paper illustrates appropriate expression training. It represents an ongoing trend toward combining the philosophy of humanism and the organized and verifiable techniques of behaviorism.

THEORETICAL CONSIDERATIONS

The theoretical rationale for the effectiveness of assertion training is two-fold. First, appropriate behavior usually facilitates a favorable response from other people. For example, if one knows that a raise is deserved and asks the boss for one, it is more likely to be received. The comic stereotype of the effect of daring to be so forward pictures the boss screaming and throwing the person out head first. The fact is that people are usually accepting and demonstrate more respect for people who express themselves appropriately, so that an assertive person will usually receive favorable feedback.[1] Within a behavioral paradigm this feedback is a form of positive reinforcement and increases the probability that this expressive behavior will occur again in a similar situation.

Secondly, the behavioral paradigm proposes that: (a) there will be learning at the emotional level by extinction of a classically conditioned response of the negative affective state elicited by particular situations, and (b) permanent modification by repetitions of appropriate behavior within a particular context. For example, if one is habitually experiencing anxiety when burdened by demands, and as a consequence acquiesces, then this interchange may be analyzed in learning terms as follows. Anxiety responses have been conditioned to refusing others, so that when the situation arises in which refusal is appropriate, anxiety is triggered. At this point, previously learned avoidance behavior (avoidance of anxiety-producing expression of refusal) is called out, which in this case is acquiescence. Anxiety is immediately reduced although many negative feelings about oneself may follow as a consequence of being "used." We know from laboratory experiments that immediate reduction of anxiety far outweighs delayed consequences so that the same pattern of behavior may be expected to persist if no intervention occurs. The avoidance

---

[1] Of course it is sometimes necessary to give feedback as to the inaccuracy of the client's perceptions and render aid in determining what is and is not likely to be a realistic expectation.

continues to be reinforced by fear reduction. If the client can be brought to refuse appropriately, with repetitions the anxiety response extinguishes if there are no negative consequences of the refusals. In addition, the process of change is facilitated by the immediate positive feelings which accompany a refusal action consonant with the motivational state.

DIMENSIONS OF NONEXPRESSIVENESS

If we wanted to characterize people on a continuum of appropriate expressiveness, at one extreme we would have people who are generally unassertive, that is, people who have a great deal of difficulty expressing themselves in any situation. These people are often described as having low self-esteem, little self-confidence, or a poor self-image. They tend to see other people as very powerful and themselves as not having any influence over their environment. They appear to be passive people in their interactions with others. They tend to have certain attitudes which have developed simultaneously with their behavior, e.g., "the meek shall inherit the earth" and "one ought not to be pushy." They may also be very angry people having bitter thoughts like, "if anything in this world needs changing, it is the aggressiveness of other people who walk all over me." These people often suffer from psychosomatic problems, e.g., headaches, or gastrointestinal disorders. Toward the other end of this continuum there are people who are generally assertive but who have particular difficulty interacting with a specific class of people. For example, someone who gets along very well in the world and interacts successfully with most people but who has difficulty in dealing with authority figures so that there is constant difficulty dealing with the boss or with older, self-confident people. These generally assertive people don't have the attitudes mentioned above. They will come in for consultation saying: " I am not able to say what I am feeling because I am very uncomfortable around these people. I am not able to get what I deserve on my job because I am not able to ask for a raise; and, I'd really like to do something about it." These people are more aware that being nonexpressive is a problem, in contrast to those people who are generally unassertive and who do not connect nonexpression in any way with their symptoms. Most of us fall somewhere between these examples, so that it is a rare exception when a client does not suffer from some degree of lack of self-expression.

There are various cues that indicate that expression training would be appropriate and useful. A great deal of information will be obtained from interaction during consultation; for example, the degree to which the client seems to be appropriately expressing herself or himself while dealing with the therapist about fees, or being late for appointments, and various other issues which are important in the therapy interaction. Another indication that expression training is appropriate can be derived from questionnaires, for instance, the Willoughby Personality Schedule (1934) or the Bernreuter Self-sufficiency Scale (1933) which have many questions about interpersonal interactions. In the process of an interview the questionnaires can be followed up with questions like: What do you do when you see someone whom you casually know approaching on the street? Some people will say, "Well, I ignore them," or "I turn and walk the other way because I don't want to bother them and I feel uncomfortable when I go up to someone I don't know very well. I don't know what they are going to say and I don't know how to respond to them." Another helpful question to ask is: When you find yourself a dollar short on your change after purchasing something from a store, do you go back and ask for it? or What is your response to a clerk who is putting pressure on you while helping you try on suits by saying, "that really looks good on you, etc."? Many people will buy a suit that they don't like because they have trouble dealing with clerks. These kinds of questions elicit a good deal of information about the degree to which people are able to assert themselves in casual interactions. Perhaps a more subtle, and in many ways more important, area that should be inquired about is close personal relationships.

For example, it is important to pay attention to how one expresses needs and how disagreements are handled. Such information elicited in detail can help define the targets for expression training. Also, people who feel a lot of anger or guilt or report being "paranoid" or having a terrible temper are usually people who lack the ability to appropriately express themselves.

TECHNIQUES OF EXPRESSION TRAINING

Once the situations which need to be dealt with have been isolated there are several ways in which one can go about working with a person to modify these responses. However, the very first task is to get the person to understand that his or her behavior is related to the problem that he or she came to have changed. There needs to be an understanding that self-expression will make some positive differences in his or her life. A person who comes in with a psychosomatic complaint, for example, will not be likely to have made the connection between his or her presenting complaints and lack of self-assertion. A person who comes in and says, " I have a terrible time with my boss and several other people and I have to do something about it " needs very little convincing. Whatever the situation, it is essential that there be an understanding between the therapist and the client as to the value of the therapeutic suggestion. The two people involved must be working in a co-operative venture to deal with the problem.

It is usually helpful if the client keeps a diary noting each time he or she is feeling uncomfortable and all of the circumstances at that time. Through this process reliable patterns show themselves, usually within several weeks. For example, it may be noted that stomach distress follows any display of anger. The therapist and the client together approach this task of discovering the relationship between environmental events and unpleasant responses with open minds and come to conclusions based on observations. The person has to be aware of the connection of behaving in a particular way and the symptoms in order to be motivated to work at the recommended tasks. It is important to point out to people, for example, that indeed their headaches are related to situations in which they didn't handle themselves in the way they would like to, and that their feeling of not being worthwhile is contingent upon the way they handle situations in their environment. Generally clients think that they have to build up their self-esteem and strengthen their egos in order to be able to go out and act effectively. However, the fact is that one strengthens ego by acting effectively. The feedback one receives from the environment determines the feeling about oneself. Frequently it is necessary to give reassurance concerning the consequences of self-expression. For example, it is permissible to say to your mother that you are left feeling guilty when she says, " This is what I get after all I have done for you." Your remark is not going to totally devastate her and you are entitled to let her know how she is making you feel. You have the right to express your feelings and not allow yourself to be manipulated by guilt-inducing statements of others. This concept is one of the most difficult to get across because there is often a feeling that expressing oneself and becoming an autonomous individual is impossible because of the intransigence of the antagonist or that it will result in injury to the other. A response to this suggested expression may be, " But if I were to say, ' Mother, you are making me feel guilty ', she would say to me, ' Well, you should feel guilty after what you've done to me.'" The client's thought is that it is impossible to win. It might then be suggested that standing on one's feelings is something we are all entitled to, and it is not subject to argument. One might then say to mother, " Even so it is making me feel guilty and I don't enjoy being with you when I feel this way,"[2] or something to that effect. The idea is that the therapist should impress upon the client that one can deal effectively with people, and his or her relationship will not necessarily deteriorate but probably improve. Being disowned is not likely to follow; mother is not going to have a heart attack as a result. In fact, this new way of behaving opens up the possibility for their relationship to change from one of mother–child to one between two autonomous adults.

After reaching agreement as to the necessity of self-expression it is important to reassure the client that the process will be guided by the degree to which the client is able to proceed. There will be no pressure to do things the client feels unready or unable to do at that time. The client should begin with behaviors which have a very high probability of being reinforced. It would be a disaster to send someone out the first time into a really significant situation in which one stands a good chance of failing. Before suggesting some action the therapist should be fairly sure that the consequences are going to be positive, particularly at the outset. Only after building a base of successes will the client be able to continue being expressive in the face of occasional negative consequences.

Record-keeping often proves helpful to the client in relating feelings about oneself and environmental events. Usually, it is worthwhile to request that the client keep records of situations in which he either expressed feelings appropriately or did not; the criterion being how one feels after it happens. If the person goes away feeling abused or seething with anger or having obsessive thoughts about what should have been said or feeling guilty, then further work at becoming more expressive is indicated. Once started the client will usually report with glee how well a situation was managed which had not been managed before. On the other hand, the client may report that it was a terrible week, and although the knowledge of what to do was available it was found to be impossible to perform. However, with records it is possible to see long term progress in the face of discouragement over one bad situation. After one bad situation a person will say, "It is not doing any good, I wasn't able to handle that." But if the therapist is prepared to say, "Look, you took care of four out of five this time, and that's very good because it was only three out of five the last time," then the therapist has some way of reinforcing the behavior in the face of perceived failure. Of course, it must be kept in mind that it is not necessary to constantly express oneself purely as an exercise. For instance, it is

---

[2] Specific sentences are sometimes suggested to clients but the emphasis is upon having clients assert appropriately in their own style and vernacular rather than parroting the therapist.

not necessary to call someone down who steps in front of you in a line if it truly does not bother you. Nor is it necessary to express every little flash of annoyance with a family member; such feelings must be expressed only if they are persistent and interfering.

One of the several things that can be done in the therapist's office to facilitate this process is behavior rehearsal—using role reversal and modeling. Let us use examples based on an actual case from the author's practice. Someone has a great deal of anxiety about doing something that has been agreed upon. The client says during a session " Next week my mother-in-law is coming to visit me, and every time she comes to visit the minute she gets in, she says something about the baby not eating. I hold back and don't say anything at the time, but before she leaves I explode with rage, then she doesn't speak to us for six months and my husband gets angry with me." In this case it should be pointed out that a person explodes with rage because she doesn't express at the appropriate time the feelings she has in a particular situation. She stores it up until the pressure becomes so great that she goes into a rage over something which on the surface appears insignificant. Other people react to this with feedback that the person is being irrational, and the feeling of needing to control her temper comes into play, leading her to again suppress her feelings until they reach uncontrollable proportions. The client usually sees this point very quickly. In the office we can prepare for dealing with the mother-in-law:

Client: I know what she is going to say as soon as we sit down to dinner. " He's not eating. He's not being given the proper food." She says that every time.

Therapist: Well, how do you feel about what your mother-in-law says?

Client: Well, it really makes me angry. It makes me feel like she doesn't respect me as a mother for my child, as if I am incompetent for the job.

Therapist: Fine, what could you say to her in order to express those feelings?

Client: There is nothing I can say to her. You can't argue with that woman.

Therapist: You know your mother-in-law better than I do. Why don't we swap roles? You play your mother-in-law, and I'll play you. Give me an idea of how she does this.

First, she does know her mother-in-law better than the therapist does. And, second, when the therapist takes her role he does not have to react as she would. He can play the role as appropriately as he is able, and the client is able to enact the worst possible images she has of what her mother-in-law might say, and she will be able to watch the therapist deal with it.

> *Client* (*mother-in-law role*): Look at that, you don't give the proper food to your family. The child looks as though he is losing weight. You aren't feeding him well.
>
> *Therapist* (*client role*): I can understand your concern about that Mother, but at the same time it really does annoy me that you keep harping about it. I think we would enjoy being with each other much more if you would not continually bring it up.
>
> *Client:* I don't know what she would say to that. I've never said anything like that to her.
>
> *Therapist:* Well, what is the worst thing she could do?
>
> *Client:* She could get very angry with me, and stomp away from the table, and then I would feel terribly guilty.
>
> *Therapist:* Well, if she does you could say something like this: "I'm sorry this has upset you, Mother. We're going to finish dinner; and, if you'd like to join us we'd be glad to have you."

Eventually, therapist and client swap places, and the therapist plays the mother-in-law. The therapist has a pretty good fix on the mother-in-law now so that he can play the part making it progressively more difficult for the client, as she is able to handle it. Each time she conquers one step, she is congratulated but a suggestion is made that she do it again in order to see if mother-in-law could come up with something else. Each step is practiced as many times as necessary for her to be able to do it comfortably and with conviction. The scene is practiced again incorporating something more difficult until the client is able to handle every conceivable difficulty. When the mother-in-law does come for a visit, the therapist asks that the client call in regularly to talk over how things are going; and certainly when she comes in for a session the therapist will inquire about it and rework any interactions which led to the client feeling defeated. The process is very concrete and specific and varies with the individual with whom one works.

There are some general rules that have proved helpful in the author's experience. The first is that one should not allow oneself to be controlled by guilt. Everytime someone tries to do this it is best to label it and tell the other person how it makes you feel.

Another rule of thumb is to instruct the client to preface his or her statements with "I feel." The way in which most people inappropriately assert themselves is to say something synonymous with "you son of a bitch." This kind of statement is totally nonproductive because it triggers each person into making self-defending statements or into attacking the other person. An example is a typical situation wherein a husband forgets to bring home a loaf of bread which his wife asked him to pick up. She might say, "What do you mean, you didn't bring the bread home? All I asked you to do was one simple thing—to bring home bread and you couldn't do it." That is nonproductive because he will probably justify himself by saying, "If you would keep the house a little neater, maybe I would remember to do things for you." And they may end up arguing over whether she really does keep house properly. However, the issue is not that he did not bring home bread or that she does not keep the house neat; the issue is that she feels as though he doesn't care about her when he forgets these things, and this is what she should be expressing to him. "I'm really disappointed, it leaves me feeling as though I'm not cared for."

Beginning a sentence with "I feel" helps to undercut the necessity for defensive maneuveurs and in fact opens him up to being understanding, although he may not be accustomed to being confronted with such open statements and may not be able to handle them at first. But if he says something like, "You're always complaining," she can re-emphasize her point. It is only observable to her; he can not make any factual statements about the way she feels nor can he argue her out of it, which illustrates another rule of thumb: stand on your feelings.[3]

Another helpful practice is to avoid evasive questions and make direct statements. For example, if a husband inquires of his wife, "Are you very tired tonight?" it is fairly obvious that he is not worried about the state of her fatigue. But she may answer, "Yes, I'm very tired," and he is stopped. He is seething and thinking that there is something the matter with his wife because she is never interested in sex. (She may be unsure as to whether he wants sex or was simply offering because he thought *she* wanted it.) He feels so badly about this that he is going to stay up half the night and then turn on the light and read simply to let her know how distraught he is. It would be much more

---

[3] A reviewer of this manuscript made the following comment, with which this author agrees. "Intransigence may result when a person deals with what is accessible only to him/her personally. The partner simply is left out of the discussion, since he/she does not know, cannot feel, and does not understand. When people stand on their feelings, why not caution them to think, to fit their feelings into a matrix of environmental circumstances, so that there can be some rapport?"

productive to say, " I'd really like to make love tonight." Then she can say she really doesn't feel like it; but at least they can discuss why that is, and he has expressed his feeling, and the real issue is in the open.

RESEARCH

The largest contribution of behavior therapy may prove to be the introduction of the scientific method to the field of psychotherapy, thus opening the way for development of the field from a philosophical trade union to one in which demonstrable results become the *sine qua non* for acceptance of method, a scientific base upon which broader theory can be developed.

While the early publications of the use of behavior therapy were largely case reports and retrospective evaluations of outcomes by clinicians using their own case loads, now there are a number of well-controlled studies in print and an apparent trend toward a geometric progression of them. The course of events has usually been of this nature in behavior therapy: (1) clinical reports, (2) well-controlled analogue studies, (3) well-controlled clinical studies. (See Feldman and MacCulloch, 1971; Marks *et al.*, 1971, for examples of this process in the use of aversive techniques and in flooding).

Research in assertive training has reached the well-controlled analog state which is exemplified by the work of McFall. McFall and Marston (1970) and McFall and Lillesand (1971), using as subjects college student volunteers, have demonstrated that behavioral rehearsal is effective in producing significantly more appropriate assertive behavior in subsequent life situations. Of three main components of behavior rehearsal, i.e., overt or covert response practice, verbal modeling, and therapeutic coaching, covert rehearsal tended to be the most influential factor. A recent spate of analog studies have focused on both process and outcome variables (Friedman, 1971; Eisler *et al.*, 1973a,b,c; Rathus, 1973; and Kazdin, 1974. For a more complete list and brief discussion of each, see Hersen *et al.*, 1973).

A great number of studies have supported the hypothesis that modeling affects assertive behavior positively. For a review of these studies see Bandura (1969). Research with clinical populations is now being reported (Hersen *et al.*, 1973; Weinman *et al.*, 1972). It may be said that these studies strongly support assertion training, but of course more research is needed. In light of other developments in behavior therapy, it is reasonable to assume that the next few years of research will give us a solid base for training methods.

SUMMARY

All of these operations rest upon usually unstated assumptions which are attributable to the philosophy espoused by humanistic psychology. Some of these assumptions are: (1) that while it is not alright to act on everything you feel, whatever you feel is OK; (2) the suppression of the recognition of feelings leads to conflict, discomfort, and a variety of symptoms; (3) to mix idioms, it is intrinsically reinforcing to behave in congruence with one's feelings, and conversely, it is uncomfortable and anxiety provoking for incongruence to exist between feelings and actions.

In the past humanistic psychology has presented a highly attractive philosophy, while behaviorism has presented a highly effective technology. They are not incompatible and in fact are quite complementary.

The Compatibility of Humanistic and Behavioristic Approaches in a State Mental Hospital[1]

SUSAN CURTISS

Department of Counselor Education, Boston University, Boston, Mass.

INTRODUCTION

The compatibility of humanistic and behavioristic treatment is being explored in an experimental token economy unit in a state mental hospital in central New York. This discussion presents data on the inadequacy for both staff and patients of applying either approach separately, and it offers a description of the practical issues and problems in attempts at combining the two. First, diagnostic evaluations and intervention strategies in the behavior modification unit which reveal difficulties in both approaches are described. This research, which explores relationships between humanistic attitudes and behaviors, was undertaken as part of an attitude change project run by a team of organizational development consultants who were committed to exploration of the viability of the humanistic model in the hospital setting. Although the staff of the behavior modification unit is less humanistically oriented than other units of the hospital, both patients and staff have difficulty operating within a strict behavioristic therapeutic program and have concerns, which can be described as humanistic, for reorienting their program.

The efforts of the consulting team to integrate the two approaches within the token economy unit are described in the second section. The information comes from a three year association with the hospital which has involved the team in extensive interviewing, system diagnosis, and varied intervention strategies, including the running of decision making and process consultation workshops for staff and patients. We see these consulting activities as the

[1] This investigation was supported by PHS Training Grant No. 02-T-000, 024-03 (Region II, Department of Health, Education, and Welfare).

essential methods through which the openness, mutuality, and internal locus of control central to the humanistic model can be achieved through a behavioristic technology. We have found that the use of the individual and group contract is the key technique for linking the two approaches.

THE TOKEN ECONOMY UNIT AND ITS SETTING

The mental hospital where these consulting activities took place is over 100 years old. The geographic area served by the hospital comprises eight counties and is roughly equivalent in size to the State of Connecticut. The largely geriatric population numbers over 100. Employees come chiefly from two neighboring villages, the economies of which are largely supported by the hospital. With the exception of the physicians and the majority of the administrative staff, many of the employees come from local families who have been involved in patient care at this hospital since it was founded. Ways of treating patients have been passed down from parents to children for generations and the hospital often employs several generational levels of the same family. This creates a stability to be envied in more urban areas, but the physical isolation of the communities tends to perpetuate attitudes toward mental illness and patient care which are no longer viable with new treatment modalities. Carrying keys and being in control at all times are the traditional ways for staff to be in this hospital.

As a part of its efforts to modernize its treatment approaches, the hospital has undertaken a five year process of decentralization. First, eight geographically based treatment units were set up. Each had its own treatment team and acute and chronic patient populations. When the consulting team was hired three years ago, the staff throughout the hospital had been struggling for two years with the transition from an authoritarian, hierarchical, and centralized power structure to a decentralized and democratic structure emphasizing the development of the multidisciplinary treatment team felt to be critical to establishing the therapeutic milieu (Cumming and Cumming, 1962) envisioned by the architects of unitization. As consultants our task was to discover the barriers preventing the development of more therapeutic and less custodial attitudes and behaviors on the part of the staff in the clinical treatment units. Our intervention strategies were aimed at creating an organizational climate with two-way communication, shared decision-making, and social values that explicitly reflected the new attitudes and beliefs of the hospital system. We hoped to build multidisciplinary teams where leaders would be designated on the basis of natural abilities and leadership qualities rather than formal education or status. We also sought significant roles on such teams and units for nonprofessionals and patients as well as a climate where social interaction could take place among all levels of staff and with patients, consistent with the therapeutic community model developed by Jones (1968) and Jones and Bonn (1973).

The consultants developed diagnostic and intervention strategies for assessing the specific needs of each clinical treatment unit. Applying these procedures in the behavior modification unit gave us important data on the need for a combination of humanistic and behavioristic approaches. The Token Economy Unit was established approximately two and a half years ago under the direction of the hospital's chief psychologist. At the time the unit was set up no behavioristic techniques were used on any of the units. This unit, with a capacity for approximately 20 patients and 18 staff members, is unique in the hospital in that it is headed by a psychologist rather than a physician. It selects its patients from among the other units of the hospital. With its dependence on behavior modification techniques to resocialize patients, it is the only unit in which all staff share a common technology other than drugs which they personally can use in the therapeutic process.

The treatment philosophy of the unit emphasizes both the importance of the therapeutic milieu in the rehabilitation of patients and the efficacy of a behavioristic approach (Mandel, 1973). The program manual describes the theory and practice of operant conditioning, positive and negative reinforcement, timing, pairing, and scheduling. Pathological and distorted patterns of living are learned and can be "remedied by a new living experience which emphasizes mutuality, cooperativeness, and the conviction that patients must take responsibility for their own lives." The importance of staff acting as models, a technique shared by both humanistic and behavioristic approaches, is stressed, as is the need to constantly explore ways of involving the patient actively in his or her own treatment process. The overall thrust of the program is seen as eclectic with the token reinforcement system as a structure for a variety of approaches. Mutual feedback among staff and patients is to be encouraged and there are to be no secrets between staff and staff, patients and staff, and patients and patients. More explicitly, the manual states that "we will reinforce openness, sharing, responsibility understanding, participation, and the need for constant effort to change behavior. We appreciate that insight and understanding have little meaning unless linked and geared to actual changes in life styles and behavior." The goal of the unit is a responsible patient and a staff group which continues to grow in its capacity to be authentic and responsible. The means by which the growth process is to be achieved is a behavioristic technology.

At least on paper the Token Economy Unit aims at realizing humanistic sounding goals. The patient who leaves this program to re-enter the community will hopefully not only have dropped his institutionalized behavior but also have become more self-responsible, authentic, and capable of choosing growth-enchancing ways of being for himself. To achieve this the Token Economy Unit's therapeutic program must make a transition in the locus, source, and mechanism of therapeutic change (Gold, p. 253). The patient is initially placed in an environment controlled by token reinforcements, and operant conditioning is used to extinguish maladaptive behavior. The locus, source, and mechanism of change are all found in the environment. Staff want to create trusting relationships with patients, but consistency in controlling the token system is given a higher priority than exploring personal history or sharing in a mutual way. Giving staff such an explicit means of being in control is compatible with traditional hospital approaches to treatment. The relationship between staff and patients is not seen as a critical mechanism of change. The issue is whether behavioristic technology can also be used by the patients as they relearn how to take responsibility for their own lives. If a patient chooses to use this technology the locus of change has become internalized. Patients then can use behavioristic means to achieve their own humanistic goals.

DIAGNOSIS AND INTERVENTION STRATEGIES IN THE TOKEN ECONOMY UNIT

Our three major diagnostic and intervention strategies clearly indicated the desirability and difficulty of using behavioristic means to achieve humanistic goals. The diagnostic attitude survey we designed as the beginning of our project revealed that the Token Economy Unit deviated from the rest of the hospital in at least two important ways. The survey contained a scale to assess the degree of staff humanistic therapeutic orientation. The Humanistic Therapist Attitude Scale (HTAS, see Appendix I) was constructed using the scale discrimination techniques of Edwards and Kilpatrick (1948). The items on the scale explored the degree to which staff shared with patients, were willing to give them responsibility, valued genuineness, and saw therapy as a mutual process from which therapists as well as patients could grow. The scale was incorporated into the system-wide survey and administered to approximately 90% ($N = 968$) of the hospital employees. The unit which was significantly lowest in degree of humanism on this measure was the Token Economy Unit ($t = 4.59; p < 0.01$). It had a group mean score of 38.4 ($SD = 5.31; N = 18$) on the HTAS compared to a staff mean for all the clinical treatment units of 44.5 ($SD = 7.57; N = 569$).

The survey was also designed to explore some theoretical issues. One hypothesis governing the use of the HTAS was that humanistic attitudes would be associated with humanistic behaviors. The humanistic approach to therapy is essentially an experiential rather than an insight-oriented method of working on problems. The therapist invites and models the way for the client to experience herself more authentically and more openly. Through experiencing herself more fully the client's behavior and her ideas about her choices and possibilities will change. The movement appears theoretically to be from new behaviors to ideas about new behavior, thus suggesting that new behavior generates new attitudes and that behavior predisposes a person to attitudes about herself rather than vice versa (Bem, 1970). We hypothesized that if experience had taught the staff the efficacy of the humanistic approach, attitudes and behaviors would be clearly associated.

Two criterion variables were developed for the survey to explore the attitude–behavior linkage. One measure tested the importance of optimism to the constellation of humanistic attitudes. Staff were asked to estimate the percentage of patients on their units who could improve enough to be able to return to the community. We hypothesized that humanistically oriented staff members, in contrast to more custodially oriented staff, would expect a higher percentage of the patient population to improve, consistent with the belief in the capacity of people to grow beyond their existential impasses. The second measure was an activities checklist comprised of the major daily tasks in which staff members on the clinical units might engage. On this self-report behavioral checklist, three preferred activities were to be chosen. We hypothesized that humanistically oriented staff would prefer activities directly related to patients, thus giving the most frequent opportunities for mutual hearing, openness, and self-disclosure.

The results did not support these hypotheses. There was a clear but reverse relationship between the criterion variables of optimism and HTAS score ($r = -0.15$, $N = 599$, $p < 0.001$) and activities preference and HTAS ($r = -0.17$, $N = 599$, $p < 0.001$) among the clinical units. These negative relationships were found with little variation for all disciplines, units, shifts, or job categories. In other words, the more humanistically oriented people, as measured by the HTAS, were significantly less optimistic about patients being released and preferred not to spend time on direct patient-related activities. Those staff who were most humanistic in theory tended to be least humanistic in practice. Less humanistic staff were more optimistic about returning patients to the community and enjoyed interacting with them more than humanistic staff.

These negative relationships were also found on the Token Economy Unit, but staff there were considerably more optimistic than the rest of the clinical treatment units. They stated on the average that 46% of the patients on their unit could be released compared with the hospital average of 20%. Although this unit was clearly less humanistic in its orientation it was considerably more optimistic about the efficacy of its treatment program. There is sound evidence indicating that such expectations for therapeutic improvement will be conveyed to patients with favorable results in treatment outcome (Goldstein, 1962). A critical factor in creating optimism appears to be the presence of a therapeutic technology in this unit compared to other units of the hospital.

Despite their optimism regarding patient improvement and release, the staff of the Token Economy Unit was not satisfied with the behavioristic technology it was using. The first evidence of discontent was voiced in the summer of 1972 when the token program had been running for approximately a year. The consulting team was invited to do a staff development workshop which was one of our major intervention strategies aimed at increasing the capacity of the unit to function as a multidisciplinary team. Extensive interviewing of the staff on all shifts took place in preparation for the workshops. The interviews revealed that problems in communication and role expectations were being exacerbated by difficulties staff had in running meetings, sharing responsibility, and reaching decisions with enough consensus to ensure their being carried out.

In the two day workshop the staff voiced many complaints. Generally the dissatisfactions centered on the token system and the degree to which operating it controlled the staff. The program had been taught to all nursing and attendant personnel in a didactic manner. The staff psychologist then acting as program director kept a large white rat in his office and used it to demonstrate the use of operant techniques. Staff were dismayed and upset by this; they felt they were robots carrying out a program which gave them little room for discretion and decision making. In airing these feelings it was revealed that none of the line staff had volunteered for work on the unit as the program director had thought. Thinking that they were all volunteers, the directors of the unit had done little to develop commitment to the token system on the part of the staff. Jokes were made about the lack of positive reinforcement for the staff. The program had not been in operation long enough to prove its viability in extinguishing maladaptive, institutionalized behavior in patients.

During the ensuing year, staff discontent led to a high staff turnover, and by the next summer part of the nursing service personnel and all the professional staff with the exception of the chief psychologist had transferred to other units. Despite these changes, morale was still low and the consulting team was again invited to do a workshop. A contract was made with the unit to focus on evaluating the therapeutic climate. The evaluation instrument for this intervention was the Ward Atmosphere Scale (WAS, Moos, 1971). The WAS is given to both staff and patients to measure perceptions of real conditions on the treatment wards and ideals for these conditions. The WAS has 99 true and false questions which are organized into ten subscales measuring relationship, treatment, and administrative variables (see Appendix II). It was administered to all staff and patients on the unit, and for the first time in the history of the hospital eight of the 20 patients then on the unit joined the staff in the workshop. When taking the questionnaire patients had the opportunity to vent some of their frustrations. The feeling was shared among patients that the staff seemed very anxious about remaining in control at all times. Patients felt they had little opportunity to share on a personal level. A few patients described the token system as just a game that wasn't really helping them. These feelings were concretely reflected in the results of the WAS. Patients felt the greatest difference between their real and ideal concerns occurred in the area of personal problem sharing. This subscale measures the extent to which patients are encouraged to be concerned with their feelings and problems and to seek to understand them. Ideally, patients also wanted much more support from each other and the staff and more spontaneity on the ward so that they could act more openly and freely express their feelings.

The staff also felt there was a sizeable discrepancy between real and ideal levels of support and spontaneity as well as a need for more involvement, more program clarity, and more order and organization. The dilemma which the Token Economy staff felt is clearly reflected in these findings. They believed that their behavioristic technology worked and they wanted it to be clearer, more organized, and more involving for patients. On the other hand, they wanted to be more supportive and spontaneous and less controlling in their relationships with patients than they had been able to be up to the time of the workshop.

These findings reflect deep concern among patients and staff for the quality of their relationships, a factor considered of major importance to humanistically oriented therapists. Staff want less mechanistic ways of interacting with patients at the same time that they also want to be clear and consistent in the areas where they retain control. Although staff on this unit were optimistic that behavioristic technology would return their patients to the community, the humanistic concern for a better quality of authentic human relationships was felt by both staff and patients. The WAS revealed that neither were content with behavioristic approaches alone as they were practiced on this unit and both saw the humanistic emphasis on the therapeutic value of relationship as an essential ingredient in their treatment milieu.

This data and these feelings were shared in the workshop. Then the participants chose the areas of order and organization, spontaneity, and support as areas needing the most attention in the therapeutic milieu. Force-field analyses were done by small patient–staff groups for each area and solutions were devised using a simple problem-solving model. Staff and patients had never before participated together in a problem-solving, decision-making workshop. The contract made among unit members with each other and the consulting team included involving patients actively in program planning, working out role conflicts among key adminstrative personnel on the unit with consultants acting as facilitators, setting up counseling skill sessions for further training of staff, and establishing a " let it all hang out " rap session to improve dialogue and get feedback exchanged among the staff. In explaining the reasons for lack of spontaneity or a personal problem-insight oriented approach to problems, staff stated that they felt they should be able to answer patient's questions and solve their problems. They frequently felt that if a patient voiced a problem, they should know how to solve it. If they could not solve the problem or if it related directly to a problem with which they are also wrestling, they felt they were not giving the adequate professional help they felt committed to offering. A frequent resolution of this dilemma had been failure to encourage patients to share their personal problems.

Individual interviews with staff have clarified somewhat the conflict the staff feels between relating to the patients through the behavioristic technology or in more authentic, less-controlling humanistic ways. At least three of the staff feel that 80% or more of the patients on token economy can be released to the community. In the first year of the program 19 out of 32 patients in the program (64%) were given community placement. Staff are justifiably proud of this rate and consequently believe very strongly in the efficacy of the behavior modification approach. The success of their patients is the positive reinforcement for which the staff is working. They are also aware that the program actively involves every patient and every staff member. Staff who have worked on other units point out that the sharing of group leadership of the different levels of the program keeps people from destroying each others' efforts through fear of rate busting. They also feel responsible for all the patients and know that the token system ensures their interacting with everyone and becoming aware of the target behaviors to be remedied. The token program charts highlight any progress that patients make, and staff feel that patients build self-esteem through seeing that they can accomplish something. The program director stresses the role of social reinforcement by the staff in the system as well as the fact that patients can help each other grow through the program.

Some of the staff feel that if they are not careful to model correct behavior or consistently give out correct reinforcements the program would not be successful. Success in the program comes from the consistent exercise of control. The staff rather than the patients have this control. Staff are not clear about how the patients can grow beyond taking responsibility for their everyday living problems although most of them see that the capacity for making their own choices is crucial for patients. Some hope that learning will generalize from taking care of everyday small concerns to large ones. Some staff fear that if patients are given decision-making power and responsibility in the unit the token system will be destroyed and patients will continue to make the bad decisions that brought them to the hospital in the first place. Staff are having difficulty giving much control to patients at this point.

INTERNALIZING CONTROL AND DEVELOPING SPONTANEITY THROUGH CONTRACTS

The humanistic orientation places the locus of control for growth, self-actualization, and responsible decision making with the person who can evolve to the degree that she experiences her intentionality and ability to make choices and becomes internally committed to this responsible way of being in the world. The Token Economy Unit must grapple with how their patients will develop an internal locus of control and become responsible enough to leave the hospital if control remains so externalized in the behavior modification approach. The compatibility of the two approaches for this unit depends on whether the transition from external to internal locus of control can be made. The unit has recently been exploring the development of internal commitment to more free, responsible behavior through the personal contract.

The unit accepts patients from other units of the hospital after a screening process. Frequently the patients who are referred have disturbing behaviors which are unusually upsetting to the rest of their unit. The Token Economy Unit thus becomes, in the words of one staff member, the "last resort hotel" for chronic patients whose institutionalized behavior is very difficult to handle. The first part of the personal contracting process begins when the patients come to the unit for an introduction to the program. Patients are not accepted for treatment unless they can voice some commitment to joining the token economy system. Most patients do not indicate what will be positively reinforcing for themselves or the behaviors they want to eliminate; both are initially the recommendation of the referring unit.

Once a patient has chosen the Token Economy Unit he or she is reinforced for "normal" behavior in a sequence of steps moving through appropriate personal hygiene and ward-cleaning responsibilities to social behaviors among patients and staff, and finally to learning the behaviors and skills related to holding a job and functioning in an autonomous way in the community. If the patient also has particular behavior problems, which could range from bed-wetting to suicidal gestures, staff may design individual behavior modification plans (IBMPs) for the patients. As the unit has become more established more patients are contracting with staff for IBMPs based on their own desire to eliminate certain troublesome behaviors.

According to the program director, individual IBMPs are developed when a patient has reached a fairly high level in the system but seems to be making no further progress. The patient may be confronted in a supportive way by a staff member if the patient is wondering why progress is not continuing. The patient is told which of his behaviors prevent him from being released. The patient and staff member then draw up a contract for the IBMP with the patient setting out the specific behaviors and in what sequence they are to be remedied. The patient may also indicate what might be reinforcing for him to try to achieve this. For example, one woman patient on the unit had become very distressed by her own pattern of suicidal acting out. On several occasions staff had discussed her suicidal behavior as the chief reason for her continued stay in the hospital. Finally, this woman came to the program director and asked him to help her draw up an IBMP regarding this behavior. The two agreed that if there were no suicidal gestures or talk for a week a staff member would take her out to lunch on the weekend. This contract operated successfully for many weeks.

The behavioristic technology of reinforcement can thus become a technique to reach personal goals set by the patient. The program director is convinced that the relatively few patients who contract for their own IBMPs have had the best chance for community placements or discharge, although no evaluative data is now available. Attempts to run controlled studies comparing outcome for patients who do or do not enter into their own contracts have so far been thwarted by the small size of the unit and difficulty in controlling for other influences. Although acceptance of these contracts among staff and patients is growing, their use on the unit is still in the early stages.

Contracting is also used with staff to encourage the development of a more open, spontaneous atmosphere on the unit. When staff are able to identify problems in the unit they are encouraged to use an open contract among all staff members as a way of developing and sharing responsibility for solving the problems that arise. For example, after the WAS workshop, a contract was established with a facilitator from the consulting team to run rap sessions where staff members could air their feelings more openly. It was hoped that this would help the unit become a therapeutic community and develop the mutual openness central to the humanistic model. The first sessions were characterized by testing and complaints. After a few weeks of structured exercises including a blindfolded trust session and some dyadic encounters, staff began to open up, members started sharing their feelings and giving each other honest feedback, and group identification was built. The group decided to take responsibility for itself and made a contract to do its own trouble shooting and run its own grievance session. The specific contract was initiated by the nurse in charge of the ward. Different team members agreed to tell this woman when things were not running smoothly. She in turn agreed to take responsibility for calling a staff meeting and airing the difficulty.

CONCLUSION

The crucial issues that must be solved before the staff can run an open humanistically oriented therapeutic community with a behavioristic technology are those of sharing control, learning to be open and authentic, and building the patients' ability to take responsibility for their own behavior. Staff must first learn how to be self-disclosing and spontaneous among themselves so that patients can share more with them. Without the experience of mutually self-disclosing relationships staff will be unable to model this behavior or invite patients to become more open. Unless the fear of losing control is tackled, the patients and staff will never be able to seriously engage in mutual decision making where power is actually shared. In addition, the staff is unwilling to risk the success of the token economy by giving up their control of the reinforcements.

Attempts to involve patients in the more open climate are still meeting with resistance. Although total unit community meetings are being held on a bi-weekly basis, the staff is in conflict about how to respond to patients' input. Attendants and nurses have vacillated between dominating the meeting to get a task accomplished to not participating in the comunity meeting at all and only voicing their opinions later in a staff critique session. When staff and patients decided to try to bring up suggestions that would lead to more spontaneity among all members of the unit, the staff made no suggestions while the patients brought up nine proposals. The unit attempted to work on one. It consisted of having patients decide the items that they wanted to have available for purchase in the token store. Staff are currently quite resistant to giving patients much input in this area and are raising objections to most of the items requested by patients. The patients are persisting and continue to test the staff through this issue to see how much real decision-making power they will be allowed to have.

The present strategy for working on these difficulties involves encouraging staff to be open, to learn how to observe their own process, and to increase their skills as counselors. The consulting team continues to contract for these activities and to encourage staff and patients to make individual and group contracts for change in different areas of unit function. We hope that the experience of using contracts and evaluating their success or failure will lead to greater acceptance of patient contracts for IBMPs. The locus of control over the program could then be experienced as shared by both staff and patients and the success of contract making could facilitate giving more responsibility to patients.

Recently evaluation procedures for the consulting activities in the Token Economy Unit reveal distinct gains in a number of key areas. The original diagnostic survey had shown that compared to the rest of the hospital morale was low, tension was high, cliques were present, conflict in the team was suppressed, and the leadership was considered weak. The second administration of the survey seven months after the WAS workshop showed improved morale, better communications, fewer cliques, conflict more out in the open, stronger and better leadership, and a marked decrease in tension. Therapeutic attitudes likewise showed important gains. The measures of optimism concerning patient release, already the highest in the hospital, gained ten percentage points to 56%. The HTAS score rose 2.5 scale points but it is still below the hospital average. This indicates to us the value of the use of contracts for staff development activities.

In summary, in this hospital most staff with humanistic attitudes feel little optimism, distance themselves from patients, and lack a successful technology for putting their humanistic views into practice. The presence of a successful technology in the behavior modification unit provides an opportunity for a new humanistic approach. Even here, however, staff and patients are not relating as openly as both want to.

APPENDIX I

THE HUMANISTIC THERAPIST ATTITUDE SCALE (HTAS)

We chose the humanistic model for several reasons. Previous attitude research in the state mental hospital setting had delineated staff ideology as either humanistic or custodial and found a strong association between humanism in ideeology and effectiveness in therapeutic role performance. The scale which Gilbert and Levinson (1957) constructed was bi-polar and discriminated degrees of custodialism more clearly than humanism. Carstairs *et al.* (1957) and Pine and Levinson (1957) developed a role performance inventory which described custodial and humanistic behaviors and gave it to supervisory staff to use as a rating device for attendants. A correlation of 0.46 was found between role effectiveness and degree of humanistic ideology as measured by Gilbert and Levinson's scale. However, our examination and pretesting of the instruments used by these researchers showed that the items which defined custodial and humanistic orientations were outdated. Advances in the articulation of humanistic theory and its therapeutic application as well as the gradual movement of mental hospitals away from a custodial stance made it necessary for us to develop a new scale with few custodial and many humanistic items.

Another reason for exploring the humanistic model was its relevance to the behavior necessary to make a therapeutic community viable. It advocates an immediacy of contact, an openness and a mutuality that militates against a norm of professional distance in the therapeutic setting. Nondefensive personal involvement and willingness to acknowledge one's own values, feelings, ideas and experiences in an authentic way are required of therapists in a therapeutic community in order that shared decision making and mutual growth for staff and patients can occur (Jones, 1968). Research by Carkhuff (1971) shows that unless staff can be models of authentic behaviors their clients will not become more interpersonally effective.

The importance Jourard (1973) and other humanistic psychotherapists place on the capacity of people to grow beyond their existential impasse and the need for the therapist to believe in this possibility even when the patient does not was also felt to be a compelling reason for using the humanistic model. In working with a largely chronic and geriatric population, we saw the need for staff optimism and persistence in working for even small gains as essential to prevent further institutionalization. There is compelling evidence (Rosenthal, 1966; Rosenthal and Jacobson, 1968; Goldstein, 1962) that the expectations held by teachers, experimenters or therapists, are communicated to their pupils, subjects of clients whether acknowledged directly and openly or communicated in an indirect or subtle manner. If the staff develops a humanistic orientation their attitudes and values will become a part of the therapeutic process. Patients would then be able to see themselves as capable of growth and improvement.

Other aspects of the humanistic model seemed to be in direct opposition to the care offered in the state hospital. Some humanistic psychotherapists recommend the approach chiefly with neurotic disorders (Waldman, 1971; Corlis and Rabe, 1969). The majority of patients at the state hospital had been diagnosed as psychotic or had organic disorders. The orientation of the hospital toward use of a wide range of diagnostic and medical approaches seemed to argue against a simplistic humanistic approach to etiology and treatment. We reasoned that the chronicity and serious disturbance in the state hospital setting might make it difficult to sustain optimistic humanistic attitudes. In addition, interviews had revealed that despite the modern therapeutic stance urged under decentralization, the staff was being reinforced for completing custodial tasks. Also, the hospital staff gave patients few choices and few opportunities to take responsibility either for themselves or for others. The realities of the hospital system suggested that staff with a humanistic orientation might find difficulty in putting it into practice.

The scale we developed to measure the humanistic orientation is reproduced below. Staff were asked to choose responses of strongly agree, agree, neutral, disagree and strongly disagree (scored 1 to 5 respectively). Scoring was reversed so that a high score would mean a greater degree of humanism. Scores from this population ranged from 24 to 66. The total HTAS score includes all items except 9 and 16 which were combined in a custodial subscale.

A Spearman-Brown split half rank order reliability coefficient was calculated for all 20 items on the scale. The coefficient was 0.40.

This is the first setting in which the scale has been tested.

1. A good therapist is able to share his own experience with his patient when appropriate.
2. Patients should have some choice about the kinds of therapeutic programs they enter.
3. If the mental hospital staff treats its patients as though they can improve, they are more likely to get better.
4. A mental patient is in no position to make decisions about even everyday living problems.
5. By hiding our feelings from other staff members, we encourage patients to hide their feelings.
6. Many people become mentally ill because they've been prevented from meeting their own basic needs.
7. Sometimes patients can help therapists as much as therapists can help patients.
8. The long-range goal of therapy is to increase a patient's ability to make his own choices.
9. Drug treatment is the only kind of therapy that seems to do mental patients much good.
10. Patients sometimes know what's good for them better than the staff does.
11. Patients should have a role in deciding when other patients can be discharged from the hospital.
12. Sometimes I've experienced problems in myself that I see patients having on a larger scale.
13. In the long run it's more therapeutic for a staff member to acknowledge his feelings of inadequacy in dealing with patients than to deny these feelings.
14. It's really important within the hospital to give patients as much responsibility as they can handle.
15. It's just as important for me to be a genuine person to my patients as it is to be a doctor, nurse, or therapy aide to them.

16. With many of the patients we have here, it's usually not worth the time it takes to explain the reasons behind an order or procedure.
17. The therapist should avoid taking responsibility for the patient so that the patient can choose to be responsible for himself.
18. The best therapists are in touch with their own dreams, fantasies, and sense experiences.
19. The most effective way to do therapy is to focus attention on what is going on in the actual relationship between the therapist and the patient as it unfolds.
20. It's usually healthier for the staff to be honest about their feelings with their patients.

APPENDIX II

WARD ATMOSPHERE SCALE (WAS)
FORMS C (REAL WARD) AND I (IDEAL WARD)

SUBSCALE DESCRIPTIONS

1. *Program involvement:* measures how active and energetic patients are in the day-to-day functioning of the ward, i.e., interacting socially with other patients, spending time constructively, being enthusiastic, and developing pride and group spirit in the ward.
2. *Support:* measures the extent to which patients are encouraged to be helpful and supportive towards other patients, and how supportive the staff is towards patients.
3. *Spontaneity:* measures the extent to which the ward atmosphere encourages patients to act openly and to freely express their feelings.
4. *Practical orientation:* assesses to what extent the patient's environment orients him towards preparing himself for release from the hospital. Such things as training for new kinds of jobs, looking to the future, and setting and working towards goals are considered.
5. *Autonomy:* assesses how self-sufficient and independent patients are encouraged to be in making their own decisions about their personal

affairs (what they wear, where they go) and in their relationships with staff.

6. *Personal problem orientation:* measures the extent to which patients are encouraged to be concerned with their feelings and problems, and to seek to understand them.

7. *Anger and aggression:* measures the extent to which a patient is allowed and encouraged to argue with patients and staff, to become openly angry and to display other aggressive behavior.

8. *Order and organization:* measures how important order and organization is on the ward, in terms of patients (how they look), staff (what they do to encourage order) and the ward itself (how well it is kept).

9. *Program clarity:* measures the extent to which the patient knows what to expect in the day-to-day routine of his ward and how explicit the ward rules and procedures are.

10. *Staff control:* assesses the extent to which the staff use measures to keep the patients under necessary controls, i.e., in the formulation of rules, the scheduling of activities, and in the relationships between patients and staff.

Affective Behaviorism: A Synthesis of Humanism and Behaviorism with Children

GILDA H. GOLD

Human Development and Family Studies, Cornell University

Behaviorism is popularly perceived as the antithesis of humanism. Humanistic aims, goals, and methods are viewed as opposite in nature to those of behaviorism. This article hopes to illustrate that this need not be the case. Primarily, it aims to show that humanistic elements should, and can, be incorporated into behavioral frameworks. Concrete methods for achieving such incorporation with children will also be depicted. In speaking of humanistic orientations theories emphasizing relationship or nondirective factors will be utilized. The nondirective theories have been chosen as they maximally emphasize exactly those elements frequently ignored by behaviorists.

If they are considered as opposite extremes, humanistic and behavioristic approaches to remediation might be polarized along three dimensions, namely: (1) *locus of change*, (2) *mechanism of change*, and (3) *source of change*. Regarding *locus of change*, remediation foci tend to reflect an internal orientation for humanists and an external orientation for behaviorists. Organismic changes such as changes in self-concept (Axline, 1969) and restoration of self-esteem (Moustakas, 1959) are stressed by humanists, whereas change in behaviors, such as increase in approach behaviors in phobias, are emphasized by behavior modifiers. Concomitant with the focus on inner organismic change, humanistic orientations (Axline, Moustakas) reveal a belief in man's holistic drive to grow and become all that he can be, i.e., to self-actualize. For behaviorists, issues of holism and internal or psychic drive are frequently deemed irrelevant.

The differential internal–external foci of humanists versus behaviorists can be seen when definitions of abnormality are pursued. To a behaviorist, abnormal behavior is "... behavior that deviates from an arbitrary and relative social norm when it takes place under certain conditions and if it occurs with a frequency or intensity that the child's social environment deems either too high or low" (Ross, 1971, p. 1). In contrast, the thwarting of the growth process toward self-actualization is emphasized by humanists such as Axline and Moustakas.

The *mechanism of change* is another frequently noted source of difference between humanists and behaviorists. The relationship between the therapist and child is highlighted as the major vehicle in humanistic remediation efforts. In fact, to Moustakas (1959), ". . . the relationship is both means and end. The relationship is the significant growth experience (Preface, XIV)." In contrast, the therapeutic relationship is ignored or downplayed by behaviorists. Active ingredients of change deriving from learning theories are stressed. These ingredients include techniques such as operant conditioning, classical conditioning and modeling.

Another difference relating to the mechanism of change is the format of treatment that is emphasized. Play therapy is frequently advocated by humanists. Play is considered the natural communication medium for children. Through play, the world of the child can be learned and remedied. Understanding the child from his point of view and helping him grow at his own pace, in a medium with which he is comfortable, toward becoming all that he can become is the hallmark of humanistic approaches with children. Play may also be used by behaviorists, but the reasons are different. Play is used only if behavioral analysis indicates that the behavior targeted for change can best be altered in a playroom situation. In contrast with the humanist whose major therapeutic medium will be play because play is the natural arena for growth of children, the behaviorist will utilize other approaches, such as direct desensitization, modeling, and operant conditioning, when their prescription seems warranted.

A third dimension along which humanists and behaviorists frequently differ speaks to the issue of *source of change.* For humanists, the child is the active source of change. The therapist facilitates change through providing a beneficial atmosphere and reflecting feelings back to the child. However, it is the child who determines his direction of growth or change. The therapist is cautioned to move with the child, rather than lead him (Axline, 1969). In contrast, in behavior modification it is the child who plays a follower role. Contingencies are frequently determined and implemented by the behavior modifier.

Summing up, humanistic and behavioristic approaches to treatment with children might be polarized along the three dimensions of locus of change, mechanism of change, and source of change. Humanistic approaches have tended to emphasize internally derived changes (such as changes in self-concept), the importance of the therapeutic relationship and the playroom, and the child as the active determiner of his growth. Behavioristic approaches are noted for focusing on external changes, the importance of learning variables, and the behavior modifier as the determiner of change.

The behaviorist focus on behavior has proved fruitful in work with children. It was necessary for the field to learn the utility of actions as a target of remediation. Behaviorism is now ready to expand its emphasis and consider the usefulness of a broader approach to human change. More specifically, the time has come for behaviorism to recognize and consider the humanistic viewpoints (as well as vice versa). To some extent this has increasingly occurred *vis-à-vis* the recognition of relationship factors. Behaviorists have increasingly recognized that effects of a behavioral treatment program may be dependent upon nonspecific humanistic factors, such as the relationship between therapist and patient. Conceptually, relationship factors have been incorporated within behavioral matrices by considering the therapist as a dispenser of positive reinforcement. In behavioristic terms the humanistic therapist who provides unconditional acceptance may be conceptualized as providing the positive reinforcers of warmth and empathy (Krasner, 1969). Within a social learning theory framework, the therapeutic relationship may also be viewed as a variable contributing to the enhancement of modeling and imitation learning effects. Increased attention to modeling behavior is likely to occur when the model is viewed in positive terms, thereby increasing the probability of acquisition of new behaviors. Incentive to perform behaviors already within the child's behavior repertoire is also increased when the model is viewed favorably (Bandura, 1971d).

Incorporation of humanistic variables related to source and locus of change also merits consideration by behaviorists. Regarding source of change, Rotter (1966) has noted that people vary in their subjective perceptions of the source that controls their behavior. Some people, termed externals, perceive the locus of control of their behavior as being external to them. Agents in the environment (e.g. luck, chance, powerful others) are viewed as the major determinants of the reinforcements they receive. Internals, on the other hand, perceive themselves as responsible for the reinforcements they receive. Considerations of perceived locus of control suggest that a behavioral change where contingencies have been determined by an external person may reinforce perceptions of external control in a child who already perceives the environment as being in control of his actions. On the other hand, including the child as part of the behavioral change process may enhance self-control perceptions, which in turn may accelerate behavior changes.

Recent evidence in the remediation of disruptive disorders also supports the active incorporation of the child in the change process. It appears that disruptive behavior may be monitored at least as well through self-regulation as through the regulation by others (Bandura, 1971d).

Regarding the third dimension, locus of change, advances in personality and social psychology indicate that inner-person variables should be considered by behaviorists as viable loci of change. For instance, formulations by Schachter (1964), Valins and Nisbett (1971), and Bem (1972) underscore the interdependence of arousal, cognition, and behavior, and the need to consider cognitions as a goal of change. Schachter (1964) has emphasized the interaction of arousal and cognition. He indicates that emotions are a joint function of physiological arousal and the cognitions that are applied to interpret the state of arousal. The cognitions are determined by past experience and existing situational cues. Valins and Nisbett (1971) have highlighted effects of cognitions on behavior. They state that erroneous attributions or cognitions about oneself can produce behavior that would be considered bizarre or pathological by external observers. They also suggest a cognitive or reattribution therapy that corrects misattributions through supplying corrective attributions. Bem (1972) has emphasized the effects of behavior on emotions and cognitions. He notes that, to some extent, persons infer their emotions and attitudes from their overt behavior and the circumstances under which the behavior occurs, especially when internal cues are weak or ambiguous.

Schachter highlights the impact of cognitive interpretations on arousal; Valins and Nisbett further indicate the possible effects of cognition on behavior; and Bem points out effects from behavior to emotions and cognition. Conjointly, the three approaches yield a resultant of arousal–cognition–behavior interaction. Arousal–cognitions determine the subjective experience of emotion or affect; cognitions influence behavior; and behavior contributes to emotions and cognitions. The interaction of arousal–cognition–behavior, which can also be called affect and behavior, suggests that remediation may be sought when either of the elements or their links fall short of an accepted standard of reference. For example, a youngster, commonly considered "aggressive," may have a low threshold of arousal. Alternatively, or in addition, he may be mislabeling or even not labeling his arousal state. Third, he may be appropriate regarding arousal level and labeling, but may lack appropriate prosocial responses in his behavioral repertoire. An interactional approach would require careful perusal of all the elements and their connections for remediation purposes; and such an interactional analysis might result in focusing on "feelings" or affect—a locus of change that is usually considered humanistic. Focusing on affect and behavior, which this author terms an "affective-behaviorism" approach, therefore, becomes a feasible way to synthesize humanism and behaviorism. Furthermore, the focus on affect might, in turn, involve arousal, affect labeling, and subjective affect as targets of remediation.

Turning to children and the interaction of arousal–cognition with behavior, the very young may be observed to have little "insight" into their behavior. For instance, a toddler with provocation may take a swipe at his provocateur. Arousal has led to action in circumstances which lead adult observers to interpret the arousal as "anger." Yet, the toddler most likely has not applied the anger label or any label. Labeling of affect will probably develop at a later stage. To some extent, the labeling of arousal will be taught directly or indirectly by others who will supply a verbalization to fit the situation. The verbalization accompanying the arousal state will become associated with the state. If during the process of learning arousal is provided with accurate interpretation when it occurs, then the motive label will be appropriate. However, the child may be subject to conflicting labels, inappropriate labels, or he may be deficient in his ability to acquire the labels (due to attentional, motivational, intellectual, or other deficits). If such situations are sufficient in number and severe enough in impact, behavior disorders may arise. For instance, the child may be subject to conflicting labels. The toddler in our hypothetical situation may be told by one parent that he is justifiably angry and by the other parent that he is unjustifiably mean. Given a sufficient number of such conflicting cognitions by inconsistent parents, the toddler may well develop a set of inconsistent cognitions related to arousal and behavior. He might develop into a child perceived as "unpredictable," i.e., a child who is usually calm and good but who sporadically erupts into violent behavior. Furthermore, if his cognitive handles over arousal are ambiguous, the child may have little awareness or "insight" into his internal state. In addition, his cognitive self-statements or self-evaluative attitudes which humanists might term self-concept (Bandura, 1971d) may become derogatory.

A toddler may be exposed to consistent but inappropriate labels. Such a youngster may develop erroneous affect cognitions related to his internal states and himself. A child who is told that only bad boys fight might learn to equate his arousal with being a bad boy. Depending on the strength of arousal, reinforcement conditions, and modeling influences, he might continue to fight. Fighting might then further reinforce the interpretation of arousal as innate badness and self-concepts of evil. On the other hand, it is also possible that a child might learn to escape or avoid situations that would evoke arousals and even the arousal itself. A withdrawn, timid child with little awareness of arousal states and his emotions might then develop. His self-concept might incorporate elements of anxiety or inferiority.

The child who is deficient in intellectual or attentional capacity may also have difficulty in developing cognitive labels related to arousal. For instance, a child who is hyperactive may not sit still long enough to develop reliable explanations of his emotions. Moreover, the lack of understanding may exacerbate his arousal and hyperactivity.

Of course, the development or exacerbation of behavior and personality problems in children is not as simplistic as described above. The major purpose of the exposition was to outline how arousal and cognition may interact with behavior in children; and to direct the behaviorist to consideration of inner organism variables, such as affect labeling, as viable loci of change.

In line with an interactional focus, this author has commenced a number of projects which explore the theoretical and practical soundness of an affective-behaviorism approach with behavior problem children. One series of studies examines affect labeling in behavior problem children. If behavioral disorders are viewed as an arousal–cognition–behavior resultant rather than as behavior *per se*, then one possible area of deficit lies in the cognitive link. Believing that this may indeed be the case, the ability of behavior problem children to label affect was investigated. In one project, three groups, each group containing eight boys between the ages of 10 and 12, were compared in their ability to label the emotions of anger, sadness, happiness, and love from an audiotape in accordance with a procedure developed by Dimitrovsky (1964). Children in regular elementary school classes who were identified as not having any particular problems with self-control served as controls. A second group of children were also children in regular classes but these youngsters were identified as having self-control difficulties. The third group consisted of children in special classes for the emotionally disturbed who were considered by school personnel to have substantial difficulties with self-control. The results indicate a significant deficit in the ability of the behavior problem children in the special classes to label affect as compared with the other two groups ($p > 0.05$). The special class children were significantly lower in their ability to label affect. The other two groups were not different from each other. The study suggests that problems of self-control that are extreme enough to warrant special placement may include an affect labeling deficit. Behavior problems that are less extreme do not seem to reflect a labeling deficit, at least by age 10. Perhaps at younger ages, when labeling of these affects is not yet well solidified, self-control problems include affect labeling difficulties to an even greater extent. In pursuit of this issue, an investigation currently in progress explores the correlation between affect labeling and impulsivity in preschoolers. Preliminary data suggests that reflectives, as identified by performance on Kagan's Matching Familiar Figures test, are more adept at affect labeling than impulsive children of the same age.

Dimensions along which humanistic and behavioristic approaches differ have been presented. The desirability of incorporating humanistic elements into behavioral frameworks has been discussed. The particular desirability of considering an interactional affective-behaviorism approach with children has been highlighted. Attention is now directed to specific avenues by which humanistic goals can be incorporated into behavioral orientations.

Several routes to inner change can be utilized. "Reflection of feeling" frequently espoused by humanists (Axline, 1969) is one vehicle, although such reflections can be reconceptualized in affective behaviorism as the provision of cognitive labels for internal states. This approach makes sense for the child who may have been misdirected or thwarted in developing proper emotional labels. It provides a therapeutic goal that focuses on feelings and a therapeutic process that seeks to provide appropriate labels for arousal. However the degree of efficiency of the approach, particularly its nondirective canon, merits further investigation. It may be that direct training in emotion labeling might be more effective, especially with older children. After an initial assessment period during which he defines situations that elicit arousal, and categorizes the emotions elicited by the situation, the therapist may discuss assessment findings and their resultant emotional labels with the child. Together, therapist and child can then refine the labels in subsequent therapeutic discussions. Such subsequent discussion can utilize arousing events of the week as therapeutic material.

An affective-behaviorism remediation program is currently being implemented in special classes for emotionally disturbed youngsters (Gold, in preparation). In this program, which incorporates humanistic considerations into a behavioristic matrix, both internal loci (related to affect) and external loci (related to behavior) are targets of remediation. Also, the child is an active source of change, and a variety of techniques are utilized. Relationship factors, play, and behavior check lists are systematically applied.

In terms of loci of change, youngsters are taught to recognize and label their internal emotional states. They are also taught appropriate alternative self-regulated behaviors to arousing situations. For instance, many of the children have extreme difficulty with self-control. Thus, they are taught how to control their own behavior by a systematic step-by-step progression of learning to label impulses and control actions. Initially, the teacher maintains control over child behavior as the children do not have the control themselves. She also teaches the children to trust that she will be reasonable and always carry through on her promises. In this way relationship factors are an integral part of the program. When the children develop faith in the teacher and start to feel comfortable, i.e., when the teacher becomes a positive reinforcer, she then begins to label the impulses that accompany behavior. At the next stage she helps the children to label the impulses by themselves. Finally, she teaches the children how to take steps to control the impulses that stir the maladaptive actions. For instance, a child learning self-control first is taught, through concrete example, that the teacher can control his behavior. When his behavior is desirable she rewards it, and when it is undesirable she takes away rewards. Once the child has learned that his teacher will consistently react to his behavior, the teacher begins labeling his impulses when he starts acting out.[1] Thus, if he acts out when another child bothers him, she might say, "Calm down. Sit in your chair. You are upset because X is bothering you." Very gradually the child learns to recognize some of the situations that make him act out. The next step is to teach the youngster to label his own impulses and the situations that trigger the impulses. When he becomes restless, he might learn to say, "X is making me angry." Then the child is taught to anticipate his own restlessness and to develop concrete coping behaviors. For instance, in one class when he feels restlessness coming on, he could freely ask for an egg timer. With the egg timer he could then go outside into a circumscribed area of the hall and sit until the timer ran down. By this time he would be feeling calmer and could return to class.

The child as an active source of change is also incorporated into the remediation program. In addition to the teaching of self-control that has been outlined above, weekly conferences are held between teacher and child. During these conferences the child's difficulties and progress are discussed in concrete terms. Problem foci for the following week(s) are delineated and procedures for handling difficulties are outlined. At first, the child may have difficulty initiating goals and delineating helping procedures. If so, he is

---

[1] It is important that the teacher label the impulses appropriately. Otherwise mislabeling with consequent increase in arousal and maladaptive behavior may occur.

gradually helped by the teacher to learn to express himself in these areas. In such situations, one of the goals of teacher and child often is helping the child to become an active source of change.

Regarding mechanisms for change, the primary framework is behavior modification. A check mark system contingent on desirable work and inter-personal behaviors is used where needed.[2] Checks are accumulated and traded in for articles purchased at the weekly "store." More desirable items cost more check marks. In addition to tangible positive reinforcement, withdrawal of positive reinforcement (e.g., privileges) and time out procedures are utilized. Shaping, fading, modeling and role playing are other behavioral procedures that are used. In addition, play is incorporated. Play is a positive reinforcement in itself. In addition, it provides a sphere within which compe-tent interpersonal behaviors can be learned.

Thus, the program incorporates elements that are frequently considered humanistic into a behavioristic matrix. Internal loci of change, the child as an active source of change, and the mechanism of play, are included in a frame-work that is basically behavioristic in orientation.

The affective-behaviorism program, with some variations, has been in existence for three years. Fifty-five children, ages 7–14, have been in the classes during this time. When these children are independently rated as improved, worse, or the same by at least two school personnel the following statistics emerge: 83.7% of the 55 children have improved, 3.7% are worse and 12.7% are the same. Additional analysis indicate that 35% of the 83.7% improved children have improved to the extent that they have been able to transition (transfer), or are in the current process of transitioning, to a regular class. An additional 7% have transitioned to a class containing children with less severe problems. These children will probably transition to a regular class within 1–2 years. Of the remaining children rated as improved, 28% represent youngsters who have additional handicaps such as retardation. These children have also improved sufficiently to transition out of a class for the emotionally disturbed to a class appropriate for their residual handicaps (e.g., a class for educable retarded youngsters). Thus, 70% of the children rated as improved have actually been able to transition to a more desirable placement.

Control classes were not available during the three years. However, some internal comparisons can be made. For instance one of the classes shifted to the affective-behavioral approach after one year of a modified Axlinian (non-directional) approach where relationship factors and reflection of feeling were

[2] After awhile, tangible rewards are not needed and social reinforcements are sufficient.

highlighted. There were nine children in the class the first Axlinian year. Three of these youngsters were rated as improved at the end of the year; three were the same; and three were worse. If the nine children are divided into those with substantial aggressive behavior problems and those without such problems, the improvements breakdown indicates that all three of the improved children did not have any substantial behavior problems. In contrast, the remaining six children all had aggressive behavior problems; and none of these youngsters improved under the Axlinian approach. In fact, the behavior of three of the children deteriorated dramatically. All six of these behavior problem children have received yearly ratings of improvement since the class has shifted to an affective-behavioral program. In fact, next year five of the six children will be in a regular class or improved special class situation. These data suggest that a conjoint affective-behavioral approach may be more effective than a more traditional humanistic approach with children who have aggressive behavior problems. As for the three nonaggressive children mentioned above, they continued to improve when the class shifted to an affective-behavioral approach. No differential rate of improvement under the Axlinian and affective-behavioral approaches is apparent. It appears that both approaches are equally effective with children who do not manifest substantial aggressive or conduct problem behaviors.

The results of the affective-behaviorism program in the emotionally disturbed class containing the most difficult children should also be discussed. Eight children were in this class at the inception of the program three years ago. The behavior of these children had been deteriorating before placement in this class. After one year of the affective-behaviorism program, three of these children had not only reversed their previous pattern of steadily declining behavior, but had improved sufficiently to leave the class for a class containing children with less severe problems. Since then, all three children have maintained their progress; and two of them probably will be in regular classes next year.

The three children under discussion all displayed conduct problems. Three of the remaining five children also manifested substantial aggressive behavior as well as other problems. Two of these children have improved substantially and will be in an improved special class placement next year. In sum then, five of the six behavior problem children with a previously deteriorating behavior baseline have not only reversed their declining trend but have improved substantially. The remaining two children do not display many aggressive or conduct problem behaviors. One of these children is rated as improved; and one is rated as the same. These ratings suggest once again that the affective behaviorism is particularly helpful for aggressive as compared with nonaggressive children.

The usefulness of affective behaviorism as compared with a straightforward humanistic approach with behavior problem children has been discussed. Issue could also be raised about the relative utility of the affective-behaviorism program and a behavior modification approach that does not highlight affect labeling training. Data concerning this issue is not presently available. However, as affective behaviorism incorporates many of the standard behavior modification features, it is anticipated that its effectiveness should at least be equal to the more standard approach. In addition, by its active incorporation of the child in the change process, affective behaviorism offers an avenue for increasing the contribution of the child in the behavior change process. It offers a concrete method for integrating humanism and behavior modification tenets in remediation efforts with children.

*   *   *   *   *

The Gilda Gold Memorial Fund has been established at Syracuse University to support work in areas consistent with Gilda Gold's research interests. Data about the fund and its projects can be obtained from Dr. Arnold P. Goldstein, Department of Psychology, Syracuse University, Syracuse, New York 13210.

PART VII

Humanism and Behaviorism in Broader Perspective

INTRODUCTION

The psychosocial perspectives in this part argue that the behaviorists' emphasis on the environment and the humanists' emphasis on the person are limited. Both approaches are seen to have serious dysfunctional effects in understanding human nature, application in therapy, and intervention in society. Despite the behaviorists' theoretical emphasis on environmental contingencies and a person's past history of reinforcement as influencers of behavior, behaviorists tend, in practice, to ignore the person's past. What do behaviorists mean by the environment—is it the natural environment, the manmade physical environment, the social environment, the interpersonal environment, the community, or the environment the person has constructed for himself by his past behaviors at crucial choice points? The behavioristic definition of the environment as contingencies of reinforcement is an apparently specific, yet really vague, definition. Systematic knowledge concerning each of the above environments and the interdependencies between systems is needed to more fully understand the role of environments.

While humanists concentrate on the inner person and the development of inner potential, problems of nongrowth are also attributed to inhibiting factors in the environment which prohibit the person from attaining his potential (e.g., Jourard's paper). The environment is seen as separate and less important than the person. The next four articles argue that the humanistic view of the person and the environment are both impoverished and this separation "alienates" the person from his world. Mischel made a similar point earlier in the book.

The psychosocial perspectives of life history, sociology, behavioral ecology, and social learning theory attempt to broaden and supplement both humanistic and behavioristic views of man and his environment. Each article suggests integrations which would strengthen understanding of the person in his environment. This increased understanding should, in turn, increase the effectiveness of therapeutic interventions.

If a person's past and future are ignored how does this limit our understanding of the person and psychological change? "A life history perspective on personality looks at human growth and decline over the whole life span, in the context of the entire social and physical environment." This naturalistic approach is in part a reaction to systematic oversights in both behavior therapy and humanistic therapy, e.g., foreshortening of vision and failure to study long term integrative efforts within the person. Ricks and Fleming examine the context and effects of behavior therapy and humanistic therapy as they impact on a person's ongoing life. What segments of the patient's behavior and experience does the therapist engage? What are the short and long term consequences of therapy? What kinds of patients seek what kinds of therapists, and what about the therapist's characteristics make him effective or ineffective? A life history perspective also focuses attention on both patient and therapist: who is each of these people, why are they here, what were their routes into being a patient or therapist or both?

Are the psychological perspectives of humanism and behaviorism overlooking the fact of man as a social being? Devereux, focusing specifically on Jourard and Wolpe, offers a sociological perspective and criticizes the two for being sociologically naive and occasionally psychologically naive. Devereux argues that Wolpe's approach is needed but insufficient. The goals of therapy are not explicit—why are we " fixing " this person and putting him back in the world that created the problem and may do the same to other people? Devereux's sociological critique of Jourard is more pointed because of Jourard's emphasis on transcending and circumventing the " facticity " of reality of society. Devereux stresses the importance of understanding that society needs a complex fabric of social roles and differentiation to fill the myriad needs of people. Devereux also argues that Jourard and other humanists have ignored the extent to which identity and esteem are derived from adequate performance of social roles—could the transparent self be a content-free self?

Devereux argues that the responsible change agent must work within an explicit and empirically critiqued framework of values and must predict and evaluate, as far as possible, the consequences of his intervention. Using three kinds of criteria—effectiveness, efficiency, and functional adequacy—

Devereux discusses how empirical knowledge may be used to critique values.

When interventions are made by humanists and behaviorists, and when the interventions are "effective," what other repercussions occur in the systems within which the person is a part? Alexander, Dreher, and Willems analyze the humanistic and behavioristic approaches from a behavioral ecology perspective, studying the complex interdependencies between organisms and their environment over long periods of time. The authors illustrate issues that should be taken into account in study and intervention into human problem areas including: (1) Are the designer's goodwill or technologist's respect or love for his client enough to ensure positive results? (2) Are the criteria of intervention picked with care and a longitudinal perspective, even though they may have to contradict common sense and accepted social theories? (3) Are the complex interdependencies of systems including the physical environment, short range behavior and long range outcomes taken into account? Like Devereux, they maintain that before we intervene we must try to understand the relationship between man and society and how our interventions may affect a society which has interconnecting and interpenetrating levels. Their questions for behavioristic approaches include: Is there a need to study unanticipated consequences? When do we intervene? What is the relationship between outcome and antecedent conditions? A study by Willems and his colleagues demonstrates how a behavioristic approach may be valuably combined with systems analysis.

Like the life history psychologists, Alexander, Dreher, and Willems emphasize the importance of a longitudinal perspective. They question the humaneness of humanism on two issues. (1) Is a person-centered orientation humane? Often problems are due to the context or situation rather than the person and the person is wrongly blamed. (2) Are the humanists vulnerable to the issue of cumulative entrapment? The authors argue that what may be good and permissible for an individual in the short run may not be good for either the individual or society in the long run, if all individuals do it.

Bandura's article demonstrates that some behavioral theorists are grappling with the social implications of their work. Bandura presents new social learning viewpoints which require us to re-evaluate and broaden our interpretations of humanism and especially behaviorism. He criticizes the critics of behavior theory as dealing with outmoded stereotypes, the radical behaviorists as presenting incomplete views of man, and the humanists' view of potential and actualization as shortsighted. Bandura raises the issue of whether it is appropriate to equate behavior theory with conditioning and thus with salivating dogs (e.g., as Jourard does on page 42). Is learning in humans mechanical and reflexive or are the effects of most reinforcements cognitively mediated? Bandura criticizes the radical behaviorists for discussing only the role of external sources of reinforcement and ignoring the role of self-reinforcement, self-regulated behavior, and observational learning. (Gold's work and Curtiss work are examples of programs which combine external reinforcement and self-regulation.) Several of the humanists' views are examined by Bandura. For example, can a society rely on control by conscience to ensure moral and ethical conduct?

In the second half of his paper, Bandura presents social learning views to deal with the humanistic issues of freedom, determinism, and dignity. Bandura, like Mischel, argues that psychology has to deal with the reciprocal influence by which each person plays an active role in creating his environment, which will in turn have strong effects on his next behavior. In his conclusion, Bandura discusses his view of the relationship between psychology and personal and social change.

Humanistic and Behavioral Approaches from a Life History Perspective

DAVID F. RICKS

University of Cincinnati

AND PATRICIA FLEMING

Counseling Center, Queens College, Flushing, NY 11367

Like humanism and behaviorism, life history psychology is more an orientation than a unified set of scientific facts. But in recent years many American and European investigators have found that a life history framework can serve to comprehend and organize data from fields as diverse as biology, psychiatry, psychology, sociology, and history (Waddington, 1968; White and Watt, 1973; Lidz, 1968; Baltes and Schaie, 1973; Ricks *et al.*, 1974). We will begin by outlining a few principles of life history research and their implications for all systems of psychotherapy. We then explore what these principles suggest for behavioral and humanistic approaches to intervention in life processes. Although we will make some particular value judgments, our general aim will not be to evaluate the two approaches. The main contribution of a life history perspective is to open up new ways of thinking about both.

THE LIFE HISTORY PERSPECTIVE

Our observational unit is the whole human life, from conception and birth through development of attachments, commitments, and skills to decline, disengagement, and death. Change is continuous throughout life, and apparent homeostasis in adult life or any other period often represents ignorance of homeorhesis, i.e., time extended, biologically and socially regulated processes (Levinson *et al.*, 1974; Vaillant, 1974) that in fact take place. Life history researchers aim to describe lives in as much detail as is necessary to represent

269

their complexity and organization. The research worker's observations are likely to be naturalistic rather than laboratory-based. Comprehension and prediction, rather than control, is usually the main test of theory. As an empirical science, life history research is particularly concerned with observation, multiple sources of information, hard data. Rather than concerning itself with the opinions and the hopes of therapists of various schools, life history research asks a humbling question: What is the evidence? What are the normative outcomes for people who suffer from a particular disorder at a particular age, and what differences from the expected outcomes are produced by psychotherapy?

From a life history perspective, the interplay of age, sex, institutions, and life tasks is crucial. Early autism and symbiotic disorders involve inability to establish a relationship with a person, or to get beyond a single exclusive attachment—and such problems develop in particular kinds of families (Speers and Lansing, 1965). Problems such as learning disabilities and school phobia are diagnosed in relation to societal demand for school attendance and learning. Delinquency and drug abuse reach peaks of incidence in late adolescence, apparently in relation to peer influences in that developmental period. Schizophrenia seems a particular danger of young adult life, the time at which one is severing family ties and getting out into the adult world. From this perspective, then, the timing and setting of psychotherapy become major issues. Do we treat only adults who come to us, or do we intervene in childhood, in the hope that work during this sensitive, malleable period may prevent later pain as well as alleviate current problems? An adequate sense of where the patient is, in terms of his own particular life trajectory, becomes central. Different therapies may be differently appropriate for different ages and stages of life. They may also complement or conflict with the institutions most involved with those stages. Can a behavior therapist, for instance, become an unwitting agent of an oppressive school system when he undertakes to shape children into calm and disciplined achievement? May a humanistic therapist set himself against legitimate family goals when he promotes the autonomy and self-determination of a child patient? Does psychotherapy enhance and support life, or can it become a substitute for living, an endless and ultimately damaging prolongation of youth and dependency into periods of life more properly concerned with adult endeavors and relationships? (Brody, 1973).

The trajectory of an individual's development can be understood only in the context of his particular epigenetic landscape. Psychotherapy is one influence among many. Parental expectations and one's own abilities, one's place or lack of place in a peer group, educational and job movement form the context of therapy. Access to other helping persons may do more than a particular treatment to determine outcome (Groeschel, 1974). When a therapist and patient enter into a therapeutic contact, each brings with him his own reference groups. Whether the patient is a member of the "friends and supporters of psychotherapy" (Kadushin, 1969), or a reluctant child forced to choose between psychotherapy and institutional placement, can determine much of what goes on between therapist and patient.

Social movements, among them schools of psychotherapy, are as much involved in the web of history as are individual patients. Why are we devoting attention to humanistic and behavioral methods in this volume to the neglect of psychoanalysis? Our guess is that most psychoanalytic propositions are true in the sense that the curative processes discovered by Freud and his successors can be observed reliably in a particular set of patients under the special conditions of psychoanalysis, i.e., lying on a couch for several 45 or 50 minute sessions per week, talking to a specially trained, usually older, usually male, analyst. But the group of patients who are both suitable for psychoanalysis and interested in it seems to be dwindling (Malan, 1973), and the psychoanalytic procedure has not, in 70 years of use, shown its relevance for numerous clear and present human problems. The topics most hotly debated in current psychoanalytic seminars are schizoid phenomena, depression, and narcissism, all issues important to a person, or a movement, undergoing social withdrawal. Psychoanalysis has not failed in any scientific or intellectual sense, but because of its degeneration into a small priestly caste, with esoteric and costly rites that put it out of the reach of people who are overly old, overly young, too poor, or not verbal enough, it is failing in terms of broad contribution to human welfare. The king has not been driven out, but he seems to be trying to abdicate, and what we are investigating in this book is the claim to succession of two lusty, growing offspring.

For patient and therapist alike, life begins well before therapy, and it ends long after (hopefully). We can visualize therapy as a period in which the developmental trajectory of a patient intersects with that of a therapist. The period, however lengthy, is never indefinite. Like education, tax consultation, or prostitution, psychotherapy is understood to be time-limited, one episode in a life. This distinguishes psychotherapy from those relationships like marriage, parenthood, or membership in the Republican party, that are ideally considered to be life long commitments open to termination only under extreme duress. How one comes to be a patient, and what happens afterward, are as important to our understanding as what happens within the period of therapy. From a life history perspective, we have to ask why people come to a therapist, what they expect to get, and whether their expectations are fulfilled (Strupp, *et al.*, 1962; Balkin, 1974). We can also ask if they find benefits that they did not anticipate. Levinson (1974) has suggested that a therapist may be a mentor, and that if this is so, then one important period in therapy can come in the years after the relationship formally terminates. The ex-patient now tests out, in the laboratory of his own ongoing life experience, ideas and ways of the therapist introjected years earlier. This post-therapy effect is one of the best reasons for considering psychotherapy as an episode with an end point rather than an end in itself.

There is also a career line leading into, and sometimes beyond, therapist-hood (Levinson, 1972; Kopp, 1971; Dumont, 1968; Henry *et al.*, 1971). We can fruitfully investigate life history differences between psychotherapists who choose different approaches, e.g., between the antecedents and attitudes of humanistic and behavioristic therapists (Schaeffer, 1971). It is also becoming practical to look at a psychotherapy relationship as a system, and to ask which patterns of therapist–patient relationship are typical, which approach an ideal, and which result in trouble (Orlinsky and Howard, 1975). Different therapists seem to help or harm different people, an issue we will examine in more detail later.

The question of adequate conceptual models for therapist and patient is particularly complex for the life history psychologist. To understand oneself is a hard enough task for most people, and to construct a model that permits comprehensive understanding and prediction for another, with a minimum of distortion and bias, is a supreme task. There is little evidence that most therapists ever approach a full understanding of any particular patient. (Of course, to a behavior therapist this may not even be a sensible task or a useful one.) One therapist's inadequacy in this regard was brought home to him near the conclusion of a young woman's therapy. She brought him her diary, saying that he knew her only in terms of her troubles and conflicts. Now that she was finishing, she wanted her therapist to get at least a glimpse of her love of music, her joy in her fiancee, her pleasure in dancing. Reading that diary, he did in fact sense a person he had hardly glimpsed before. Was his experience unique?

Since our experience of another person is always partial, biased by our own perspectives and the special behavior we elicit and respond to, we always intervene in selective, biased ways. This is simply part of the human condition, and therapists are no more immune to it than surgeons, teachers, or parents. We can, however, be aware of this bias, and different therapies and their practitioners can be evaluated as to the degree of bias or distortion in their conception of the patient. One of the authors recently spent many hours in the company of a young man about whom authoritative psychiatrists are in perfect agreement. He is schizophrenic and from this follows a regimen of drug treatment and hospitalization appropriate to current understanding of that diagnosis. But long conversations with this intelligent, self-centered, mocking adolescent suggest that his institutional caretakers see only a part of him. Like Hamlet, he is crazy when he thinks the situation demands it, but the rest of the time he seems no more out of contact than those who approach him through the conceptual constrictions induced by the rubric of schizophrenia.

In the following sections, some of the models used by different therapies will be examined. Looking to the evidence, we will also ask whether different therapies get the results at which they aim. And if they do get these results, do they get them for the reasons they themselves give? For example, many psychoanalysts think that behavior therapists reduce symptoms primarily because they have developed a systematic method for exploiting positive transference. Their cures are therefore real, but liable to later regression, since they depend upon an ongoing unanalyzed relationship with the therapist. Behaviorists sometimes claim that humanistic therapists do not cure real symptoms, but only provide a 20th century form of religious conversion and identity. From a life history perspective these are questions not only for debate, but for information. Science proceeds by the intrusion of data into controversy.

REFLECTIONS ON BEHAVIOR THERAPIES[1]

On what part of a human life does the behavior therapist focus? How broad is this focus? Contrary to most observers, though not all (Locke, 1971), we think that the primary focus of Wolpe's behavior therapy is on the patient's *inner life*. Not since Titchener has anyone worked as hard as Wolpe to differentiate subtle gradations of inner experience. His method is not Watsonian, Hullian, or Pavlovian, but a neo-Titchenerian concern with sensation and emotion. And Wolpe further narrows the focus. Rather than looking at a broad range of human emotions (Wessman and Ricks, 1966) he concentrates on gradations of a particular emotion, anxiety. We would not argue that all

[1] The following discussion of behavior therapy, and particularly Wolpe's approach, owes much to conversations with Paul L. Wachtel and Jeanne Marachek.

behaviorists are so concerned with inner sensations as Wolpe is. Peterson (1968), for instance, does a magnificent job of analyzing the current life situations of his patients, and the research of many behaviorists on situational determinants of behavior (Mischel, 1968) is far from introspective. Inspection of Wolpe's (1969) dialogues with patients shows that the uninformed bias that his methods are shallow, superficial, concerned only with overt responses, is simply wrong. Narrow, yes. Shallow, no.

It may be helpful to differentiate behavior therapists as to the amount of inner life they accept and are willing to engage. At one extreme would be dedicated Skinnerians, devoted to the idea of the empty organism emitting hard little units of countable behavior. Wolpe is far from this extreme, but he is by no means the most "internal" of the behavior therapists. This position might be reserved for those interested in broad spectrum therapies (Lazarus, 1971), in the interpersonal relationship set up in therapy (Bergin, 1967a,b), and in the phenomena of self-regulation (Franks and Wilson, 1973; Gold, this book). Here we find a concern with commitment, choice, and cognition that is almost directly opposed to the early Skinnerian model. Since these are crucial long term determinants of behavior, concern with them is evidence that behavior therapy is reaching responsible maturity.

Another hallmark of Wolpe's approach, as central as concern with dreams in psychoanalysis, is his work with the patient's fantasy. He uses fantasy narrowly, as an approach to the understanding and control of anxiety arousal, and not as a naturally occurring event of great human interest, as Murray (1938), McClelland (1961), and Singer (1966) understand it. But again, the concern is with inner life. This emphasis on fantasy is equally striking in Lazarus' (1971) development of behavior rehearsal techniques. From a life history standpoint, this concern with fantasy is to be applauded. Like emotion, fantasy is a long term integrator and organizer of personality. Any therapy hoping to have long term effects and to understand them has to take such internal variables into account.

What kind of influence does the therapist attempt to exert? In the life space of the patient, what earlier or later persons does he resemble? What kind of attachment does he expect his patients to form to him? The methods for locating a therapist inside the patient's interpersonal world exist (Kelly, 1955; Ricks, 1972), but little research has been done on the problem. Psychoanalysts expect transference reactions to reflect the immediate family group of the patient—father, mother, elder siblings—and there is much clinical evidence to support this. Who does the behavior therapist resemble? It is apparent in Wolpe's discussion that he hopes to be seen as an expert, similar to dentists, physicians, and similar problem-solvers who have been presented with particular pains and symptoms in the patient's life and made them better. There is no attempt here to be any kind of new parent to the patient, nor does Wolpe give evidence of any grandiose rescue fantasies. We imagine that Wolpe would be embarrassed if a follower were to refer to him the way Freud's followers sometimes do, as "the master" (Brill, 1938). Unlike humanistic therapists, with their emphasis on self-disclosure, Wolpe has no need to aspire to a goal of great wisdom, of living an exemplary life, for he has a more modest technical goal, that of being a skilled healer of particular focal problems. There is much to admire in anyone who aspires to be a good craftsman, a skilled worker. This is a limited goal, but one that can be achieved. What is missing in Wolpe's work, though not in that of Bergin or Lazarus, is a systematic theory of the therapeutic relationship, how it is formed, maintained, used for the benefit of the patient, and terminated.

What career line leads one into the particular situation of consulting a behavior therapist? This issue has not been studied as much as the comparable question of what leads one to see a psychoanalytically or somatically oriented psychiatrist (MacIver and Redlich, 1959; Kreitman, 1962). Our impression is that many behavior therapy patients are like two groups often seen by somatically oriented psychiatrists: one group is adult, poor, female, and low in educational level; the other group consists of children who raise social problems or provoke authorities. The adult patients are people for whom submission to authority may be more often enforced than it is for most of us, while the children are often rebellious but faced with authoritative pressures to change their behavior. In both groups behavioral transformations are expected to occur rapidly, with minimal personal investment of effort, and often for the sake of people other than the patient. A study of the attitudes of people who would choose to see a behavior therapist (Jacobson, 1970) indicates that they are dependent, authoritarian, and looking for induced cure rather than a corrective emotional experience. Perhaps PADUFA (poor, authoritarian, dependent, undereducated, female, adult)[2] and SLODS (slow learning, overactive, disorganized schoolboy) can join YAVIS (young, attractive, verbal, intelligent, successful) (Schofield, 1964) in the pantheon of patients.

What is the career line of the behavior therapist? We know of no research comparable to that done by Henry and his colleagues (1971) on the origins of

---

[2] An important exception may be the growing number of middleclass men and women who are referred to behavior therapists for removal of specific sexual inhibitions.

other therapists. Our observations suggest that behavior therapy has so far had more appeal to psychologists than to psychiatrists or social workers. And within psychology its appeal has been particularly to people whose earlier work was in experimental psychology and learning. Training in experimental psychology biases one toward thinking mainly about observable data, and not positing underlying processes or structures. In contrast, Freud's and Goldstein's training in neurology, like Murray's in surgery, embryology, and biochemistry, made them comfortable with ideas about underlying long term needs and internal organizers.

This brings us to the model through which the patient is interpreted. Psychoanalysis has always coexisted with, and tried to provide understanding for, the traditional psychiatric categories of neurosis, psychosis, and character disorder. This heritage has been an asset when it required attention to observable differences between patients, and thus lent an empirical, observational quality to a discipline prone to deal in hypothetical relationships between posited internal entities. But psychiatrically trained psychoanalysts sometimes let their concepts frame too strictly the information they gather, so that a patient is seen as a "compulsive," "character disorder," or "schizophrenic," not as a human being at a particular point in his life, facing his own set of problems, in a unique network of relationships, showing symptoms only suggestive of a given syndrome. To the extent that Wolpe uses a traditional psychiatric perspective he inherits the values and the limitations of this system. Behavior therapists who have emphasized the degree to which each person's behavior is immediately responsive to his personal environment, on the other hand, are beginning to develop new interactive ways of conceptualizing human behavior patterns. There is value in traditional psychiatric models, but it ought to be recognized that they were developed to think about cohorts of patients different from those today, living in institutions unlike those of the last couple of decades, and so are less useful now than the newer models being developed.

It is of course possible that a therapist can misunderstand a patient, interpret the patient's problems in biased and inappropriate ways, and yet somehow, by caring, believing in what he is doing, and simply trying, make a positive difference in the patient's life (Fish, 1973). This is what all therapists do much of the time. Do behavior therapists help more than therapists trained through other routes? Their literature has much more rhetoric about science than that of other groups, some of it quite extreme in tone (Eysenck, 1970). The evidence for behavior therapy has been thoughtfully reviewed (Franks and Wilson, 1973) and the various therapies compared (Bergin, 1971). We will not duplicate these reviews here. Our conclusion is that these methods do help, and our view of the literature of behavior therapy over time shows an impressive cumulative curve, with increasingly sophisticated designs, more work on real problems (overweight, smoking, alcoholism, high blood pressure, compulsions, sexual dysfunctions, stuttering) and less on minor and unimportant phobias. We are also impressed with the willingness that behavior therapists have shown to criticize their own work and the work of other behavior therapists. Improving methods of therapy is a pressing need for all therapists, and there can be no real improvement in our work without honest discussion of failures, improvements that fail to last, or improvements that come unexpectedly and for reasons we fail to understand.

We can hope in the next few years to read reports of effective new behavioral techniques for helping hyperactive and slow-learning children, two groups we can diagnose with increasing sophistication but frequently fail to help after diagnosis. We can also hope that there will be increasing study of how to modify negative emotions other than anxiety, for example, studies of behavior therapy with problems of hostility, depression (Seligman, 1973) and apathy. And though it may make the neat designs of behavior therapists look fuzzier, we hope that they will study each case to see whether they get results in addition to those intended.

A few years ago a student was in behavioral treatment to cure her fear of flying. She reported that during the last phases of her therapy she not only achieved this particular goal, but also (a) became more able to stand up for herself with her parents, brother, and husband, (b) found herself talking up in class, and volunteering to make reports, for the first time in her life, and (c) became much more sharing with other women and less competitive with them. These changes had brought several new satisfactions, so that they had a very good likelihood of lasting. But it was also apparent that she positively worshipped the therapist who had produced all of these changes in her life. This aspect of her cure is less than ideal, but the rest of her changes were impressive.

Since one of the speculations of critics has been that behavior therapy increases dependency by exploiting positive transference, and therefore fosters depressed and hopeless feelings, changes like the initiative and assertiveness of this student are important evidence—if they are fairly common and if they last. There is as yet little long term follow-up research on the results of behavior therapy. Lazarus (1971) reports a disappointingly high rate of recurrence of symptoms, while some follow-ups of other forms of therapy (Balkin, 1974) present a contrasting picture of continued growth and happiness.

REFLECTIONS ON HUMANISTIC PSYCHOTHERAPIES

The language of humanistic psychologists suggests a much broader focus, and a longer perspective, than we have been discussing. Humanistic therapists talk about optimal personality functioning, self-realization of potentials and capacities, personal integration, psychological freedom, transcendence of the immediate demand character of the environment, and development of an internal locus of control (Mahrer and Pearson, 1971). These terms suggest a long view of life: optimization of any function is likely to be a matter of extensive trial and refinement of controls, self-realization is a long term project, freedom is the classic goal of education and citizenship. "You shall know the truth, and the truth shall make you free." But in contrast to traditional humanistic beliefs, there is also in this movement a focus on the here and now. Particularly in the work of Perls (1969) and in the encounter group movement, we find rejection both of past history and of future plans, in favor of immediate sensory awareness. This may be only an adaptation to an emerging California life style built around permanent transience. But we think it goes deeper. The core of humanistic psychotherapy is coming into touch with one's own emotions. History and anticipation are dismissed because both are thought to draw attention away from present feeling. But there is evidence that emotion is in fact not limited to present experience—few adults can recall an angry or loving parent without strong emotion, and to deny human beings the pleasures and pains of anticipation would make us dull indeed. An emphasis on emotion here and now is, of course, an extremely helpful *technique* in all forms of psychotherapy, whether one is talking about transference and resistance, constructing a hierarchy of anxiety-evoking stimuli, or commenting on the white knuckles of the young man who has just been telling you he bears you no ill will whatsoever. But humanistic psychotherapists are unique in combining insistence on the importance of emotion and restriction of focus to emotions at the present moment. This is a major flaw, and one likely to be corrected only when humanistic psychotherapists stop reacting against what they perceive as the Freudian emphasis on the past and begin constructing a truly comprehensive psychology of experience that will integrate past, present, and future. The primitive, debased conception of emotion apparent in therapies that consist of screaming, hitting, and kicking the floor in mindless "discharge" is far from furthering the noble goals of self-realization and development of a mature character. What we have in this offshoot of the human potential movement is not a scientific advance, but a reaction we think best interpreted in political terms. As Freudian psychology has become progressively more intricate, cognitive, focused on interpretation and working through rather than spontaneous abreaction, an increasingly one-sided psychology of the ego, not the person, this reaction has emphasized the emotional side of human life. Commenting on a similar earlier movement in philosophy, J. S. Mill (1869) said: "It is one of the characteristic prejudices of the reaction of the nineteenth century against the eighteenth, to accord to the unreasoning elements in human nature the infallibility which the eighteenth is supposed to have ascribed to the reasoning elements." A wholistic view of human nature must take both into account, and can accord infallibility to neither reason nor feeling. This is what Kraepelin meant when he wrote about the "higher integrative emotions, such as love and hope," and it is what humanistic psychologists like Tomkins (1963a,b) and Stotland (1969) are concerned with in their discussions of how emotions integrate impulse and control, the push of bodily needs and the resistant push of social demands.

Their therapeutic focus on the immediate present has led many humanistic therapists to a theoretical position that is as ahistorical as the outmoded, and now discarded, behavioristic position that the symptom *is* the neurosis. This leaves the humanistic therapist, like early behavior therapists, no comprehensive way of responding to the patient who is striving toward an integration of past and present selves ("I used to have all of these friends, and we did things together, but now I want to do things on my own.") Nor does it help the therapist understand people who sense in themselves a kind of mourning for lost potentials ("I used to think I would be a really good painter, but now I seem to lose interest."). Above all, it makes it impossible to understand those times, frequent in any therapy, when a patient regresses or goes back to earlier ways, usually to form a new base for further maturation, sometimes to stay regressed. From a life history point of view, any adequate theory of psychotherapy must be able to comprehend changes in behavior and feeling as having a temporal dimension. Personality is formed over time, and it is changed over time. To put all of one's energies into the immediate present simply ignores too much of human life to be helpful on more than a short term basis.

Is there a particular age, or social group, to which humanistic therapies seem particularly appropriate? The answer can be sought in terms of the strengths and the weaknesses of the humanistic approach. Are there people, then, who are not suffering any clear behavioral deficits, not showing any cognitive disturbances, and yet seem out of touch with experience and feeling? The answer to this is a clear " yes." The main group in question is composed of intelligent late adolescents and young adults, cognitively well educated, who have submitted to social programming so thoroughly that they have lost touch with themselves and so suffer excruciating problems of commitment and choice (Fagen and Shepherd, 1973). To such young people, a Rogerian " you feel" is often not only a depth interpretation, it is a revelation. Learning to base choice and action on feeling is for them an intensely curative experience. In psychoanalytic psychotherapy such people can intellectualize endlessly. One once wrote a class paper in which he catalogued and carefully distinguished 42 different defenses. Another went into psychoanalysis at age twenty-six because she could not bring herself to marry " the man I am madly in love with." At age twenty-nine, still in analysis and unmarried, she made a decision—to go to social work school and become a psychotherapist. Psychoanalysis, in its current refined state, is often of limited service to such young people. But humanist psychotherapies, with their emphasis on getting in touch with immediate feelings and experiencing them in all of their fascinating depth, are as specific to this disorder as a dietary supplement is to its specific deficiency disease. Whether humanistic therapies can be modified in ways that will make them equally useful to children (Axline, 1964; Moustakas, 1959) or to that vast mass of people overlooked or shoved aside by modern technological societies (Ryan, 1966) remains to be demonstrated conclusively, but the possibility is there. The best current evidence for this scope is the schizophrenia project of Rogers *et al.* (1967). Humanistic psychotherapies may also be especially useful in helping older people and dying people to come to terms with life before it ends for them.

Most studies of humanistic psychotherapy have shown little concern for long term outcome. It has not been clear what general criteria should be used, since each client might have a unique goal and a unique outcome. But in the Wisconsin schizophrenia research one traditional psychiatric criterion for the treatment of schizophrenia, number of days spent out of the hospital, was carefully evaluated during successive six month periods for nine years (Truax and Mitchell, 1971). No evidence anywhere in psychotherapy research is more convincing than their clear demonstration that schizophrenic patients who worked with therapists capable of accurate empathy, nonpossessive warmth, and simple human genuineness (something like Jourard's transparency), got better and stayed better, while control patients improved more slowly and patients seen by less capable therapists finished the follow-up period more often hospitalized than the controls. Note that the characteristics that made this difference were not variables of training, degrees, or technical skills. Any intelligent, patient, and diligent person can in time possess academic or professional degrees. Skills can be modeled and taught. A good deal of research has been devoted to whether the special qualities of personality involved in accurate empathy, nonpossessive warmth, and emotional honesty can be enhanced through training. The conclusion seems to be that they can. But this involves us in a larger issue. If a person aims to become a physicist, his plan can involve courses to take, skills to master, concepts and apparatus to be understood. On the other hand, if a person aspires to empathy and warmth, he may be planning changes in his whole personality and life style. Perhaps the only way to get good therapists in adequate numbers is to facilitate the process of change by selecting already gifted pupils, as advanced music teachers do. But do we know how to select for empathic talent? Even more threatening is the possibility that the only way to teach these qualities is to model them for students. But how many teachers of therapists have this capacity? This is not so large an issue in forms of psychotherapy that focus on role, technique, or environmental change, but for the humanistic psychotherapist it is all important. Here the therapist must not only do something helpful, he must *be* a helpful person. He is not a technician, however high level, but a model, mentor, and exemplar. The demands on the therapist are extreme, and they are made worse by the lack of any systematic theory of transference reactions and ways of resolving them. The result can be un-recognized dependency of the client on the therapist, and extreme difficulty resolving this dependency. Rogers (1967) has provided a very personal and moving account of his own struggles with a dependent client who put him in this dilemma.

What is the experiential line that leads one into the chair opposite a humanistic therapist, into a human potential group, or perhaps into an Esalen pool? We have mentioned that the patient tends to be young and intelligent and at loose ends. Often the route into clienthood goes through the doors of a college counseling center. Other clients are recruited through public lectures or demonstrations. Unlike the current generation of psychoanalysts, humanistic therapists tend to have a temporary but intense "star quality" like that of popular entertainers. A few years ago we attended three crowded lectures by one of the stars, Ronald Laing, and were much impressed by the empathy between Laing and his audience. Last year, at another

Laingian lecture, we found a new audience surprisingly out of touch with Laing. Many people walked out early, and when the lecture ended most of the questions had to do not with Laing's ideas but with his opinions of a newer but much less-gifted man. Why is there this worship, and why is it so fleeting? Our impression is that many of the recruits to humanistic therapy and to its sets of groupies are from Protestant or nonreligious backgrounds, usually middle class, and often alienated from their parents. Having cut loose from traditions and parental authority, but not having fully developed inner autonomy or personal moral authority, they are looking for a guiding voice. For the past few years, humanistic psychotherapy has provided many of "this year's" gurus.

The pathway to becoming a humanistic psychotherapist has often been through an early commitment to the Protestant clergy, followed by a decision to work in a more secular vein (e.g., Rogers, May), or through finding the human immediacy of student counseling more rewarding than the intellectual tasks of teaching. It is not surprising, then, that some humanistic therapists aspire to deliverance more than to the modest goal of delivering helping services. Other humanistic therapists have moved into psychotherapy from social work, or from school guidance. For these ex-ministers, ex-teachers, and social workers the openness of the humanistic approach, with its lack of an explicit diagnostic framework and prescribed therapeutic behavior, may serve as a loose umbrella for feelings of rejection of the establishment and an intense desire to rescue personally some of its outcasts.

What is the model through which the client is interpreted and what biases does it introduce? Probably the most general point on which humanistic therapists agree is that there is an innate growth potential possessed by every human being. This may be interpreted as modestly as Goldstein's (1940) belief that a patient's striving toward re-integration after a brain injury is at least as important as the neurological facts of the wound. Or it may be interpreted almost mystically, as a kind of healing magic within the client. Belief in this kind of growth potential justifies a relatively passive style of therapy, one that concentrates on creating a climate in which growth can take place rather than actively striving to bring about growth. The second main belief is that each person has a unique self, and that this self is organized at all times so as to achieve inner harmony, even at the expense of shutting off sensory and emotional awareness. Since being out of touch with oneself leads to painful experiences of incongruity, the job of the therapist is to get empathically in touch with the unexperienced feelings and to facilitate the client's contact with the closed off part of himself. This is probably valuable for anyone, and especially valuable for young people who are so out of touch with themselves as living organisms that mechanical terms like being "programmed" or "turning on" can feel like adequate descriptions of personal experience.

We commented earlier on the short time span involved in the humanistic focus on immediate awareness. The other major bias is the systematic neglect of all that is not felt, but merely thought, believed, or decided.

One of us once played to a psychotherapy class a therapy recording in which a woman wanted advice about whether to send her son to summer camp. The therapist spent most of the hour reflecting this desire for advice, and the client spent most of the hour reiterating her request. The result was a therapeutic impasse, mounting anger apparent in the voice of the client, and resigned negativism increasingly apparent in the therapist. The teacher was at that time an advocate of the form of therapy being demonstrated. The class had better judgment. They told the teacher that if this was psychotherapy they saw no value in it.

Humanistic psychotherapies have also been slow to help people cope with real life concerns such as poverty, racism, dangerous streets, garbage, and sick children. Many clients are looking for survival strategies in psychotherapy, and to such clients coping with everyday life is more important than sorting out one's feelings about it. Empathy is not enough in such situations. The therapist must go beyond empathy to develop concern, mutual action, and even confrontation with those who have a stake in maintaining things as they are.

Do humanistic therapies help, then? The conclusion from the best available review is that they do (Bergin, 1971). And they help not only the young, intelligent, emotionally insulated people who are their primary clients, but also deeply disturbed people. Humanistic therapists working with Rogers, or influenced by him, have done impressive work both on the measurement of therapeutic improvement and on the conditions that bring it about. Until the recent growth of behavior therapy studies, they had done more research on psychotherapy than any other group. Like behaviorists, humanistic therapists have done almost no work on primary prevention of mental disorders and not much on early intervention. However, Project Re-ED (Lewis, 1971) comes out of a humanistic framework, and its success demonstrates a potential for early intervention. Since prevention of disorder has a far broader and longer term impact than treatment, this is a most promising step.

BEYOND SCHOOLS

Doctrine and observation have a reciprocal relationship. When we lack empirical guides for conduct we look for guidance in dogma. As we accumulate experience, understand relationships, and gain in ability to predict from data, we find less need for doctrine. When we are able to throw away the crutches of elaborate theory, we recognize that a therapist is simply one person doing his best to help another person. Theories support us as we begin this task, since they alert us to things that we might not have looked for without them, but at some point any theory becomes constricting. We need to know enough to discard theories and base our intervention paradigm on what a particular person tells us about his particular problems or concerns.

The comparable movement in research is to look beyond comparisons of schools or doctrines to the practices of particular psychotherapists with particular clients. In one project, for example, we observed some impressive changes in young delinquent men, and measured some of these changes systematically (Ricks *et al.*, 1964). Since we have the data to prove it (Shore and Massimo, 1973) we can confidently assert that the therapist who worked with these boys was highly effective. However, we are not sure that his own theories could account for his effectiveness. His impact with delinquent boys might have been just as dependent on his athletic grace, his style of dress, his taste in expensive cars and intimate knowledge of their workings, his distrust of office routines and schedules. These are matters of life style, and we have little research evidence about the effect of such variables on therapeutic outcomes.

In another study, we were at first disturbed to find that most of our good outcomes were accounted for by a small group of therapists, one of whom seemed particularly adept at keeping highly vulnerable young men from becoming psychotic adults. We were interested in the characteristics of children and their families that might predict later disorder. This effect of intervention was not our concern, and its power was a complication we could have done without. But eventually it became apparent that we would be ignoring information if we did not study the methods of the most effective therapist and contrast them with the work of other people whose effects were less impressive. These methods are described in detail in another article (Ricks, 1974). What we want to emphasize here is that this effective therapist is extremely different from the other. He is a quiet, reticent New England Yankee, very calm, extremely realistic, the kind of person one sees on the street and asks for directions with implicit faith that the directions will be clear and direct. The children with whom he was most effective were quite different from those seen by Massimo, victims rather than angry and rebellious, scared of other people rather than frightening to those around them. The criteria for outcomes were also different. Judging from the fates of our control group boys, not working with Massimo meant a 70% chance for being arrested later. Not being clients of Young, given the movement that this sample had made toward psychosis, was likely to mean later hospitalization.

The findings in these studies have brought us to a position similar to that of Jourard (p. 37), that therapeutic influence probably reflects the personality and life style of the therapist. After an extensive review of the research literature, Bergin comes to a similar conclusion.

" Our faith is that whatever is powerful in traditional therapy resides in the work of a minority of its practitioners . . . We assume that there is little reason to reinforce or reassure the ordinary practitioner of psychotherapy, for we expect future research to show that his labors must be revised toward matching the behavior of a few successful peers who actually obtain most of the therapeutic results. It is also likely that observation of their styles will eventually yield completely new techniques focused around the actual therapeutic agents that are identified and extracted from their practice." [Bergin, 1971, p. 263.]

To many practitioners this position holds nothing new. They may conclude only that researchers, being slow learners, have finally begun to realize something long talked about among therapists—that psychotherapy is an art and like all artistic performances requires a talent that is widely admired (e.g. Fromm–Reichman, Axline, Mahler, Perls), frequently aspired to and seldom possessed. As a side effort in one psychotherapy study, we once asked their colleagues to rank the effectiveness of a number of therapists for whom we could construct outcome ratios based on several patients. It was reassuring to find that colleagues not only agreed with each other (which may have reflected an unusually high amount of interstaff consultation practiced in the excellent institution studied) but that their pooled assessment of competence agreed exactly with our outcome data. So in part we are only saying that research supports clinical practice. But we also mean to go well beyond current clinical practice. We need to do many more systematic, long term, life history comparisons of psychotherapists in terms of their therapeutic impact and its converse, deterioration effects. And following these, we need to do intensive case studies of those few therapists whose results indicate that they might be models and mentors to us all. Our emphasis in clinical research has generally been on only one participant in the clinical interaction. As psychotherapists, we know more about our patients than we know about ourselves. Often we are like Polonius, saying things that suggest practical wisdom and then behaving foolishly. No wonder that psychoanalysts have replaced mothers-in-law and ministers as the favorite subject for cartoons! Luckily the cure for this disharmony is well known to psychotherapists. It consists of listening carefully to others, particularly to one's critics, and then doing some thoughtful self-searching. Much of this self-searching can be carried out in one's own psychotherapy, in conversation with a good therapy supervisor, or with colleagues. Part of it may come in symposia like the one in which we participate here.

CONCLUSION

A life history perspective on personality looks at human growth and decline over the whole life span, in the context of the entire social and physical environment. Life history psychology aims to be an empirical science, emphasizing as its methods naturalistic description and long term prediction. From this perspective psychotherapy is seen as an episode in the life of the patient or client, one influence among many competing or complementing influences. Any one patient is also one episode in the life of the psychotherapist, and the period in which patient and therapist influence each other is always time limited.

We have been concerned with the segment of the patient's behavior or experience with which the therapist makes contact, the context of therapy, the kind of influence that the therapist tries to effect, the model he uses to help him perceive and understand the patient, and the evidence for whether he helps or not.

Implicit in all of the comparisons drawn above is an emerging life history oriented way of thinking about, doing, and studying psychotherapy. The life history orientation may be best exemplified at this point by Lidz or Erikson. Such a therapist would understand his patient in terms of the patient's current position in his own personal life trajectory. He would use a comprehensive and minimally biasing life history model. He would try to understand himself as well as his patient in terms of origins, developmental lines, and likely outcomes. He would have the clinical wisdom, and the research competence, to study his clinical style and methods, and to discover which patients he helped, which he left unchanged, and which he harmed. Knowing this, he would modify his caseload appropriately, referring those patients he could not help to others who might be more useful to them. He would be as much concerned with long term outcomes as with the immediate details of his clinical interactions. He would be interested in primary prevention of distress and early intervention to prevent later distress, rather than only waiting for problems to be brought to him in adult life.

As these therapists come into being, they are likely to find much they can use in the analytic tradition of studying therapeutic relationships, much of value in techniques of behavioral intervention, much in humanistic thought that helps them comprehend their patient's inner lives. But such a therapist will work within a framework broader than any of these. Like ethology and ecology, with which it shares its general philosophical stance, life history psychology does not reject narrower disciplines but incorporates them into a broader, more inclusive framework. It is not a new school, but it already gives a new perspective to the work of all of the current schools.

Models for Man, Value Systems, and Intervention Strategies: A Sociological Critique of Wolpe and Jourard[1]

EDWARD C. DEVEREUX

Department of Human Development and Family Studies
Cornell University, Ithaca, NY 14850

In the present essay I propose to examine the underlying value orientations and therapeutic goals of Drs. Jourard and Wolpe from a sociological perspective. This approach may seem a bit unfair, since neither of them claims to be a sociologist. Both are primarily therapists, and my impression is that, in their very different ways, both are effective in these roles.

In one limited sense, as I feel Dr. Wolpe would agree, the therapist may be likened to a skilled garage mechanic. Both are experienced tinkerers who have developed some facility at dealing with the specific problems or "presenting symptoms" of the automobile or patient committed to their care. We may judge their effectiveness pragmatically: did their efforts result in the car's running better, in the patient's feeling better? In this case, the values of the customer or patient are accepted, uncritically, as "given."

But in a broader sense, the parallel rather quickly breaks down. Most garage mechanics do not write and talk about their work in general terms, and we do not expect them to come up with a general analysis of transportation systems and their functional or dysfunctional attributes. Therapists, on the other hand, are highly articulate and presumably responsible professionals, given to talking and writing about their work and contributing in their way to

[1] The author acknowledges with thanks the thoughtful criticisms and comments made by Professor Henry Alker and by the editors of this volume on earlier drafts of this paper. While the present draft has been influenced by their critiques, not all of their suggestions could be met, and the author accepts full responsibility for arguments presented in this paper.

289

our growing body of knowledge and theory about man and society. Certainly both Wolpe and Jourard have written extensively, and we have a fair sample of how they talk about their work in the symposium papers included in this book.

While neither of the participants attempted to set forth any general theory of man and society in the present symposium, I feel it is fair to review their work in such a broad perspective for two reasons. First, each has become identified as a representative of a more general position in social science—Wolpe with the general domain of behaviorism and its application in behavior modification, Jourard with the domain of humanistic psychology. Both schools have many other advocates who do not limit their work to therapy. Thus on the behaviorist side we have writers, like Skinner and Homans, who have attempted to construct general theories of man and society on the basis of the "laws of learning," and practitioners who have attempted to apply the techniques of behavior modification to education, to marriage, to politics, and to social reform generally. Similarly, on the humanist side we have the more general theories of spokesmen like Allport, Fromm, and Maslow, and attempted applications for reform in education or society generally from writers like A. S. Neil and Paul Goodman.

Second, I would argue that any responsible therapist must be guided by some either explicit or implicit theory of man and society. Whether or not he attempts to generalize from his own work, some such theory must necessarily influence the value system in terms of which he conducts his practice. For while the garage mechanic may perhaps accept the stated values of his customer, uncritically, as "given," the responsible therapist cannot and in fact usually does not. For a therapist cannot be responsive only to the stated needs and values of his client. Like the lawyer, he is also a licensed agent of society, and is obliged to take its values and interests into account.

In the present article, my thesis will be that anyone who would function as a responsible change agent—whether as therapist, social reformer, or revolutionist—must necessarily take into account not only the best available knowledge about the empirical relationships among the realities he is dealing with, but also must work within an explicit, sophisticated, and empirically critiqued framework of values; he must be able, so far as possible, both to predict and evaluate the consequences of whatever intervention he undertakes. I will argue that such a framework must necessarily take into account sociological as well as psychological variables, and that neither the behaviorist perspective of Dr. Wolpe nor the humanist perspective of Dr. Jourard is sociologically adequate.

VALUE SYSTEMS, INTERVENTIONS
STRATEGIES, AND EMPIRICAL SCIENCE

Before turning to my specific critique of the value orientations of these two therapists, I must explicate the framework I propose to employ. In what ways are value systems held to be relevant? In what ways may they be empirically critiqued? Why should therapists, working with individual patients, be expected to take sociological variables into account?

There are, of course, some behavioral scientists who hold that values are simply irrelevant for behavior; it is argued that behavior is entirely shaped and controlled by environmental contingencies, and that values, goals, attitudes, etc., are at best epiphenomena of no causal or explanatory significance. This extreme behaviorist position is most ably represented by B. F. Skinner; he scoffs at the notions of "freedom and dignity" still employed by philosophers and social scientists who form a part of what he calls the "mentalistic underground." Skinner's own behavior, in my opinion, definitively refutes his theory. His book *Beyond Freedom and Dignity* (1971) bristles with his own values and prejudices, and with proposed programs of intervention designed to move society in the directions he prefers. Environmental contingencies, skillfully manipulated by Skinner and his followers, may indeed be sufficient to shape and control some of the behavior of pigeons and even of people. But what controls the behavior of the manipulator himself? To this writer it seems quite plain that even the most radical behaviorists reserve for themselves the right and ability to design and manipulate the "independent," stimulus variables in their experiments and the "freedom" to choose the goals in terms of which they would shape behavior. Hence, in the final analysis, even the most radical behaviorists turn out to be voluntarists after all. But of course I will not begrudge them their "freedom" to protest this.

Another position, somewhat more difficult to cope with, acknowledges that values and attitudes are causally relevant, but holds that they are inherently arbitrary, matters of free individual choice, like my preference for pickles more than poetry. Indeed, Parsons (1935, 1937) has demonstrated that there are adequate empirical and theoretical grounds to require the assignment of at least some element of "freedom" in the selection of values and value systems if we are to talk about action instead of mere behavior.[2] Without this

---

[2] While all action is behavior, not all behavior is action. The theory of action is concerned with a special class of behavior which, it is argued, can be analyzed and understood only by taking

element of value freedom, action systems lose their voluntaristic character entirely, and values—together with all other subjective processes—become causally irrelevant. Were it not for this vital "freedom" assumption, all therapists would quickly be out of business. For even if the patient merely "behaves," as Skinner would maintain, surely the therapist or behavior-modifier is "acting," with reference to some kind of value system.

If we hold that values are relevant for behavior, and that the actor has at least some freedom in choosing his own values and in setting his priorities among them, how then may values and value systems be empirically critiqued? Here I would propose that there are three kinds of criteria with reference to which empirical knowledge may be employed to critique values: these I will label the criterion of *effectiveness*, the criterion of *efficiency*, and the criterion of *functional adequacy*.

The criterion of effectiveness is the simplest to explain. It is based on the observation that many things which people value are valued not in and of themselves but rather as means to other, more ultimate values. Such inter-mediate, instrumental values are usually backed by belief systems regarding the efficacy of the things which are thus valued. A mother, for example, may place a certain value on spanking as a child-rearing practice. Pressed, she would probably say that she believes that spanking is an effective means for getting a child to give up some undesirable behavior—for example hitting his little brother. If someone with fuller knowledge can now demonstrate to her, empirically, that spanking may actually increase rather than decrease a child's tendency to behave aggressively toward siblings, presumably she will revise her evaluation of spanking. All instrumental values are thus continually open to empirical critique.

The criterion of efficiency is concerned with the relationships among the different values of the same actor. For example, it might appear that we are free to choose whatever values we like, and to put them in whatever priority ranking we prefer—work before pleasure, etc. In practice, however, such priority systems are also open to empirical critique. To demonstrate this, I would draw upon what I may call the "postulate of empirical interconnec-tedness." This postulate states, as a generalization from experience, that almost any change in the state of one variable will probably have ramifying

---

explicitly into account a subjective process of orientation in which the actor defines, structures and evaluates the situation in which he finds himself and shapes his behavior in the situation with reference to various ends, goals, values, and normative standards (Parsons and Shils, 1951). Radical behaviorists and traditional S–R theorists, of course, deny the relevance of the entire action-schema; for them, there is no action, only behavior.

consequences for many other variables, because of the ecological embeddedness of phenomena in the empirical world. It follows that action taken in behalf of any one value or interest, whether or not it achieves its intended result, may also produce a number of other ramifying consequences or side effects. At least some of these are likely to implicate other values of the same actor, and hence must be counted either as secondary gains or as costs in evaluating the action taken. To pursue the example used before, even if it is shown that spanking is effective in producing an intended effect of obedience, if someone with fuller knowledge can demonstrate, empirically, that this form of discipline may produce a number of other side effects which the mother would not approve, had she been aware of them, the place of spanking in her hierarchy of child-rearing values will presumably be altered.

More generally, we may say that every increment of empirical knowledge which enables us better to predict the ramifying consequences of our actions will provide some leverage for critiquing our value systems. For such information continually changes the parameters in terms of which we estimate the costs and benefits of action taken in pursuit of our goals. In planning responsible intervention strategies, therefore, judgments about the empirical *effectiveness* of a particular means for a particular end can rarely if ever be taken as a sufficient criterion. Responsible, rational intervention strategies must always follow some judgment about the relative efficiency of alternative strategies for the total set of values of the actor. The minimum framework thus involves some kind of cost–benefit calculus, in which an attempt is made to decide, on empirical grounds, which strategy promises the greatest net balance of gain for all the values which stand to be affected.

We should observe in passing that, while the effectiveness criterion applies only to intermediate, instrumental values, the efficiency criterion applies equally well to ultimate values directly pursued. For action taken directly on behalf of final values also entails various side effects or costs. Thus, if I discover that my love of peanuts, a final but not very important value, is making me fat and worsening my health, I may come to love them less.

Until now I have said nothing whatever of the content of values. I have been dealing solely with the values of a single actor and I have been assuming, for purposes of argument, that these were arbitrarily and freely chosen and ordered by the individual. I have tried to demonstrate that, even under those assumptions, value systems are susceptible to continual revision in the light of every increment of empirical knowledge. But what of the objective content or reference of value systems? Can these too be subjected to empirical critique?

On this, I am admittedly on much less sure ground. As a committed voluntarist, there is a part of me which is bound to say: let every fool choose whatever foolish values he pleases. Let the martyr starve himself to death; let the ascetic forego sex; let the masochist flog himself bloody, or let the sadist flog a consenting other. If these people are fully aware of the consequences of their behavior and find a net balance of gain, for their own particular value systems, in the courses of behavior they pursue, can empirical science find any basis for critique?

It is in this connection that I would invoke my third criterion, the criterion of functional adequacy. This criterion is designed to critique the relevance of values, and of actions taken in their behalf, for the needs of various kinds of systems. For example, food values and habits may be appraised, empirically, against whatever is known about the nutritional needs of the human organism as a biological system. Child-rearing values and practices may be appraised, empirically, in terms of our growing knowledge of the psychological needs of young children, and also in terms of the needs of social systems for "socialized" adults with appropriate kinds of competencies and commitments.

Here I must invoke yet another postulate, concerning the embeddedness of systems. Simply put, man is simultaneously, both as an individual and a component of a species, a biological animal, a psychological animal, and a social animal. These three orders of systems, moreover, are empirically interpenetrating in such a way that most of any action taken is likely to have consequences relevant to the needs of all three kinds of systems. What are scored as gains with reference to the needs of one order of system must often be counted as costs for the needs of another. For example, while "free sex" may serve the biological and psychological needs of some individuals, this practice—if made general in the population—might prove dysfunctional for the maintenance of viable family systems appropriate for the socialization needs of young children.

If we look for the source of human values, it is clear that most of them are not spun, whole cloth, out of thin air or blind hedonism. We can say, with Skinner, that man tends to value whatever is reinforcing. But to stop here short circuits the analysis, and leaves it empirically sterile. Should we arrange our lives simply to maximize our opportunities for reinforcement? Or should we ask, Why are some kinds of behaviors experienced as reinforcing? As Skinner himself observes, in a very crude way we tend to get reinforcement for behaviors which are adaptive or functional in service of our needs as biological and psychological systems. But this relationship easily gets out of adjustment, so that behavior in the service of short term reinforcement—for example, the alcoholic with his drink—may prove dysfunctional for our total, long run needs. An empirical analysis of man's biological and psychological needs thus promises to provide some empirical leverage for a critique for the functional relevance of his values.

But man cannot be for himself alone. Like most other organisms, his innate programming suggests an overriding concern, in nature's design, for the survival of the species more than that of the individual. Without such cooperative social performances as sexual intercourse and parental care of the helpless young, the species would quickly perish. It is therefore fortunate and functional that we should find the relevant behaviors in this domain reinforcing and that we should value them. But man's involvement as a social animal goes far beyond the base survival needs of the species. Through long evolutionary processes we have become so embedded in society that social living is essential not just to our survival as individuals and as a species, but also to the meeting of virtually all our other needs as well. Indeed, many of our most central psychological needs—for example, love, esteem, approval, etc.—have an inherently social reference. Outside of society man would not be recognizably human.

Since man is committed to live in society, it is clear that he must also be committed to the survival of society. In fact Skinner goes so far as to make the survival of culture his final goal. While it's evident that some kind of sociocultural environment must survive if man himself is to endure, I cannot accept mere cultural survival as a sufficient final criterion. If Hitler's Thousand-year Reich had made it—and for a while we thought it might—Skinner would be forced to say: this is it![3] As a humanistic sociologist, I prefer to believe that the ultimate criterion must be the efficiency of alternative patterns of social organization and culture for meeting man's human and social needs. If we can define man's essential needs adequately, we have a powerful empirical criterion for critiquing society.

This, of course, is precisely what the humanistic psychologists, including Dr. Jourard, have been trying to do. However, much of their critique, in my opinion, is sociologically naive, because it fails to take into account the complex empirical interdependencies which characterize societal systems, and because it fails to recognize that social systems also have needs of their

[3] Skinner, who seems to me to be a closet humanist, would undoubtedly object to this, preferring the milder, less aversive controls envisioned in his Walden II. But does this preference for nonaversive controls really rest on hard-nosed empirical evidence, or is it, at least in part, a carefully rationalized value preference? If cultural survival is the only acknowledged criterion, and if a totalitarian, repressive regime can indeed survive, Skinner would be logically bound to accept it. I would be pleased to welcome him to membership in our mentalistic underground.

own which must be taken into account by responsible change agents. Moreover, the ways in which societies function to meet the needs of their people are often exceedingly indirect. Social living requires many kinds of cooperative performances which are concerned more with the adaptation, survival, and goal attainment of the social system as a whole than they are with the needs of the individual members. To take an obvious example, the United States Navy does not exist primarily to provide satisfactions for the officers and men who must play its various roles. A little reflection will reveal that virtually all social systems, including even the family, perform functions relevant to societal needs, generate system needs at their own levels, and require behaviors or role performances from their participants which may have little direct bearing on their personal needs or wishes.

Just as individuals find reinforcing and hence tend to value behaviors which are functional for their needs, so societies become organized about types of role behaviors which are believed to be adaptive or functional for the social system. Such behaviors are socially valued and become the focus for social rules and norms (Homans, 1950, 1961). In addition, traits of personality deemed to be relevant also became focal for social evaluation and sanction. For example, in war-making tribes, not just combat behavior but also aggressiveness and bravery are socially valued. The task of socialization thus always involves a heavy, culture-specific load, in which efforts are bent to shape in the growing child, and to maintain in adults, the culturally preferred character traits, behavior systems, and value configurations.

Certainly, social systems must be critiqued, and efforts must continually be made for responsible reform. I would agree with the humanistic psychologists that one set of standards for any proposed social reform should be the relevant consequences for fulfilling human needs more humanely and with fewer crippling strains and side effects. But psychological considerations are never, by themselves, sufficient criteria for any responsible intervention or reform. For whatever we do is certain to have sociological as well as psychological consequences. And since man is destined to live in some kind of social system—the present one or any modification thereof—these too must be predicted, taken into account, and evaluated.

How does all this bear upon the role and responsibilities of the therapist? As noted above, the therapist is a licensed practitioner, and this license requires him to act as a responsible agent of society. In addition to his own personal values, and those of his clients, he is also obliged to take society's interests and values into account. Can a therapist safely assume, for example, that anxiety is a "bad thing" and ought to be got rid of, without giving due consideration to the possible functionality of certain levels of anxiety in maintaining socially required performances? Even if the inhibition of free sexual and aggressive expression is shown to involve some cost to mental health, the responsible therapist must take some heed to the societal functions of such inhibitions.

I do not mean, of course, that the therapist must take current social structures and cultural value-systems as given and unmodifiable. I merely mean that society's interests and needs must be given responsible consideration. And this proposition does not depend alone on legal or moral grounds; for if the therapist's goals for his patient are inconsistent with the functional needs of the society, there may be empirical backlashes for his patient.

But here I would once again call attention to the fact that therapists, unlike garage mechanics, are not merely practitioners. Many of them also attempt to be articulate contributors to our growing body of general knowledge about the nature of man and society. If their work is guided by an adequate and empirically critiqued general theory, hopefully we should find in it some points of leverage for responsible reforms of both man and society.

ON THE VALUE PERSPECTIVES OF
WOLPE AND JOURARD

In terms of this needed dual perspective, giving heed both to sociological and psychological considerations. I find the formulations of doctors Wolpe and Jourard insufficient.

To begin with Wolpe, let me say that, together with other participants in the symposium, I emerged with enormous respect for his "magnificence" as a person—to use Jourard's term—and for his competence and integrity both as a scientist and as a practicing therapist. There is no doubt in my mind that he does get impressive results and that he can document them with hard-nosed data. Alas, poor Freud! Something really important is obviously going on here, and it is essential that findings and results like these be incorporated and properly assimilated into our growing body of scientific knowledge and theory about human behavior.

On the surface, at least, Dr. Wolpe's goals for his patients would seem simple enough and noncontroversial. He would do what he can—evidently quite a lot—to relieve them of suffering at precisely the points where the shoe pinches tightest, whether it be in helping to remove a phobic fear of snakes, of crowds, or of elevators. Tantrum behavior, bed-wetting, bad study habits, stuttering, tobacco addiction, and frigidity are all included among the "presenting symptoms" to which Dr. Wolpe applies his therapeutic efforts. All such problems, Dr. Wolpe asserts, are clearly causing pain and suffering for his patients, as they themselves recognize in applying for his help. They represent not only unpleasant experiences and behaviors, but also they are maladaptive and hence functionally inefficient. Moreover, they may all lead to more persistent and general anxieties, and hence form the basis for more debilitating neurotic behavior. By helping his patients get rid of such phobic fears or maladaptive habits, Dr. Wolpe hopes not only to relieve their suffering but also to help them live in more viable ways. These all seem like commendable goals and it would be difficult to find fault with any of them. Certainly Dr. Wolpe does not try to play God to his patients.

My main criticism of Wolpe's position concerns what it leaves out rather than what it puts in. It appears to me that Wolpe's role parallels too closely that of the skilled garage mechanic. He appears to be a tinkerer who has hit upon some things which, judged pragmatically, seem to work effectively. It appears to me that he accepts his patients' account of their complaints rather uncritically and that he deals primarily with the presenting symptoms without any real concern for causes or underlying structures. There is little here to contribute to our general understanding of mental illness or mental health.

Regarding the goals of his therapy, they seem again like those of the mechanic: fix the ailing carburetor and get the car back on the road. But why? Wolpe speaks of removing maladaptive habits and thus of enabling people to live in more viable ways. But in terms of what value system are these symptoms maladaptive? R. D. Laing and his followers might see some of them as wholly appropriate and adaptive defenses against a society gone mad. What does he really mean by making life more "viable"?

Basically, what I see in Wolpe's work is an almost total absence of any thoughtful or critical conception of man as a human being, still less of man as a social being. All we are told is that it is somehow better to live without pain. Even this is perhaps arguable: there is some evidence, for example, that lives without pain produce few great novels. Regarding what is good, we get from Wolpe only the notion that the good is whatever is experienced as reinforcing—a rather content-free, sterile, and hedonistic criterion. There is in Wolpe's discussion no concern for problems of motivation, still less for the complex and developing interdependencies which challenge the students of human development and personality. And there is no real analysis of the complex structures of social environment which produced the reinforcement contingencies his patients are responding "maladaptively" to.

Let me freely grant that, "for the time being"—to use Auden's phrase to describe the imperfect world we are stuck with at the moment—we will continue to need skilled mechanics to get our carburetors adjusted, dentists to cope with our toothaches, and therapists to help relieve our mental pains when the suffering becomes unbearable. And let me also concede that in the absence of nagging toothaches or acute mental anguish we are all un-doubtedly "freer" to pursue whatever more ultimate goals we may choose for ourselves.

But if suffering is widespread, we also need all the wisdom, scientific theory, and knowledge we can muster to help us understand how we got that way, as people and as societies. Only through such knowledge can we go about the urgent business of reshaping our world in ways which will meet our human and social needs more adequately. In Wolpe's work, I see no basis for constructing a general theory of man in society—a theory, that is to say, from which one might develop a sophisticated critique of society's impact on man, and from which one might develop responsible intervention programs.

Surely Dr. Wolpe's own claims are modest enough. He carefully avoids becoming involved in these larger issues, and perhaps it is only fair to say that, on his own very limited ground, he cannot be faulted. But the larger issues must surely be faced by our disciplines, and the question remains whether the kinds of knowledge growing out of the learning theory and behavior modification tradition can form an adequate basis for any such general theoretical system.

On this matter, I have very serious misgivings both on practical and theoretical grounds. With behavior modification techniques you can shape the behavior of a pigeon to turn in clockwise circles, of a husband to pat his spouse's fanny more frequently, of a schoolchild to remain seated at his desk—these and many other things. But in the name of what values are these learnings imposed? Unlike the patients who voluntarily apply to Dr. Wolpe for relief of some perceived suffering, the pigeon, the husband, and the schoolchild may be quite unaware either of suffering or other allegedly maladaptive consequences of their prior, unshaped behavior. And in any event, the shaping may be instigated by some second or third party, without the subject's knowledge or informed consent. Moreover, the *values* in terms of which the shaping is done are not derived from learning theory, nor perhaps from any other explicitly formulated theory.

Essentially, behavior modification is a technique rather than a theory, and one which is potentially both promising and threatening because of its devas-tating effectiveness. The danger of these techniques being used irresponsibly are very real indeed, since the whole behavior modification movement has developed in what is almost a pragmatic, antitheoretical tradition: "Don't ask me why. I just know it works, and here are some charts to prove it." Learning theory is, of course, a real theory, indeed a very sophisticated theory—about *how* learning occurs! But, by itself, it yields no propositions about *what* is learned, nor any criterion or theoretical perspectives for evaluating the results.

While the laws of learning theory are general, applying equally to pigeons and people (or so it is asserted), it is simply not of itself a general theory of man, still less of man in society. Attempts by Skinner, Homans, and others, to extend the behaviorist model to this broader domain have been, in my opinion, singularly naive and unsuccessful. They are psychologically naive because, as noted before, they provide no real analysis of the basis and content of man's needs—except for the sterile notion of a generalized need for reinforcement of any kind whatever—or of the complex and developing interdependencies in his personality structure. And they are particularly naive sociologically because of their tendency to think of the social environment blindly in terms of reinforcement contingencies, without ever asking why they got that way, and what would be the consequences for society as well as for man if they were altered.[4]

Dr. Jourard also impressed me as a person of real magnificence—to use his own term once again—and of great integrity, radiating a little less the cool competence of Dr. Wolpe, but a bit more human warmth. If I had a son with a stuttering problem or a phobic fear of crowds, I would refer him to Dr. Wolpe. But if he was plagued with doubts about his identity and personal worth, I would send him to Dr. Jourard. For Dr. Jourard is clearly not dealing with surface behaviors or symptoms but rather with the whole person. And his therapeutic strategy—it is really that, more than a specific technique—appears to be based largely on modeling. I can readily believe that Dr. Jourard would make an excellent model, from whom a perplexed and bewildered patient could draw unknown sources of strength and confidence.

Dr. Jourard, in my opinion, goes considerably beyond Wolpe in making his values explicit and in specifying the kind of person he is trying to model and mold. And he also goes much further in specifying the source of the difficulties he sees his patients and himself struggling against. Most generally, the culprit is what he calls "facticity"—a vivid term he employs to designate, I believe, something like the "reality principle:" we live in a world we did not make, and

---

[4] Skinner does go beyond mere reinforcement as a final goal when he argues that things which are experienced as reinforcing may have some "survival" value, a proposition for which there are surely myriad exceptions. And he also postulates the "survival of the culture" as a kind of superordinate goal. But what kind of culture? Homans (1961, ch. 18) goes a bit further and attempts to rought out a psychogenic theory for the origin and basis of cultural differentiation. But while his argument has a certain elegant empirical plausibility, it is sociologically sterile, for he never really considers the societal consequences of varying social arrangements, nor even their consequences for men.

the stubborn facts press everywhere upon us, demanding that we cope, escape, or somehow try to adapt and make ourselves comfortable. More specifically, the real source of our problems is the social structure itself, with its demands that we conform to its rules, play out the roles it imposes upon us, accept its values, strive for its goals, and even derive our most essential conceptions of our "self" from society's definitions. "If I were to claim a kind of magnificence for myself," Dr. Jourard observes "it's in the stubborn refusal to limit myself to other people's definitions of what my age, sex, occupational and familial roles ought to be."

All these socially imposed constraints, Jourard believes, limit our freedom to find our own best sense of personal worth and fulfillment, restrict the free flowering of individuality, force us to relate to others through masks, limit our range of potential experiences, repress our capacity to express our feelings and thoughts freely and honestly, prevent us from living fully in the immediate present, stunt our potentials for growth, weaken, cripple, and demean us as personalities. In short, socially imposed constraints have the effect of dehumanizing us.

The goal of therapy, according to Jourard, is to help individuals "transcend" these bonds of facticity and social constraint; to show them—through modeling—how to find hidden sources of strength in themselves, how to discover inner standards for self-evaluation; how to take down the masks which have constrained their relationships to others, the better to reveal themselves and to see others honestly, transparently; how to expand their capacity for experiencing life fully and spontaneously.

But the purpose of all this transcendent experience, Jourard argues, is not withdrawal or permanent escape. The purpose, rather, is to permit "re-entry" with a capacity to play out one's social roles with new degrees of freedom and creativity, with a determination to resist the passive acceptance of forces which are crippling and to struggle to reshape the world and one's situation in it, by one's own initiatives, in ways which will be more livable, life-giving, and viable.

As a sociologist who also counts himself a humanist, I find myself in general and hearty agreement with much of what Dr. Jourard is saying. I share much of his diagnosis of the social source of our discontents and most of his goals for man. Hence, I can enthusiastically wish him success in his therapy efforts.

I cannot accept it all, however, without expressing certain reservations both on sociological and on psychological grounds. I agree that societal rules and roles restrict our freedom, and hence may be experienced as crippling. But as a sociologist I must remind the reader that all societies must have some system of rules and roles to regulate the complex relationships and cooperative task performances which sustain the society, and directly or indirectly, serve the needs of its members. Not only social rules but all the stubborn facts of life in the real world—Jourard's "facticity"—do and must impose disciplines and constraints upon us all. Our struggles with the reality principle force us, in meeting our goals, to master technical skills, to defer direct gratification while engaged in necessary instrumental behaviors, and since we must usually do this cooperatively with others, to accept social disciplines and constraints as well. A world which explodes only with individual freedom and here–now spontaneity may have some difficulty in getting the crops planted, cared for, and harvested.

While all social institutions must be continually critiqued and modified, to make them more functional socially and more viable humanly, society in general can never be the generic enemy, since we are all irrevocably committed to it. Without it we would not only be unable to meet our needs; we would not even be human.

While particular social rules and roles must always be open to revision, we will not live without them altogether. Moreover, the particular rules and roles in any given society, constraining though they may indeed appear, are never wholly arbitrary and capricious. On the contrary, they tend to represent the distillation of society's long experience about the kinds of behaviors which have proven, over the very long run, to be socially functional, necessary, and rewarding.

The problem with socially defined roles is not that they exist, but that they tend to become packaged too tightly, not only with the nouns and verbs of role prescriptions, but with the adjectives and adverbs of role style as well. Moreover, these role definitions become encrusted by the cake of custom and tend to persist inflexibly through changing times. Their value prescriptions may be too easily taken for granted or come to be regarded as somehow sacred and unchangeable. In all this, we may lose sight of their initial or current instrumental and functional appropriateness. Responsible criticism and responsible intervention programs are essential if we are to keep our social role definitions in tune with the changing needs of our times. Surely, the women's liberation movement has demonstrated, with both ethical and empirical argument, that the time is ripe for a pretty thorough revamping of the sexrole prescriptions of our society. But how? Should sex be eliminated entirely as a basis for role assignment, as some have argued? Perhaps so, but one should not cast off a thousand years of history and selective evolution lightly, without making sure that an adequate alternative is provided which will better serve both society's functional needs and man's psychological needs.

Dr. Jourard's protest against social constraints is far too general; it lacks specificity and hence provides little leverage for constructive social criticism or innovation. Either escape entirely, if you can, or go back in determined to do your own thing, or perhaps fix up your own little corner of the world to make it more fit for you to live in. I see no protocol here for responsible social reform, no call here to duty in the constructive service of fellow man and society. Accept what you must; make yourself as comfortable as possible, but maintain sufficient detachment so that you can avoid being wounded and find room to nurture your own individuality. On sociological grounds, I find Dr. Jourard's perspective, together with that of most other psychological humanists, inadequate and hence irresponsible. Mental health, alone and however defined, can never be a sufficient criterion for social policy.

Curiously, I also find deficiencies in Jourard's perspective on psychological grounds as well. Basically, it seems to me that he has failed to take into account the inherently social and specifically "societal" elements in man's "human" nature. Through his long experiences with the exigencies and rewards of cooperative social living, man's basic personality structure and need-systems have been shaped in such a way that he can only realize and fulfill himself through his participation in the socially valued activities of his group (Leighton, 1959). While such participation unquestionably imposes disciplines and constraints, it also provides essential rewards in terms of security, affection, esteem, and even of identity.

Take the need for esteem as a case in point. While one may be loved by a particular other simply on the basis of one's unique personal qualities, esteem is a reward which is inherently geared to the fulfillment of specific or general performance standards set by society. From a sociological perspective, it represents society's most powerful positive sanction in motivating approved, functional, standards of behavior. Whereas every boy wants his mother's love, still more—by the time he is 12—he wants his father's approval and esteem, contingent rewards he will earn only by meeting his father's standards, whether through athletic prowess or academic success. Later he will seek approval and esteem from more generalized societal others through his efforts to achieve in terms of more general social and cultural norms.

Consider the relation of all this to the much misunderstood problems of personal identity and worth. Self-esteem is roughly the reciprocal of the esteem we receive from significant others. We cannot respect ourselves unless we earn the respect of others, in terms of their standards. An essential core of our identity is and probably must be socially derived. To a much larger extent than the humanists would admit, we become what our society makes us become through the roles it ascribes to us or enables us to achieve, and through the structures of social sanctions it provides for us. We relate to each other, not as generic human beings, but very largely as incumbents of socially defined roles—as men and women, as parents and children, as Jews and Gentiles, as psychologists and sociologists.

Our true identity carries with it a rich lode of specific cultural content and history, and we should think twice, on psychological as well as sociological grounds, before we throw it all away. Peel off all these layers of social meaning and content derived from our multiple social roles, and try to find the core of your "true self" way down inside. As some of the kids on drug trips have found, to their chagrin, maybe no one is there at all. Peel off all the masks which socially structure and define our relationships to others and try to relate directly—transparently—to others, as in current encounter group sessions. Trying to love everybody just alike because of their generic humanity, as many have reported, turns out to be difficult and also rather a bore. For the transparent self may also be a content-free self. There is simply not enough here to sustain even our basic humanity for longer than a single, desperate weekend, and certainly not enough to form a viable and enduring social system.

In short, it appears to me that even on psychological grounds, Dr. Jourard's view of the perfected and liberated state of man is a bit naive and simplistic. It places too much stress on our needs for freedom, spontaneity, and expressiveness, but not enough on our equally vital needs for security, discipline, achievement, approval, and esteem. Man's highest cultural and creative achievements, and—in my judgment—his greatest strengths of character and personality, have always come through participation in organized human societies. Rather than denying the differences which define our separate social and cultural roles, each with its elements of the distilled wisdom of our ancestors, let us stand up on the separate pedestals our traditions provide, and rejoice in the things which define our social uniqueness and speciality as well as our common humanity. Is it less human to be proud of being a Jew, a husband, a father, even though these be things which define, in part, our relations to others?

Granted that all social roles imply some discipline and constraints; granted that they establish differences among us in ways not exactly of our own design and choosing: such definitions can be blinding or crippling, but they do not have to be. As a humanistic sociologist, I will opt for pluralism every time.

What a dull society it would be if American Jews really lost their magnificent separate identity and merged, indistinguishably, with the common stream. What a pity if all the women—as the old song put it—were really transported far beyond the northern sea. Such socially defined differences do not have to stifle our struggles for personal identity—indeed we may realize our selves within them. Nor do they have to present insurmountable barriers to communication. Indeed, if we can learn to communicate, we are rather more likely to have something to say.

With respect to Dr. Jourard, I would conclude that his value system is more appropriate for a temporary therapeutic holiday than as a basis for a permanent style of life. We surely all need to step outside our roles from time to time to gain perspective on ourselves. In earlier times Saturday nights and Sunday mornings helped serve this purpose. Given these breaks to help us reassess the premises of our involvement in the workaday world, perhaps we can re-enter with renewed strength. But re-enter we must, as Jourard freely admits. Monday morning is sure to come and we can and must learn to realize our essential humanity within the frameworks of ongoing society.

In conclusion, it appears to me that while both Drs. Wolpe and Jourard have diagnosed some of the problems which plague us as individuals, and have designed effective therapies addressed to these ills, neither is successful in constructing an adequate general theory about the complex interrelationships between man and society. Hence, by themselves, neither provides an adequate basis for responsible reforms either of man himself or of the society in which he lives.

Behavioral Ecology and Humanistic and Behavioristic Approaches to Change[1]

JAMES L. ALEXANDER, GEORGE F. DREHER, AND EDWIN P. WILLEMS

Department of Psychology, University of Houston, Texas 77004

Most of the other articles in this book present either a behavioristic or humanistic approach to human behavior and experience. Some of the articles make comparative and evaluative statements across the boundaries of the two approaches. We will not participate directly in that paired comparison. Rather, we will step outside the behavioristic and humanistic points of view by presenting a third approach—behavioral ecology—and by spelling out some of the ways in which it bears on behaviorism and humanism.

Behavioral ecology is in the process of formulation as an orientation to human behavior. It relates to the work of Barker and Wright (Barker, 1965, 1968; Barker and Schoggen, 1973; Barker and Wright, 1955; Wright, 1967, 1969–1970), but, as it is presented in the present article, it also reflects the influences of other approaches to ecological problems (see Willems, 1973a, b, c; 1974; in press). The ecological perspective has important implications for the way in which psychologists do their work. Thus, one major purpose of this paper is to present the overall flavor and major assumptions and principles of behavioral ecology to the extent that they can be spelled out at present.

Behavioral ecology relates in some specific and important ways to behavioristic and humanistic views of human change. Behavior modification is a rigorous, criterion-oriented approach to behavior change. The behavioral technologist specifies behaviors he wants to modify, engages in an intervention keyed to those behaviors, obtains data on his progress, and stops when he demonstrates that he has reached his criterion of change. But, from the perspective of behavioral ecology, some serious concerns and questions should be raised about the work of the behavioral technologist, even when he

[1] Work on this paper was supported in part by Research and Training Center No. 4 (RT-4), Baylor College of Medicine and the Texas Institute for Rehabilitation and Research, funded by Social and Rehabilitation Services, USDHEW.

succeeds in achieving his aims. These issues will be spelled out in the section that follows the presentation of the ecological point of view. The reader should understand that we are not discussing behaviorism in general, but only some of its specific applications in the treatment of troubling behavior.

The humanistic orientation is quite different. As we understand him, the humanistic psychologist attaches singular importance to a rich, full representation of the psychological functioning of persons and formulates his interventions into persons' lives in such a manner as to enhance the richness and fullness of the person's life and make it psychologically and subjectively meaningful. It is not easy to specify when the humanistic psychologist does this successfully. However, from the vantage point of behavioral ecology, some serious and troubling questions must be asked of the humanist, even when he gives the impression of achieving his therapeutic goals. These issues will be raised after the section on behavioral technology.

Does a paper on behavioral ecology belong in a discussion of behavioristic and humanistic psychology? We believe it does because part of our intent, beyond the presentation of a point of view, is to stimulate thought, discussion, evaluation, and amplification regarding professional psychology and its attempts to understand and alleviate human problems. The challenge is to clarify and strengthen our theories and our strategies of intervention. Such clarification and strengthening will follow from presentation of the ecological perspective and discussion of its points of articulation and disagreement with behavioral technology and humanism. We agree with Bruhn (1974, p. 120) when he says that:

> "...the systems approach begins when one discipline begins to see the world through the eyes of another, realizing that any given discipline has a restrictive view of the whole system. The systems perspective respects the concern of each discipline to treat its subject matter as a distinct entity, but only when these separate entities are fitted together is a holistic view of human behavior possible."

THE ECOLOGICAL PERSPECTIVE

People everywhere are worried about behavioral problems. A syndicated columnist, after reciting a long list of troubling aspects of day-to-day life in New York City, concluded recently that "New York's problem is not economic. New York ranked fourth among... 18 cities in per capita income adjusted for cost-of-living differences.... *New York's problem is behavior*"

(Jones, 1973) (italics added). Ordinary, everyday human behavior and, especially, its emergence into troubling forms are serious threats to persons, societies, and the human species. Uneasiness over crime and social disintegration, the sense of deterioration of daily behavioral and social life, the sense of things not working right or even coming apart, and the forbidding and growing sense of vulnerability to the acts of persons and to daily events over which one has no direct control are, perhaps, even more widespread than apprehension over lung cancer, auto-accidents, or heart trouble.

When persons turn to psychology and its allied disciplines for assistance, they confront an irony. Most research in psychology deals with relatively small, discrete problems and with modest objectives. When we stretch these bits to fit a comprehensive framework and use them to elucidate everyday problems of behavior, the bits and pieces wear poorly. They also wear poorly for those persons who try to use the understanding in a treatment or technology to solve an individual or community problem and for architects and planners who strain to use the models in designing large, everyday systems. Human behavior—what persons *do*—is inextricably bound up in the larger conditions of human living. By and large, the fragments of our research domain in psychology have not begun to approach the scale and complexity of those systems. "... simple arguments seem to be easier to comprehend and embrace than complex ones which may be better" (David, 1972, p. 93).

Psychology and its allied disciplines must overcome their sense of futility about understanding and changing the seemingly pell-mell course of problems of human behavior. These disciplines must develop the means to influence and shape the course of human behavior in more reflective, purposeful, and humane directions. Otherwise, their venerable traditions may disappear and "...become like those of a buggy whip factory, interesting and nostalgic but totally useless" (Thoreson *et al.*, 1972, p. 134). Apart from the future of any specific scientific movement, problems of human behavior must be solved and we must deal with the survival of meaningful social and behavioral life. A necessary condition for these developments will be the mobilization of a new willingness to change our old modes of thinking about human behavior in favor of an approach that accepts and understands the complexity and interdependency of the ecological systems in which behavior is embedded.

Ecology has its origins in the biological sciences. It refers traditionally to the study of relationships between living things and their habitats and the formalization of the natural rules by which those interactions are governed. Complex interdependencies involving organisms and their environments over extended periods of time are the scientific focus of the ecologist and tremendous advances have been made in understanding such interdependencies in areas outside of psychology (Benarde, 1970; Chase, 1971; Colinvaux, 1973; Dubos, 1965, 1968; Margalef, 1968; Shepard and McKinley, 1969; Smith, 1966; Wallace, 1972; Watt, 1966, 1968).

These advances are important, but the development of the ecological perspective is still very spotty. On the one hand, the scientific community has begun to grasp the complexity, interdependency, and delicacy of the physical and biological ecosystems in which human beings are embedded—the networks of forces, energies, and vectors involving toxins, nutrients, and biological health and pathology. "Before he is Christian or pagan, liberal or conservative, ...rich or poor, pacifist or warrior, man is a biological entity " (Chase, 1971, p. 3). Much is known about the ways in which man's biological functioning and well-being are caught up in webs of the environments he inhabits; e.g., injudicious use of insecticides, effects of pollution, the ebb and flow of infectious diseases. In fact, ecological principles have become the grounds for understanding biological health and the quality of life, as well as for planning preventive measures and new legal statutes. Just as importantly, this general ecological view has generated a sophisticated conservatism, a sensitized conscience, and an ecological awareness of the many ways in which simplistic intrusions into these man–environment systems can produce unintended and unpleasant effects and that widespread and long term harm may follow from short term or narrowly defined good.

In contrast, we have only a beginning conceptual grasp of the ways in which human *behavior* and its deteriorations are implicated in complex systems involving persons and environments. In the rapid and faddish formulation of ecological science, we seem to have forgotten that, in addition to being biological organisms that are subject to complex exchanges of energy with their environments and thus are governed by the biological laws of ecosystems, humans are also *behaving* organisms and that *behavioral* regularities are intimately involved in the ways in which persons function in their environments. Just as much as they are biological entities, persons are also "Christian or pagan, liberal or conservative, rich or poor, pacifist or warrior," skilled and unskilled, active or passive, aggressive and altruistic, self-destructive and happy, cooperative and antagonistic. Indeed, behavior is the principal means by which persons carry out transactions with their habitats. By comparison to the ecological and epidemiological aspects of biological health, we know very little about the ecological aspects of behavior and behavioral difficulty. For example, much is known about the relations among traffic patterns, industrial patterns, population density, air pollution, and diseases of the lungs and about the relations among spillage of nondegradable poisons into waterways, the characteristics of the waterways, the assimilation of the pollutants by fish and shrimp, and the damage done to persons who eat the fish or shrimp. However, very little is known about the relations among environmental systems, the use of those systems by human beings, and the emergence of behavioral problems. We have scarcely begun to formalize the system-like regularities and laws that bind human behavior to its habitat over time.

Behavioral scientists try to offer models and remedies that can be applied to human problems in some direct fashion and to intervene, directly or indirectly, in phenomena whose complexity they often do not understand. One need not be an alarmist to recognize that understanding human behavior in relation to the environmental systems people inhabit will not only be adaptive for us, but will have survival value as well. While it is tempting to retreat from such complexity into the simpler and more comforting issues of our separate approaches, we need just the opposite—to confront the complexity and disarray and to formulate principles to manage them.

Macro-ecology

Humane efforts to apply proven technology and to alleviate human suffering on a large scale can go awry in the most surprising and vexing ways. The building of large dams leads to increased rates of infectious disease, decreases in fish harvests, and disruptions of social and cultural patterns (Murdock and Connell, 1970; Sterling, 1972). The green revolution, which involves breeding crops toward genetic uniformity, increases the vulnerability of the crops to epidemics (Wade, 1972). The large scale use of pesticides and the introduction of new species of animals into an area lead to new, ecologically volatile problems. There is something pervasively wrong with our available understanding of environment–inhabitant systems and the impact of singular intrusions into those systems. In the cases of crops, insecticides and other pesticides, and large dams—indeed, in many cases outside the behavioral sciences—we have learned that they are ecological phenomena whose complexity was not anticipated. We know now what happened and we have discovered the principles that govern such events. When it comes to human *behavior*, an analogous kind of ecological perspective has not been formalized as yet, primarily because, with few exceptions, behavioral scientists and ecologists have not conceived of human behavior as being implicated in complex ecological systems.

In a most disquieting way, Turnbull (1972) describes the social and behavioral disintegration of the Ik, a group of hunter-gatherers who inhabit part of the Kidepo Valley in Northern Uganda (see also Calhoun, 1972). Turnbull, who lived among the Ik and observed them for 18 months, reports that the traditional way of life among the Ik involved highly cooperative forms of hunting across the reaches of the valley and living in small, widely dispersed bands. Terrain, rituals, traditional beliefs, and day-to-day behavior all combined to form an interrelated whole over time. Then, partly in the interests of wildlife conservation, the Ugandan Government defined the Kidepo Valley as a national park, herded the Ik to the edges of the park, set up police outposts to keep the Ik out of the valley, and encouraged the Ik to take up farming on the mountain slopes. The social and behavioral fabric of the Ik society fell apart completely. Malicious competition replaced cooperation. Hostility and treachery replaced kindness. Laughter became a raucous response to the misfortunes of people, rather than an expression of good will and humor. Members of the group were left to die and sometimes goaded to die instead of being nursed and helped. Strong isolation in booby-trapped enclaves and suspicion replaced openness and companionship between people. Members of the group starved, even though ample food was sometimes available a short distance away.

The case of the Ik is disturbing because it reflects a society that has deteriorated to malevolence and behavioral disturbance. However, it also displays the effects of fundamental disruption of ecological links between habitat and social and behavioral adaptation. Even more disturbing are some suggestive parallels between the ways the Ik now live and the ways that many 20th century members of industrialized society live. Many of the complaints of present-day city dwellers about the degradation and disorientation of daily life sound very much like the developments for the Ik. "People who call themselves free are living in areas where they are afraid to take a long walk or a deep breath because of the levels which crime and pollution have reached" (Wittcoff, 1973, p. 67). Zimbardo (1970) argues that "Reason, premeditation, the acceptance of personal responsibility, the feeling of obligation, the rational defense of commitments, appear to be losing ground to an impulse-dominated hedonism bent on anarchy" (p. 240) and that present-day American life represents "...a fundamental change in the quality of individual and mass hostility, aggression, and inhumanity" (p. 247). All around us we see and hear about new forms of behavioral pathology that bewilder us because our traditional assumptions and our traditional psychological models offer no means to understand them or attribute motives to them. Perhaps the behavioral pathology that threatens to overwhelm many persons is fueled by disruptions of the relationships between habitat and living style which we do not recognize only because they occur much more gradually than the upheaval of the Ik.

Micro-ecology

Organism–behavior–environment systems whose complexity and subtlety surprise us also occur on a small scale. The single example cited here is so rich with implications that it is almost like a major parable of behavioral ecology. An ornithologist with a European zoo wished to add a small, rare bird called the bearded tit (sometimes called the reedling) to the zoo's collection (Robert B. Lockard, personal communication). Noting that other attempts to maintain the bird in captivity had been unsuccessful, he devoted a great deal of time and effort to summarizing what was known about the tit's habitat and life style. Armed with all this information, including many photographs, the ornithologist built an extensive setting for the tits in his zoo, being careful to include exactly the right proportion and distribution of shrubs, trees, grasses, rocks, arrangements for feeding, nesting materials, and lighting. After the designed environment satisfied him, he introduced a male and female to it. The birds sang, ate, drank, flitted about, groomed, mated, built an appropriate nest, laid eggs, hatched babies, and fed them. If birds can be said to enjoy their environments, then, by all these behavioral criteria, the ornithologist had designed an environment whose habitability the bearded tits enjoyed thoroughly.

Within a day or two, however, he came to check the tits, only to find the babies dead on the ground. Since the parents were still so clearly enjoying themselves, he assumed that some accident or illness had befallen the infants, and he waited for the reproductive cycle to recur. When a new brood was hatched, the ornithologist observed carefully and found, to his dismay, after a period of time, that the parents pushed the babies out of the nest, onto the ground, where they died. This cycle, beginning with mating and ending with the babies dead on the ground, repeated itself over and over again.

The ornithologist tried modifications, but none forestalled the systematic infanticide. In desperation, he went back out to observe tits in the wild. After many hours of observation, he noted three clear patterns of behavior. First, throughout most of the daylight hours, the parent tits were almost frantically active at finding and bringing food for the infants. Second, the infants, with whose food demands the parents could hardly keep pace, spent the same hours with their mouths open, apparently crying for food. The third pattern was that any inanimate object, whether eggshell, leaf, or beetle shell, was quickly shoved out of the nest by the parents.

With these observations in hand, the ornithologist went back to observe his captive tits and what he found astounded him because of its subtlety, and yet, its clarity. During the short time a new brood of infants lived, the parents spent only brief periods feeding them by racing between the nest and the food supply, which the ornithologist had supplied in abundance. After a short period of such feeding, the infants, apparently satiated, fell asleep. The first time the infants slept for any length of time during daylight hours, the parents shoved them (two inanimate objects, after all) out of the nest.When he made the food supply *less* abundant and *less* accessible and thereby made the parents work much longer and harder to find food, the ornithologist found that the infants spent more daylight time awake, demanding food, and that the tits then produced many families and cared for them to maturity.

Infanticide is a behavior problem and this story points to several important issues. The first is that neither the designer's good will nor the technologist's respect or love for his clients will themselves ensure his creating the right environment. Good intentions by agents of change do not necessarily lead to habitability. The second issue is more complex and points to the criteria we use in making evaluative inferences about our efforts. All the indicators in the behavior of the parent tits suggested that their captive environment was congenial and hospitable and that it fulfilled their needs. Yet, the long range criterion of survival of the captive representatives of the species (a surprise, a shock to the ornithologist) pointed to a very different conclusion about the environment. If we think anthropomorphically, the parent birds probably enjoyed the ease of the first captive environment much more than the effort required by the second environment. The parents had to work much harder in the second environment than in the first, but their babies survived in the second and not in the first. We must pick our criteria with care, perhaps flying in the face of what common sense, accepted social wisdom, and popular psychological theories tell us is humane, important, and worthwhile.

The third issue points to methodology. Since it involves behavior and behavior–environment relations, the case of the bearded tit and its human analogs are of direct interest to the psychologist and other behavioral scientists. However, our traditional methods of research on humans hardly put us in a position to elucidate the real-life interdependencies of behaviors and environments. We say that systems concepts, complex dependencies, reciprocity, and extended time-related cycles must be entertained as descriptive and explanatory terms, but they almost never show up in the actual reports of our research. By and large, we continue to study behavior as though its important phenomena were simple, single file, relatively short term, largely organism-based, and most amenable to research by means of short-cut methods such as questionnaires, interviews, and simple experiments.

The fourth issue involves even more speculation. It is the reminder, supported by many examples outside psychology, that the complicated systems comprising everyday environments, their human inhabitants, and the links among them probably involve lawful interdependencies whose subtlety has eluded us completely. In the case of the bearded tits and environmentally induced infanticide, the interdependencies involved (a) some aspects of a total physical environment, (b) the ongoing short range individual and social behavior of the birds, e.g., child-rearing practices and characteristic ways of dealing with the environment, and (c) a long range outcome. Who knows, for example, what aspects of personal, familial, neighborhood, and general social behavior and their environmental surroundings combine to account for troublesome symptoms such as irritability, alcoholism among housewives, drug abuse, vandalism, child abuse, high divorce rates, truancy, motiveless murder, interpersonal and intergroup tension, and the deterioration of human amenities? We do not know. Unless we find out, we may make changes that only create new and unanticipated problems, no matter how humane and decent the reasons for making the changes.

Some General Implications

From this general ecological awareness and from more fully developed disciplines outside of psychology, a central theme and some important implications emerge for behavioral ecology and for psychology. Benarde (1970) presents this theme succinctly: "The significant feature is that the social, physical, and biological components function as an integrated system, and any tampering with any part of the system will affect each of the other parts and alter the whole" (p. 24).

It is becoming clear in the ecological literature that "we can never do merely one thing" (Hardin, 1969), that every intervention, every human artifice, has its price, no matter how well intentioned the agent of intervention may be (Bateson, 1972). Most of the cases cited above (e.g., large dams, crops) illustrate that this point recurs with painful regularity. Positively motivated intrusions into interdependent systems can lead to all sorts of unanticipated effects, many of which are unpleasant and pernicious. To label these unintended effects as "side effects" only compounds the problem. The epidemic of schistosomiasis among the people of the Nile is no more a "side effect" of the Aswan Dam than is the capability of flood control. Both are effects of building the dam. There are no such things as side effects.

In our growing awareness of ecological phenomena, we are reluctant to introduce new biotic elements and new chemicals into our ecological systems, but we display dismal irresponsibility when it comes to intervening in behavioral and behavioral–environmental systems. Amost every day we hear of projects or technologies being changed, slowed down, stopped, or disapproved on ecological grounds, because of the known complexity or delicacy of ecosystems. The location of a proposed factory is switched, a bridge is not built, a planned freeway is rerouted, a smokestack is modified, someone is restrained from introducing a new animal into an area, or a chemical is taken off the market. Those who think that no changes are required in the behavioral sciences, or that arguments for a new effort in behavioral ecology are just so much window dressing, should ask just one question: How often have I heard of a program or project whose target is human behavior being changed, slowed down, stopped, or disapproved on *behavioral*–ecological grounds, because of the *known* complexity and delicacy of eco-behavioral systems? The answer should sober us quickly. It is quite foreign to psychologists (as well as many other social scientists) to think of the physical and behavioral environment as inextricable parts of the behavioral processes of organisms and as relating to them in ways that are extremely complex. Two results that follow are (a) relatively splintered, bit-like attempts to understand large scale, complex phenomena, and (b) blithe forms of bit-like tinkering in complex, interdependent systems.

Until a few years ago, technologists believed that most of their developments would be useful in a direct and simple sense. We know now that this is not necessarily true—feasibility and even intrinsic success are not sufficient grounds for immediate application.

"With each decade, scientific findings translated into technology radically reshape the way we live. Technical capacity has been the ruling imperative, with no reckoning of cost, either ecological or personal. If it could be done, it has been done. Foresight has lagged far behind craft manship. At long last we are beginning to ask, not *can* it be done, but *should* it be done? The challenge is to our ability to anticipate second- and third-order consequences of interventions in the eco-system before the event, not merely to rue them afterward. [Eisenberg, 1972, p. 123.]

This widening awareness—the ecological perspective—suggests that many things that *can* be done either should not be done or should be done most judiciously and that more technology will not provide solutions to many technologically induced problems (Chase, 1971; Dubos, 1965, 1970–1971).

This line of argument may well lead to a conservatism with regard to intervention in behavior–environment systems and the suggestion that the most adaptive form of action may sometimes be inaction. The problem is that we know little as yet about the circumstances under which the price for a particular action outweighs the price of inaction and vice versa. If we give the above examples and arguments a slight interpretative twist, we arrive at another conclusion that is even more important: we need a great deal more basic research and theoretical understanding that takes account of the ecological, system-like principles that permeate the phenomena of behavior and environment, a basis to plan environmental designs, behavioral interventions, and technologies in such a way that they will not produce unanticipated negative costs in behavior–environment systems. We might protest that science is supposed to be the search for unifying and *simplifying* principles. Simon (1969) notes that "The central task of a natural science is to make the wonderful commonplace: to show that complexity, correctly viewed, is only a mask for simplicity" (p. 1). For psychologists, the masking process usually is more like putting on blinders; the *assumption* that the phenomena are simple is made before the search for simplicity even begins.

THE STANCE OF THE BEHAVIORAL ECOLOGIST

Partly because it is still in its early stages of development and partly because it is never likely to comprise a single theory or a single set of methods, behavioral ecology is difficult to define precisely. At present, it is a general orientation or a set of values, beliefs, and assumptions that leads one to view the worlds of behavior, behavior change, and research on behavior in a distinctive way. Despite the imprecision about behavioral ecology, it can be characterized by means of some of its major emphases, assumptions, and programmatic implications. This section presents 14 such earmarks which, taken together, converge on behavioral ecology as an approach to the study of behavior and the environment.

Behavior and Environment. Behavioral ecology emphasizes the mutual and interdependent relations among organism, behavior, and environment. Craik (1970), Barker (1963a, 1965, 1968, 1969), and Gump (1968, 1969) have discussed what this means and most of the examples cited above address this issue.

> "... both organism and environment will have to be seen as systems, each with properties of its own, yet both hewn from basically the same block. Each has surface and depth, or overt and covert regions ... the interrelationship between the two systems has the essential characteristics of a 'coming-to-terms.'... It follows that, much as psychology must be concerned with the texture of the organism or of its nervous processes and must investigate them in depth, it also must be concerned with the texture of the environment as it extends in depth away from the common boundary." [Brunswik, 1957, p. 5.]

Thus, one of the central conceptual issues of behavioral ecology is the transactional character of organism–environment systems. Behavior is a transactional phenomenon that always points two ways, or relates in two directions—organism and environment—and to mediating processes between them. Behavior represents the "coming-to-terms" across the boundaries of organism and environment in organism–environment systems. It is partly on such grounds that the behavioral ecologist thinks in terms of organism–environment–behavior systems. Bits of behavior or bits of environment taken independently (as in an S–R model), the "independent" and "dependent" variables of most experiments, and the bits and pieces of behavior with which we tinker so indiscriminately in psychotherapy, counseling, operant behavior modification, and behavioral pharmacology are all abstractions that have lost much of their scientific and practical meaning because they are separated from the larger, contextual interdependencies in which they occur in the lives of people. What is worse, when changing such abstracted bits of behavior, we may create unintended effects in the ecological systems with which the behaviors are linked. The credo of behavioral ecology is that behavior is a property of ecological systems rather than simply an attribute of the individual (Rhodes, 1972).

Site Specificity: The Importance of Place. A striking fact emerges from descriptive studies of everyday behavior: a high degree of predictability from place, or setting, to behavior. To the behavioral ecologist, *where* organisms are located is never unimportant or accidental because behavior and place concatenate into tightly lawful, functioning systems (Barker, 1963a; Moos, 1973; Wicker, 1972; Willems, 1965). "The correlation between site and activity is often so high that an experienced ecological psychologist can direct a person to a particular site in order to observe an animal exhibiting a given pattern of behavior" (King, 1970, p. 4).

In their discussion of basic assumptions regarding the influence of the physical environment on behavior, Proshansky *et al.* (1970a) argue that actual, observed molar "patterns of behavior in response to a physical setting persist regardless of the individuals involved" (p. 30). Barker (1963a, 1968) also points out that place–behavior systems have such strong principles of organization and constraint that their standing patterns of behavior remain essentially the same though individuals come and go. Wicker (1972) calls this "behavior–environment congruence." Barker (1968) calls it "behavior–milieu synomorphy," and argues that the appropriate units of analysis for studying such synomorphic relationships are *behavior settings*, whose defining attributes and properties he has spelled out in detail (1963a, 1968, pp. 18–33).

These principles are illustrated in a research program in which we have been involved in a comprehensive rehabilitation hospital in Houston, Texas. Adults with injuries to the spinal cord, resulting in severe functional impairments, are our target population. From direct observations of patient behavior we can extract measures of behavioral *independence*, i.e., the proportion of behavioral events which patients initiate and engage in alone, and behavioral *complexity*, i.e., the proportion of time that patients do more than one thing at once. Because increases from very low rates in these measures reflect a relative normalizing of the patients' behavior repertoires, both relate closely to important goals of the hospital's treatment system. We find, first, that behavioral independence and complexity vary dramatically when patients move from one hospital behavior setting to another (LeCompte and Willems, 1970). Second, differences between settings (places in the hospital) account for far more variance in patient independence than do differences between patients (Willems, 1972a). Finally, and most interestingly, differences between early patients (near admission) and advanced patients (near discharge) in independence and complexity are much larger in some settings than in others

(Willems, 1972b); there are powerful behavior setting dependencies in the rate of growth or progress in patient behavior.

A further example is found in the work of Raush and his colleagues in their studies of normal children and children who had been diagnosed as hyperaggressive or disturbed (Raush, 1969; Raush *et al.*, 1959a, b, 1960). By observing the children for extended periods of time in various settings and then examining the frequencies of various kinds of behavior by the children toward peers and adults, the investigators were able to demonstrate several aspects of place dependency. First, the interpersonal behavior of all the children varied strongly from one setting to another. Second, and perhaps most revealing, the place dependence of behavior was much stronger for normal children than for disturbed children; i.e., the influence of the setting was greater for normal children. Finally, as the disturbed children progressed in treatment, the place dependence of their behavior came to approximate the normal children more and more.

Molar Phenomena and Nonreductionism. The ecological perspective tends, generally, to place more emphasis upon *molar* phenomena than upon *molecular* ones. Closely related is a relative emphasis upon environmental, behavioral, and organismic holism and simultaneous, complex relationships. This is so in part because, all the way from survival of a species, through adaptive functioning, down to day-to-day and moment-by-moment adaptive processes, the emphasis is upon the organism's and the population's behavioral commerce with the environmental packages they inhabit. Adaptation to everyday settings and long range, functional performance in them places focus on coming to terms with the environment, on what Powers (1973) calls *results* rather than more molecular movements. Even though it might be possible, in principle, to study the ecology of eye-blinks (a relatively molecular phenomenon), the behavioral ecologist usually focuses on larger, setting-sized, functional behavior episodes, e.g., cooperation, conflict, solving problems, social interactions, transporting, etc. (Barker, 1963a, 1965, 1969; Sells, 1969; Wicker, 1972; Wright, 1967).

Behavioral Focus. Traditionally, psychologists have studied many aspects of human functioning: thoughts, feelings, moods, structures of personality, habits, motives, judgments, cognitions, self-concepts, beliefs, choices, neurochemical processes, endocrinal processes, perceptions, sensory processes, ego strengths, and a host of traits and dispositions. Many have focused much less on subjective, internal, dispositional properties of persons and have devoted their investigative efforts to the study of behavior, on what persons *do* in the overt sense in relation to the environment.

The focal point for the behavioral ecologist is individual and collective behavior—e.g., where persons go, what they do with their time, how they use resources, how they interact with each other. Such an emphasis has not occurred in a vacuum. The great strides made in animal ecology and ethology have had an influence (Eibl-Eibesfeldt, 1970; Lorenz, 1970, 1971; Hutt and Hutt, 1970). In those areas, investigators have been forced to focus on overt behavior because the subjects cannot verbalize their feelings and internal, subjective states. Second, professional behavioral scientists (e.g., industrial psychologists), whose responsibility has been to select persons for the degree to which they will fit into complicated, real-life tasks (e.g., a job in industry), have become somewhat disenchanted with their traditional dependence on measures of personality, values, and attitudes as the basis of selection (see Dunnette, 1963; Wernimont and Campbell, 1968). There has been a shift away from measures or selection in terms of internal, dispositional variables toward selection in terms of how job candidates *perform* on tasks that approximate or sample the kinds of situational demands that they would face on the job.

Finally, not only do attempts to measure subjective, dispositional variables often evolve into psychometric jungles of checking, cross-checking, and validation, but, more distressingly, they often yield very weak correlations to behavior (Mischel, 1968; Wicker, 1969, 1971; Willems, 1967). On the basis of his review of the attitude–behavior field, Wicker (1969, p. 75) concludes that there is

"... little evidence to support the postulated existence of stable, underlying attitudes within the individual which influence both his verbal expressions and his actions.... Most socially significant questions involve overt behavior, rather than people's feelings, and the assumption that feelings are directly translated into actions has not been demonstrated."

Transdisciplinary Emphasis. The behavioral ecologist assumes and *acts* on the assumption that the phenomena of behavior participate in a much larger network of phenomena, descriptions, and disciplines. In fact, as Smith (1966) points out: "The ecologist is something of a chartered libertine. He roams at will over the legitimate preserves of other scientists and "poaches" from other disciplines" (p. 5). Ecology tends to be highly eclectic and the ecologist tends to borrow and lend concepts, methods, and hypotheses freely, with little sense of preciousness about boundaries between disciplines, because he believes that the sciences of behavior thrive on polygamy. The need for eclecticism and professional symbiosis arises because of the nature of the phenomena and partly because of the nature of professional specialization.

Behavior, the principal means by which organisms carry on commerce with the environment, is embedded in and relates to phenomena at many levels, which themselves form hierarchies of embedded systems, e.g., molecules, cells, tissues, organs, organ systems, organisms, settings, facilities, institutions, political systems, economic systems. Behavior is a mid-range phenomenon; what organisms *do* is the principal means by which they relate to the various levels of context. Thus, the full contextual understanding of behavior requires models and approaches developed by persons who study the various levels of embeddedness (Barker, 1969; Boulding, 1968; Chase, 1971; Sells, 1969; Shepard and McKinley, 1969).

Systems Concepts.   It is common for the ecologist to couch much of what he does and thinks about in the terminology and concepts of systems. This happens for several reasons. Sometimes it is because of the extensiveness of the phenomena under study, sometimes because of their complexity or because of the emphasis on interdependence of many variables at many levels, sometimes because systems theory brings to bear an appropriate and powerful set of formal principles, and sometimes simply because *system* is the best metaphor or image the ecologist can conjure up to communicate what he is trying to say. As science and technology have grown in complexity, the use of systems theory and terminology has become more widespread. Thus, it is only reasonable that ecologists would turn to this formal discipline for tools of conceptual representation and analysis. There is a growing awareness that we need new and sophisticated forms of analysis and synthesis that are not amenable to the traditional, either/or methodology that permeates Western scientific thinking. Systems theory and its various derivatives offer the tools for representing *interdependence* and simultaneous, time-related complexity (Berrien, 1968; Buckley, 1968; Laszlo, 1972; von Bertalanffy, 1968).

One clear example of the interrelated nature of behavior–organism–environment systems is found in the work of Proshansky *et al.* (1970b, chapters 3 and 43) in their report of an attempt to increase the therapeutic effectiveness of psychiatric facilities through appropriate design. They focused their efforts on one ward of a mental hospital—a ward with severely disturbed adult women. The ward was laid out on a long corridor, with a nurses' station at one end, near the entrance, and a solarium at the other end, with bedrooms, a bathroom, and a dayroom in between. When the psychologists came, the solarium, which was meant to be a place of relaxation and recreation, was overheated, poorly furnished, and generally unappealing, with intense sunlight pouring in through a bank of uncovered windows. It was used very little, even though there was a TV set there. Just about the only thing patients did consistently in the solarium was to stand alone for long periods of time in a state of preoccupation, detachment, and withdrawal—that singular behavior pattern in which severly disturbed persons engage so much. This isolated standing was one of the behavior patterns that the hospital staff wished to change.

The psychologists changed the solarium by adding furniture, drapes, and other accessories. Soon, larger numbers of patients began spending longer periods of time there, and the solarium took on the air of a pleasant recreational and social area. More importantly, the rate of isolated standing behavior went down so that very little of it was now occurring in the solarium. The psychologists had achieved their purpose—for the solarium. However, all they had succeeded in doing was to change the *location* of the isolated standing behavior—a great deal of it now took place at the other end of the corridor, by the nurses' station. Luckily, these environmental designers did not restrict their behavior observations to the solarium, but studied a whole environment–behavior *system*, of which the solarium was only one component.

Habitability.   More than many of his peers in behavioral science, the behavioral ecologist devotes a great deal of attention to the question of *habitability*; that is, to the issue of what kinds of environments are fit for human beings to inhabit. The ecologist not only does this because it sets the stage for human design and social engineering, but because he believes that when he leaves his preoccupation with phenomena that are often called "basic" and that are convenient from the investigative point of view—e.g., measures of time, latency, errors, number of trials, thresholds, bar-pressing, and molecular physiology—and concerns himself with such messy and molar everyday problems as safety, convenience, comfort, satisfaction, adjustment, long term functional achievement, adaptation, and cost, he may well be on the most direct path to basic theoretical understanding as well (see Benarde, 1970; Chase, 1971; Chapanis, 1967; Moos and Insel, 1974).

Ecological Diagnosis.   Diagnosis is a process that begins with careful scrutiny of a set of indicators and ends with a judgment, a statement, regarding the events to which those indicators point. For example, a certain pattern among indicators such as fever, respiratory congestion, joint pain, and malaise can lead to a judgment that influenza is occurring. In psychology and psychiatry, judgments of what is wrong (diagnoses) are often highly constrained by prior theoretical commitments that lead one to look for the underlying problem inside the person. It is important to recognize this tradition because diagnostic judgments usually carry with them either implicit or explicit strategies of intervention. If the underlying problem is seen to lie inside the person, then remedial steps will usually be focused on the person. The bearded-tit story cited above and much of what has been outlined in this section raise some fundamental conceptual questions about the use of behavior as a source of indicators, the process of diagnostic judgment, and the targets of intervention.

After he had confirmed his suspicion that the parent tits were engaging in infanticide, the ornithologist could have followed the example provided by diagnosticians of human affairs. That is, he could have assumed that the mainsprings of the behavior resided inside the skins of the parents and he could have diagnosed *them* as crazy or sick and in need of some form of help, perhaps psychotherapy. Instead, he used a series of careful observations to scrutinize the organism–environment system and to converge on a contextual, ecological diagnosis of the problem. Then, he engaged in an ecological course of remedial action that makes great sense in retrospect; i.e., he intervened with the accessibility of the food supply. We have little difficulty accepting this kind of ecological, contextual approach to infra-human animals, but we manage to blind ourselves to its implications for human behavior. The problem lies in our models, theories, and research, which are preoccupied with the unity and integrity of persons taken one at a time and are preoccupied with what goes on inside them, rather than with behavior-environment systems. After all, it is the *person* who behaves, whose behavior we must understand, who misbehaves, and it is the *person* who comes or is referred for help because of some serious internal disturbance, isn't it? This is the way it has been in psychology, but psychology needs much more if it is to deal effectively with human problems.

Naturalistic Emphasis.   Behavioral ecology is largely naturalistic in its methodological orientation; "largely" because it is not defined by any particular methodology and because this is an emphasis rather than a necessary condition. Pluralism of methods is crucial to behavioral ecology, but the ecologist's methodological statement of faith has two parts. First, with Keller and Marian Breland (1966), the ecologist says: "...you cannot understand the behavior of the animal in the laboratory unless you understand his behavior in the wild" (p. 20). Second, contrary to widely held canons in psychology, the ecologist believes that the investigator should manipulate and control only as much as is absolutely necessary to answer his questions clearly, an argument which has been made by many writers (Barker, 1965, 1969; Brandt, 1972; Gump and Kounin, 1959–1960; Lockard, 1971; Menzel, 1969; Willems, 1965, 1969). The ecologist works with the continual reminder that holding experimental conditions constant while varying a limited phenomenon is a figment of the experimental laboratory which may result in the untimely attenuation of both findings and theories. The ecologist recommends more dependence on direct, sustained, naturalistic observation of human behavior and less on shortcut methods based upon verbal expression and the handiest investigative location, which so often is the experimental laboratory.

Distribution of Phenomena in Natural Systems.   Behavioral ecology concerns itself with the distribution of phenomena in nature; upon the range, intensity, and frequency of behavior in the everyday, investigator-free environment (Barker, 1965, 1968, 1969; King, 1970; McGuire, 1969; Willems, 1969; Wright, 1969–1970). Ethologists and many European students of behavior recognize the importance of this procedural issue, but it is one of the most poorly understood issues in all of American psychology. Part of the basis for this misunderstanding may be the feeling that simply observing, counting, measuring, tallying, and classifying everyday phenomena is too commonplace, too mundane, and too unimaginative.

Observing, counting, measuring, and tallying behavior is not simple at all; it is an arduous, time-consuming, painstaking process that probably taxes the scientist's commitment to science more than anything else. Perhaps this is why studying the distribution of behavioral phenomena in natural systems has not received more attention. Hutt (1970) points out that the reasons may also be partly historical. The founders of psychology and most of their followers have seen psychology as an *analytic* science that follows the model of Newtonian physics. In the process, psychology "... appears to have forgotten that physics also enjoyed a long history of naturalistic observation before it entered its analytical stage" (p. 6). Barker argues (1968, pp. 2 and 3):

"Although we have daily records of the oxygen content of river water, of the ground temperatures of cornfields, of the activity of volcanoes, of the behavior. We must know how the relevant conditions are distributed there have been few scientific records of how human mothers care for their young, how teachers behave in the classroom (and how the children respond), what families actually do and say during mealtime, or how children live their lives from the time they wake in the morning until they go to sleep at night. Because we have lacked such records, we have been able only to speculate about many important questions.... Before we can answer these kinds of questions, we must know more than the laws of behavior. We must know how the relevant conditions are distributed among men."

Taxonomy.   Behavioral ecology concerns itself with one of the great voids in American psychology—the problem of taxonomy. Together with naturalistic description of the distribution of behavioral phenomena, basic taxonomic research has been grossly neglected by psychologists (Frederiksen, 1972). It is sometimes argued that behavior is too ephemeral, too spontaneous, and too malleable to be fitted into taxonomies. That is an evasion, because the fleeting and malleable qualities of many chemical and biological phenomena have not prevented the creation of useful taxonomies.

Taxonomies are important for several reasons. First, there is the aesthetic pleasure that accompanies scientific orderliness. Second, systems of classification represent the only comprehensive way to avoid being smothered by a great host of splintered, separate facts (Altman, 1968; Studer, 1972). The development of comprehensive theory depends upon a coherent classification of the empirical domain. Third, a good taxonomy "can provide a standard metalanguage to describe all concepts and variables in a field" (Altman and Lett, 1970, p. 182). Such translation into a common system permits comparison of various findings and concepts with each other. Fourth, as Altman and Lett point out (1970), an effective taxonomy can help scientists pinpoint well-established results, confused or contradictory results, and areas of research that have been neglected; i.e., missing data. Fifth, Altman and Lett also argue that a taxonomy can lead to predictions of new relationships that have not become obvious from separate studies. Sixth, a generally used taxonomy allows any particular investigator to classify what he is working on and to classify it with sufficient precision in a general system so that he is fully aware of how his phenomenon relates to what other investigators are working on and it allows him to communicate it with enough precision so that other investigators know what he is working on.

Long Time Periods.   In keeping with the characteristics of behavior-environment systems and the kinds of behavioral dimensions with which he often works (e.g., adaptation, accommodation, functional achievement, long range behavior, and sometimes even survival), the ecologist not only allows, but sometimes demands, unusually long periods and time dependencies in his research. For generations, behavioral scientists involved in development—child development, personality development, cultural development—have tried to demonstrate how events at one time can function as remote antecedents of something that occurs later (e.g., amount of social and environmental stimulation during infancy and childhood as a remote antecedent of later intelligence). Over and above this traditional search for early antecedents, the ecologist advocates truly longitudinal research that monitors interdependencies continuously, or nearly continuously, for extended periods of time. At least three concerns lead to this emphasis. First, sequential phenomena that emerge over time are among the most important properties of behavior (Barker, 1963b; Raush, 1969). Second, ecosystems in general (and, therefore, probably behavioral–ecological systems) follow rules of succession and internal distribution in which the phases and changes in the systems over time become the critical issue. Third, we know by now from other areas (e.g., crop diseases, pollution, insecticides) that empirical monitoring of very long sequences can be both scientifically illuminating and pragmatically critical. The behavioral ecologist would argue that human behavior and its emergent relations to its contexts must also be studied in such long term perspective. The fact that the behavioral sciences cannot match the sophistication of ecological biochemistry or agronomy is no excuse to wait.

Of course, not all of the important phenomena of human functioning and behavior require very long periods of study. However, the *ecological* problem is that behavioral scientists are distressingly unwilling to differentiate those behavioral issues that require the emergent time frame from those that do not and even less willing to knuckle down and tackle those that do. We would much rather do several discrete studies each year than work on a phenomenon whose important properties unravel and cycle over a period of months or years.

Small Rates.   The behavioral ecologist is more willing than many of his peers to depend upon rate measures across whole populations in drawing conclusions. Americans and American behavioral scientists look for *whopper* effects; we tend to respond most readily to large increases and decreases in things. We are used to viewing things as effective or ineffective, important or unimportant, good or bad only if they lead to big changes in rate. Another way of saying this is that we do not view things from an ecological perspective. The ecologist lets himself view certain matters in terms of whole populations and in terms of small changes in rates in those populations. A change in a few parts per million in the occurrence of a chemical in the environment can mean the difference between a rate that preserves life and a rate that destroys it. Small increases in percents or even fractions of percents in such phenomena as tuberculosis, metallic poisoning, bubonic plague, cholera, or schistosomiasis can bear unambiguous information that something is wrong in the environment and in the relations between persons and the environment.

If this is so, then why should it be different with social and behavioral phenomena? Does nearly everyone in a population have to be involved in rape, murder, suicide, drug addiction, alcoholism, assault, irritability, depression, malaise, uncooperativeness, child abuse, or lack of social amenity before we conclude that there is something fundamentally wrong in the environment or in the interaction of that population with it? Probably not. However, we are not prepared to take small rates measures seriously enough, partly because we know so little about the general adaptive and maladaptive value of behavior phenomena (we know so little about its symptomatic value in various contexts) and partly because we do not yet have the models and theories that lead us to depend upon such rate measures to tell us something important. These are ecological problems and they are ecological problems for the behavioral sciences.

Evaluation of Natural Experiments.   The final aspect of behavioral ecology is one which, to date, has done most to bring general ecology to the attention of the public. Many events—e.g., introduction of insecticides, building dams, introduction of contraceptive techniques, increase in pollutants, use of new seed crops, lumbering, introduction of organisms into new areas—are out of the direct control of ecologists and, therefore, represent natural experiments whose various effects they are able to study. Such natural experiments, when evaluated by ecologists, have provided data and generalizations that have made ecology a faddish and controversial enterprise and they are phenomena on which ecologists have been able to test models and strategies of investigation.

Behavioral ecology has begun to recognize the potential scientific value of natural experiments and should realize that the possibilities are almost infinite, e.g., institutional reforms, refurbishing programs, social change programs, changes in trafficways and transportation systems, disruption of neighborhoods, increases in population and crowding, shifts from single-family to multi-family dwellings, programs of behavior modification.

BEHAVIORAL TECHNOLOGY IN ECOLOGICAL PERSPECTIVE

The ecologist sees a world of complexity rather than simplicity, a world that obeys laws of balance, reciprocity, and interdependency rather than a world in which independent events occur in isolated fashion, a world in which environment and organism are linked inextricably, a world in which many crucial events and their relations evolve over time. Viewing behavioral technology within the ecological framework will help to clarify the technological and ecological positions and will raise some serious questions for the technologist.

Technology is the systematic application of tested scientific principles to pragmatic, real-life tasks and problems. On these terms, applied behavior analysis, or behavior modification, is a behavioral technology par excellence. In fact, the basic research paradigm is also the basic treatment paradigm and the basic research manipulation—contingency management—is also the treatment manipulation. This close coordination of the treatment model to the research process surrounds applied behavior analysis with an enviable degree of explicitness, rigor, and precision.

Once developed, technologies are usually applied and the tendency to use them increases in proportion to the precision with which they can be applied. Thus, we can anticipate phenomenal growth in the array of behavior problems, settings, age groups, and diagnostic groups to which behavior modification will be applied, partly because its precision and specificity will continue to increase and partly because its developers and users display an unusual amount of zeal and optimism about their work. The purpose of this section of the paper is to view behavioral technology within the larger ecological framework. It will be argued that simple strategies of behavior change need to be evaluated and planned within this framework before their true potential will be realized.

Commonalities

The ecological and technological points of view often seem to operate from quite different values and assumptions, but they also may be similar and complementary in many ways. Eight commonly shared values will be presented, with the clear implication that the technologist and ecologist will find value in new forms of cooperative effort, joint-event research, or piggybacking.

(1) *Empiricism and objectivity.* In general, the ecologist and the applied behavior analyst both place a great deal of emphasis upon empirical data, especially if they must choose between complex, speculative theories and an empirical base. Both prefer the direct measurement of what individuals do behaviorally in specific settings to the measurement of theorized internal states. For both, the ratio of empirical data to theory is higher than it is for many other subdisciplines and both prefer to base their generalizations on extensive data sets. However, if the criteria of explicitness and rigor are used in the comparison, the behavior analyst holds a clear advantage. The behavior analyst's objectivity and precision are admired by the behavioral ecologist, who often works within domains that make these criteria more difficult to meet.

(2) *Environment as selective.* Both emphasize a transactional view of behavior; i.e., that the organism's functioning is mediated by behavior–environment interaction. This transactional credo, which is foreign to many scientists, is so dear to both that Skinner might as well be speaking for both when he says: "The environment is obviously important, but its role has remained obscure. It does not push or pull, it selects, and this function is difficult to discover and analyze...the selective role of the environment in shaping and maintaining the behavior of the individual is only beginning to be recognized and studied" (1971, p. 25). Two implications of this view that are accepted by the behavioral ecologist and behavior analyst are (a) that behavior is largely controlled by the environmental setting in which it occurs, and

(b) that changing environmental variables results in the modification of behavior.

(3) *Importance of site specificity.* Both the behavioral ecologist and the behavior analyst assume the site specificity of behavior. The behavioral ecologist's position was described in a previous section. The behavior analyst offers the behavioral ecologist a very promising model—operant contingency control—for understanding site specificity.

(4) *Baseline data on behavior.* The collection of baseline data is a common value that follows from a mutual focus upon the description of what organisms do. Behavioral technologists and ecologists attach fundamental importance to gathering extensive, reliable, relatively atheoretical data as a starting point for their work. While both document the frequency and distribution of behavior (see Bijou *et al.*, 1968), there is a fundamental difference in this descriptive process. This distinction has important implications for both the diagnostic process and the evaluation of interventions. Collection of baseline data for the behavioral ecologist represents a long range monitoring of the complex situational and behavioral environment. Usually, specific target behaviors are not selected on an *a priori* basis and while the behavioral ecologist sometimes chooses behaviors of interest, he views them within this larger contextual framework. The behavioral technologist does not emphasize long range monitoring and he usually limits baseline description to one, or at best, a relatively small number of target behaviors.

(5) *Environmental measurement.* Closely related to the baseline observation of behavior is the emphasis of both groups upon explicit documentation, measurement, and recording of the environment of behavior. The fact that they conceptualize the environment differently is less interesting than the fact that both actually carry out environmental measurement as part of their work.

(6) *Commonplaceness.* This is somewhat different than a shared procedure; it is a shared interest and belief in what is important. Both the behavioral ecologist and the behavior analyst accept common, ordinary, everyday behaviors as primary phenomena to be described, counted, understood, and explained. Both proceed on the basis that "science advances by relentless examination of the commonplace; that some of its greatest discoveries have been made through fascination with what other men have regarded as not worthy of note" (Henry, 1971, p. xix). Thus, the naturalistic observation of the ecologist and the baseline observation of the applied behavior analyst bulge with reference to such ordinary phenomena as location of persons, eating, talking, resting, fighting, reading, holding and handling objects, parti-

cipating in activities, making mistakes, etc. These are primary data for both and are offered in contrast to highly abstract, rarified concepts.

(7) *Common sense and principles of behavior.* Everyone has some intuition regarding his behavior and the behavior of others. Conventional social wisdom and commonsense principles of how things work and what is right, good, and humane permeate what people say about behavior and behavior change. The behavioral ecologist and behavior analyst seem to display an unusual openness to accepting, pursuing, and discovering explanations and governing principles that are counterintuitive and violate common sense. Once the principles have been found to hold, both seem willing to promote programs that do not coincide with conventional, commonly held views. Making food supplies less abundant and less accessible (the bearded-tit example cited earlier) is not an intuitive solution to the problem of infanticide. Displaying love and caring for individuals hardly seems inhumane, but when viewed within the context of reinforcement principles, loving and caring responses can serve unfortunate ends. Baer (1969) describes a four-year-old girl who developed normally, but after the births of two younger brothers began to crawl extensively and display other pre-four-year-old responses. Her behavior was attributed to her new, peripheral position in the family and was interpreted as regressive. Her preschool teachers assumed that insecurity at home contributed to her crawling and other withdrawn behaviors and when crawling was observed, comfort and caring were offered. When she was moving and walking normally, they assumed that, for the moment, her needs were being met and left her and attended to others. They responded with the most humane of intentions and their practices were "impeccable from the point of view of the logic of need" (Baer, 1969, pp. 137–138). But, the girl's behavior did not improve until viewed within a reinforcement model; i.e., until love and attention were made more strictly contingent upon appropriate walking performances.

(8) *Intervention and its effects.* The applied behavior analyst is very successful in achieving categorical outcomes in behavior by means of dimensional management of contingencies. His approach, using a highly specific remedy to alleviate a specific troublesome behavior, satisfies a fundamental principle of applied ecology: strategies of intervention and control that are as specific as possible to particular troubling events are always preferable (see Odum, 1963, pp. 106–107). However, a second principle of applied ecology emphasizes the necessity to predict the results of intrusions in ecological systems. If we are to avoid the removal of vital behaviors or the inadvertant addition of dysfunctional ones, longitudinal monitoring of intact behavior–environment

systems is required. The work of the behavior modifier clearly fulfills the first ecological principle, while the work of the behavioral ecologist emphasizes the second. The behavioral ecologist and the behavior modifier need to link efforts to fulfill both principles.

Some Important Problem Areas

Even though the behavior modifier, more than other practitioners of behavior change strategies, tends to comply with certain ecological principles, many crucial differences emerge that have implications for practice. Stating these differences and problem areas may help to stimulate research, sharpen the perspective of differing points of view, and lead to concrete areas for action.

(1) *Long time periods.* The ecologist has learned from other areas that empirical monitoring of very long sequences can be both scientifically illuminating and pragmatically critical. Participation in long range research is a fundamental issue for the behavioral ecologist. Psychologists often rely upon static accounts of what their subjects do, feel, or think. The widespread use of interviews, questionnaires, and behavioral checklists during one-time data collection sessions support this notion. The behavioral technologist has carried the measurement process forward. He will typically collect baseline data, intervention phase data, and will also monitor behavior during a subsequent maintenance phase.

However, this approach needs to be extended. The behavioral technologist must be willing to participate in even longer range research. Some behavioral interventions might unwittingly disrupt desirable things or set undesirable things in motion that become clear only over very long periods of time. The contingency model can easily become self-serving. When undesirable events follow a behavioral intervention, the behavioral technologist's reply will probably be: "Whatever happens before or after my technological intervention, whether good, bad, or indifferent, is a function of chaotic or unfortunate programs of contingency or, at the least, programs of contingency that are out of my explicit control. Ergo, those occurrences are none of my business, by definition." This is precisely the kind of short-sighted view that has led to technologically induced problems in many areas.

(2) *"Other" data.* One serious ecological problem is the distinct possibility of unanticipated accompaniments of successful interventions. The operant technologist argues eloquently for his simple solutions to many pressing

social and behavioral problems. However, the power and precision with which he works is also the reason for greatest concern from the ecological point of view. Despite some significant exceptions, the work of behavior modifiers has been focused very narrowly—one or a few behavioral categories at a time, one organism at a time, one circumscribed place at a time, and one set of reinforcers or punishers at a time. As the procedures of technological intervention become more powerful, more sophisticated, more precise, and more narrow, their *intended* effects become easier to specify. However, most technological interventions also have *unintended* effects. When an unexplained or undesirable outcome follows an intervention, the behavior modifier often responds that what is needed is more technological ingenuity and more rigorous programming and contingency control. The behavioral ecologist would prefer that operant technologists become involved in clarifying the profoundly complicated and theoretical nature of the simplified interfaces they arrange between organisms and environments.

Arguing against a simplistic interpretation of operant behavior control, Wahler (1972, p. 5) raises the possibility of *indirect* contingency control.

"Indirect, in this case, refers to reinforcers that might control behavior despite the fact that they do not occur as immediate consequences of that behavior. According to this assumption, one might observe a child behavior that is consistently produced in the absence of likely reinforcers. Despite this fact, it is possible that the behavior could be maintained by reinforcers directly applied to other behaviors produced by that child."

Upon first consideration, what Wahler is describing fits nicely into a chaining model of behavior. However, this explanation requires ordered sequential relationships. A study by Buell *et al.* (1968) demonstrated that some behavior covariations are not easily explained within the chaining model. They used teacher social attention to reinforce a withdrawn girl's use of equipment in an outdoor preschool play setting. The intervention was successful, but it also affected behaviors involving interactions with other children (touching, verbalizations, and cooperative play). In his review of this study, Wahler (1972) maintains that it is highly unlikely that this complex array of behaviors always occurred in the same temporal order.

A partial replication of Buell *et al.* by Bradley (1971) was also reviewed by Wahler (1972, p. 10).

"When Bradley made teacher social approval contingent upon a withdrawn preschool girl's cooperative play with peers, a correlated increase was also apparent in the girl's verbalizations. However, an examination of sequential relationships between these two behaviors showed no consistent order of occurrence; sometimes cooperative play preceded verbalizations; sometimes the reverse occurred."

The chaining model does not seem sufficient and additional research is certainly needed. Wahler (1972) uses the term, *response class*, to denote naturally occurring, covarying, functional units of behavior which arise by means of processes that are unknown at present. Wahler *et al.* (1970) showed that parents' successful efforts to reduce nonspeech deviant behaviors by their children also led to reductions in stuttering and that this "side effect" was not due to differences in direct reinforcement of stuttering and fluent speech.

Another clear example comes from the work of Sajwaj *et al.* (1972), who found various "side effects" of manipulating single behaviors in a preschool boy. They arranged for the teacher to ignore the child's initiated speech to her (nagging) in one setting of the preschool. This tactic was successful in reducing the nagging, but produced systematic changes in other behavior by the child in the same setting and in another setting as well. Some of the "side effects" were desirable (increasing speech initiated to children, increasing cooperative play) while some were undesirable (decreasing task-appropriate behavior, increasing disruptive behavior) and some were neutral (use of girls' toys). The investigators were able to show that the covarying effects were not due to differential attention by the teacher applied directly to those behaviors, but were somehow (as yet, mysteriously) a function of modifying another single dimension of behavior. Sajwaj *et al.* consider it distinctly possible that modifying one behavior modifies the properties of the larger setting, thus changing the system of contingencies and the opportunity for reinforcers to contact behaviors.

Finally, in the Probation Department of Los Angeles, some explicit use has been made of token systems and other behavior modification techniques in dealing with deviant behavior among adolescent boys (Caldwell M. Prejean, personal communication). The probation officers were successful in reducing the rates of petty vandalism, such as stealing hubcaps and items from stores. However, as the petty vandalism went down, the rates of more serious offenses, such as stealing cars and destroying property, went up.

It goes without saying that such phenomena beg for further research before any definitive statements can be made about their causal linkages. However, that is precisely the point: the phenomena beg for research, but they beg for research (a) that admits the possibility of unanticipated complexities, (b) that uses models that lead us to look for them and define them as important phenomena, worth our attention, and (c) that adds procedures that allow their detection and measurement when they occur.

(3) *Diagnostic observation.* The least publicized and least explicit part of most behavior modification studies—the observational process by which the investigator views complicated behavior systems, selects certain dimensions for study, and bets successfully that they will be amenable to contingency control—represents an extremely important process. This skill and ingenuity needs to be made more public and explicit and it needs to be subjected to study. It is diagnosis par excellence, and both the technologist and ecologist could benefit greatly from more explicit rules for analyzing the critical aspects of behavior–environment systems and diagnosing the specific ways in which they function suboptimally.

(4) *Setting behavior linkages.* The behavioral ecologist emphasizes the relationship between behavior and the physical environment. This process is poorly understood and needs to be evaluated within the context of other environmental conditions. The delivery of interpersonal reinforcers is currently emphasized by behavior modifiers, but an expanded view is necessary. For example, we might consider the ways in which particular behavioral and educational outcomes in a classroom evolve as a combined function of (a) shape, distribution, and crowding of furniture; (b) mutual delivery of interpersonal reinforcers and punishers; (c) proxemics; and (d) classroom activity format. The designing of functional environments awaits such information, which should be of interest to both the behavioral technologist and ecologist.

(5) *When to rearrange.* The question of when to rearrange follows directly from the problem of unintended effects or "other data." The issue could be subsumed under that heading, but it suggests important metamethodological and ethical considerations that need to be discussed briefly. Zelazo *et al.* (1972a) describe an early infantile walking response that can be transformed from a reflexive to an instrumental action. Stimulation of this response during a period beginning in the second week after birth and continuing through the eighth week resulted in significant reductions in the ages of infants at which they first began to walk alone. The authors described a variety of possible benefits that could result from the development of early mobility. For example, " a major benefit of retaining the walking response and encouraging early mobility may be that it promotes an earlier sense of competence " (Zelazo *et al.*, 1972a, p. 315).

In a reply to Zelazo *et al.*, Gotts (1972) suggested that to accelerate the onset of walking might prove quite undesirable. For example, "at the naturally occurring mean age for solo walking... the average infants' posterior fontanel is closed and his anterior fontanel is closed or nearly closed.... To accelerate the onset of walking would thus unnecessarily expose younger children, who have less complete fontanel closure, to possible central nervous system injury" (Gotts, 1972, p. 1057). In reply to Gotts, Zelazo *et al.* (1972b) emphasize that their desire was to encourage more research on newborn walking and not to encourage all parents to accelerate the ages at which their newborns walk.

The point is well taken that more research is needed before intervention is prescribed. However, when to intervene is a critical question that needs to be considered with more care. While the example just cited is only one specific case, the resulting dialogue represents a needed process (for an interesting discussion of the control of the developmental process, see Baer, 1973).

(6) *Outcomes vs. antecedent conditions.* This last area for concern is basically a theoretical issue, but it also has applied implications. Applied behavior modification involves more than a technology. It participates in a theoretical movement whose view of behavior rests on assumptions of environmentalism, instrumentality, and contingency control. One of the pitfalls here is that information gleaned from interventions into troubling behavior may lead to misleading inferences back to the general model of behavior. The potential error lies in building and confirming a model of behavior on the basis of what works in treatment, or inferring causes from effectiveness of treatment. " To demonstrate that a likely dispenser of stimulus events (such as a parent) can operate as a reinforcer in the modification of a child's deviant behavior is not proof that the dispenser was directly responsible for the prior maintenance of that behavior " (Wahler, 1972, p. 3). It is entirely possible that there are fundamental differences between the conditions under which an organism comes to behave in a certain way and the conditions under which he can be made to behave. We need more wisdom about such matters and they are matters of concern for both the technologist and the ecologist. More complete contextual understanding of troubling behavior can only lead to increased predictability and success in intervention.

A Substantive Illustration

We have been arguing that the ecologist and technologist need to acquire the capability to work together on problems of mutual concern. The opportunities for such a process are many and varied. The material that follows is intended only to illustrate how this might happen.

Behavior technologists often work within institutional settings. The collection of baseline data allows them to make a behavioral diagnosis and follow-up data allow them to evaluate the effectiveness of a technological intervention. The evaluative design requires the monitoring of behavior before, during, and after the intervention phase. But, as Wahler (1972) has pointed out, there is, at present, no *a priori* basis for choosing behaviors to monitor. The behavioral ecologist has called for long range monitoring of the rich and extremely complex situational and behavioral environment. It has been argued that only within this contextual framework can the behavioral technologist evaluate and generate effective programs of behavior change.

Earlier, it was mentioned that in 1968 a comprehensive program of ecologically oriented research was initiated at a unique rehabilitation facility in Houston, Texas (LeCompte and Willems, 1970; Willems, 1972a, 1973d; Vineberg and Willems, 1971). Adults with spinal cord injuries represent the target population and they are observed in their natural setting. During one particularly important phase of this research, trained observers followed a patient continuously for an 18 hour day by rotating in two hour observational shifts. Using small, battery operated cassette recorders, observers dictated a continuous narrative description of the target patients' behavior. Teams of coders then analyzed typed transcripts of the behavior. By this process, protocols were obtained from 12 patients in 1968, totalling 216 hours, and from 15 patients in 1971, totalling 270 hours. In both years, the patients observed comprised all of the patients who were involved in the hospital's program of comprehensive rehabilitation. This resulted in a very rich source of data. Behavioral indicators of progress in rehabilitation were quantitatively derived and evaluated. The ways in which the hospital's system of health care meets the patients and ways in which these relationships change over time were also studied systematically.

There were no behavior technologists at the hospital when the data were collected in 1968 and 1971, but there was an intrusion into the system. Between the two sets of observations, the hospital's system for delivering care was changed. Through 1968 and until a few months before the observations in 1971, the treatment program and the resulting care delivery system were run along fairly traditional lines. The hospital's administration intruded into the system by establishing a Spinal Cord Center in 1971. The Center, which had its own location in the hospital, housed a group of 15 to 20 patients. A core team of persons from various staff categories was assigned to the Center and its patients, and the responsibilities and affiliations of the team resided with the Center patients rather than with their own professional groups and locations. Under this arrangement, all members of the Center's core team were to be directly involved in all aspects of a patient's program: diagnosis, assessment, treatment plan, delivery of treatment, and modification of treatment program. Underlying this arrangement was the prediction that the assignment of a multidiscipline core staff to a patient, to a location, and to a cross-disciplinary responsibility would enhance and optimize the care that patients received, with results in terms of individualization of care, better adaption, better progress, shorter hospitalization time, better understanding of disability, and better preparation of the patient and family for life outside the hospital. It was assumed that there should follow a general intensification of the rehabilitation program and its independence training for patients and that through a more coordinated focusing of staff effort and involvement, patients should be caught up earlier in behavioral performances that were oriented toward their readjustment and functional independence. In other words, one of the purposes of the Spinal Cord Center was to *redistribute* patient behavior over the course of hospitalization.

The important point for present purposes is that the research was operated under the guiding belief that a complex system involving persons, environment, facilities, and programs was being monitored and that the change to the Spinal Cord Center changed the relations among the components of that system. With a complicated set of data, the task was to document both anticipated and unanticipated changes and check them against the goals of the Center.

First, some aspects of the distribution of patient behavior remained invariant through the change. Across all patients and across kinds of behavior, both the proportion of patient behavior that occurred in various parts or settings of the hospital and the frequencies of various kinds of behavior remained constant through the change to the Center. Furthermore, the proportion of time that late patients (near discharge) spent in complete idleness (lying in bed, etc.) was much lower than the proportion for early patients (nearer admission and earlier in the rehabilitation process) and the difference between late and early patients remained the same through the change.

Second, a number of aspects of the system changed in positive directions, in directions hoped for. Two examples illustrate these positive changes. From the observational data, it was possible to calculate the proportion of patient behaviors in which various kinds of other persons were directly, behaviorally involved (e.g., help with a transfer, help with eating a meal). Before the change to the Center, aides and orderlies carried the largest burden of such involvements by far. One goal of the Center arrangement was to change this distribution of involvements so that more advanced staff members would be directly involved with patients more often. Also, in the interests of better preparing patients and family members for life outside the hospital, another goal was to create conditions under which visitors, such as spouses and other family members and friends, would become directly involved with patients more often. Table 1 indicates that these purposes were achieved to some extent. The rate of direct involvement with patients by aides and orderlies went down while the rates for nurses, physical therapists, and visitors went up.

TABLE 1. PROPORTION OF PATIENT BEHAVIORS IN WHICH FOUR KINDS OF OTHER PERSONS WERE DIRECTLY INVOLVED

	1968	1971	Percent change 1968 to 1971
Aides and orderlies	0.41	0.24	−41%
Nurses	0.11	0.14	+27%
Physical therapists	0.10	0.14	+40%
Visitors	0.04	0.10	+150%

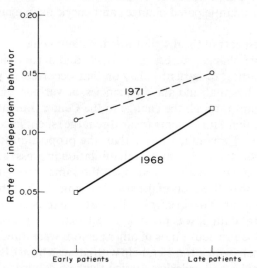

FIG. 1. Proportion of time that early and late patients displayed behavioral independence in 1968 and 1971.

Another example of a positive change occurred in the independence of the patients. From the observational data, those behaviors which the patients themselves initiated and carried out alone were identified as events that reflected behavioral independence. Calculating the proportion of time for such behaviors to total time for the day yielded the rate of independence for each patient. Figure 1 shows the results before and after the introduction of the Center. As had been hoped, not only were patients generally more independent after the change, but they displayed the independence earlier.

Finally, against the background of constancies and some positive changes, the system also took back some things and produced some negative and unanticipated effects. These can be illustrated with two examples. One of the purposes of behavioral rehabilitation at the hospital is to prepare the patient for life outside the hospital. One way to do that is to make sure that as patients progress over time and regain some behavioral independence, they practice their new independence skills in more and more settings of the hospital and practice carrying out many different behaviors in independent fashion. Figures 2 and 3 indicate that that was precisely what was happening in 1968, before the change to the Center (see solid lines in both figures). In 1968, late patients performed independently (their own initiative and no help from others) in far more of the hospital's settings (Fig. 2) and in a greater number of

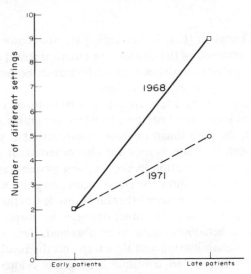

FIG. 2. Number of different hospital settings in which early and late patients performed independently in 1968 and 1971.

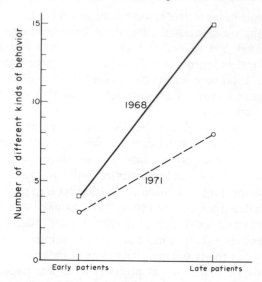

FIG. 3. Number of different kinds of behavior which early and late patients performed independently in 1968 and 1971.

different kinds of behavior (Fig. 3) than early patients. However, this picture changed with the creation of the Center; the environmental and behavioral range of the late patients' independent performance became much more restricted (see the dotted lines in both figures).

These data represent only a few discrete illustrations of a more complex analysis of a system made up of persons, facilities, programs, behaviors, and settings. However, the data illustrate how research that is guided by ecological principles can lead one to look for phenomena that might be overlooked otherwise. An intervention in the ongoing system resulted in some constancies and some gains. But these constancies and gains were also linked interdependently with losses in some other functions, losses that may not have been apparent unless the system-like functioning of the hospital was assumed and unless extensive behavioral data were obtained. This research at the Texas Institute for Rehabilitation and Research and the resulting climate or orientation that lends itself to continuing program evaluation has been described to illustrate the need and potential for cooperation. The behavioral ecologist and behavioral technologist can and need to work together.

HUMANISTIC PSYCHOLOGY IN
ECOLOGICAL PERSPECTIVE

Viewing the humanistic orientation in psychology within an ecological framework is more difficult because the humanistic position is not stated with the explicitness of behavioral technology. We wonder what transcendence of the environment really means, or how insightful, self-actualizing individuals can be viewed within an ecological perspective. The material that follows describes (a) how a behavioral ecologist might view humanistic psychology, (b) some perceived commonalities between the two movements and some important areas of disagreement, (c) the humaneness of humanistic psychology, and (d) the impact of the person centered approach.

The behavioral ecologist and the humanist share a common concern. Both are reacting against some traditional trends in American psychology. The behavioral ecologist maintains that we are not ready to understand everyday behavior, to plan appropriate conditions for human living, or to alleviate human suffering effectively. Neither our current models nor our arsenal of research tools match the realities of everyday behavior. On the surface, this sounds very much like Carl Rogers' discussion of the emerging humanistic perspective: "... the trend of which I am speaking will attempt to face up to all of the realities in the psychological realm. Instead of being restrictive and inhibiting, it will throw open the whole range of human experiencing to scientific study" (1963, p. 80). This reaction against narrow, constricted approaches is even more clearly characterized by Maslow (1965, p. 24):

> "It is easy enough to develop a sound theory of the learning of nonsense syllables, or of rats running in mazes, or of conditioning of the dog's salivary reflex. To integrate these miniature theories into the whole fabric of psychology is another matter. To relate them to love and hate, to growing and regressing, to happiness and pain, to courage and anxiety, exposes the weakness of nibbling away at the edges of reality instead of making reconnaissance flights over the whole of it."

While both behavioral ecology and humanistic psychology represent protest movements, there is a subtle quality about the Rogers and Maslow arguments that causes the behavioral ecologist to pause. Rogers states clearly in the 1963 paper that the humanistic approach in psychology "will explore the private worlds in inner personal meanings ..." (p. 80), and Maslow echoes this need by his choice of examples. Both seem to suggest that the humanness of life needs to be rekindled and that this process is tied to certain inner, experiential qualities. The behavioral ecologist feels much more comfortable when the word humanness is used in a different context. Dubos (1968) speaks for ecology when he says that "The humanness of life depends above all on the quality of man's relationship to the rest of creation—to the winds and the stars, to the flowers and the beasts, to smiling and weeping humanity" (p. 8).

Commonalities

But it is not enough to describe a vague discomfort with the humanistic orientation and then to offer a poetic rejoinder. More specific agreements and disagreements between the two points of view will be discussed in the material to follow. Initially, points of agreement will be described, but the agreement slowly vanishes and areas of disagreement are discussed in the succeeding section.

(1) *Molar phenomena and nonreductionism.* For Maslow (1965), miniature, compartmentalized approaches in psychology represent a "nibbling away at the edges of reality..." (p. 24). The behavioral ecologist would agree wholeheartedly and would certainly be delighted with Maslow's choice of words. If we are going to create the conditions that lend themselves to human well-being, interdependencies within the man–environment system must be examined carefully.

While the notion of the whole being greater than the sum of its parts is shared by the ecologist and humanist, one important distinction seems to surface continually. Maslow (1965) also says that, "The lessons of Gestalt psychology and of organismic theory have not been fully integrated into psychology. The human being is an irreducible unit..." (p. 32). This suggests that nonreductionism for the humanist emphasizes organismic variables. The humanist uses this orientation to argue for the uniqueness of the individual. The ecologist would more readily promote the notion "that the individual is not a skin encapsulated ego but an organism–environment field" (Watts, 1969, p. 140). The humanist argues for a nonreductionistic science and yet his emphasis on the individual violates this stance. The humanist suggests that an individual cannot be understood if he is viewed as a fragmented grouping of components. But humanistic psychology is arguing for a self-regulating, autonomous component (the "whole individual") and therefore represents only a quasi-nonreductionism.

(2) *Naturalistic emphasis.* The ecological position suggests that the investi-

gator (or therapist) should manipulate and control only as much as is absolutely necessary to answer his questions (or to promote change with a client). The behavioral ecologist is not a therapist, nor does he typically take on the role of a change agent. He is a researcher and the nonmanipulative basis for his research generates distinguishable research activities (Willems and Raush, 1969). Barker (1965) sees a difference between data resulting from experimenter manipulation (here the psychologist is characterized as an operator) and data collected within a naturalistic framework (here the psychologist is characterized as a transducer). "In short the data which psychologists produce as operators and as transducers refer to nonoverlapping classes of psychological phenomena" (p. 4).

Poppen and Wandersman (1973) suggest that a "humanistic therapist can be ... characterized as a passive catalyst" (p. xxi). Taking this view, the behavioral ecologist and humanist are more closely related than the humanist and behavioral technologist. The active manipulative role of the behavioral technologist distinguishes his activities from the passive catalyst role of the humanist and the nonmanipulative, transducer role of the behavioral ecologist. The behavioral technologist does not hesitate to intervene and, as an active change agent, he accepts the responsibility for a client's progress. The humanistic therapist is also a change agent, but since an individual's development is seen as an internal process, his role is very different. Usually, he will not tell his client what to do or how to do it with the forcefulness displayed by the behavior technologist. He sees himself in a more gentle, more "natural," human-to-human interactive role. He will help his client develop and grow, but he will not attempt to set up all of the sufficient conditions for that development.

The behavioral ecologist is not a therapist. His skills are more adapted to the collection and interpretation of information that will give meaning to the developmental process and specify the conditions under which desired change will take place. He is cautious of narrow, single dimension intrusions into a man–environment system. He is more of an observer and interpreter than an active therapeutic agent. If he acts as an agent of change, he is greatly concerned about the natural interdependencies into which he intrudes.

(3) *Evaluation of natural experiments.* The behavioral ecologist and the humanist share a concern for the direction and tempo of change within our society. The ecologist's concern for technological advance is characterized by Dubos (1968) when he stresses "that technological advances endlessly create new dilemmas, since every innovation has unforeseen consequences. Social regimentation, traffic jams, environmental pollution, constant exposure to

noise and other unwanted stimuli are but a few of the undesirable accompaniments of economic and technological growth" (p. 13). The behavioral ecologist has begun to recognize that the monitoring and evaluation of change that is out of his direct control is a valuable and crucial enterprise. Increases in population and crowding, shifts from single-family to multi-family dwellings, and an endless array of social reform programs represent examples of events that require systematic evaluation. Campbell (1969) advocates such research and suggests that we need to continue or discontinue programs on the basis of assessed effectiveness. Since the humanistic psychologist is particularly sensitive to the dangers of our present technological society, cooperative research efforts should come naturally for the humanist and ecologist.

(4) *Transdisciplinary emphasis.* The traditional boundaries of psychology are not important to the behavioral ecologist, and the humanistic perspective also suggests an opening up, a fresher, wider perspective. Rogers (1963) is clearly critical of the inhibited, traditional approaches in psychology when he describes how the humanistic trend will affect the practitioner: "In this respect I believe that the psychologist will experience a new burst of creative freedom, such as has occurred in other sciences when old bonds and boundaries have been broken. No problem, no method, no perspective, will be out of bounds" (p. 81). Some humanistic psychologists have argued that compartmentalized departments of psychology within our universities have created unhealthy orientations. Bugental (1963) states that "our pattern of many specialities—clinical, counseling, industrial, child—is proving more self-defeating than implementing" (p. 565).

In important ways, the behavioral ecologist would concur with Bugental and Rogers, but, while agreement within this realm is considerable, there is still a difference in thrust. Associated with humanistic psychology are terms such as "phenomenological" and "existential." The humanist draws heavily from a certain philosophical tradition. The behavioral ecologist is more clearly aligned with the systems analyst, sociologist, urban planner, and biological ecologist in his emphasis on organism-behavior-environment systems.

Problem Areas

Beyond this base of general agreement, there are also crucial disagreements. Each of the arguments regarding differences between behavioral ecology and humanistic psychology has implications for the way in which humanists conduct their business.

(1) *Behavioral focus.* The behavioral ecologist emphasizes overt molar behavior as it relates to the environmental contexts in which it occurs. The focus of the humanist is "experience," the internal subjective feelings or reactions of individuals. The ecologist does not argue against the reality of subjective internal states; rather, the disagreement is a matter of emphasis in the attempt to understand human functioning. The ecologist's relative emphasis on overt behavior involves more than a simplistic advocacy of behaviorism as well. Some approaches to behaviorism argue that overt behavior, directly observable and physically defined, is more *real* than internal psychological states, feelings, and dispositions. On the other hand, the humanist does not seem to particularly value the behavior, but rather the independent, internal, subjective aspects of life. To philosophical behaviorists, such events are epiphenominal and uninteresting, if anything at all. The position of the behavioral ecologist is somewhat different. For him, overt behavior is the more *important.* For him, it is more important to know how parents *treat* their children than how they feel about being parents; more important to observe whether passersby *help* someone in need or not than what their beliefs are about altruism and kindness; more important to note that a person *harms* someone else when given an opportunity than to know whether his self concept is that of a considerate person; more important to know what people *do* with trash than to measure their attitudes about trash; more important to know what one *does* in the way of consumption of alcohol or hiring of women than to infer community attitudes with regard to alcohol or women. To the behavioral ecologist, person–environment–*behavior* systems represent problems to be understood and solved that are simply more important than person–environment–*cognition* systems or person–environment–*attitude* systems. Even though he may sometimes employ concepts and measurements relating to internal, subjective events to help to explain a relationship between environment and behavior, the behavioral ecologist will emphasize the behavioral domain as the primary one, the one to be explained.

The humanist's concern for such things as creativity, self-growth, development, responsibility, and psychological health, sound good to most persons, including behavioral ecologists, but they need to be specified with much more clarity. What sorts of overt behaviors, occurring when, in what environmental circumstances, and with which individuals depict a peak experience? What sorts of behaviors characterize self-growth? These questions and countless similar ones should be an important part of the humanistic psychologist's professional work. The internal, subjective aspects of experience are only part of the picture and the humanist has ignored the behavioral part for too long. A complete picture of the full possibilities inherent in man and the ways in which these possibilities can be actualized will be achieved only if overt behavior is seen as belonging not only to the same coin as internal subjective responses, but to the same coin as the environment.

(2) *Systems.* From the behavioral ecologists' point of view, systems concepts are not only important, but they pervade his thinking and work. Humanists also recognize the utility of the systems view and systems concepts appear in much of the literature of humanistic psychology. However the use of a systems approach can be misused and misunderstood. For example, Fromm (1968, p. 4) asserts:

> "The present social system can be understood a great deal better if one connects the system 'Man' with the whole system. Human nature is not an abstraction nor an infinitely malleable and hence dynamically negligible system. It has its own specific qualities, laws, and alternatives. The study of the system Man permits us to see what certain factors in the socio-economic system do to man, how disturbances in the system Man produce imbalances in the whole social system. By introducing the human factor into the analysis of the whole system, we are better prepared to understand its dysfunctioning and to define norms which relate the healthy economic functioning of the social system to the optimal well-being of the people who participate in it. All this is valid, of course only if there is agreement that maximal development of the human system in terms of its own structure— that is to say, human well-being—is the overriding goal."

The opening assumption of Fromm's statement would be very palatable to the ecologist. However, the closing comment represents a fundamental misconception. Many of the vivid environmental problems now confronted by mankind follow from trying to enhance the personal and collective well-being of man as if such enhancement could come about independently of the complex exchanges of energy to which man is subject. Even though the illustrations and analogies are not as clear in the behavioral realm, one purpose of this paper has been to argue that the imperialism of behavioral and psychological well-being as an overriding goal can (and probably will) lead to many dismal outcomes when the well-being is conceived too narrowly, when the targets of treatment and change are not seen as inextricable parts of larger systems. With what is known today about the nature and functioning of eco-systems, it is clear that man must view himself as related interdependently to all other aspects of his environment. Maximizing the human subsystem in terms of its own structure at the expense of other interrelated components can lead, in the long run, to suffering for mankind, not development of his potential. In the shorter run, this conceptual confusion accounts for the unpleasant aftereffects of some of our most humane actions. Maximum development of the human potential is only a dream if we continue to ignore man's system-like interrelatedness with his environment. Dubos (1968, p. 165) argues that:

"Ideally, all aspects of the environment should form an integrated ecological system in which the welfare of any part of the system is dependent upon the welfare of all the others. In the light of ecological theory, man is part of the total environment and therefore cannot achieve and maintain physical and mental health if conditions are not suitable for environmental health. For this reason, it is ecologically and indeed logically impossible to define an optimum environment if one has only man in mind."

(3) *Behavior–environment*. Extending the argument from the focus on behavior and the use of systems concepts leads to a point of major conceptual concern for the behavioral ecologist in relation to the work of the humanistic psychologist. Behavior is the means by which organisms and environments are mutually and interdependently related. Organisms and environments are part of the same system, with behavior being the major interface between them. Watts (1969, p. 140) points out:

"If you will accurately describe what any individual organism is doing, you will take but a few steps before you are also describing what the environment is doing...we can do without such expressions as 'what the individual is doing' or 'what the environment is doing,' as if the individual was one thing and the doing another. If we reduce the whole business simply to the process of doing, then the doing, which was called the behavior of the individual, is found to be *at the same time* the doing which is called the behavior of the environment."

This transactional nature of behavior and environment is widely accepted by many psychologists. Behaviorists, of course, are quite explicit in their formulations of behavior–environment interactions. Although with somewhat less precision, the humanists seem to pay lip service to the transactional nature of behavior and environment. For example, Maslow's hierarchy of needs, culminating in self-actualization, is based on behavior–environment interdependence at the lower and middle levels. The basic needs necessary to sustain life, such as food, water, clothing, and shelter must be met continually before progressing to middle level needs such as love and esteem of peers. All of these middle and lower level needs are satisfied through interrelated, reciprocally functioning organism–behavior–environment systems. However, Maslow (1961) seems to become myopic about this point when he discusses optimal mental health: "I feel we must leap ... to the clear recognition of transcendence of the environment, independent of it, able to stand against it, to fight it, to neglect it, or to turn one's back on it, to refuse it or adapt to it" (p. 2). Maslow carefully explains that transcendence is an hierarchical–integrative concept "which implies simply that the higher is built upon, rests upon, but includes the lower" (p. 2).

The myopia involved in this best of intentions argument represents the fundamental misconception in the position of humanistic psychology mentioned above. In the first place, it seems contradictory to speak of an individual transcending his environment when the transcendence being advocated is "built upon," "rests upon," and "includes" the individual in an organism–behavior–environment system. In addition, for the ecologist, the individual is never outside of or somehow beyond his environment; the environment is as much a part of the individual as is his nose.

The behavioral ecologist's emphasis on behavior and environment perhaps agrees somewhat with the humanists' reaction to the extreme behaviorists' contention that man is merely a passive agent in a controlling environment. However, advocating transcending the environment does not lead to understanding the nature of man's functioning. The ecologist's position is more nearly aligned with Bandura (1971c, p. 40) when he states:

"...man is neither driven by inner forces nor buffeted helplessly by environmental influences. Rather, psychological functioning is best understood in terms of a continuous reciprocal interaction between behavior and its controlling conditions.... Behavior partly creates the environment and the resultant environment, in turn, influences the behavior."

(4) *Site specificity of behavior.* The behavioral ecologist's emphasis on behavior and environment is closely related to the phenomenon of site specificity in behavior. Humanists sometimes point to Mischel's (1968) reports of low intercorrelations between measures of personality traits and low correlations between traits and behaviors as supporting their advocacy of the uniqueness of the individual. While the ecologist accepts the fact that individuals are unique, he tends to agree with Mischel (1968, p. 295) when he states:

"No one challenges the fact that response potentiality resides in persons; situations may evoke behavior but they do not perform it. Living organisms are not empty and their repertoires of potential behavior exist nowhere outside their own skins....After agreeing on this point, however, it also seems that it is not the critical issue. *The key question, rather, is how to study, understand, predict, and modify these human responses."* [Italics added.]

An important implication of Mischel's (1968) findings is that the site specific nature of many behaviors often accounts for a far larger proportion of the total variance in behavior than do measures of personality traits or individual dispositions. In the conduct of everyday affairs, not only is location specificity in behavior depended upon for predictability and social order, but departures from such correlations often lead to persons being labeled or diagnosed as sick, crazy, deviant, hyperactive, depressed, etc., and in need of help or control. Person-based concepts and variables, inside the skins of persons, may help us to understand the limits of human adaptation, but they will not allow us to explain the everyday diversity of behavior. This diversity is patterned by place dependencies; it is manifested in behavior because of adaptation across the diversity of the environments through which persons pass. Barker (1968) presents this argument from a slightly different vantage point:

> "When environments are relatively uniform and stable, *people* are an obvious source of behavior variance, and the dominant scientific problem and the persistent queries from applied fields are: What are people like? What is the nature and what are the sources of individual differences? ... But today *environments* are more varied and more unstable than heretofore, and their contribution to the variance of behavior is enhanced [p. 3]. ...a beam has many strengths depending especially upon its structural context. The same is true, too, of the meaning of words. Words have a range of meanings, the precise one being determined by the context in which it occurs. A good dictionary gives a number of these meanings, the modal meanings; but for greatest precision it uses the word in revealing contexts. A person is like a beam or word: he has many strengths, many intelligences, many social maturities, many speeds, many degrees of liberality and conservativeness, and many moralities" [pp. 5–6].

(5) *Long time periods.* The humanist is a catalyst and an initiator of what he calls processes of growth. He may help individuals to master key developmental tasks or he may hope to minimize discontinuity in the stages of his clients' growth. One thing is certain—he wants his interventions in a client's life to have long-lasting and far-reaching effects. In contrast, the behavioral technologist is criterion oriented. That is, he specifies what he wants to achieve

and, when his goals are accomplished, he stops. His intervention may have long-lasting, complex effects, but he at least does not intend to implement unspecified change. The humanist assumes that his intervention strategy is dynamic and that his client will build upon initial growth and strive toward further actualization in ways that are not specified at the outset. This basic assumption suggests that humanists (more than other agents of change) should be very concerned about and understand effects that emerge over time. For the humanist to understand the effects of his intervention, it is critical that the unfolding of a sequential pattern of change be viewed within a longitudinal perspective. There is little evidence that he accepts this longitudinal perspective on evaluating his work, but it is crucial that he accept it. The ecologist and humanist could combine skills fruitfully to understand the process of human change more clearly and monitor it more explicitly.

(6) *Habitability.* The issue of what sorts of environments are best suited for human habitation is a major concern of the behavioral ecologist. This interest stems naturally from his emphasis on person–behavior–environment systems and it is not a purely academic concern. Engineers, architects, and other agents of environmental planning and policy more and more frequently are turning to the social sciences with various forms of the question: How do we design this environment so that it is best suited for its human inhabitants?

What we know at present about the habitability of environments is pitifully thin and leaves us with more questions than answers. We know what has not worked, retrospectively, and we can point to some existing conditions that create problems. For example, Dubos (1971a) discusses the new town of Skarholmen, near Stockholm, Sweden. Skarholmen was built to incorporate the most advanced architectural technology. Among its 20,000 inhabitants, particularly among its children and teenagers, there is an alarming rate of restlessness, aggressiveness, and withdrawal that is correlated with nearness to the center of town and the density of living arrangements. Behavioral scientists studying and evaluating the new town have suggested that the antisocial behaviors are related to population density and the highly austere form of architecture. Whether this specific explanation is correct or not, it would appear that the behavioral problems are symptomatic, not of personal problems, but of problems in the relationship of habitat and behavior.

Newman (1972) reports an extensive set of data on the relations between the size of housing projects and what persons do in them. For example, in projects with 1000 or fewer units and six or fewer stories, the rate of felonies and misdemeanors is 47 for each 1000 persons. In projects with the same limits on numbers of units, but with more than six stories, the rate of similar crimes moves upward by 8.5%, to 51 per 1000 persons. However, in projects with more than 1000 units *and* more than six stories, the crime rate jumps by 43%, to 67 per 1000 persons. In other words, increasing population size and increasing height somehow interact to correlate with sharp increases in rates of crime. Newman presents further data on felonies alone. As the height of the housing project increases from three to sixteen stories, the rate of felonies jumps by 130%, from 8.8 per 1000 persons to 20.2 per 1000. As the height of projects increases from three to twenty stories, the rate of robberies and muggings shoots up by 475%!

Such numbers sound abstract and distant. However, when we translate them into probabilities—the likelihood that innocent persons will be victimized and affected—we can see why many persons develop a bewildering sense of vulnerability and a feeling that things have come apart in ways that mystify them. What would the humanistic psychologist do if faced with issues of this sort? He proclaims proudly that his primary concern is a scientific approach to maximizing the development of the human potential. Yet, the question of what sorts of environments enhance the probabilities of reaching this end does not appear in the humanistic literature. Habitability is a real-life problem without simple solutions. The question of which environments are good for human habitation involves selecting criteria that have long range implications; it also involves understanding the nature of the human animal and the ways in which he is linked with his environment. However, the potential payoff, the collective benefit to mankind, which would result from a better, more complete understanding of the habitability of human environments, is enormous. Likewise, our failure to address this problem adequately has frightening, negative consequences. Dubos (1970, p. 87) points out:

" Man is not on his way to extinction. He can adapt to almost anything. I am sure that we can adapt to the dirt, pollution and noise of New York City or Chicago. That is the real tragedy—we can adapt to it. As we become adapted we accept worse and worse conditions without realizing that a child born and raised in this environment has no chance of developing his total physical and mental potential. It is essential that we commit ourselves to such problems as a society and as a nation, not because we are threatened with extinction, but because, if we do not understand what the environment is doing to us, something perhaps worse than extinction will take place—a progressive degradation of the quality of human life."

The ideals to which humanists subscribe should be brought out of the armchair, out of the constriction of single-person interventions and into the messy, difficult, trying world of problems which are in urgent need of immediate attention. The humanist's compassion for his fellow man should spur him to deal with the issues that lie at the roots of the human condition. In discussing our relations to the present socially and technologically created environment, Dubos (1971b) argues that man should ". . . design environments really adapted to his nature. He should not be satisfied with palliative measures treating the effects of objectionable conditions, but instead change the conditions" (p. 53).

(7) *Ecological diagnosis.* The classical mode of diagnosis, in which the person is seen as the repository of the problems, can lead easily to results that are too facile, too quick-and-dirty in their execution, as well as pernicious in their results. The ease with which this can happen is illustrated by the work of Rosenhan (1973). In Rosenhan's study, eight sane persons gained admission to twelve different mental hospitals over a period of time. Without the hospitals' knowledge that they were pseudopatients, the eight persons called the hospitals for admitting appointments. They used pseudonyms and falsified employment information, but, in the admitting–diagnostic routine, they did not alter other characteristics of their life histories or personal circumstances except for one thing. During the admitting procedure, they complained of hearing voices, which they described as "unclear," "empty," "hollow," "thud," and as being unfamiliar to them. All were admitted with a diagnosis of "schizophrenia" except one. The investigators who arranged the study told each pseudopatient that he would have to get out of the hospital by his own devices. The average length of stay was 19 days, with a range from 7 to 52 days. Even though several of the hospitals had excellent reputations, other patients—never staff members—were the ones who spotted the pseudopatients as pretenders. To top it off, each of the pseudopatients was discharged with a diagnosis of "schizophrenia in remission." Note that they were not judged never to have been insane; they were judged to have been insane and somehow remitted. In other words, the original label stuck.

Rosenhan reports other data and his study certainly has far-reaching implications. The important point for present purposes is to note how simplistic and facile—but dangerous—the classical mode of diagnosis can be. Assuming that the person carries around the roots of his problems inside him, the classical mode often involves only a few logical steps (and a few shortcuts) to respond to a simple set of verbal signals about what is presumably going on inside the person and conclude, diagnostically, that his life is fouled up. What such a process disregards about the person's behavioral life and his function-ing beyond the simple verbal, inward-pointing signals should give us all pause.

As Calhoun has argued (1967), the ecosystem and its members can collude in processes that are systematically or ecologically disharmonious and destructive; that is, they can become involved reciprocally in "ecological traps." The fact that some persons manifest the problems while others do not, that the disturbance process has varying concentrations and is not necessarily distributed equally throughout the ecological system should not divert us from the principle that we ". . . cannot speak only of the disturbance of the individual, but . . . must speak of the disturbance of the system" (Rhodes, 1972, p. 559). Our traditional models lead us to focus on persons. The points in the ecological system in which we sample determine where we locate the behavioral problem. Scientists and practitioners alike, "We are, so to speak, fishing in the stream of life, and bring up only that for which we have appropriate bait" (Rhodes, 1972, p. 563). Thus, when our pet models lead us to attach our disturbance detectors to the individual, we will detect disturb-ance in the individual and we will make him our target of intervention and change. In the process, we disregard the fact that the problem or the disturb-ance may lie at the level of an ecological system of which the individual is only one component and that our scientific understanding of behavior, our principles of diagnosis, and our interventions must be adjusted to that level of complexity.

What's So Humane About Humanism?

The humanistic and ecological movements are both protests against the more traditional areas of psychology. Other similarities, sometimes only superficial and sometimes only potential areas of agreement, were pointed out above. However, the commonalities seem weak and tenuous when compared to the areas of disagreement. These differences can be sharpened by raising two final issues.

Is a Person-centered Orientation Humane? If we are to answer important questions about human well-being, it is imperative that we look for answers in the right places. The humanistic psychologist believes that his views and models provide a particularly rich and representative picture of human problems and a particularly humane approach to solutions. These models emphasize person-centered, organismic variables. As Caplan and Nelson (1973) and Ryan (1971) have pointed out so eloquently, (a) person-centered variables have been the chief focus of psychologists and other behavioral scientists involved in solving human problems, (b) the person-centered approach, the "psychologizing" approach, has dominated treatment and remedial efforts for too long, and (c) we need to shift to contextual definitions and diagnoses of human problems because person-centered ones frequently lead to modes of action that not only evade the location of the problem but may even compound the problem. When people behave in inappropriate or troubling ways, it is common for researchers and therapists to focus "on 'person-centered' characteristics (these that lie within the individual), while ignoring situationally relevant factors (those external to the individual)" (Caplan and Nelson, 1973, p. 199).

The general attenuation of social involvement displayed by many inhabitants of large cities exemplifies a problem that can easily be viewed within the person-centered framework. Milgram (1970) describes a variety of behavioral characteristics that are most striking in cities. Bystanders are less likely to intervene in a crisis, city dwellers are less likely to trust and assist strangers, and "Even at the most superficial level of involvement—the exercise of everyday civilities—urbanites are reputedly deficient" (Milgram, 1970, p. 1463). When an individual fails to assist another or behaves with a general coldness in his interactions with others, it could be argued that *he* needs to develop interpersonal skills, to become more open, caring, and concerned. This suggests that the individual needs to change, grow, and become a fuller person. But efforts directed at this personal growth process may not only reduce the possibility of understanding systemic causes, but may compound problems by avoiding the real problems.

The behavioral ecologist would maintain that many of the behavioral differences between city dwellers and small-town dwellers can only be understood adequately when the characteristics of the city and not the inhabitants are viewed as causing the social attenuation. Milgram (1970) agrees and suggests that "contrasts between city and rural behavior probably reflect the responses of similar people to very different situations, rather than intrinsic differences in the personalities of rural and city dwellers. The city is a situation to which individuals respond adaptively" (p. 1465). Probably in far more ways than we have even begun to imagine, the troubling, sad, and uncomfortable symptoms that appear in the everyday lives of persons point to problems to be solved at the level of *contexts* rather than at the level of *persons*.

It is for such reasons and for reasons discussed earlier ("Ecological diagnosis", "Habitability") that we ask: What is so humane about a movement which (a) sees human difficulty essentially as a person-based matter, (b) disregards the *inextricable* links between environmental systems and human functioning, including behavioral and psychological functioning and, as a result, (c) makes the internal, subjective affairs of the individual the primary targets of intervention and amelioration?

Cumulative Entrapment.   The behavioral ecologist's emphasis on long time periods provides another way to look at the question: What is so humane about humanistic psychology? The humanist's interventions into persons' lives are directed at processes whose essential nature is long term. The issue from the ecological perspective is not as simple as pointing out that the humanist should consider a longer time frame in his work. The behavioral ecologist questions the humaneness of humanism because the appropriate criteria for evaluating what is good for human beings—what is humane—can be determined *only* if a long time perspective is considered. Most of the examples and illustrations offered in this paper demonstrate that short term criteria of good are frequently misleading.

A classic argument regarding cumulative entrapment is found in Hardin's article, "The tragedy of the commons" (1968). One example of a *commons* is public grassland available to all the local herdsmen for grazing their cattle. It is to the immediate advantage of each individual cattleman to increase the number of cows in his herd and feed them by grazing on the grassland. In the short view, each individual profits by taking advantage of the free good, the commons. However, if all the herdsmen follow the same relentless logic, the effect is that the common grasslands are overgrazed and eventually destroyed in the long run. The long run result of a short run, individual good is negative for both the group and each individual.

The ecological point is that not only do many of our positive but short-sighted views of good lead to serious, negative consequences in the long run, but these reversals typically occur because of the synergistic workings of the organism–behavior–environment systems within which individuals are immersed. The selection of criteria for evaluating the humaneness of our interventions into complex systems must take cognizance of the interrelated nature and functioning of these systems over time. Platt (1973) applies this logic to human behavior in a reinforcement paradigm.

Another dramatic present-day example is the deadly sludge that is creeping along the ocean floor toward New York. Over a period of 40 years, New York and neighboring cities have dumped more than 200 million cubic yards of industrial wastes, pesticides, sewage, and other wastes about 20 miles out into the ocean. It has been assumed at best that the dumped wastes would disappear by some process of degrading or, at worst, that they would just stay out there. Instead, a true environmental horror seems about to be visited back upon the cities. According to accounts in various news media, the dumped wastes have accumulated into a black, disease-ridden sludge that is creeping back toward shore at a rate of about one mile per year. In the water above the sludge, the count of coliform bacteria has run as high as 542,000 per milliliter. The level considered safe for swimming is about 70 per milliliter. Furthermore, the sludge contains many toxic metals and the viruses of hepatitus, encephalitis, and polio.

One important point for present purposes is that the problem has developed in frightening form over a very long time frame—four decades. Dumping some barge loads of waste in the huge ocean back in the 1930s seemed innocuous enough, but the combination of continued dumping, some biological and oceanographic laws, and a long period of time for them to operate has produced a scary rebound effect on the children of the perpetrators and upon the whole state. The second important point is that our views of human *behavior* and its articulation with environmental systems seldom even consider the possibility of such synergistic effects over time. Thus, we generally do not even ask in a systematic way whether our ways of "dumping" persons into typical residential systems, penal and correctional institutions, schools, industrial facilities, and hospitals, or subjecting them to our favorite forms of treatment will lead to negative results that will be visited back upon them and their children over the long haul. Part of the problem here is that the immediate and short term effects may be misleading in that they appear just as innocuous and serene as the ocean system with a few years' worth of waste dumped into it back in the 1930s.

CONCLUDING COMMENTS

By means of examples, analogies, assertions, and propagandistic statements, we have presented an emerging ecological perspective on human behavior and its implications for behavioral technology and humanistic psychology, two approaches to human change. Our first purpose is heuristic—to reveal and juxtapose the assumptions and working principles of the three movements for comparison. The second purpose is to stimulate the kind of discussion, cross-seeding, and cooperation needed to develop more complete and effective approaches to human functioning and human change. As Kaplan (1964) points out in his brilliant essays on philosophy of science, "The division of labor in the economy of science is, after all, a historical product and not the reflection of logical necessity. As a science progresses, old partnerships . . . are dissolved, and new ones . . . come into being" (p. 31).

Several things have nagged at us during the preparation and writing of this paper. First, we have often wished either that behavioral ecology were spelled out more clearly and more definitively or that we possessed the kind of incisiveness and astuteness necessary to develop it more fully. This paper offers what we can now see and touch with enough clarity to share. Second, in ways that we probably do not fully apprehend, both general issues and the positions of others have at times been presented in caricature. Past experience leads us to expect that we will be advised of such lapses in effective ways. In the process of such exchange, we hope that we and others will learn something new about our favorite subject matter—human behavior—and our respective ways of dealing with it. Finally, perhaps inevitably, position papers and comparative papers are written from a vantage point and they tend to communicate a particular spirit: What's mine is mine and what's yours is negotiable. What would appear to be ours in this paper is mostly not ours to begin with. We have marshalled our argumentative resources to present behavioral ecology. We give it away freely because, not only will its maturation depend upon the contribution of many persons, but, to the extent that its principles and message are viable, they should permeate the thinking and professional style of all of us.

Behavior Theory and the Models of Man[1]

ALBERT BANDURA

Department of Psychology, Stanford University,
Stanford, California 94305

The views about the nature of man conveyed by behavior theory require critical examination on conceptual and social grounds. What we believe man to be affects which aspects of human functioning we study most thoroughly and which we disregard. Premises thus delimit research and are, in turn, shaped by it. As knowledge gained through study is put into practice, the images of man on which social technologies rest have even vaster implications. This is nowhere better illustrated than in growing public concern over manipulation and control by psychological methods. Some of these fears arise from expectations that improved means of influence will inevitably be misused. Other apprehensions are aroused by exaggerated claims of psychological power couched in the language of manipulation and authoritarian control. But most fears stem from views of behaviorism, articulated by popular writers and by theorists themselves, that are disputed by the empirical facts of human behavior.

In the minds of the general public, and of many within our own discipline, behavior theory is equated with "conditioning." Over the years the terms behaviorism and conditioning have come to be associated with odious imagery, including salivating dogs, puppetry, and animalistic manipulation. As a result, those who wish to disparage ideas or practices they hold in disfavor need only to label them as behavioristic or as Pavlovian precursors of a totalitarian state.

Contrary to popular belief, the fabled reflexive conditioning in humans is

[1] Presidential address presented at the meeting of the American Psychological Association, New Orleans, August, 1974. Copyright 1974 by the American Psychological Association. Reprinted by permission.

largely a myth. Conditioning is simply a descriptive term for learning through paired experiences, not an explanation of how the changes come about. Originally, conditioning was assumed to occur automatically. On closer examination it turned out to be cognitively mediated. People do not learn despite repetitive paired experiences unless they recognize that events are correlated (Dawson and Furedy, 1974; Grings, 1973). So-called conditioned reactions are largely self-activated on the basis of learned expectations rather than automatically evoked. The critical factor, therefore, is not that events occur together in time, but that people learn to predict them and to summon up appropriate anticipatory reactions.

The capacity to learn from correlated experiences reflects sensitivity, but because Pavlov first demonstrated the phenomenon with a dog, it has come to be regarded as a base animalistic process. Had he chosen to study physiological hyperactivity in humans to cues associated with stress, or the development of empathetic reactions to expressions of suffering, conditioning would have been treated in a more enlightened way. To expect people to remain unaffected by events that are frightening, humiliating, disgusting, sad, or pleasurable is to require that they be less than human. Although negative effects such as fears and dislikes can arise from paired experiences of a direct or vicarious sort, so do some of the enobling qualities of man. The pejorative accounts of learning principles, which appear with regularity in professional and lay publications, degrade both the science of psychology and the audiences that the offensive rhetoric is designed to sway.

It is well documented that behavior is influenced by its consequences much of the time. The image of man that this principle connotes depends upon the types of consequences that are acknowledged and an understanding of how they operate. In theories that recognize only the role of proximate external consequences and contend they shape behavior automatically, people appear as mechanical pawns of environmental forces. But external consequences, influential as they often are, are not the sole determinants of human behavior, nor do they operate automatically.

Response consequences serve several functions. First, they impart information. By observing the effects of their actions individuals eventually discern which behaviors are appropriate in which settings. The acquired information then serves as a guide for action. Contrary to the mechanistic metaphors, outcomes change behavior in humans through the intervening influence of thought.

Consequences motivate, through their incentive value, as well as inform. By representing foreseeable outcomes symbolically, future consequences can be converted into current motivators of behavior. Many of the things we do are designed to gain anticipated benefits and to avert future trouble. Our choices of action are largely under anticipatory control. The widely accepted dictum that man is ruled by response consequences thus fares better for anticipated than for actual consequences. Consider behavior on a fixed-ratio schedule (say, 50 : 1) in which only every fiftieth response is reinforced. Since 98% of the outcomes are extinctive and only 2% are reinforcing, behavior is maintained despite its dissuading consequences. As people are exposed to variations in frequency and predictability of reinforcement, they behave on the basis of the outcomes they expect to prevail on future occasions. When belief differs from actuality, which is not uncommon, behavior is weakly controlled by its actual consequences until repeated experience instills realistic expectations (Bandura, 1971a; Kaufman *et al.*, 1966).

Had humans been ruled solely by instant consequences, they would have long become museum pieces among the extinct species. Not that our future is unquestionably secure. The immediate rewards of consumptive lifestyles vigorously promoted for short term profit jeopardize man's long term chances of survival. But immediate consequences, unless unusually powerful, do not necessarily outweigh deferred ones (Mischel, 1974). Our descendants shall continue to have a future only because those who foresee the aversive long term consequences of current practices mobilize public support for contingencies that favor survival behavior. Hazardous pesticides, for example, are usually banned before populations suffer maladies from toxic residues. The information processing capacities with which humans are endowed provide the basis for insightful behavior. Their capacity to bring remote consequences to bear on current behavior by anticipatory thought supports foresightful action.

Explanations of reinforcement originally assumed that consequences increase behavior without conscious involvement. The still prevalent notion that reinforcers can operate insidiously arouses fears that improved techniques of reinforcement will enable authorities to manipulate people without their knowledge or consent. Although the empirical issue is not yet completely resolved, there is little evidence that rewards function as automatic strengtheners of human conduct. Behavior is not much affected by its consequences without awareness of what is being reinforced (Bandura, 1969; Dulany, 1968). After individuals discern the instrumental relation between action and outcome, contingent rewards may produce accommodating or oppositional behavior depending on how they value the incentives, the influencers and the behavior itself, and how others respond. Thus reinforcement, as it has become better understood, has changed from a mechanical strengthener of conduct to an informative and motivating influence.

People do not function in isolation. As social beings, they observe the conduct of others and the occasions on which it is rewarded, disregarded, or punished. They can therefore profit from observed consequences as well as from their own direct experiences (Bandura, 1971b). Acknowledgment of vicarious reinforcement introduces another human dimension—namely, evaluative capacities—into the operation of reinforcement influences. People weigh consequences to themselves against those accruing to others for similar behavior. The same outcome can thus become a reward or a punishment depending upon the referents used for social comparison.

Human conduct is better explained by the relational influence of observed and direct consequences than by either factor alone. However, behavior is not fully predictable from a relational coefficient because social justifications alter the impact of outcome disparities. Inequitable reinforcement is willingly accepted when people are graded by custom into social ranks and rewarded according to position rather than performance. Arbitrary inequities are also likely to be tolerated if the underrewarded are led to believe they possess attributes that make them less deserving of equal treatment. Persuasively justified inequities have more detrimental personal effects than acknowledged unfairness because they foster self-devaluation in the maltreated. Negative reactions to inequitable reinforcement, which is acknowledged to be unwarranted, can likewise be diminished by temporizing. If people are led to expect that unfair treatment will be corrected within the foreseeable future, it becomes less aversive to them.

Theories that explain human behavior as the product of external rewards and punishments present a truncated image of man because people partly regulate their actions by self-produced consequences (Bandura, 1971b; Thoresen and Mahoney, 1974). Example and precept impart standards of conduct that serve as the basis for self-reinforcing reactions. The development of self-reactive functions gives humans a capacity for self-direction. They do things that give rise to self-satisfaction and self-worth, and they refrain from behaving in ways that evoke self-punishment.

After self-reinforcing functions are acquired, a given act produces two sets of consequences—self-evaluative reactions and external outcomes. Personal and external sources of reinforcement may operate as supplementary or as opposing influences on behavior. Thus, for example, individuals commonly experience conflicts when rewarded for conduct they personally devalue. When self-condemning consequences outweigh rewarding inducements, external influences are relatively ineffective. On the other hand, if certain courses of action produce stronger rewards than self-censure, the result is cheerless compliance. Losses in self-respect for devalued conduct can be abated, however, by self-exonerating justification. We shall return to this issue shortly.

Another type of conflict between external and self-produced consequences arises when individuals are punished for behavior they regard highly. Principled dissenters and nonconformists often find themselves in this predicament. Personally valued conduct is expressed provided its costs are not too high. Should the threatened consequences be severe, one inhibits self-praiseworthy acts under high risk of penalty but readily performs them when the chances of punishment are reduced. There are individuals, however, whose sense of self-worth is so strongly invested in certain convictions that they will submit to prolonged maltreatment rather than accede to what they regard as unjust or immoral.

External consequences exert greatest influence on behavior when they are compatible with those that are self-produced. These conditions obtain when rewardable acts are a source of self-pride and punishable ones are self-censured. To enhance compatability between personal and social influences, people select associates who share similar standards of conduct and thus ensure social support for their own system of self-reinforcement.

Individualistic theories of moral action assume that internalization of behavioral standards creates a permanent control mechanism within the person. Restraints of conscience thereafter operate as enduring controls over reprehensible conduct. The testimony of human behavior, however, contradicts this view. Much human maltreatment and suffering is, in fact, inflicted by otherwise decent moral people. And some of the most striking changes in moral conduct, as evidenced, for example, in political and military violence, are achieved without altering personality structures or moral standards. Personal control is clearly more complex and flexible than the theorizing implies.

Although self-reinforcing influences serve as regulators of conduct, they can be dissociated from censurable deeds by self-exonerating practices (Bandura, 1973). One device is to make inhumane behavior personally and socially acceptable by defining it in terms of high moral principle. People do not act in ways they ordinarily consider evil or destructive until such activities are construed as serving moral purposes. Over the years, much cruelty has been perpetrated in the name of religious principles, righteous ideologies, and regulatory sanctions. In the transactions of everyday life euphemistic labeling serves as a handy linguistic device for masking reprehensible activities or according them a respectable status. Self-deplored conduct can also be made benign by contrasting it with other flagrant inhumanities. Moral justifications and palliative comparisons are especially effective because they not only eliminate self-generated deterrents, but engage self-reward in the service of reprehensible conduct. What was morally unacceptable becomes a source of self-pride.

A common dissociative practice is to obscure or distort the relationship between one's actions and the effects they cause. People will perform behavior they normally repudiate if a legitimate authority sanctions it and acknowledges responsibility for its consequences. By displacing responsibility elsewhere, participants do not hold themselves accountable for what they do and are thus spared self-prohibiting reactions. Exemption from self-censure can be facilitated additionally by diffusing responsibility for culpable behavior. Through division of labor, division of decision making, and collective action, people can contribute to detrimental practices without feeling personal responsibility or self-disapproval.

Attribution of blame to the victim is still another exonerative expedient. Victims are faulted for bringing maltreatment on themselves, or extraordinary circumstances are invoked as justifications for questionable conduct. One need not engage in self-reproof for committing acts prescribed by circumstances. A further means of weakening self-punishment is to dehumanize the victim. Inflicting harm upon people who are regarded as subhuman or debased is less likely to arouse self-reproof than if they are looked upon as human beings with sensitivities.

There are other self-disinhibiting maneuvers that operate by misrepresenting the consequences of actions. As long as detrimental effects are ignored or minimized there is little reason for self-censure. If consequences are not easily distortable, distress over conduct that conflicts with self-evaluative standards can be reduced by selectively remembering the benefits and forgetting the harm of one's acts.

Given the variety of self-disinhibiting devices, a society cannot rely on control by conscience to ensure moral and ethical conduct. Though personal control ordinarily serves as a self-directive force, it can be nullified by social sanctions conducive to destructiveness. Indoctrination and social justifications give meaning to events and create anticipations that determine one's actions. Control through information, which is rooted in cognitive processes, is more pervasive and powerful than conditioning through contiguity of events. Cultivation of humaneness therefore requires, in addition to benevolent personal codes, safeguards built into social systems that counteract detrimental sanctioning practices and uphold compassionate behavior.

A conceptual orientation not only prescribes what facets of man will be studied in depth, but also how one goes about changing human behavior. Early applications of reinforcement principles, for example, were guided by the then prevalent belief that consequences alter behavior automatically and unconsciously. Since the process supposedly operated mechanically, the reinforcers had to occur instantly to be effective. Participants in change programs were, therefore, uninformed about why they were being reinforced and, in an effort to ensure immediacy of effects, reinforcers were presented intrusively as soon as the requisite responses were emitted. The net effect was a tedious shaping process that produced, at best, mediocre results in an ethically questionable manner. In many public and professional circles, reinforcement still connotes furtive control even though reinforcement theory and practices have progressed well beyond this level.

Realization that reinforcement is an unarticulated way of designating appropriate conduct prompted the use of cognitive factors in the modification of behavior. Not surprisingly, people change more rapidly if told what behaviors are rewardable and punishable than if they have to discover it from observing the consequences of their actions. Competencies that are not already within their repertoires can be developed with greater ease through the aid of instruction and modeling than by relying solely on the successes and failures of unguided performance.

As further research revealed that reinforcers function as motivators, consequences were recognized as sources of motivation that depend heavily for their effectiveness upon the incentive preferences of those undergoing change. Hence, people do not indiscriminately absorb the influences that impinge upon them. Outcomes resulting from actions need not necessarily occur instantly. Humans can cognitively bridge delays between behavior and subsequent reinforcers without impairing the efficacy of incentive operations.

At this second evolutionary stage, reinforcement practices changed from unilateral control to social contracting. Positive arrangements affirm that if individuals do certain things they are entitled to certain rewards and privileges. In the case of negative sanctions, reprehensible conduct carries punishment costs. The process is portrayed in reinforcement terms, but the practice is that of social exchange. Most social interactions are, of course, governed by conditional agreements though they usually are not couched in the language of reinforcement. Describing them differently does not change their nature, however.

Contingencies vary in the human qualities they embody and in the voice individuals have in decisions concerning the social arrangements that affect their lives. Reflecting the salient values of our society, reinforcement practices have traditionally favored utilitarian forms of behavior. But conditions are changing. With growing reservations about materialistic lifestyles, reinforcement practices are being increasingly used to cultivate personal potentialities and humanistic qualities. These emerging changes in value commitments will probably accelerate as people devote fewer hours to working for income and have more leisure time for self-development.

Another change of some consequence is the renewed concern for individual rights. People are seeking a collaborative role in the development of societal contingencies that affect the course and quality of their lives. As part of this social trend, even the actions taken in the name of psychotherapy are being examined for their ethics and social purposes. These concerns have provided the impetus for prescripts to ensure that reinforcement techniques are used in the service of human betterment rather than as instruments of social control.

A closely related issue is the relative attention devoted to changing individuals or to altering the institutions of society to enrich life. If psychologists are to have a significant impact on common problems of life, they must apply their corrective measures to detrimental societal practices rather than limit themselves to treating the casualties of these practices. This, of course, is easier said than done. Practitioners, whatever their specialty, are reinforced more powerfully for using their knowledge and skills to further the interests of existing operations than for changing them. Socially oriented efforts are hard to sustain under inadequate reinforcement supports.

The methods of change discussed thus far draw heavily upon external consequences of action. Evidence that people can exercise some control over their own behavior provided the impetus for further changes in reinforcement practices. Interest began to shift from managing conduct to developing skills in self-regulation. In the latter approach, control is vested to a large extent in the hands of individuals themselves. They arrange the environmental inducements for desired behavior; they evaluate their own performances; and they serve as their own reinforcing agents (Goldfried and Merbaum, 1973; Mahoney and Thoresen, 1974). To be sure, the self-reinforcing functions are created and occasionally supported by external influences. Having external origins, however, does not refute the fact that, once established, self-influence partly determines what actions one performs. Citing historical determinants of a generalizable function cannot substitute for contemporaneous influences arising through exercise of that function.

The recognition of self-directing capacities represents a substantial departure from exclusive reliance upon environmental control. But the emerging self-influence practices are still closely rooted in physical transactions—the self-administered consequences are, for the most part, material. Eventually changes in form, as well as source, of reinforcement will appear as the insufficiency of material outcomes is acknowledged. Most people value their self-respect above commodities. They rely extensively on their own self-demands and self-approval as guides for conduct. To ignore the influential role of covert self-reinforcement in the regulation of behavior is to disavow a uniquely human capacity of man.

Proponents who recognize only external consequences restrict their research and practice to such influences and thus generate evidence that reinforces their conceptions. Those who acknowledge personal influences as well tend to select methods that reveal and promote self-directing capabilities in man. The view of man embodied in behavioral technologies is therefore more than a philosophical issue. It affects which human potentialities will be cultivated and which will be underdeveloped.

The preceding remarks addressed the need to broaden the scope of research into the reinforcement processes regulating human behavior. Much the same might be said for the ways in which human learning is conceptualized and investigated. Our theories have been incredibly slow in acknowledging that man can learn by observation as well as by direct experience. This is another example of how steadfast adherence to orthodox paradigms makes it difficult to transcend the confines of conceptual commitment. Having renounced cognitive determinants, early proponents of behaviorism advanced the doctrine that learning can occur only by performing responses and experiencing their effects. This legacy is still very much with us. The rudimentary form of learning based on direct experience has been exhaustively studied, whereas the more pervasive and powerful mode of learning by observation is largely ignored. A shift of emphasis is needed.

The capacity to represent modeled activities symbolically enables man to acquire new patterns of behavior observationally without reinforced enactment. From observing others, one forms an idea of how certain behavior is performed and on later occasions the coded information serves as a guide for action. Indeed, research conducted within the framework of social learning theory shows that virtually all learning phenomena resulting from direct experience can occur on a vicarious basis by observing other people's behavior and its consequences for them (Bandura, 1969). The abbreviation of the acquisition process through observational learning is, of course, vital for both development and survival. Modeling reduces the burden of time-consuming performance of inappropriate responses. Since errors can produce costly, if not fatal, consequences, the prospects of survival would be slim indeed if people had to rely solely on the effects of their actions to inform them about what to do.

In many instances the behavior being modeled must be learned in essentially the same form. Driving automobiles, skiing, and performing surgery, for example, permit little, if any, departure from essential practices. In addition to transmitting particular response patterns, however, modeling influences can create generative and innovative behavior. In the latter process, observers abstract common features from seemingly diverse responses and formulate generative rules of behavior which enable them to go beyond what they have seen or heard. By synthesizing features of different models into new amalgams, observers can achieve through modeling novel styles of thought and conduct. Once initiated, experiences with the new forms create further evolutionary changes. A partial departure from tradition eventually becomes a new direction.

Some of the limitations commonly ascribed to behavior theory are based on the mistaken belief that modeling can produce at best mimicry of specific acts. This view is disputed by growing evidence that abstract modeling is a highly effective means of inducing rule-governed cognitive behavior (Bandura, 1971c; Zimmerman and Rosenthal, 1974). On the basis of observationally derived rules, people alter their judgmental orientations, conceptual schemes, linguistic styles, information-processing strategies, as well as other forms of cognitive functioning. Nevertheless, faulty evaluations continue to be mistaken for weaknesses inherent in theory.

Observational learning has recently come to be accepted more widely, but some theorists are willing to grant it full scientific respectability only if it is reduced to performance terms. As a result, enactment paradigms are used which are rooted in the traditional assumption that responses must be performed before they can be learned. Instant reproduction of modeled responses is favored, thereby minimizing dependence upon cognitive functions which play an especially influential role when retention over time is required. The issue of whether reinforcement enhances modeling is pursued to the neglect of the more interesting question of whether one can keep people from learning what they have seen.

When learning is investigated through observational paradigms a broader range of determinants and intervening mechanisms gains prominence. Learning by observation is governed by four component processes; attentional functions regulate sensory input and perception of modeled actions; through coding and symbolic rehearsal, transitory experiences are transformed for memory representation into enduring performance guides; motor reproduction processes govern the integration of constituent acts into new response patterns; and incentive or motivational processes determine whether observationally acquired responses will be performed. Studied from this perspective, observational learning emerges as an actively judgmental and constructive, rather than a mechanical copying, process.

Since observational learning entails several subfunctions that evolve with maturation and experience, it obviously depends upon prior development. Differences in theoretical perspectives prescribe different methodologies for studying how the capacity for observational learning itself is acquired. When modeling is conceptualized in terms of formation of stimulus–response linkages, efforts are aimed at increasing the probability of imitative responses through reinforcement. Modeling can be increased by rewarding matching behavior, but such demonstrations are not of much help in identifying what exactly is being acquired during the process, or in explaining imitation failures under favorable conditions of reinforcement. From a social learning view, the capability for observational learning is developed by acquiring skill in discriminative observation, in memory encoding, in coordinating ideomotor and sensorimotor systems, and in judging probable consequences for matching behavior. Understanding how people learn to imitate becomes a matter of understanding how the requisite subfunctions develop and operate. Capacity for observational learning is restricted by deficits, and expanded by improvements, in its component functions.

Over the years proponents of the more radical forms of behaviorism not only disclaimed interest in mentation, but also marshaled numerous reasons why cognitive events are inadmissible in causal analyses. It was, and still is, argued that cognitions are inaccessible except through untrustworthy self-reports, they are inferences from effects, they are epiphenomenal, or they are simply fictional. Advances in experimental analysis of behavior, it was claimed, would eventually show them to be unnecessary. Empirical evidence, however, has shown the opposite to be true. A large body of research now exists in which cognition is activated instructionally with impressive results. People learn and retain much better by using cognitive aids that they generate than by repetitive reinforced performance (Anderson and Bower, 1973; Bandura, 1971c). With growing evidence that cognition has causal influence in behavior, the arguments against cognitive determinants are losing their force.

These recent developments have shifted emphasis from the study of response learning to analyses of memory and cognition. From this effort we have gained a better understanding of the mechanisms whereby information is acquired, stored, and retrieved. There is more to learning, however, than the acquisition and retention of information. Behavioristic theories addressed themselves to performance but de-emphasized internal determinants, whereas the cognitive approaches remain immersed in thought but divorced from conduct. In a complete account of human behavior internal processes must eventually be tied to action. Hence, explanations of how information eventuates in skilled performance must additionally be concerned with the organization and regulation of behavior. Social learning includes within its framework both the processes internal to the organism as well as performance-related determinants.

Speculations about man's nature inevitably raise the fundamental issues of determinism and human freedom. In examining these questions it is essential to distinguish between the metaphysical and the social aspects of freedom. Many of the heated disputes on this topic arise as much, if not more, from confusion over the dimensions of freedom being discussed as from disagreements over the doctrine of determinism.

Let us first consider freedom in the social sense. Whether freedom is an illusion, as some writers maintain, or a social reality of considerable importance depends upon the meaning given to it. Within the social learning framework, freedom is defined in terms of the number of options available to people and the right to exercise them. The more behavioral alternatives and social prerogatives people have, the greater is their freedom of action.

Personal freedom can be limited in many different ways. Behavioral deficits restrict possible choices and otherwise curtail opportunities to realize one's preferences. Freedom can therefore be expanded by cultivating competencies. Self-restraints arising from unwarranted fears and stringent self-censure restrict the effective range of activities that individuals can engage in or even contemplate. Here freedom is restored by eliminating dysfunctional self-restraints.

In maximizing freedom a society must place some limits on conduct because complete license for any individual is likely to encroach on the freedom of others. Societal prohibitions against behavior that is socially injurious create additional curbs on conduct. Conflicts often arise over behavioral restrictions when many members of society question conventional customs and when legal sanctions are used more to enforce a particular brand of morality than to prohibit socially detrimental conduct.

The issue of whether individuals should be allowed to engage in activities that are self-injurious but not detrimental to society has been vigorously debated over the years. Prohibitionists argue that it is difficult for a person, other than a recluse, to impair himself without inflicting secondary harm on others. Should self-injury produce incapacities, society usually ends up bearing the treatment and subsistence costs. Libertarians do not find such arguments sufficiently convincing to justify a specific prohibition because some of the self-injurious activities that society approves may be as bad or worse than those it outlaws. Normative changes over time regarding private conduct tend to favor an individualistic ethic. Consequently, many activities that were formerly prohibited by law have been exempted from legal sanctions.

Some groups have their freedom curtailed by socially condoned discrimination. Here, the alternatives available to a person are limited by skin color, sex, religion, ethnic background, or social class, regardless of capabilities. When self-determination is prejudicially restricted, those who are subordinated remove inequities by altering practices that compromise or temporize the professed values of society.

Freedom deals with rights as well as options and behavioral restraints. Man's struggle for freedom is principally aimed at structuring societal contingencies so that certain forms of behavior are exempted from aversive control. After protective laws are built into the system, there are certain things that a society may not do to an individual, however much it might like to. Legal prohibitions on societal control create freedoms that are realities, not simply feelings or states of mind. Societies differ in their institutions of freedom and in the number and types of behaviors that are officially exempted from punitive control. Social systems that protect journalists from punitive control, for example, are freer than those that allow authoritative power to be used to silence critics or their vehicles of expression. Societies that possess an independent judiciary ensure greater social freedom than those that do not.

In philosophical discourses, freedom is often considered antithetical to determinism. When defined in terms of options and rights there is no incompatability of freedom and determinism. From this perspective, freedom is not conceived negatively as the absence of influences or simply the lack of external constraints. Rather, it is defined positively in terms of the skills at one's command and the exercise of self-influence upon which choice of action depends.

Psychological analyses of freedom eventually lead to discourses on the metaphysics of determinism. Are people partial determiners of their own behavior, or are they ruled exclusively by forces beyond their control? The long-standing debate over this issue has been enlivened by Skinner's (1971) contention that, apart from genetic contributions, human behavior is controlled solely by environmental contingencies, for example, "a person does not act upon the world, the world acts upon him" (p. 211). A major problem with this type of analysis is that it depicts the environment as an autonomous force that automatically shapes and controls behavior. Environments have causes as do behaviors. For the most part, the environment is only a potentiality until actualized and fashioned by appropriate actions. Books do not influence people unless someone writes them and others select and read them. Rewards and punishments remain in abeyance until prompted by appropriate performances.

cies are partly of a person's own making. By their actions people play an active role in producing the reinforcing contingencies that impinge upon them. Thus, behavior partly creates the environment, and the environment influences the behavior in a reciprocal fashion. To the oft-repeated dictum, change contingencies and you change behavior, should be added the reciprocal side, change behavior and you change the contingencies.

The image of man's efficacy that emerges from psychological research depends upon which aspect of the reciprocal control system one selects for analysis. In the paradigm favoring environmental control, investigators analyze how environmental contingencies change behavior $[B = f(E)]$. The personal control paradigm, on the other hand, examines how behavior determines the environment $[E = f(B)]$. Behavior is the effect in the former case, and the cause in the latter. Although the reciprocal sources of influence are separable for experimental purposes, in everyday life two-way control operates concurrently. In ongoing interchanges one and the same event can thus be a stimulus, a response, or an environmental reinforcer depending upon the place in the sequence at which the analysis arbitrarily begins.

A survey of the literature on reinforcement confirms the extent to which we have become captives of a one-sided paradigm to map a bi-directional process. Environmental control is overstudied, whereas personal control has been relatively neglected. To cite but one example, there exist countless demonstrations of how behavior varies under different schedules of reinforcement, but one looks in vain for studies of how people, either individually or by collective action, succeed in fashioning reinforcement schedules to their own liking. The dearth of research on personal control is not because people exert no influence on their environment or because such efforts are without effect. Quite the contrary. Behavior is one of the more influential determinants of future contingencies. As analyses of sequential interchanges reveal, aggressive individuals actualize through their conduct a hostile environment, whereas those who display friendly responsiveness produce an amicable social milieu within the same setting (Raush, 1965). We are all acquainted with problem-prone individuals who, through their aversive conduct, predictably breed negative social climates wherever they go.

It should be noted that some of the doctrines ascribing pre-eminent control to the environment are ultimately qualified by acknowledgment that man can exercise some measure of countercontrol (Skinner, 1971). The notion of reciprocal interaction, however, goes considerably beyond the concept of countercontrol. Countercontrol portrays the environment as an instigating force to which individuals react. As we have already seen, people activate and create environments as well as rebut them.

People may be considered partially free insofar as they can influence future conditions by managing their own behavior. Granted that selection of parti-cular courses of action from available alternatives is itself determined, indivi-duals can nevertheless exert some control over the factors that govern their choices. In philosophical analyses all events can be submitted to an infinite regression of causes. Such discussions usually emphasize how man's actions are determined by prior conditions but neglect the reciprocal part of the process showing that the conditions themselves are partly determined by man's prior actions. Applications of self-control practices demonstrate that people are able to regulate their own behavior in preferred directions by arranging environmental conditions most likely to elicit it and administering self-reinforcing consequences to sustain it. They may be told how to do it and initially be given some external support for their efforts, but self-produced influences contribute significantly to future goal attainment.

To contend, as environmental determinists often do, that people are con-trolled by external forces and then to advocate that they redesign their society by applying behavioral technology undermines the basic premise of the argument. If humans were in fact incapable of influencing their own actions, they could describe and predict environmental events but hardly exercise any intentional control over them. When it comes to advocacy of social change, however, thoroughgoing environmental determinists become ardent expon-ents of man's power to transform environments in pursuit of a better life.

In backward causal analyses, conditions are usually portrayed as ruling man, whereas forward deterministic analyses of goal setting and attainment reveal how people can shape conditions for their purposes. Some are better at it than others. The greater their foresight, proficiency, and self-influence, all of which are acquirable skills, the greater the progress toward their goals. Because of the capacity for reciprocal influence, people are at least partial architects of their own destinies. It is not determinism that is in dispute, but whether it is treated as a one-way or a two-way control process. Considering the interdependence of behavior and environmental conditions, determinism does not imply the fatalistic view that man is but a pawn of external influences.

Psychological perspectives on determinism, like other aspects of theorizing, influence the nature and scope of social practice. Environmental determinists are apt to use their methods primarily in the service of institutionally prescribed patterns of behavior. Personal determinists are more inclined to cultivate self-directing potentialities in man. The latter behavioral approach and humanism have much in common. Behavioral theorists, however, recognize that "self-actualization" is by no means confined to human virtues. People have numerous potentialities that can be actualized for good or ill. Over the years, man has suffered considerably at the hands of self-actualized tyrants. A self-centered ethic of self-realization must therefore be tempered by concern for the social consequences of one's conduct. Behaviorists generally emphasize environmental sources of control, whereas humanists tend to restrict their interest to personal control. Social learning encompasses both aspects of the bi-directional influence process.

When the environment is regarded as an autonomous rather than an influenceable determinant of behavior, valuation of dignifying human qualities and accomplishments is diminished. If inventiveness emanates from external circumstances, it is environments that should be credited for people's achievements and chastised for their failings or inhumanities. Contrary to the unilateral view, human accomplishments result from reciprocal interaction of external circumstances with a host of personal determinants including endowed potentialities, acquired competencies, reflective thought, and a high level of self-initiative.

Musical composers, for example, help to shape tastes by their creative efforts and the public in turn supports their performances until advocates of new styles generate new public preferences. Each succeeding form of artistry results from a similar two-way influence process for which neither artisans nor circumstances deserve sole credit.

Superior accomplishments, whatever the field, require considerable self-disciplined application. After individuals adopt evaluative standards, they expend large amounts of time, on their own, improving their performances to the point of self-satisfaction. At this level of functioning, persistence in an endeavor is extensively under self-reinforcement control. Skills are perfected as much, or more, to please oneself as to please the public.

Without self-generated influences most innovative efforts would be difficult to sustain. This is because the unconventional is initially resisted and gradually accepted only as it proves functionally valuable or wins prestigious advocates. As a result, the early efforts of innovators bring rebuffs rather than rewards or recognition. In the history of creative endeavors, it is not uncommon for artists or composers to be scorned when they depart markedly from convention. Some gain recognition later in their careers. Others are sufficiently convinced of the worth of their work that they labor indefatigably even though their productions are negatively received during their lifetimes. Ideological and, to a lesser extent, technological advances follow similar courses. Most innovative endeavors receive occasional social support in early phases, but environmental conditions alone are not especially conducive to unconventional developments.

The operation of reciprocal influence also has bearing on the public concern that advances in psychological knowledge will produce an increase in human manipulation and control. A common response to such apprehensions is that all behavior is inevitably controlled. Social influence, therefore, is not a question of imposing controls where none existed before. This type of argument is valid in the sense that every act has a cause. But it is not the principle of causality that worries people. At the societal level, their misgivings center on the distribution of controlling power, the means and purposes for which it is used, and the availability of mechanisms for exercising reciprocal control over institutional practices. At the individual level, they are uneasy about the implications of psychotechnology in programming human relations.

Possible remedies for exploitative use of psychological techniques are usually discussed in terms of individual safeguards. Increased knowledge about modes of influence is prescribed as the best defense against manipulation. When people are informed about how behavior can be controlled, they tend to resist evident attempts at influence, thus making manipulation more difficult. Awareness alone, however, is a weak countervalence.

Exploitation was successfully thwarted long before there existed a discipline of psychology to formulate principles and practices of behavior change. The most reliable source of opposition to manipulative control resides in the reciprocal consequences of human interactions. People resist being taken advantage of, and will continue to do so in the future, because compliant behavior produces unfavorable consequences for them. Sophisticated efforts at influence in no way reduce the aversiveness of yielding that is personally disadvantageous. Because of reciprocal consequences, no one is able to manipulate others at will, and everyone experiences some feeling of powerlessness in getting what they want. This is true at all levels of functioning, individual and collective. Parents cannot get their children to follow all their wishes, while children feel constrained by their parents from doing what they desire. At universities the administrators, faculty, students, and alumni all feel that the other constituencies are unduly influential in promoting their self-interests but that one's own group is granted insufficient power to alter the institutional practices. In the political arena, Congress feels that the executive branch possesses excessive power, and conversely the executive branch feels thwarted in implementing its policies by congressional counteraction.

If protection against exploitation relied solely upon individual safeguards, people would be continually subjected to coercive pressures. Accordingly, they create institutional sanctions which set limits on the control of human behavior. The integrity of individuals is largely secured by societal safeguards that place constraints on improper means and foster reciprocity through balancing of interests.

Because individuals are conversant with psychological techniques does not grant them license to impose them on others. Industrialists, for example, know full well that productivity is higher when payment is made for amount of work completed rather than for length of time at work. Nevertheless, they cannot use the reinforcement system most advantageous to them. When industrialists commanded exclusive power they paid workers at a piecerate basis and hired and fired them at will. Reductions in power disparity between employers and employees resulted in a gradual weakening of performance requirements. As labor gained economic coercive strength through collective action, it was able to negotiate guaranteed wages on a daily, weekly, monthly, and eventually on an annual basis. At periodic intervals new contractual contingencies are adopted that are mutually acceptable. In the course of time, as better means of joint action are developed, other constituents will use their influence to modify arrangements that benefit certain segments of labor and industry but adversely affect the quality of life for other sectors of society.

As the previous example illustrates, improved knowledge of how to influence behavior does not necessarily raise the level of social control. If anything, the recent years have witnessed a diffusion of power, creating increased opportunities for reciprocal influence. This has enabled people to challenge social inequities, to effect changes in institutional practices, to counteract infringements on their rights, and to extend grievance procedures and due process of law to activities in social contexts that hitherto operated under unilateral control. The fact that more people wield power does not in and of itself ensure a humane society. In the final analysis the important consideration is the purposes that power serves, however it might be distributed. Nor does knowledgeability about means of influence necessarily produce mechanical responsiveness in personal relations. Whatever their orientations, people model, expound, and reinforce what they value. Behavior arising out of purpose and commitment is no less genuine than improvised action.

The cliché of *1984*, and its more recent kin, diverts public attention from regulative influences that pose continual threats to human welfare. Most societies have instituted reciprocal systems that are protected by legal and social codes to prevent imperious control of human behavior. Although abuses of institutional power arise from time to time, it is not totalitarian rule that constitutes the impending peril. The hazards lie more in the intentional pursuit of personal gain whether material or otherwise, than in control by coercion. Detrimental social practices arise and resist change, even within an open society, when many people benefit from them. To take a prevalent example, inequitable treatment of disadvantaged groups for private gain enjoys public support without requiring despotic rule.

Man, of course, has more to contend with than inhumanities toward one another. When the aversive consequences of otherwise rewarding lifestyles are delayed and imperceptibly cumulative, people become willful agents of their own self-destruction. Thus, if enough people benefit from activities that progressively degrade their environment then, barring contravening influences, they will eventually destroy their environment. Although individuals contribute differentially to the problem, the harmful consequences are borne by all. With growing populations and spread of lavish lifestyles taxing finite resources, people will have to learn to cope with new realities of human existence.

Psychology cannot tell people how they ought to live their lives. It can, however, provide them with the means for effecting personal and social change. And it can aid them in making value choices by assessing the consequences of alternative lifestyles and institutional arrangements. As a science concerned about the social consequences of its applications, psychology must also fulfill a broader obligation to society by bringing influence to bear on public policies to ensure that its findings are used in the service of human betterment.

PART VIII

Humanism and Behaviorism: Toward New Syntheses

Humanism and Behaviorism: Toward New Syntheses

DAVID F. RICKS

University of Cincinnati

ABRAHAM WANDERSMAN

Center for Community Studies, George Peabody College, Nashville, Tennessee 37203

AND PAUL J. POPPEN

Department of Psychology, George Washington University, Washington, D.C. 20006

Our goal has been to stimulate a discussion between humanism and behaviorism and to examine its implications. Beginning with systematic presentations of the ideas and therapeutic approaches of two exemplary therapists, one a humanist and the other a behaviorist, we have carried through a diologue between the two men, two ways of thought, two ways of collecting and interpreting information. Do we now know both approaches better, and can we see signs of mutual respect and possible mutual help? The reader will answer this for himself, and different readers will reach different conclusions. We will present our own conclusions here, but we will expect and welcome different judgments of the papers in this book.

Our principal interest will be the degree to which the humanist and behaviorist positions, each of which has its own integrity and theoretical coherence, may be converging into a new synthesis. We do not expect humanism and behaviorism to come completely together, nor do we think it would be productive if they did. But as we worked on this project we were surprised to find much more agreement than either common stereotypes or our own original judgments could have predicted. Both groups are clearly beyond the name calling, suspicion, and rhetoric that polarized humanists and behaviorists from the middle 1950s to the early 1970s. We seem to be on the verge of a creative synthesis that can unite the two approaches, or at least large parts of them, into a *broader social developmental view of the human being as an active organizer of his own particular environment over time.* The intellectual power of such a new synthesis, already suggested in recent work by Krasner and Ullman (1973) and by Bandura's article in this book, is impressive in its own right. It promises to revitalize our understanding of human nature, choice, freedom, and the meanings we can give to life. It has also given a new vitality to thinking about psychotherapy and behavior change.

Attempts have been made to diminish or disregard the dichotomies that have separated humanism and behaviorism. Some of the efforts have merely tacked on the term humanism to a behavioristic program when they apparently meant humanitarian, while others have attempted to integrate ideas from humanism and behaviorism. Thoreson and Mahoney (1974) point in the direction of a "behavioral humanism" which is "a scientific approach to human behavior that neither ignores nor de-emphasizes cognitive phenomena" (p. 6). Work in this area has been progressing under the social learning label. Thoreson (1973) has attempted to translate humanistic ideas into admittedly simple statements of human action (position 4 in Part I). For example, the humanistic idea of having new and unusual thoughts, physical sensations, and images is translated into increasing the frequency and variety of low probability responses. Despite its oversimplistic appearance, Thoreson suggests that this approach may be empirically useful. In this book, we have encouraged a dialogue which included a synthesis of parts of humanism and behaviorism as a goal, e.g., behavioristic methods for humanistic goals (Goldstein) and programs including humanistic methods and goals and behavioristic methods and goals (Gold) (position 5 in Part I). In Part VII, which viewed humanism and behaviorism in broader perspective, the potential of integrating humanism and behaviorism with other perspectives is suggested with the aim of producing a more comprehensive understanding of the relationship between man and society and more efficient and functional interventions towards the improvement of the quality of life (position 6 in Part I).

Most of the papers assembled here have emphasized interpretation and understanding, getting ideas into perspective and thinking them through, rather than gathering new data. This emphasis might mislead a reader into thinking that we see only a small role for new research data and information. Not so. Unlike those theorists who believe that the paradigm clash between humanism and behaviorism can only be resolved on nonempirical grounds, we hold for the solution of controversy by careful search for evidence. In part, the evidence can come from new experiments such as Alker developed for self-observation and Rychlak invented for studying reinforcement value. In part it can come from clinical research on the pragmatic values of helping children label and control their own emotional arousals (Gold) or helping an institution become a more person-centered place (Curtiss). "I would maintain that science in the broadest sense can and does discover what human values are, what the human being needs in order to live a good and happy life, what he needs in order to avoid illness, what is good for him and bad for him" (Maslow, 1966, p. 125).

Devereux argued to the same type of conclusion, that the fulfillment of values, and to some extent the values themselves, could be studied empirically. Psychotherapy and behavior change provide a real life observation post for the study of human nature. Readers interested in the research background of the ideas debated here can find increasingly sophisticated research reports of what goes on in psychotherapy, and what its outcomes are, in Bergin and Garfield (1971), Bergin and Suinn (1974), Franks and Wilson (1974), and Orlinsky and Howard (1975).

We will now put our conclusions into four simple declarative sentences and show some of the evidence for each.

1. *Neither behaviorism nor humanism is reducable to the other, and neither can be completely incorporated into the perspectives or language of the other.* A popular strategy among behaviorists has been to translate other approaches into the presumably more precise language of behavioral theories (Sears, 1943; Dollard and Miller, 1950; Thoresen, 1973). This approach has some values. It may be useful, for instance, to study empathy as a particular kind of positive reinforcement. The problem is that the narrow scope of behaviorism has trouble encompassing much that is important to humanists, such as self-realization, self-evaluation, and emotional involvement.

There is clearly a movement toward incorporation of cognition, fantasy, affect, and self-awareness into behavior theory, and in the articles in this book these tend to be called by their common English names, not the neologisms of earlier behavior theory. This growth in the scope of behavior theory is probably due to its current involvement in real life problems. As behavior therapy grapples with the problems of anxious children, depressed adults, and complicated human relationships it can be expected to show increased comprehesion of traditionally humanistic concerns. But similarity is not incorporation, and many humanistic ideas, such as self-actualization, can still be best expressed in humanistic language.

One striking illustration of this lack of specificity when behaviorists try to deal with humanistic concerns is the continued use of the global term "nonspecific factors" to describe the therapist's personal contribution to psychotherapy. Since humanistic therapists have been able to be quite specific and operational about what they mean by warmth, empathy, genuineness, transparency, etc., behavior therapists should now follow their lead, discard this tired old umbrella term, and try to be as precise about the person of the therapist as they are about his methods.

Humanists have argued that their ideas are necessary in order to understand how human beings can live proactively as well as reactively, can transcend immediate environments through memory and imagination, and can create their own environments through choices over time. Like G. H. Mead contemplating Watson, they can say that they find the behavior of the psychologist studying the rat more interesting than they find the rat itself. It does not seem likely that behavioral perspectives and language can soon encompass all of this range of inner life.

Behaviorism cannot be reduced to humanism because the humanistic position has no way of incorporating the many techniques of behavior therapy, at least without being considerably changed in the process. The humanist claim to incorporation of behaviorism within a more comprehensive understanding of human nature differentiates behavior in different environments. Behavioristic notions are interpreted as valuable only in showing how organisms respond to clearly structured, coercive environments, such as a Skinner box or Mischel's example of a red traffic light. In Maslow's hierarchy of needs, the bodily needs studied by behaviorists are not denied, but the organism is seen as responsive to higher needs as soon as these simple needs are satisfied. The trouble with this position is that the behaviorism it incorporates is too often a simple stereotype, rather than the more comprehensive and flexible scheme of a Bandura or Mischel. These theories not only provide a technology for behavior change; they are complex paradigms in their own right, and while humanists can learn from them, no humanistic theorist has succeeded in comprehending social learning theory within his own broader system.

The essays in this book suggest a halt to further efforts at territorial aggrandizement. The field of therapy would be diminished without humanists such as Jourard, and it would be equally diminished without behaviorists such as Wolpe. People who come to treatment want "to be left alone or talked to as a human being," as Jourard says, but they also want to be relieved of their symptoms, inhibitions, and anxieties. What is needed is not submission of one system to the other, or translation of the language of one approach into the language of the other, but a creative synthesis of the two. Alexander, Dreher, and Willems suggest that this is already under way, with each system complementing and filling in weaknesses in the other.

2. *Humanism and behaviorism are reconcilable.* We offer this conclusion in opposition to those who argue that the two represent diametrically opposite views, as well as those who argue that coexistence or détente is the closest approach the two can tolerate. Consider the Rychlak–Mischel debate. Both the humanist and the behaviorist point the way to understanding each human being as an active, aware problem solver, accommodating to his environment, but also assimilating it in his own way, influenced, but also influencing.

Whether this active organism must require a final cause, and this cause must be a self, remains open to debate. We have tried to hear both sides, the dialectical approach that Rychlak advocates in difficult situations. But we do not need to keep on seeing the two sides as opposites if we can find areas of agreement. The mainstream of modern thought is breaking down old dichotomies such as male vs. female, black vs. white, us vs. them. Are the humanist and behaviorist still so far apart? Isn't it likely that both are concentrating on complementary parts of some larger ecological or social or life span whole?

Of the several possible syntheses, the most popular continues to be one with a long history, the use of behavioristic techniques to reach humanistic goals. This strategy is most explicit in the program Curtiss used to redevelop a traditional mental hospital. Token economies have often been seen as the purest form of Skinnerian behaviorism. But in the hands of a humanist, these techniques were used to modify and enliven a tradition dominated ward. Supporting Skinner's contention that behaviorism is a humanism that works, staff with behavioristic orientations were more optimistic about patient outcomes and preferred to spend more time with patients. "Those staff who were most humanistic in theory were least humanistic in practice" (p. 240). The goals set in this program, "internalizing controls" and "developing spontaneity", were thoroughly humanistic. And while the technology used was primarily behavioristic, the method of individual contracts based on mutual decisions of patient and therapist shows the respect for individual choice that is the hallmark of humanism.

Goldstein also demonstrates a reconciliation of humanistic goals, in this case emotional awareness and expressiveness, with a behavioral technology. Mischel and Bandura bring cognition into the "empty organism" of classical behaviorism. Goldstein goes further, introducing not only emotion (which may or may not be expressed), but also a self (which is asserted in self-assertion). From the patient's point of view, there may not be much difference between Goldstein's behavioral instruction to try to begin statements with "I feel" and Rogers' empathic humanistic "You feel." A long run comparative study might make the prediction that both techniques would result in people focusing on feelings and becoming increasingly aware of their own emotional states.

Gold's use of behavior therapy methods, interpreted within a cognitive developmental framework, and directed toward the humanistic goal of helping the child reach accurate understanding of his emotional arousals, is an even more strongly bonded synthesis. Humanistic theorists have focused on emotion as their particular concern, but they can hardly ignore the effectiveness of Gold's behavioral methods in making emotions open to awareness, discussion, and control. (Though they might argue for transparency and expression rather than control, once the child is aware of the feeling.) Since Gold's whole concept of human nature is so consistent with humanistic positions, we might even think of her approach as a synthesis of a humanistic *therapist* with a cognitive behavioral technology.

Coexistence will of course continue to flourish, with thoughtful therapists exploring combinations of methods that will emphasize behavior therapy for behavior problems and humanistic therapy for problems of experience and meaning. This mutual toleration will probably continue to take the form of "You treat your patients and I'll treat mine, and may we both be helpful." Or it can take the form of comparative studies of the efficiency of the two methods in reaching common goals, such as self-regulation, without too many unwanted side effects. This is the dominant stance of true believers in both fields today, but we believe that several of the authors in this volume have been able to go beyond collaboration toward integration and synthesis. Gold's comparative data, small scale as they are, suggest that even the most dedicated Rogerian, confronted with an actively aggressive child, might well adopt her behavioral methods.

Lambert and Bergin show another way in which reconciliation is coming about. Early debates on method had a childish "My therapist can lick your therapist" flavor. As therapy research moved from dramatic case reports to careful data collection and controlled studies, claims became less strident and extreme. The field of psychotherapy research now seems finally ready to begin providing reliable answers to what we might call its fundamental question, "What specific therapeutic interventions produce change, in what particular clients, under what specific conditions?" Psychotherapy research has had at this point a disturbingly small impact on practice. At one time this might have been due to the small amount of relevant research and its poor quality. At this point, however, any remaining inability to use research results in refining the therapeutic effort must be seen as at least in part due to ingrained habit, stupidity, or dogmatism on the part of practising therapists. The facts are beginning to be obvious, and those unwilling to use them have to ask themselves why. The importance of the issue is especially clear in the case of deterioration effects. If therapy doesn't help, we can at least feel that we have tried—but if a therapist harms his patient because of his own unwillingness to learn and grow, he really has no place in the therapeutic endeavor.

Harding's classification of behavior therapy methods provides another illustration of their growing reconciliation with humanistic approaches. If we use his categories to set up a fourfold table, and then classify particular behavioristic methods within the table, we get this result:

	GOAL	
	Increase the frequency of desired responses	Decrease the frequency of undesired responses
Requires cooperation	Behavior rehearsal Modeling Assertion training	Desensitization
Does not require cooperation	Behavior shaping	Aversive conditioning

METHOD

The first cell contains three methods that work toward the increase of desirable behavior, with the cooperation of the patient. Among the behavior therapy methods, these are operationally the most humanistic.

Classification of humanistic methods is not so easy as classifying the methods of behaviorists. The relevant classification might be in terms of relationship factors such as those Lambert and Bergin discussed, or perhaps even the therapists themselves, as Jourard suggests. We might then classify therapists according to the problems they had encountered and the solutions they had reached. It might be possible to define a few ideal types of therapists—a Rogers type, a Perls type, a Jourard type, etc.—and to see to what extent each particular humanistic therapist blended these in his work. Gold's research offers an example of a method of work that might be considered the type of humanism closest to behaviorism on this spectrum. If we can begin to understand the varieties of therapists, not according to ideological labels, but according to what they are and do, we can go on to study their particular effects. Ricks and Fleming offer evidence that case studies of therapists can help us to understand their varieties, and perhaps even select appropriate therapists for particular patients. If they are correct, the best type of therapist for one population may be quite different from the optimal therapist for another. In one of his finest papers, Jourard (1971c) described the lethal factors in the male role in American society. There may be comparable lethal factors in striving to be a therapist who can help everybody. The intense effort at self-improvement evident in Jourard's paper is matched in some of the papers by Rogers (1967) and in papers by humanistic therapists like Raskin (1975). It would probably be more practical for each therapist to take a long hard look at his work and its effects, and to say something like: "All right, I am not really much help to this set of people (narcissistic depressives, delinquent boys, bored middle aged housewives, or whatever) but I really seem to understand and help these others. So be it. This is where my future efforts will go."

Alker's paper suggests that self-observation can proceed in the laboratory as well as in the clinic. More generally, he proposes that integration of humanism and behaviorism can come about by developing new ways of thinking about research and new ways of gathering information. This is not a simple "let the facts decide the issue" but a sophisticated attempt to discover how to find the facts that can open up the possibility of decision. Alker's paper suggests that inventive researchers may be able to test many of the basic propositions of the humanistic position. Among these (Szasz, 1965) are:

(a) The person is capable of making a rational choice for which he should be held responsible and the therapist should not influence or guide the person and should have limited responsibility.
(b) It follows that the person will act according to his own values and that is good.
(c) It is good to express feelings and emotions.

3. *Existing areas of agreement provide the growing points around which new syntheses of humanism and behaviorism are already developing.* Both are concerned with humane goals. While it is easy to exploit the clang association that equates "humanism" with "humane," the evidence in this book indicates that behaviorists are just as interested in alleviating suffering and promoting development as their humanistic peers. In fact, reading Wolpe, one can gain new respect for the much maligned medical model, which really seeks control over pain, not over people, and removal of symptoms, not removal of the patient's autonomy or pride.

Both humanists and social learning therapists are concerned with the person as an active organism. As Curtiss shows, a concern with behavior does not necessarily exclude efforts to promote spontaneity and self-control of one's own environment. Recent developments in social learning theory, which emphasize self-awareness and social effects of behavior, put an even stronger emphasis on the person in the person–environment interaction.

The methods of humanists and behaviorists may lead to quite similar results. We mentioned earlier the common outcomes we might expect from Goldstein's and Rogers' particular ways of focusing on emotions in therapy. The analysis can be carried much further. Suppose, for example, we agree that it is well for people to feel less inhibited and anxious, and that one common sign of this is a feeling of increased freedom and openness, of having more alternatives open in one's life and more ready access to those alternatives. This freedom might be reached through several different therapy approaches. Gold might produce it by helping people to recognize their emotional states and gain control over them; Goldstein might help them to become more appropriately expressive; Rychlak might help them to recognize the reinforcements they were working for. An increased sense of freedom might also come from a Maslovian examination of one's need hierarchy, or from work with an empathic Rogerian therapist concerned with feelings.

A fourth area of agreement is the willingness to subject clinical impression and experience to the sobering test of research results. Rogers and his students pioneered the empirical study of therapy and its outcomes, but behavior therapists have been even more willing than the Rogerians to submit their ideas to the discipline of natural consequences, and to be governed by these consequences, not by dogma.

4. *Broader perspectives may incorporate both humanism and behaviorism into more comprehensive positions.* Both traditional humanism and laboratory based behaviorism were in trouble as soon as they tried to conceptualize the interactions of the person with his natural environment. The current sophisticated work of social learning theorists and those behaviorists interested in the design of environments is making up for this deficiency in the behavioral approaches. Other than Laing's residences and groups like Esalen, humanists seem to have no corresponding development. This lack of concern for the environment may account for the solopsistic quality of many humanistic interior journeys. Humanists might do better here if they remained aware of the human environment, and of man as a social animal whose autonomy grows as he increases his options in society, not as he withdraws from it.

Goldstein offers a good example of the value to the behaviorist of seeing people in context. Some of the early assertiveness training and rational-emotive therapy brought about an unmitigated aggressiveness that later associates of the patient found extremely grating. A therapist has not helped his patient a great deal if he has only changed him from a person who gets ulcers to a person who gives them.

The main argument in each of the larger perspectives is "the postulate of empirical interconnectedness" (Devereux), which may also be expressed as the ecologist's "you can never do just one thing." All of the papers in the last section of the book were concerned with what both behaviorism and humanism fail to account for or leave out of their systems. They argue that Wolpe leaves out the context of the symptom he is removing—not the immediate behavioral context, but the human context (what function this symptom plays in the overall life of the patient) and the social context (its role in the family life and work life he is involved in or retreating from). Suppose, to use one of Wolpe's examples, a therapist removes a young man's fear of approaching women, but fails to help him to become socialized in the complicated rituals of sexual conduct. He might have cured an inhibition, but at the cost of freeing a potential rapist. Humanistic ignorance of the environment has often led to a naive radicalism, in which the environment is simply treated as an obstacle to self-realization, rather than the arena in which the self will either be realized or lost.

All of the broader perspectives are oriented around some conception of the person's development over time, "the complex and developing interdependence of the personality structure," in a society that is itself changing. Desire to remove the human being from his everyday context, the better to control and change him, has a long history. Asylums were originally supposed to provide a retreat from life's demands, and became in time the human warehouses we now call mental hospitals. Jails were originally "time out" for troublesome people, and became our current institutions for training in crime. We have learned from these experiments and others like them that there is no alternative to trying to cope with the person's problems where he is, in his own context. In practice this proves to be less convenient for the therapist but more effective for the patient. A systems view looks to change the system anywhere it shows inadequate functioning and some elasticity. Sometimes this may be in the parents, the school, or the job situation, not in the designated patient.

The broader perspectives remind us that a really shocking lack in current theories of phychotherapeutic change is their insulation from the growing corpus of knowledge about biological, cognitive, and social development. The life history perspective particularly emphasizes locating problems early, and work with high risk populations to lower the odds on later trouble rather than waiting for fully developed problems to be presented to the passively waiting therapist.

The most developed framework is the ecological perspective outlined by Alexander, Dreher, and Willems. An ecological systems approach appears to comprehend all of the narrower systems, and it not only puts them in relation to each other, but gives each part a new specificity and relevance by including it into a larger, more articulated whole. A proper respect for the ways in which people fit into their biological and social systems prevents the ecologist from falling into the "anti-society" stance of the more radical humanists. The ecologist will strive to improve a society, but he will never assume that his patient can live without one.

One of the converging areas for learning theory, life history research and ecology is study of the changing nature and availability of reinforcements through the life span. These seem to begin with attachment, safety, and appetitive needs, proceed through development of social and cognitive competence, culminate in mating and parenthood, then trail off into the milder reinforcements of later maturity and old age. A learning approach has to recognize that any organism learns what it is biologically biased and maturationally primed to learn. Study of different species suggests that primates, including humans, have the same propensity for learning relationships with fellow primates that rats have for learning mazes and dogs have for learning to salivate on cue. A therapy based on human learning, then, will have to make learning about human relationships a primary focus. Older learning theories based on rats or dogs or pigeons are not likely to be so relevant. And as learning theories focus on how relationships are learned they converge toward areas traditionally considered humanistic.

IMPLICATIONS FOR PSYCHOTHERAPY AND BEHAVIOR CHANGE

Who is to do psychotherapy? If we hold to traditional ways of thought, we have no general answer. Those trained in psychoanalysis hold that only the analytic route makes one fully analyzed, learning theorists argue that only their training makes one fully effective, and humanists may say that only their approach can make the therapist and his patient fully human. (If this sounds like parody, the authors are prepared to point to statements by true believers in each school that are even more extreme.) We believe that the evidence in this book justifies a belief that no one approach is likely to have the breadth of applicability, the flexibility, or the therapeutic effectiveness achieved by a judicious combination of methods. The best therapists are likely to be people who have a thorough grounding in psychoanalysis, humanism, and behaviorism. Unlike traditional behaviorists, they are likely to be quite precise as to how they themselves enter into the therapeutic experience of their clients—and, unlike traditional psychoanalysts and humanists, they are likely to be able to do a good many kinds of active intervention.

In training, humanists have tended to emphasize encounters, experiences, growth within the therapist. Behaviorists have emphasized a range of methods. Training programs for psychotherapists have a challenging task ahead as they try to combine training in technical skills with experiences that promote personal growth.

How is therapy to be done? The message of this book is clear: get beyond paper credentials and schools and take what helps people from each approach, without undue regard for intellectual paternity. The most creative therapists will find excitement in developing individual approaches that fit the age and problems of each patient and the setting of the therapeutic program. The section on broader perspectives suggests, however, that therapists ought to check carefully for the generalizability of their findings before applying them on a large scale in new settings and with new age groups. Maturation and environment are powerful influences that easily defeat insensitive transfer of methods from one age group or local setting to another.

Much of the most important new work in therapy will be design of environmental programs, in which the whole institution or agency is planned on therapeutic principles. In such settings the therapist can become an activist, an advocate for those he wants to help.

The growing literature on psychotherapy research indicates that the responsible therapist must find out who he helps, who he leaves untouched, who he hurts. And he must ask further whether some aspect of his personality is responsible for his effect, or whether some aspect of his methods or of the therapeutic setting is more important.

How are we to judge what help and hurt are, and how they can be measured? Are any criteria general enough to apply to the outcomes of all schools of therapy, in ways that will not bias comparisons? Some criteria for change, e.g., insight and recovery of early memories, are identified with psychoanalysis, while others, such as spontaneity and immediateness, are identified with some humanistic approaches. Our search in this book has been for a more general framework.

The ordinary medical criteria for cure provide a starting point for the criteria we will discuss. Medical treatment is expected to preserve life, to decrease pain and other symptoms, to restore normal function, and to strengthen the organism so that the disorder will not recur. If we add to these treatment criteria the public health goals of early intervention to reduce risk for later disorder, and of preventing the conditions that cause the disorder in the first place, we have a comprehensive ecological model for looking at intervention efforts. We will try to adapt this model to the problems of psychological intervention. We will propose a hierarchy of goals, ranging from simple, minimal criteria with extremely broad applicability, to other criteria that are still broader than those in general use.

Criterion I. Survival. Expected survival rates can be calculated for any defined group of people. For some groups, such as elderly patients, suicidal and depressed people, and those who are addicted to drugs or alcohol, death rates are strikingly high. Robins (1972) and Groeschel (1974) have demonstrated that they are also high in groups not often thought to be at risk for early death, such as young delinquent boys.

It seems likely that any therapy that reduces the weight of depression can lower the rates for suicide (and for addiction to pain muffling drugs). Cognitively oriented therapies and assertion training, for instance, can apparently change the ways one evaluates one's self and the kinds of cues one evokes from other people. If desensitization or insight reduces anxiety, and so reduces the risk of high blood pressure in stress situations, it should reduce the frequency of sudden breakdown of heart functions. Therapies that make emotion conscious and bring impulses under control probably reduce the likelihood that a person will get himself knifed or shot during an uncontrolled aggressive outburst. Sexual therapies that keep the elderly active by night as well as by day are likely to result in happier and longer lives.

Eysenck (1952) included people who had died in his category of therapeutic failures. We do not have to agree with Eysenck's other ideas to note that here he seems to have made a thoughtful decision.

Criterion II. Effective reproduction, parenting, and survival of the culture or subculture the patient group represents. Survival of the culture may seem a value beyond the modest goals of psychotherapy, but people as diverse as Freud, Skinner, and Devereux agree on its value as a criterion for the broad effects of psychotherapy. Effective reproduction and parenting is a general criterion for biological viability. One criterion for therapy, then, would be its capacity to remove the inhibitions and anxieties that prevent effective reproduction and competent mothering or fathering. The criterion does not lend itself to simple counting—the issue is not how many children are produced, but whether patients can have the children they want and raise them well. Weissman and her colleagues (1972), among others, have indicated some of the criteria for adequate mothering, and some of the ways in which psychological handicaps can interfere with mothering.

Criterion III. Decreased vulnerability to inner and outer sources of stress. Vulnerability is measurable in terms of physiological indicators like pulse rate, breathing rate, skin conductance, and chemical changes in the blood. It is also commonly reported to therapists, e.g., "After yesterday, I just don't think I can go out and face another customer." A huge body of research, ably summarized by Garmezy (1974), has described the characteristics of children vulnerable to schizophrenia. Risk rates can be calculated for various groups, such as those born to schizophrenic parents, children with low intellectual ability, those rejected by peers, and those involved in intense family conflict. If psychotherapy can reduce the risk for breakdown in such children it makes a major social contribution. Evidence from the Judge Baker studies (Ricks, 1974), the Wisconsin studies of Rogers and his colleagues (1967), and Myers and Bean's (1968) follow-up of discharged patients suggests that good therapists can strikingly reduce the risk for schizophrenia. It seems likely that desensitization to help one cope with anxiety, behavior rehearsal for situations of upcoming stress, insight into old roots of present problems, and growth of self-awareness and secure identity can all have the effect of reducing vulnerability.

Vulnerability to antisocial behavior has also been extensively studied (Robins, 1972; Roff, 1974). These children are vulnerable in a different sense than those vulnerable to schizophrenia. While many have a tough veneer, they generally feel unable to conform to the demands of families, schools, and employers well enough to make a go of life and get what they want legally. For these children, a practical criterion of decreased vulnerability is getting back into the ordinary spectrum of developmental tracks well enough to stay out of trouble with the law and out of jail.

Criterion IV. Increased competence and " good fit " to one's behavioral niche in the environment. There are many arenas in which competence or lack of competence can show itself: school, work, social relationships, family living. Society provides a useful measure of competence in the employment history— whether an ex-patient has been able to get jobs, hold them, be promoted, and take responsibility are important criteria for outcome. Social competence can be measured by sociometric methods in childhood (Roff *et al.*, 1972) and by social activities in adult life. Myers and Bean (1968) show that ability to hold a job is a better predictor of ex-patients staying out of mental hospitals than any other single criterion. The therapies that most emphasize competence have been the various educational methods, Massimo's vocational guidance techniques, and those behavioral therapies that have emphasized self-awareness, self-regulation, and teaching alternatives to long term patterns of learned helplessness.

Criterion V. Feeling better. Strupp *et al.* (1962) asked people why they had entered therapy and what changes they had experienced. Generally, people had come to therapy because they felt bad: depressed, anxious, guilty, sick, and so on. What they got from therapy was decreased depression and anxiety, increased enjoyment, and greater feelings of satisfaction, well-being, and self-esteem, together with a general increase in awareness of all emotions. Balkin (1974) used a set of feeling scales, filled out every night for a month, to measure more precisely how people felt before and two years after psychotherapy. His results suggest that therapy can result in marked improvement in daily feelings. In rare moments, at their best, the pre-therapy group reached the level of happiness, energy, sociability, and so on that the post-therapy group felt most of the time.

Criterion VI. Improved social system performance. The behavioral ecology approach suggests that the consequences of therapy for the social systems in which the individual participates must be evaluated. Devereux provides criteria of efficiency, effectiveness, and functional adequacy by which system functioning can be evaluated. For example, an acting out child who is taught self-control may not only feel better himself but may enable the systems in which he participates e.g., family, classroom, and neighborhood to function better.

Criterion VII. A reorganized personal world. The devout humanist or psychoanalyst might at this point say something like this: "So, what have you showed? You can count the numbers of ex-patients who end up in hospital or jails, and you can perhaps estimate vulnerability or competence or feeling better. But what therapy is really about is reorganization of the patient's personal world. Can you measure whether a person now perceives his mother in a totally new way, whether he has successfully resolved his Oedipus complex, whether his personality is now integrated into a new structure?" Our answer is that all of these changes are to some extent measurable now, and all are potentially measurable.

Take transference. Suppose we get from you, the reader, a set of names of all the people who have been important in your life. We might do this by getting you to give us your autobiography, and then pulling from it every name you had to mention in order to describe your own life. When we have tried this (Ricks, 1972) we have gotten from 50 to 100 people, and currently this set often contains one or more therapists. We can then ask you Q-sort these names according to all sorts of criteria—who you feel most comfortable with, who means the most to you, who you respect the most, can communicate the best with, and so on. We now correlate the sorts, factor them, and there before us we have the factorial crossroads of your unique interpersonal world, with everybody assigned his location by his positions in your various Q-sorts and the loadings of those sorts on the factors. If we do this procedure several times as you proceed through psychotherapy we can chart the emotional neighborhoods of your parents, therapist, and other significant figures. If your therapist is seen as much like Mommy or Daddy in the first year of therapy, and after therapy is seen as rather similar to a particularly valued dentist or history teacher, we have charted the emergence and dissolution of transference reactions. Our results so far suggest that there is nothing particularly mysterious or unmeasurable in this idea of restructuring of the personal world. (The method is general in scope, so that not all of the changes it can show will necessarily involve a therapist.)

Take "integrated into a new structure." Here R. Cartwright (1972) has developed methods for studying consistency across a set of relationships. The client is given precise ways for answering the question, "Am I the same person with my mother as with my father, my boyfriend, my boss, etc. ? " Psychotherapy resulted in increased consistency in 9 out of 10 clients in one study, and these findings were confirmed and extended on replication. Cartwright's results demonstrate that the concept of structure can be empirically related to consistency, order, and stability.

According to these criteria, a long term follow-up of therapy, by therapists of any persuasion, should show that a treated group has greater survival rates than matched controls. They should also show more effective reproduction and parenting, should show less vulnerability to breakdown or extremes of acting out, be more competent in learning, work, and social life, and be more able to deal with stress. Finally, they should feel better, and they should have reorganized their personal lives in ways that show more integrative structure. All of these have been measured in one or more studies, and the bulk of the evidence on all of the criteria is at least mildly confirmatory of the value of psychotherapy. However, these results are group trends, and in almost all studies research can also detect some patients who fail to move toward the criteria and some who deteriorate. No study of therapeutic trends is adequate without attention to these therapeutic failures. Our successes confirm us in our work, but it is from our failures that we learn the lessons we most need to learn.

Applied together, these criteria can provide a comprehensive assessment of any program in psychotherapy, either individual therapy or intervention in a system. The criteria are doctrine free—they can apply equally to all forms of psychotherapy and behavior change, even though each owes its origins mainly to one or another school. The idea of feeling better as a result of psychotherapy, and the various measures of self-ideal correspondence, self-satisfaction, etc., are associated with humanistic therapies, but it may be that behavioristic methods can help patients reach these goals faster and more efficiently than humanistic therapies can. Humanistic therapies may decrease extreme sensitivities (e.g., to ridicule) more than behavior therapies can. These are empirical issues calling out for research solutions.

Presentation of this set of criteria does not imply that we think that all of the criteria will apply equally in all therapeutic situations. Any particular program of therapy might emphasize certain criteria, drop others, and modify those that they keep to fit their particular patient population. We would also suggest that therapy can be seen in terms of interest groups, and that the interests of patients, which we concentrated on here, may not always coincide with the interests of therapists or of funding agencies.

The criteria are proposed primarily for evaluating psychotherapy and behavior change. However, we do not believe that they are limited only to this area. They may provide standards for evaluation of many kinds of human change programs, e.g., innovations in education and in community design.

WHERE ARE WE HEADED?

The optimism and the strength to struggle and change systems that Curtiss noted in the behavioral unit in her study seems to permeate much of the discussion of behavior therapy in this book and in the current world of psychotherapy. Behavioral methods are in a heady period of innovation, growth, and proliferation into new areas. As they broaden their scope, they seem to cope as well with the complex systems of institutions and social expectations as they did earlier with the simpler surroundings of the laboratory. Much of what behaviorists are doing can only be viewed with admiration for their vitality and their innovations.

The situation in humanism does not justify so much optimism. The great men and women of humanism often came to their full development late in life, and currently Bühler, Maslow, Rogers, and Perls are either dead or retired. In the work of younger humanists such as Jourard (whose untimely death occurred while this book was in progress) there is an admirable movement toward a greater operationalism and specificity, some fine scholarship, and some interesting research—but few really new ideas or programs. We do not see among current humanists the enthusiastic therapeutic explorations of the behaviorists. Many of their new explorations are in directions that broaden therapeutic methods in ways that are hard to describe or study. Other than their explorations of new ways for selecting and training therapists (Carkhuff, 1971) and the occasional studies of therapist personality and talent, there is little new work going on. Changes in humanistic theory seem to be neither systematic nor cumulative. It is hard not to agree with Koch, himself a humanist, that current humanism is showing signs of simultaneously hardening into intellectual dogmatism and deteriorating into methodological anarchy (Koch, 1969). Encounter groups and sensitivity training may offer a way out of this cul de sac. Like the written work of Rogers, May, Maslow, and Perls, they bring many recruits to humanism. But humanism seems more in need of new ideas than of new recruits. Rychlak, Jourard, and Alker offer some new directions, and perhaps these models can be a basis for an evolving humanism over the next few years. Another basis for an enlarged humanism is developmental psychology and the psychology of the life span of human development—a fact that Bühler grasped a long time ago, but one that has not yet had its full impact in humanistic thought.

LEARNING FROM EACH OTHER

The main function of dialogue is mutual learning, and the test is whether we now see familiar facts in new ways. What behaviorists can learn from humanists, and vice versa, might be suggested by what we have learned from each other and from our authors in the course of doing this book.

The broadening scope of behaviorism is evidence that behaviorists are learning from psychoanalysts, humanists—and perhaps most of all, from their patients. But we believe that they have not yet fully digested the research news that the whole personality and life style of the therapist is relevant to therapeutic process and outcomes. Behaviorism badly needs to study the therapist and his own reinforcers.

Like other people intoxicated by the partial victories of technology, behaviorists need to develop a greater respect for the system properties of human nature and the social order. Skinner's "humanism that works" requires two further questions: Works for what? Works for who? Here behaviorists can learn from humanists, who have always been concerned with human nature and human values. Ecological research shows that it is impossible to isolate real life change. Changes in symptoms lead to changes in family life, in jobs, in all sorts of human relations. As behaviorists become more aware of this they are less likely to go on developing programs that arouse the fury of civil libertarians.

Humanists need to learn from behaviorists a respect for doing as well as being. What the therapist is cannot fail to be important, but what he does is crucial to the well-being of his patient. Suppose a particular therapist is genuine, transparent, and incompetent. Will he help his patients, or only meddle in human lives in an enthusiastic but uninformed way?

Related to this is a second lesson, flexibility in methods. Current behavior therapists have many methods available, and if one does not work they can switch to another. Gold, for example, could show that when Axline methods failed to work with aggressive children she could switch to active affective teaching, which did work.

After an impressive early start in research on psychotherapy, with Rogers and his students, humanistic research in psychotherapy has in recent years fallen behind behavioristic research. This seems to us to be a regressive movement. Humanists can learn from behaviorists, or learn once again, that there is no substitute for patient investigation. Although behaviorists are not strangers to personal antagonisms and irrelevant controversy, their record here is a good example to humanists interested in maintaining viable systems of human service.

So long as we stay out of the day to day work of psychotherapy, in the quiet of the study or library, it is easy to think of psychotherapists as exponents of competing schools. When we actually participate in psychotherapy, or observe its complexities, it loses this specious simplicity. Our work on this book, and our own experience, convinces us that the old dichotomy of humanism vs. behaviorism is dead. This book has explored several of the syntheses that result when behaviorists and humanists talk and work together.

We have also tried to look at both approaches to therapy from the broader perspective of life history research, sociological systems, and ecology. Observing human beings growing up to adulthood, in the intricate biological and social systems in which all of us develop, we get a sense of what an enormous task it is to try to influence, change, and help another human being. We share Jourard's belief that humanists and behaviorists are both admirable, even heroic. We hope this book will help them in their work together. Beyond that, we hope it will help the people into whose lives they reach.

References

ABRAMSON, Y., TASTO, D. L., and RYCHLAK, J. F. (1969) Nomothetic vs. idiographic influences of association and reinforcement value on learning. *Journal of Experimental Research in Personality* **4**, 65–71.

ADLER, A. (1964) *Social Interest: A Challenge to Mankind.* New York: Capricorn Books.

AGRAS, W. STEWART (ed.), (1972) *Behavior Modification: Principles and Clinical Applications.* Boston: Little, Brown & Co.

ALBERTI, R. E. and EMMONS, M. L. (1970) *Your Perfect Right: A Guide to Assertive Behavior.* San Luis Obispo, California: Impact.

ALKER, H. A. (1965) The concept of mental health. *Philosophy and Phenomenological Research* **25**, 534–543.

ALKER, H. A. (1972) Is personality situationally specific or intrapsychically consistent? *Journal of Personality* **40**, 1–16.

ALKER, H. A. and POPPEN, P. J. (1973) Personality and ideology in university students. *Journal of Personality* **41**, 653–671.

ALKER, H. A., TOURANGEAU, R., and STAINES, B. (in press) Facilitating Eriksonian identity achievement through audio-visual self-confrontation. *Journal of Consulting and Clinical Psychology.*

ALLPORT, G. (1937) *Personality: A Psychological Interpretation.* New York: Holt.

ALLPORT, G. (1961) *Pattern and Growth in Personality.* New York: Holt, Rinehart & Winston.

ALTMAN, I. (1968) Choicepoints in the classification of scientific knowledge. In B. P. Indik and F. K. Berrien (eds.), *People, Groups, and Organizations.* New York: Teachers College Press, pp. 47–69.

ALTMAN, I. and LETT, E. E. (1970) The ecology of interpersonal relationships: a classification system and conceptual model. In J. E. McGrath (ed.), *Social and Psychological Factors in Stress.* New York: Holt, Rinehart & Winston, pp. 177–201.

ANDERSON, J. R. and BOWER, G. H. (1973) *Human Associative Memory.* New York: Wiley.

ANDREWS, J. E. (1972) The effect of word meaning on the affective learning styles of ascendant and submissive subjects. Unpublished master's thesis, Purdue University.

ARCHER, E. J. (1960) Re-evaluation of the meaningfulness of all possible CVC trigrams. *Psychological Monographs* **74**, No. 10 (Whole No. 497).

ARISTOTLE (1952) Physics. In vol. 8 of R. M. Hutchins (ed.), *Great Books of the Western World.* Chicago: Encyclopedia Britannica.

ARNOLD, M. B. (ed.) (1970) *Feelings and Emotions.* New York: Academic Press.

AXLINE, V. M. (1964) *Dibs: In Search of Self.* Boston: Houghton Mifflin.

AXLINE, V. M. (1969) *Play Therapy.* New York: Ballantine.

AYLLON, T. and AZRIN, N. (1968) *The Token Economy: A Motivational System for Therapy and Rehabilitation.* New York: Appleton–Century–Crofts.

BACON, F. (1952) *Advancement of Learning.* In vol. 30 of R. M. Hutchins (ed.), *Great Books of the Western World.* Chicago: Encyclopedia Britannica.

BAER, D. M. (1969) An operant view of child behavior problems. *Science and Psychoanalysis.* Vol. XIV. New York: Grune & Stratton, pp. 137–146.

403

BAER, D. M. (1973) The control of developmental process: Why wait? In H. W. Reese and J. Nesselroade (eds.), *Methodological Issues in Life-span Developmental Psychology*. New York: Academic Press, pp. 185–193.

BAILEY, K. and SOWDER, T. (1970) Audiotape and videotape self-confrontation in psychotherapy. *Psychological Bulletin*, **74**, 127–137.

BAKAN, D. (1965) The mystery–mastery complex in contemporary psychology. *American Psychologist* **20**, 186–191.

BAKER, B. L. (1969) Symptom treatment and symptom substitution in enuresis. *Journal of Abnormal Psychology* **74**, 42–49.

BALKIN, J. (1974) Once more with feeling: moods before and after psychotherapy. In D. F. Ricks, M. Roff, and A. Thomas, *Life History Research in Psychopathology*, vol. III. Minneapolis: University of Minnesota Press.

BALTES, P. B. and SCHAIE, K. W. (1973) *Life-span Developmental Psychology*. New York: Academic Press.

BANDURA, A. (1969) *Principles of Behavior Modification*. New York: Holt, Rinehart & Winston.

BANDURA, A. (1971a) *Social Learning Theory*. New York: General Learning Press.

BANDURA, A. (1971b) Vicarious and self-reinforcement processes. In R. Glaser (ed.), *The Nature of Reinforcement*. New York: Academic Press, pp. 228–278.

BANDURA, A. (ed.) (1971c) *Psychological Modeling: Conflicting Theories*. Chicago: Aldine Atherton.

BANDURA, A. (1971d) Psychotherapy based upon modeling principles. In A. Bergin and S. Garfied (eds.), *Handbook of Psychotherapy and Behavior Change: An Empirical Analysis*. New York: Wiley, pp. 653–708.

BANDURA, A. (1973) *Aggression: A Social Learning Analysis*. Englewood Cliffs, New Jersey: Prentice-Hall.

BANDURA, A. (1974) Behavior theory and the models of man. Presidential address presented at the meeting of the American Psychological Association, New Orleans, August 1974.

BARKER, R. G. (1963a) On the nature of the environment. *Journal of Social Issues* **19**, 17–38.

BARKER, R. G. (ed.) (1963b) *The Stream of Behavior*. New York: Appleton–Century–Crofts.

BARKER, R. G. (1965) Explorations in ecological psychology. *American Psychologist* **20**, 1–14.

BARKER, R. G. (1968) *Ecological Psychology*. Stanford, California: Stanford University Press.

BARKER, R. G. (1969) Wanted: an eco-behavioral science. In E. P. Willems and H. L. Raush (eds.), *Naturalistic Viewpoints in Psychological Research*. New York: Holt, Rinehart & Winston, pp. 31–43.

BARKER, R. G. and WRIGHT, H. F. (1955) *Midwest and Its Children*. New York: Harper & Row.

BARKER, R. G. and SCHOGGEN, P. (1973) *Qualities of Community Life*. San Francisco: Jossey-Bass.

BARRETT-LENNARD, G (1965) Professional psychology—the control of human behavior. *Australian Journal of Psychology* **17**, 24–34.

BATESON, G. (1972) *Steps to an Ecology of Mind*. New York: Ballantine Books.

BEM, D. (1970) *Beliefs, Attitudes and Human Affairs*. Belmont, California: Brooks/Cole.

BEM, D. (1972) Self-perception theory. In L. Berkowitz (ed.), *Advances in Experimental Social Psychology*. Academic Press.

BEM, D. and ALLEN, A. (1974) On predicting some of the people some of the time: the search for cross-situational consistencies in behavior. *Psychological Review* **81**, 506–520.

BENARDE, M. A. (1970) *Our Precarious Habitat*. New York: W. W. Norton.

BERGIN, A. E. (1963) The effects of psychotherapy: negative results revisited. *Journal of Counseling psychology* **10**, 244–250.

BERGIN, A. E. (1966) Some implications of psychotherapy research for therapeutic practice. *Journal of Abnormal Psychology* **71**, 235–246.

BERGIN, A. E. (1967a) Further comments on psychotherapy research and therapeutic practice. *International Journal of Psychiatry* **3**, 317–323.

BERGIN, A. E. (1967b) An empirical analysis of therapeutic issues. In D. Arbuckle (ed.), *Counseling and Psychotherapy: An Overview*. McGraw-Hill, pp. 173–208.

BERGIN, A. E. (1970) Cognitive therapy and behavior therapy: foci for a multidimensional approach to treatment. *Behavior Therapy* 1, 205–212.

BERGIN, A. E. (1971) The evaluation of therapeutic outcomes. In A. E. Bergin and S. Garfield (eds.), *Handbook of Psychotherapy and Behavior Change: An Empirical Analysis*. New York: Wiley, pp. 217–270.

BERGIN, A. E. and GARFIELD, S. (eds.) (1971) *Handbook of Psychotherapy and Behavior Change: An Empirical Analysis*. New York: Wiley.

BERGIN, A. E. and STRUPP, H. H. (1972) *Changing Frontiers in the Science of Psychotherapy*. Chicago: Aldine–Atherton.

BERGIN, A. E. and SUINN, R. M. (1975) Individual psychotherapy and behavior therapy. *Annual Review of Psychology* 26.

BERNREUTER, R. G. (1933) The measurement of self-sufficiency. *Journal of Abnormal and Social Psychology* 28, 291–300.

BERNSTEIN, D. A. (1973) Situational factors in behavioral fear assessment: a progress report. *Behavior Therapy* 4, 41–48.

BERRIEN, F. K. (1968) *General and Social Systems*. New Brunswick, NJ: Rutgers University Press.

BIJOU, S. W., PETERSON, R. R., and AULT, M. H. (1968) A method to integrate descriptive and experimental field studies at the level of empirical concepts. *Journal of Applied Behavior Analysis* 1, 175–191.

BLOCK, N. J. (1971) Are mechanistic and teleological explanations of behavior incompatible? *Philosophical Quarterly* 21, 109–117.

BOOKBINDER, L. J. (1962) Simple conditioning vs. the dynamic approach to symptoms and symptom substitution: a reply to Yates. *Psychological Reports* 10, 71–77.

BORING, E. G. (1950) *A History of Experimental Psychology*. New York: Appleton–Century–Crofts.

BOULDING, K. E. (1968) General systems theory: the skeleton of science. In W. Buckley (ed.), *Modern Systems Research for the Behavioral Scientist*. Chicago: Aldine, pp. 3–10.

BOWERS, K. (1973) Situationism in psychology: an analysis and a critique. *Psychological Review* 80, 307–336.

BOYD, H. S. and SISNEY, V. V. (1967) Immediate self-image confrontation and changes in self-concept. *Journal of Consulting psychology* 31, 291–294.

BRADLEY, B. M. (1971) Modification of isolate behavior in preschool settings. Some response-response relationships. Unpublished thesis, University of Tennessee.

BRADY, J. P. (1972) Systematic desensitization. In W. S. Agras, (ed.), *Behavior Modification*. Boston: Little, Brown & Co.

BRANDT, R. M. (1972) *Studying Behavior in Natural Settings*. New York: Holt, Rinehart & Winston.

BRELAND, K. and BRELAND, M. (1966) *Animal Behavior*. New York: Macmillan.

BRILL, A. A. (1938) Introduction to *The Basic Writings of Sigmund Freud*. New York: Modern Library.

BRODY, B. (1973) Tales from the Vienna Woods. *The Columbia Forum*, vol. II, No. 3, Summer.

BRUHN, J. G. (1974) Human ecology: a unifying science? *Human Ecology* 2, 105–125.

BRUNSWICK, E. (1957) Scope and aspects of the cognitive problem. In H. Gruber, R. Jessor, and K. Hammond (eds.), *Cognition: The Colorado Symposium*. Cambridge, Mass.: Harvard University Press.

BICKLEY, W. (ed.) (1968) *Modern Systems Research for the Behavioral Scientist*. Chicago: Aldine.

BUELL, J., STODDARD, P., HARRIS, F. R., and BAER, D. M. (1968) Collateral social development accompanying reinforcement of outdoor play in a preschool child. *Journal of Applied Behavior Analysis* 1, 167–173.

BUGENTAL, J. F. T. (1963) Humanistic psychology: a new breakthrough. *American Psychologist* **18**, 563–567.

BUGENTAL, J. F. T. (1965) *The Search for Authenticity: An Existential–Analytical Approach to Psychotherapy.* New York: Holt.

BUHLER, C. and ALLEN, M. (1973) *Introduction to Humanistic Psychology.* Monterey, California: Brooks/Cole.

BURCHARD, J. D. (1967) Systematic socialization, a programmed environment for the habilitation of antisocial retardates. *Psychological Record,* **17**, 461–476.

BURTON, A. (1967) *Modern Humanistic Psychotherapy.* San Francisco: Jossey-Bass.

CAHOON, D. D. (1968) Symptom substitution and the behavior therapies: a reappraisal. *Psychological Bulletin* **69**, 149–156.

CALHOUN, J. B. (1967) Ecological factors in the development of behavioral anomalies. In J. Zubin and H. F. Hunt (eds.), *Comparative Psychopathology.* New York: Grune & Stratton, pp. 1–51.

CALHOUN, J. B. (1972) Plight of the Ik and Kaiadilt is seen as a chilling possible end for man. *Smithsonian* **3**, 27–33.

CAMPBELL, D. T. (1969) Reforms as experiments. *American Psychologist* **24**, 409–429.

CAPLAN, N. and NELSON, S. D. (1973) On being useful: the nature and consequences of psychological research on social problems. *American Psychologist* **28**, 199–211.

CARKHUFF, R. R. (1969) *Helping and Human Relations.* New York: Holt, Rinehart & Winston.

CARKHUFF, R. R. (1971) *The Development of Human Resources.* New York: Holt, Rinehart & Winston.

CARLSON, R. (1971) Where is the person in personality research? *Psychological Bulletin* **75**, 203–219.

CARSTAIRS, C. M. (1957) Ideology, personality, and role definitions: studies of hospital personnel. In E. Greenblatt (ed.), *The Patient and the Mental Hospital.* Glencoe.

CARTWRIGHT, R. D. (1972) The Q method and the intrapersonal world. In S. R. Brown and D. J. Brenner (eds.), *Science, Psychology, and Communication.* New York: Foresight Books, Teachers College Press.

CHAPANIS. A. (1967) The relevance of laboratory studies to practical situations. *Ergonomics* **10**, 557–577.

CHASE, A. (1971) *The Biological Imperatives.* New York: Holt, Rinehart & Winston.

CHILD, I. (1973) *Humanistic Psychology and the Research Tradition.* New York: Wiley.

COLINVAUX, P. A. (1973) *Introduction to Ecology.* New York: Wiley.

COOKE, G. (1973) The efficacy of two desensitization procedures: an analogue study. *Behavior Research and Therapy* **4**, 17–24.

CORLIS, R. B. and RABE, P. (1969) *Psychotherapy from the Center: A Humanistic View of Change and Growth.* Scranton: International Textbook Co.

COTTLE, T. J. (1967) The circles test: an investigation of perceptions of temporal relatedness and dominance. *Journal of Projective Techniques and Personality Assessment* **31**, 58–71.

COTTLE, T. J. (1969) Temporal correlates of the achievement value and manifest anxiety. *Journal of Consulting and Clinical Psychology* **33**, 541–550.

COULSON, W. and ROGERS, C. R. (1968) *Man and the Science of Man.* Columbus, Ohio: Charles E. Merrill.

CRAIK, K. H. (1970) Environmental psychology. In *New Directions in Psychology,* IV. New York: Holt, Rinehart & Winston, pp. 1–121.

CROSS, H. S. (1964) The outcome of psychotherapy: a selected analysis of research findings. *Journal of Consulting Psychology* **28**, 413–417.

CUMMING, J. and CUMMING, E. (1962) *Ego and Milieu: Theory and Practice of Environmental Therapy.* New York: Atherton Press.

DAVID, E. E. (1972) Making objectivity credible and acceptable. *American Psychologist* **27**, 91–95.

DAVISON, G. C. (1968) Systematic desensitization as a counterconditioning process. *Journal of Abnormal Psychology* **73**, 91–99.

DAVISON, G. C. (1969) Appraisal of behavior modification techniques with adults in institutional settings. C. M. Franks (ed.), *Behavioral Therapy: Appraisal and Status.* New York: McGraw-Hill, pp. 220–278.

DAWSON, M. E. and FUREDY, J. J. (1974) The role of relational awareness in human autonomic discrimination classical conditioning. Unpublished manuscript, University of Toronto.

DENIKE, L. and SPIELBERGER, C. (1963) Induced mediating states in verbal conditioning. *Journal of Verbal Learning and Verbal Behavior* 1, 339–345.

DENKER, P. G. (1946) Results of treatment of psycho-neuroses by the general practitioners. *New York State Journal of Medicine* 46, 2164–2166.

DEWALD, P. A. (1972) *The Psychoanalytic Process: A Case Illustration.* New York: Basic Books.

DIMITROVSKY, L. (1964) The ability to identify emotional meaning of vocal expressions at successive age levels. In J. R. Davitz (ed.), *The Communication of Emotional Meaning.* New York: McGraw-Hill.

DITTMAN, A. T. (1966). Psychotherapeutic processes. In P. R. Farnsworth, O. McNemar, and Q. McNeMar (eds.), *Annual Review of Psychology.* Palo Alto: Annual Reviews Inc. 16, 51–78.

DOLLARD, J. and MILLER, N. E. (1950) *Personality and Psychotherapy: An Analysis in Terms in Learning, Thinking, and Culture.* New York: McGraw-Hill.

DUBOS, R. (1965) *Man Adapting.* New Haven, Conn.: Yale University Press.

DUBOS, R. (1968). *So Human an Animal.* New York: Charles Scribner's Sons.

DUBOS, R. (1970) We can't buy our way out. *Psychology Today* 3, 20, 22, 86–87.

DUBOS, R. (1971a) The despairing optimist. *American Scholar* 40, 16–20.

DUBOS, R. (1971b) The despairing optimist. *American Scholar* 40, 565–572.

DUBOS, R. (1971c) Man overadapting to the environment. *Psychology Today* 4, 50–53.

DULANY, D. E. (1962) The place of hypotheses and intentions: an analysis of verbal control in verbal conditioning. In C. W. Eriksen (ed.), *Behavior and Awareness.* Durham, NC: Duke University Press, pp. 102–129.

DULANY, D. E. (1968) Awareness, rules, and propositional control: a confrontation with S–R behavior theory. In T. R. Dixon and D. L. Horton (eds.), *Verbal Behavior and General Behavior Theory.* Englewood Cliffs, NJ: Prentice-Hall, pp. 340–387.

DUMONT, M. (1968) *The Absurd Healer.* New York: Science House.

DUNNETTE, M. D. (1963) A modified model for test validation and research. *Journal of Applied Psychology* 47, 317–323.

EDDY, G. L., and SINNETT, R. E. (1973) Behavior setting utilization by emotionally disturbed college students. *Journal of Consulting and Clinical Psychology* 40, 210–216.

EDWARDS, A. L., and KILPATRICK, F. P. (1948) A technique for the construction of attitude scales. *Journal of Applied Psychology* 32, 374–384.

EIBL-EIBESFELDT, I. (1970) *Ethology: The Biology of Behavior.* New York: Holt, Rinehart & Winston.

EISENBERG, L. (1972) The *human* nature of human nature. *Science* 176, 123–128.

EISLER, R. M., HERSEN, M., and AGRAS, W. S. (1973a) Effects of videotape and instructional feedback on non-verbal marital interactions: an analogue study. *Behavior Therapy* 4, 551–558.

EISLER, R. M., HERSEN, M., and MILLER, P. M. (1973b) Effects of modeling on components of assertive behavior. *Journal of Behavior Therapy and Experimental Psychiatry* 4, 1–6.

EISLER, R. M., MILLER, P. M., and HERSEN, M. (1973c) Components of assertive behavior. *Journal of Clinical Psychology* 29, 295–299.

ERIKSON, E. H. (1963) *Childhood and Society.* New York: Norton.

ERIKSON, E. H. (1964) *Insight and Responsibility.* New York: Norton.

EVANS, R. (1968) *B. F. Skinner: The Man and His Ideas.* New York: Dutton.

EYSENCK, H. (1952) The effects of psychotherapy: an evaluation. *Journal of Consulting Psychology* 16, 319–324.

EYSENCK, H. (1959) Learning theory; behavior therapy. *Journal of Mental Science* 61–75.

EYSENCK, H. (1966) *The Effects of Psychotherapy.* New York: International Science Press.

EYSENCK, H. (1967) The non-professional psychotherapist. *International Journal of Psychiatry* 3, 150–153.

EYSENCK, H. (1969) Relapse and symptom substitution after different types of psychotherapy. *Behavioral Research Therapy* 7, 287–288.

EYSENCK, H. (1970) Behavior therapy and its critics. *Journal of Behavior Therapy and Experimental Psychiatry* 1.

EYSENCK, H. and BEECH, R. (1971) Counterconditioning and related methods. In A. E. Bergin and S. Garfield (eds.), *Handbook of Psychotherapy and Behavior Change*. New York: Wiley, pp. 543–611.

FAGEN, J. and SHEPHERD, I. L. (1973) *Life Techniques in Gestalt Therapy*. New York: Harper & Row.

FELDMAN, M. P. and MACCULLOCK, M. J. (1971) *Homosexual Behavior: Therapy and Assessment*. Oxford: Pergamon Press.

FISH, J. M. (1973) *Placebo Therapy*. San Francisco: Jossey-Bass.

FRAISSE, P. (1963) *The Psychology of Time*. New York: Harper & Row.

FRANK, J. D. (1961) *Persuasion and Healing*. Baltimore: Johns Hopkins.

FRANK, J. D. (1967) Does psychotherapy work? *International Journal of Psychiatry* 3, 153–155.

FRANKS, C. M. (ed.) (1969) *Behavioral Therapy: Appraisal and Status*. New York: McGraw-Hill.

FRANKS, C. M. and WILSON, G. T. (1973) *Annual Review of Behavior Therapy: Theory and Practice: 1973*. New York: Brunner/Mazel.

FRANKS, C. M. and WILSON, G. T. (1974) *Annual Review of Behavior Therapy: Theory and Practice: 1974*. New York: Brunner/Mazel.

FREDERIKSEN, N. (1972) Toward a taxonomy of situations. *American Psychologist* 27, 114–123.

FRIEDMAN, P. H. (1971) The effects of modeling and role playing on assertive behavior. In J. D. Krumboltz and C. E. Thoresen (eds.), *Advances in Behavior Therapy*. New York: Holt, Rinehart & Winston, pp. 454–469.

FROMM, E. (1968) *The Revolution of Hope*. New York: Harper & Row.

GALSTER, J. M. (1972) Affective factors in paired-associate acquisition and tachistoscopic recognition of faces and names. Unpublished Master's thesis, Purdue University.

GARFIELD, S. L. and BERGIN, A. E. (1969) Therapeutic conditions and outcome. *Journal of Abnormal Psychology* 77, 108–114.

GARFIELD, S. L., PRAGER, R. A., and BERGIN, A. E. (1971) Evaluation of outcome in psychotherapy. *Journal of Consulting and Clinical Psychology* 37, 307–313.

GARMEZY, N. (1974) Children at risk: the search for the antecedents of schizophrenia. Part 1: Conceptual models and research methods. *Schizophrenia Bulletin* 8.

GILBERT, D. C. and LEVINSON, D. J. (1957) "Custodialism" and "humanism" in mental hospital structure and in staff ideology. In Greenblatt (ed.), *The Patient and the Mental Hospital*. Glencoe.

GOLD, G. H. (1973) Humanism in behavior modification with children. *The Cornell Journal of Social Relations* 8, 97–103.

GOLD, G. H. Affective-behavioral classrooms for emotionally disturbed children (in preparation).

GOLDFRIED, M. R. and MERBAUM, M. (eds.) (1973) *Behavior Change Through Self Control*. New York: Holt, Rinehart & Winston.

GOLDSTEIN, A. P. (1962) *Therapist–Patient Expectancies in Psychotherapy*. New York: Pergamon Press.

GOLDSTEIN, A. P. (1971) Psychotherapy research and psychotherapy practice: independence or equivalence? In S. Lesse (ed.), *An Evaluation of the Results of the Psychotherapies*. Springfield, Ill.: Charles C. Thomas, pp. 5–17.

GOLDSTEIN, K. (1940) *Human Nature from the Point of View of Psychopathology*. Cambridge: Harvard University Press.

GOODALL, K. (1972) Field report: shapers at work. *Psychology Today*, November.

Goss, A. E. (1961) Early behaviorism and verbal mediating responses. *American Psychologist* **16**, 285–298.

Gottlieb, J. S. and Frohman, C. E. (1972) A probable biologic mechanism in schizophrenia. Mimeo.

Gotts, E. E. (1972) (Letter) *Science* **177**, 1057–1058.

Grings, W. W. (1973) The role of consciousness and cognition in automatic behavior change. In F. J. McGuigan and R. Schoonover (eds.), *The Psychophysiology of Thinking*. New York: Academic Press, pp. 233–262.

Groeschel, B. (1974) Social adjustment after residential treatment. In Ricks, D. F., Roff, M., and Thomas, A. (eds.) *Life History Research in Psychopathology*, vol. III. Minneapolis: University of Minnesota Press.

Gump, P. V. (1968) Persons, settings, and larger contexts. In B. P. Indik and F. K. Berrien (eds.), *People, Groups, and Organizations*. New York: Teachers College Press, pp. 233–249.

Gump, P. V. (1969) Intra-setting analysis: The third grade classroom as a special but illustrative case. In E. P. Willems and H. L. Raush (eds.), *Naturalistic Viewpoints in Psychological Research*. New York: Holt, Rinehart & Winston, pp. 200–220.

Gump, P. V. and Kounin, J. S. (1959–60) Issues raised by ecological and "classical" research efforts. *Merrill–Palmer Quarterly* **6**, 145–152.

Hardin, G. (1968) The tragedy of the commons. *Science* **162**, 1243–1248.

Hardin, G. (1969) The cybernetics of competition: a biologist's view of society. In P. Shepard and D. McKinley (eds.), *The Subversive Science: Essays Toward an Ecology of Man.* Boston: Houghton Mifflin, pp. 275–296.

Harré, R. and Secord, P. (1972) *The Explanation of Social Behavior*. Oxford: Basil Blackwell.

Heidegger, M. (1962) *Being and Time* (translated by J. Maaguerrie and E. Robinson). New York: Harper & Row.

Heider, F. (1958) *The Psychology of Interpersonal Relations*. New York: Wiley.

Henry, J. (1971) *Pathways to Madness*. New York: Random House.

Henry, W. E., Sims, J. H., and Spray, S. L. (1971) *The Fifth Profession*. San Francisco: Jossey-Bass.

Hersen, M., Eisler, R. M., Miller, P. M., Johnson, M. B., and Pinkstone, S.G. (1973) Effects of practice, instructions, and modeling on components of assertive behavior. *Behavior Research and Therapy* **11**, 443–453.

Holme, R. (ed.) (1972) *Abnormal Psychology: Current Perspectives*. Del Marr, California: CMR Books.

Homans, G. C. (1950) *The Human Group*. New York: Harcourt, Brace & World.

Homans, G. C. (1961) *Social Behavior: Its Elementary Forms*. New York: Harcourt, Brace & World.

Holme, L. E. (1965) Control of coverants: the operants of the mind. *Psychological Record* **15**, 501–511.

Hutt, S. J. (1970) The role of behaviour studies in psychiatry: an ethological viewpoint. In S. J. Hutt and C. Hutt (eds.), *Behaviour Studies in Psychiatry*. New York: Pergamon Press, pp. 1–23.

Hutt, S. J., and Hutt, C. (eds.) (1970) *Behaviour Studies in Psychiatry*. New York: Pergamon Press.

Immergluck, L. (1964) Determinism-freedom in contemporary psychology: an ancient problem revisited. *American Psychologist* **19**, 270–281.

Jacobson, R. A. (1970) Personality correlates of choice of therapist. Unpublished doctoral dissertation. Teachers College, Columbia.

Jaspers, K. (1962) *The Great Philosophers*. New York: Harcourt, Brace & World.

Jones, J. L. (1973) "Fun City" provides a lesson. *Houston Chronicle*, December 15, 1973.

Jones, M. (1968) *Beyond the Therapeutic Community*. New Haven: Yale University Press.

JONES, M. and BONN, E. M. From therapeutic community to self-sufficient community. *Hospital and Community Psychiatry* **24**, 675–680, (1973).

JOURARD, S. M. (1964) *The Transparent Self*. New York: Van Nostrand.

JOURARD, S. M. (1968) *Disclosing Man to Himself*. New York: Van Nostrand.

JOURARD, S. M. (1971a) *The Transparent Self*. 2nd edn. New York: Van Nostrand.

JOURARD, S. M. (1971b) *Self Disclosure: An Experimental Analysis of the Transparent Self*. New York: Wiley.

JOURARD, S. M. (1971c) Some lethal aspects of the male role. In *The Transparent Self*. New York: Van Nostrand.

JOURARD, S. M. (1972) The transcending psychotherapist. *Voices: The Art and Science of Psychotherapy*.

JOURARD, S. M. (1973) Changing personal worlds: a humanistic perspective. *The Cornell Journal of Social Relations* **8**, 1–12.

JOURARD, S. M. (1974) *Healthy Personality: An Approach from the Viewpoint of Humanistic Psychology*. New York: Macmillan.

JUNG, C. G. (1954) *The Development of Personality*. In vol. 17 of H. Read, M. Fordham, and G. Adler (eds.), *The Collected Works of C. G. Jung*. Bollingen Series XX. New York: Pantheon Books.

KADUSHIN, C. (1969) *Why People Go to Psychiatrists*. New York: Atherton.

KANFER, F. H. and PHILLIPS, J. S. (1970) *Learning Foundations of Behavior Therapy*. New York: Wiley.

KANFER, F. H. and KAROLY, P. Self-control, a behavioristic excursion into the lion's den. *Behavior Therapy*, 1972, **3**, 398–416.

KANT, I. (1952) *The Critique of Pure Reason*. In vol. 72 of R. M. Hutchins (ed.), *Great Books of the Western World*. Chicago: Encyclopedia Britannica, pp. 1–250.

KAPLAN, A. (1964) *The Conduct of Inquiry*. San Francisco: Chandler.

KAUFMAN, A., BARON, A., and KOPP, R. E. (1966) Some effects of instructions on human operant behavior. *Psychonomic Monograph Supplements* **1**, 243–250.

KAZDIN, A. E. (1974) Effects of covert modeling and model reinforcement on assertive behavior, *Journal of Abnormal Psychology* **83**, 240–253.

KELLNER, R. (1965) The efficacy of psychotherapy: the results of some controlled investigations. *Psychiatria et Neurologia* **149**, 333–340.

KELLNER, R. (1967) The evidence in favor of psychotherapy. *British Journal of Medical Psychology* **40**, 341–358.

KELLY, G. A. (1955) *The Psychology of Personal Constructs*. New York: Norton.

KELLY, G. A. (1970) Personal construct theory. In J. Mancuso, *Readings for a Cognitive Theory of Personality*. New York: Holt, Rinehart & Winston, pp. 27–47.

KING, J. A. (1970) Ecological psychology: an approach to motivation. In W. J. Arnold and M. M. Page (eds.), *Nebraska Symposium on Motivation*. Lincoln, Nebraska: University of Nebraska Press, pp. 1–33.

KOCH, S. (1969) Psychology cannot be a coherent science. *Psychology Today*, September.

KOPP, S. (1971) *Guru: Metaphors from a Psychotherapist*. Palo Alto: Science and Behavior Books.

KRASNER, L. (1969) Behavior modification—values and training: the perspective of a psychologist. In C. N. Franks (ed.), *Behavior Therapy: Appraisal and Status*. New York: McGraw-Hill.

KRASNER, L. (1971a) Behavior therapy. In P. Mussen (ed.), *Annual Review of Psychology*, vol. 22. Palo Alto: Annual Reviews Inc., pp. 483–532.

KRASNER, L. (1971b) The operant approach in behavior therapy. In A. E. Bergin and S. Garfield (eds.), *Handbook of Psychotherapy and Behavior Change: An Empirical Analysis*. New York: Wiley, pp. 612–652.

KRASNER, L. and ULLMAN, L. P. (1973) *Behavior Influence and Personality*. New York: Holt, Rinehart & Winston.

KREITMAN, N. (1962) Psychiatric orientation—a study of attitudes among psychiatrists. *Journal of Mental Science* **108**.

KRETSCHMER, E. (1922) *Medizinische Psychologie*. Stuttgart–Leipzig: Thieme.

KRUMBOLTZ, J. O. and THORESEN, C. E. (1969) *Behavioral Counseling: Cases and Techniques*. New York: Holt, Rinehart & Winston.

KUHN, T. (1970) *The Structure of Scientific Revolutions*. Chicago: University of Chicago Press.

LAING, R. D. (1967) *The Politics of Experience*. New York: Ballantine Books.

LANDIS, C. A. (1937) Statistical evaluation of psychotherapeutic methods. In L. B. Hinsie (ed.), *Concepts and Problems of Psychotherapy*. New York: Columbia University Press, pp. 155–165.

LANG, P. J. (1968) Fear reduction and fear behavior: problems in treating a construct. In J. M. Shlien (ed.), *Research in Psychotherapy*. Washington: American Psychological Association, **3**, 90–102.

LASZLO, E. (1972) *The Systems View of the World*. New York: Braziller.

LAZARUS, A. A. (1971) *Behavior Therapy and Beyond*. New York: McGraw-Hill.

LECKY, P. (1969) *Self-consistency: A Theory of Personality*. Garden City, NY: Doubleday.

LECOMPTE, W. F. and WILLEMS, E. P. (1970) Ecological analysis of a hospital: location dependencies in the behavior of staff and patients. In J. Archea and C. Eastman (eds.), *EDRA—2: Proceedings of the 2nd Annual Environmental Design Research Association Conference*. Pittsburgh: Carnegie–Mellon University, pp. 236–245.

LEFCOURT, H. M. (1973) The function of the illusions of control and freedom. *American Psychologist* **28**, 417–425.

LEIGHTON, A. (1959) *My Name is Legion*. New York: Basic Books.

LEVINSON, D. J., DARROW, C. M., KLEIN, E. B., LEVINSON, M. H., and McKEE, B. (1974) The psychosocial development of man in early and adulthood and the mid-life transition. In D. F. Ricks, M. Roff, and A. Thomas, *Life History Research in Psychopathology*, vol. III. Minneapolis: University of Minnesota Press.

LEVEINSON, E. A. (1972) *The Fallacy of Understanding*. New York: Basic Books.

LEWIS, W. W. (1971) Project Re-ED: the program and a preliminary evaluation. In Rickard, H. C. (ed.), *Behavioral Intervention in Human Problems*.

LIDZ, T. (1968) *The Person: His Development Throughout the Life Cycle*. New York: Basic Books.

LOCKARD, R. B. (1971) Reflections on the fall of comparative psychology: Is there a message for us all? *American Psychologist* **26**, 168–179.

LOCKE, E. A. (1971) Is "behavior therapy" "behavioristic"? *Psychological Bulletin* **76**, 318–327.

LOCKE, J. (1952) *An Essay Concerning Human Understanding*. In vol. 35 of R. M. Hutchins (ed.), *Great Books of the Western World*. Chicago: Encyclopedia Britannica.

LONDON, P. (1969) *Behavior Control*. New York: Harper & Row.

LONDON, P. (1972) The end of ideology in behavior modification. *American Psychologist* **27**, 913–921.

LORENZ, K. (1970) *Studies in Animal and Human Behaviour*, vol. 1. Cambridge, Mass.: Harvard University Press.

LORENZ, K. (1971) *Studies in Animal and Human Behaviour*, vol. 2. Cambridge, Mass.: Harvard University Press.

LUBORSKY, L. (1973) Therapeutic technology: effects of specific techniques. Paper presented at the Society for Psychotherapy Research Meetings, Philadelphia, June, 1973.

McCLELLAND, D. (1961) *The Achieving Society*. New York: Van Nostrand.

McFALL, R. M. and LILLESAND, D. B. (1971) Behavior rehearsal with modeling and coaching in assertion training. *Journal of Abnormal Psychology* **77**, 313–323.

McFALL, R. M. and MARSTON, A. R. (1970) An experimental investigation of behavior rehearsal in assertive training. *Journal of Abnormal Psychology* **76**, 295–303.

McFARLAND, K. K. (1969) The influence of reinforcement value and school achievement on a "pictorial–verbal" learning task. Unpublished Master's thesis, St. Louis University.

McGuire, W. J. (1969) Theory-oriented research in natural settings: the best of both worlds for social psychology. In M. Sherif and C. W. Sherif (eds.), *Interdisciplinary Relationships in the Social Sciences.* Chicago: Aldine, pp. 21–51.

MacIver, J. and Redlich, F. (1959) Patterns of psychiatric practice. *American Journal of Psychiatry* 115.

Mahoney, M. J. (1974) *Cognitive Behavior Modification.* Cambridge, Mass.: Ballinger.

Mahoney, M. J. and Thoresen, C. E. (1974) *Self-control: Power to the Person.* Monterey: Brooks/Cole.

Mahrer, A. R. and Pearson, L. (1971) *Creative Developments in Psychotherapy.* Cleveland: Press of Case Western Reserve University.

Malan, D (1973) The outcome problem in psychotherapy research: a historical review. *Archives of General Psychiatry* 29, 719–729.

Malan, D., Bacal, H. A., Heath, E. S., and Balfour, F. H. (1968) A study of psychodynamic changes in untreated neurotic patients. *British Journal of Psychiatry* 114, 525–551.

Mandel, R. (1973) *Manual for Token Economy Unit.* Unpublished manuscript.

Margalef, R. (1968) *Perspectives in Ecological Theory.* Chicago: University of Chicago Press.

Marks, I., Boulougouris, J., and Marset, P. (1971) Flooding versus desensitization in the treatment of phobic patients: a crossover study. *British Journal of Psychiatry* 119, 353–375.

Maslow, A. H. (1961) Health as transcendence of environment. *Journal of Humanistic Psychology* 1, 1–7.

Maslow, A. H. (1965) A philosophy of psychology: the need for a mature science of human nature. In F. T. Severin (ed.), *Humanistic Viewpoints in Psychology.* New York: McGraw-Hill, pp. 17–33.

Maslow, A. H. (1966) *The Psychology of Science.* New York: Harper & Row.

Maslow, A. H. (1968) *Toward a Psychology of Being.* New York: Van Nostrand/Reinhold.

Maslow, A. H. (1970) *Motivation and Personality.* New York: Harper & Row.

Matson, F. W. (ed.) (1973) *Without/Within: Behaviorism and Humanism,* Monterey: Wadsworth.

Meehl, P. E. (1960) The cognitive activity of the clinician. *American Psychologist* 15, 19–23.

Melges, F. T. and Fourgerousse, C. E. (1966) Time sense, emotions and acute mental illness. *Journal of Psychiatric Research* 4, 127–139.

Meltzoff, J. and Kornreich, M. (1970) *Research in Psychotherapy.* Atherton Press.

Meichenbaum, D. and Cameron, R. (1974) The clinical potential of modifying what clients say to themselves. In M. J. Mahoney and C. E. Thoresen (eds.), *Self-control: Power to the Person.* Monterey: Brooks/Cole.

Menzel, E. W. (1969) Naturalistic and experimental approaches to primate behavior. In E. P. Willems and H. L. Rausch (eds.), *Naturalistic Viewpoints in Psychological Research.* New York: Holt, Rinehart & Winston, pp. 78–121.

Milgram, S. (1970) The experience of living in cities. *Science* 167, 1461–1468.

Mill, J. S. (1869) *The Subjugation of Women.* Philadelphia: J. B. Lippincott.

Miller, G. W., Galanter, E., and Pribram, K. H. (1960) *Plans and the Structure of Behavior.* New York: Holt, Rinehart & Winston.

Mischel, W. (1968) *Personality and Assessment.* New York: Wiley.

Mischel, W. (1972) Direct versus indirect personality assessment: evidence and implications. *Journal of Consulting and Clinical Psychology* 38, 319–324.

Mischel, W. (1973a) Toward a cognitive social learning reconceptualization of personality. *Psychological Review* 80, 252–283.

Mischel, W. (1973b) *Introduction to Personality.* New York: Holt, Rinehart & Winston.

Mischel, W. (1974) Processes in delay of gratification. In L. Berkowitz (ed.), *Advances in Experimental Social Psychology,* vol. 7. New York: Academic Press, pp. 249–292.

Mischel, W. and Staub, E. (1965) Effects of expectancy on working and waiting for larger rewards. *Journal of Personality and Social Psychology* 2, 625–633.

Mischel, W., Ebbesen, E., and Zeiss, A. R. (1973) Selective attention to the self: situational and dispositional determinants. *Journal of Personality and Social Psychology* 27, 129–142.

MISCHEL, W., ZEISS, R., and ZEISS, A. R. (1974) Internal–external control and persistance: validation and implications of the Stanford Preschool I-E Scale (SPIES). *Journal of Personality and Social Psychology* **29**, 265–278.

MOOS, R. H. (1971) *Revision of the Ward Atmosphere Scales (WAS): Technical Report.* Social Ecology Laboratory, Department of Psychiatry, Stanford University and Veterans Administration Hospital, palo Alto.

MOOS, R. H. (1973) Conceptualizations of human environments. *American Psychologist* **28**, 652–665.

MOOS, R. H. and INSEL, P. M. (eds.) (1974) *Issues in Social Ecology.* Palo Alto, California: National Press Books.

MOUSTAKAS, C. E. (1959) *Psychotherapy with Children.* New York: Ballantine.

MURDOCH, W. and CONNELL, J. (1970) All about ecology. *The Center Magazine* **3**, 56–63.

MURRAY, H. A. (1938) *Explorations in Personality.* New York: Oxford University Press.

MURRAY, H. A. (1963) Studies of stressful interpersonal disputations. *American Psychologist* **18**, 28–39.

MURRAY, E. J. and JACOBSON, L. I. (1971) The nature of learning in traditional and behavioral psychotherapy. In A. E. Bergin and S. L. Garfield (eds.), *Handbook of Psychotherapy and Behavior Change: An Empirical Analysis.* New York: Wiley, pp. 709–747.

MYERS, J. K. and BEAN, L. L. (1968) *A Decade Later: A Follow-up of Social Class and Mental Illness.* New York: Wiley.

NEISSER, U. (1967) *Cognitive Psychology.* New York: Appleton–Century–Crofts.

NEWMAN, O. (1972) *Defensible Space.* New York: Macmillan.

ODUM, E. P. (1963) *Ecology.* New York: Holt, Rinehart & Winston.

O'LEARY, K. D. and O'LEARY, S. (eds.) (1972) *Classroom Management: The Successful Use of Behavior Modification.* New York: Pergamon Press.

ORLINSKY, D. E. and HOWARD, K. I. (1975) *Varieties of Psychotherapy Experience.* New York: Foresight Books, Teachers College Press.

PAGE, M. M. (1969) Social psychology of a classical conditioning of attitudes experiment. *Journal of Personality and Social Psychology* **11**, 177–186.

PAGE, M. M. (1970) Role of demand awareness in the communicator credibility effect. *Journal of Social Psychology* **82**, 57–66.

PARSONS, T. (1935) The place of ultimate values in sociological theory. *International Journal of Ethics* **45**, 282–316.

PARSONS, T. (1937) *The Structure of Social Action.* New York: McGraw-Hill.

PARSONS, T. and SHILS, E. A. (eds.) (1951) *Toward a General Theory of Action.* Cambridge, Mass.: Harvard University Press.

PAUL, G. L. (1966a) *Effects of Insight, Desensitization, and Attention Placebo Treatment of Anxiety.* Stanford, California: Stanford University Press.

PAUL, G. L. (1966b) *Insight versus Desensitization in Psychotherapy.* Stanford: Stanford University Press.

PAUL, G. L. (1969a) Outcome of systematic desensitization: I, Background procedures and uncontrolled reports of individual treatment. In C. M. Franks (ed.), *Behavior Therapy: Appraisal and Status.* New York: McGraw-Hill, pp. 63–104.

PAUL, G. L. (1969b) Outcome of systematic desensitization: II, Controlled investigations of individual treatment, technique variations and current status. In C. M. Franks (ed.), *Behavior Therapy: Appraisal and Status.* New York: McGraw-Hill, pp. 105–159.

PERLS, F. (1969) *Gestalt Therapy Verbatim.* Compiled and edited by J. Stevens. Lafayette, California: Real People Press.

PETERSON, D. R. (1968) *The Clinical Study of Social Behavior.* New York: Appleton–Century–Crofts.

PIAGET, G. W. and LAZARUS, A. A. (1969) The use of rehearsal-desensitization. *Psychotherapy: Theory, Research, and Practice* **6**, 264–266.

PINE, F. and LEVINSON, D. J. (1957) Two patterns of ideology, role conception, and personality among mental hospital aides. In Greenblatt (ed.), *The Patient and the Mental Hospital*, Glencoe.

PLATT, J. (1973) Social traps. *American Psychologist* **28**, 641–651.

POPPEN, P. J. and WANDERSMAN, A. (1973) Characterizations and descriptions of humanism and behaviorism. *The Cornell Journal of Social Relations* **8**, ii–xxviii.

POWERS, W. T. (1973) Feedback: Beyond behaviorism. *Science* **179**, 351–356.

PRICE, R. H. (1974) The taxonomic classification of behaviors and situations and the problem of behavior-environment congruence. *Human Relations*.

PRICE, R. H. and BOUFFARD, D. L. (1974) Behavioral appropriateness and situational constraint as dimensions of social behavior. *Journal of Personality and Social Psychology* **30**, 579–586.

PROSHANSKY, H. M., ITTELSON, W. H., and RIVLIN, L. G. (1970a) The influence of the physical environment on behavior: some basic assumptions. In H. M. Proshansky, W. H. Ittelson, and L. G. Rivlin (eds.), *Environmental Psychology*. New York: Holt, Rinehart & Winston, pp. 27–37.

PROSHANSKY, H. M., ITTELSON, W. H., and RIVLIN, L. G. (eds.) (1970b) *Environmental Psychology*. New York: Holt, Rinehart & Winston.

RACHMAN, S. and TEASDALE, J. D. (1969) Aversion therapy: an appraisal. In C. M. Franks (ed.), *Behavior Therapy: Appraisal and Status*. New York: McGraw-Hill, pp. 279–320.

RASKIN, M. J. (1975) Becoming a therapist, a person, a partner, a . . . . Unpublished paper.

RATHUS, S. A. (1972) An experimental investigation of assertive training in a group setting. *Journal of Behavior Therapy and Experimental Psychiatry* **3**, 81–86.

RATHUS, S. A. (1973) Instigation of assertive behavior through videotape-mediated assertive models and directed practice. *Behavior Research and Therapy* **11**, 57–65.

RAUSH, H. L. (1965) Interaction sequences. *Journal of Personality and Social Psychology* **2**, 487–499.

RAUSH, H. L. (1969) Naturalistic method and the clinical approach. In E. P. Willems and H. L. Raush (eds.), *Naturalistic Viewpoints in Psychological Research*. New York: Holt, Rinehart & Winston, pp. 122–146.

RAUSH, H. L., DITTMAN, A. T., and TAYLOR, T. J. (1959a) The interpersonal behavior of children in residential treatment. *Journal of Abnormal and Social Psychology* **58**, 9–26.

RAUSH, H. L., DITTMAN, A. T., and TAYLOR, T. J. (1959b) Person, setting and change in social interaction. *Human Relations* **12**, 361–379.

RAUSH, H. L., FARBMAN, I., and LLEWELLYN, L. G. (1960) Person, setting, and change in social interaction: II, A normal-control study. *Human Relations* **13**, 305–333.

RAUSH, H. L., BARRY, W. A., HERTEL, R. K., and SWAIN, M. A. (1974) *Communication, Conflict, and Marriage*. San Francisco: Jossey-Bass.

RAYMOND, M. J. (1956) Case of fetishism treated by aversion therapy. *British Medical Journal* **2**, 854–857.

RHODES, W. C. (1972) An overview: toward synthesis of models of disturbance. In W. C. Rhodes and M. L. Tracy (eds.), *A Study of Child Variance*. Ann Arbor: University of Michigan Press, pp. 541–600.

RICKS, D. F. (1972) Dimensions in life space: factor analytic case studies. In S. R. Brown and D. J. Brenner (eds.), *Science, Psychology, and Communication: Essays Honoring William Stephenson*. New York: Foresight Books, Teachers College Press.

RICKS, D. F. (1974) Supershrink: methods of a therapist judged successful on the basis of adult outcomes of adolescent patients. In Ricks, D. F., Roff, M., and Thomas, A., *Life History Research in Psychopathology*, vol. III. Minneapolis: University of Minnesota Press.

RICKS, D. F., ROFF, M., and THOMAS, A. *Life History Research in Psychopathology*, vol. III, Minneapolis, University of Minnesota Press, 1974.

RICKS, D. F., UMBARGER, C., and MACK, R. (1964) A measure of increased temporal perspective in successfully treated adolescent delinquent boys. *Journal of Abnormal and Social Psychology* **69**.

ROBINS, L. N. (1972) An actuarial evaluation of the causes and consequences of deviant behavior in young Black men. In M. Roff, L. N. Robins, and M. Pollack, *Life History Research in Psychopathology*, vol. II. Minneapolis: University of Minnesota Press.

ROFF, M. (1972) Childhood antecedents of adult neurosis, severe bad conduct, and psychological health. In D. F. Ricks, A. Thomas, and M. Roff (eds.), *Life History Research in Psychopathology*, vol. I. Minneapolis: University of Minnesota Press.

ROFF, M., SELLS, S. B. and GOLDEN, M. (1972) *Social Adjustment and Personality Development in Children*. Minneapolis: University of Minnesota Press.

ROGERS, C. R. (1947) Some observations on the organization of personality. *American Psychologist* **2**, 358–368.

ROGERS, C. R. (1957) The necessary and sufficient conditions of therapeutic personality change. *Journal of Consulting Psychology* **22**, 95–103.

ROGERS, C. R. (1961) *On Becoming a Person: A Therapist's View of Psychotherapy*. Boston: Houghton.

ROGERS, C. R. (1963) Toward a science of the person. *Journal of Humanistic Psychology* **3**, 72–92.

ROGERS, C. R. (1967) Carl Rogers. In E. G. Borgin and G. Lindzey (eds.), *A History of Psychology in Autobiography*. New York: Appleton–Century–Crofts.

ROGERS, C. R. and SKINNER, B. F. (1956) Some issues concerning the control of human behavior. *Science* **124**, 1057–1066.

ROGERS, C. R., and TRUAX, C. B. (1967) The therapeutic conditions antecedent to change: a theoretical view. In C. R. Rogers, G. T. Gendlin, D. V. Kiesler, and C. B. Truax (eds.), *The Therapeutic Relationship and Its Impact: A Study of Psychotherapy with Schizophrenics*. Madison: University of Wisconsin Press.

ROGERS, C. R., GENDLIN, G. T., KIESLER, D. V., and TRUAX, C. B. (eds.) (1967) *The Therapeutic Relationship and Its Impact: A Study of Psychotherapy with Schizophrenics*. Madison: University of Wisconsin Press.

ROSENHAN, D. L. (1973) On being sane in insane places. *Science* **179**, 250–258.

ROSENTHAL, R. (1966) *Experimenter Effects in Behavioral Research*. New York: Appleton Century Crofts.

ROSENTHAL, R. and JACOBSON, L. (1968) *Pygmallion in the Classroom: Teacher Expectation and Pupil Intellectual Development*. New York: Holt, Rinehart & Winston.

ROSS, A. O. (1971) *Behavior Disorders of Children*. General Learning Press.

ROTTER, J. B. (1954) *Social Learning and Clinical Psychology*. Englewood Cliffs, NJ: Prentice-Hall.

ROTTER, J. B. (1966) Generalized expectancies for internal versus external locus of control. *Psychological Monographs* **80**, (1, whole No. 609).

ROYCE, J. E. (1973) Does person or self imply dualism? *American Psychologist* **28**, 833–866.

RUSSELL, B. (1940) *An Inquiry into Meaning and Truth*. London: Allen & Unwin.

RYAN, W. (1966) *Distress in the City*. Cleveland: Press of Case Western Reserve University.

RYAN, W. (1971) *Blaming the Victim*. New York: Pantheon.

RYCHLAK, J. F. (1966) Reinforcement value: a suggested idiographic, intensity dimension of meaningfulness for the personality theorist. *Journal of Personality* **34**, 311–335.

RYCHLAK, J. F. (1968) *A Philosophy of Science for Personality Theory*. Boston: Houghton Mifflin.

RYCHLAK, J. F. (1969) Lockean vs. Kantian theoretical models and the "cause" of therapeutic change. *Psychotherapy: Theory, Research, and Practice* **6**, 214–222.

RYCHLAK, J. F. (1970) The human person in modern psycholocal science. *British Journal of Medical Psychology* **43**, 233–240.

RYCHLAK, J. F. (1972) Communication in human concordance: possibilities and impossibilities. In J. H. Masserman and J. J. Schwab (eds.), *Man for Humanity: On Concordance vs. Discord in Human Behavior*. Springfield, Ill.: Charles C. Thomas, pp. 91–101.

RYCHLAK, J. F. (1973a) *Introduction to Personality and Psychotherapy: A Theory–Construction Approach*. Boston: Houghton Mifflin.

RYCHLAK, J. F. (1973b) A question posed by Skinner concerning human freedom, and an answer. *Psychotherapy: Theory, Research, and Practice* **10**, 14–23.

RYCHLAK, J. F. and BARNA, J. D. (1971) Causality and the proper image of man in scientific psychology. *Journal of Personality Assessment* **34**, 403–419.

RYCHLAK, J. F. and TOBIN, T. J. (1971) Order effects in the affective learning styles of over-achievers and underachievers. *Journal of Educational Psychology* **62**, 141–147.

RYCHLAK, J. F., McKEE, D. B., SCHNEIDER, W. E., and ABRAMSON, Y. (1971) Affective evaluation in the verbal learning styles of normals and abnormals. *Journal of Abnormal Psychology* **77**, 11–16.

RYCHLAK, J. F., GALSTER, J., McFARLAND, K. K. (1972) The role of affective assessment in associative learning: from designs and CVC trigrams to faces and names. *Journal of Experimental Research in Personality* **6**, 186–194.

RYCHLAK, J. F., HEWITT, C. W., and HEWITT, J. (1973a) Affective evaluation, word quality, and the verbal learning styles of black versus white junior college females. *Journal of Personality and Social Psychology* **27**, 248–255.

RYCHLAK, J. F., TASTO, D. L., ANDREWS, J. E., and ELLIS, H. C. (1973b) The application of an affective dimension of meaningfulness to personality-related verbal learning. *Journal of Personality* **41**, 341–360.

RYCHLAK, J. F., CARLSEN, N. L., and DUNNING, L. P. (1974) Personal adjustment and the free recall of materials with affectively positive or negative meaningfulness. *Journal of Abnormal Psychology* **83**, 480–487.

RYCHLAK, J. F., FLYNN, E. J., BURGER, G., and TOWNSEND, J. W. Osgoodian evaluation and reinforcement value: identical or different dimensions of meaningfulness? In preparation.

RYCHLAK, J. F., TUAN, N. D., and SCHNEIDER, W. E. (1974) Formal discipline revisited: affective assessment and nonspecific transfer. *Journal of Educational Psychology* **66**, 139–151.

SAJWAJ, T., TWARDOSZ, S., and BURKE, M. (1972) Side effects of extinction procedures in a remedial preschool. *Journal of Applied Behavior Analysis* **5**, 163–175.

SCHACHTER, S. (1964) The interaction of cognitive and physiological determinants of emotional state. In L. Berkowitz (ed.), *Advances in Experimental Social Psychology*. Academic Press.

SCHAEFFER, J. (1971) Body boundary imagery and fantasy in two types of therapist. Unpublished thesis proposal. Teachers College, Columbia University.

SCHOFIELD, W. (1964) *Psychotherapy: The Purchase of Friendship*. Englewood Cliffs, NJ: Prentice-Hall.

SCHWITZGEBEL, R. (1964) *Streetcorner Research: An Experimental Approach to the Juvenile Delinquent*. Cambridge, Mass.: Harvard University Press.

SEARS, R. R. (1943) *Survey of Objective Studies of Psychoanalytic Concepts*. New York: Social Science Research Council.

SELIGMAN, M. E. P. (1973) Fall into helplessness. *Psychology Today*, June.

SELLS, S. B. (1969) Ecology and the science of psychology. In E. P. Willems and H. L. Raush (eds.), *Naturalistic Viewpoints in Psychological Research*. New York: Holt, Rinehart & Winston, pp. 15–30.

SHAPIRO, A. K. (1971) Placebo effects in medicine, psychotherapy and psychoanalysis. In A. E. Bergin and S. L. Garfield (eds.), *Handbook of Psychotherapy and Behavior Change: An Empirical Analysis*. New York: Wiley, pp. 439–473.

SHEPARD, P., and McKINLEY, D. (eds.) (1969) *The Subversive Science: Essays Toward an Ecology of Man*. Boston: Houghton Mifflin.

SHORE, M. F. and MASSIMO, J. L. (1973) After ten years: a follow-up study of comprehensive vocationally oriented psychotherapy. *American Journal of Orthopsychiatry* **43**.

SIMON, H. A. (1969) *The Sciences of the Artificial*. Cambridge, Mass.: MIT Press.

SINGER, J. L. (1966) *Daydreaming*. New York: Random House.

SKINNER, B. F. (1953) *Science and Human Behavior*. New York: Macmillan.

SKINNER, B. F. and ROGERS, C. R. (1956) Some issues concerning the control of human behavior. *Science*, **124**, 1057–1066.

SKINNER, B. F. (1971) *Beyond Freedom and Dignity*. New York: Knopf.

SKINNER, B. F. (1972) Humanism and behaviorism. *The Humanist*.

SKINNER, B. F. (1974) *About Behaviorism*. New York: Knopf.

SLACK, C. W. (1960) Experimenter–subject psychotherapy: a new method of introducing intensive office treatment for unreachable cases. *Mental Hygiene* **44**, 238–256.

SMITH, R. L. (1966) *Ecology and Field Biology*. New York: Harper & Row.

SNIDER, J. G. and OSGOOD, C. E. (1969) *Semantic Differential Technique: A Sourcebook*. Chicago: Aldine.

SPEERS, R. W. and LANSING, C. (1965) *Group Therapy in Childhood Psychosis*. Chapel Hill: University of North Carolina Press.

STAATS, A. W. (1972) Language behavior therapy: A derivative of social behaviorism. *Behavior Therapy*, **3**, 165–192.

STERLING, C. (1972) Superdams: the perils of progress. *The Atlantic* **229**, 35–41.

STEVENS, S. S. (1935). The operational definition of psychological concepts. *Psychological Review* **42**, 517–527.

STOTLAND, E. (1969) *The Psychology of Hope*. San Francisco: Jossey-Bass.

STRUPP, H. H., WALLACH, M. S., and WOGAN, M. (1962) Psychotherapeutic experience in retrospect: questionnaire survey of former patients and their therapists. *Psychological Monographs* **76**.

STUDER, R. G. (1972) The organization of spatial stimuli. In J. F. Wohlwill and D. H. Carson (eds.), *Environment and the Social Sciences: Perspectives and Applications*. Washington, DC: American Psychological Association, pp. 279–292.

SZASZ, T. (1965) *The Ethics of Psychoanalysis: The Therapy and Methods of Autonomous Psychotherapy*. New York: Basic Books.

TENBRUNSEL, T. W., NISHBALL, E. R., and RYCHLAK, J. F. (1968) The idiographic relationship between association value and reinforcement, and the nature of meaning. *Journal of Personality* **36**, 126–137.

THOMPSON, T. and GRAVOWSKI, J. (eds.) (1972) *Behavior Modification of the Mentally Retarded*. New York: Oxford University Press.

THORESEN, C. E. (1973) Behavioral humanism. In C. E. Thoresen (ed.), *Behavior Modification in Education*, Seventy-second yearbook of the National Society for the Study of Education. Chicago: University of Chicago Press.

THORESEN, C. E. (1974) Behavioral humanism. In M. J. Mahoney and C. E. Thoresen (eds.), *Self-control: Power to the Person*. Monterey: Brooks/Cole.

THORESEN, C. E. and MAHONEY, M. J. (1974) *Behavioral Self-control*. New York: Holt, Rinehart & Winston.

THORESEN, R. W., KRAUSKOPF, C. J., McALEER, C. A., and WENGER, H. D. (1972) The future for applied psychology: are we building a buggy whip factory? *American Psychologist* **27**, 134–139.

THORNDIKE, E. L. and LORGE, I. (1944) *The Teacher's Work Book of 30,000 Words*. New York: Teacher's College, Columbia University.

TOMKINS, S. S. (1963a) Left and right. In R. W. White (ed.), *The Study of Lives*. New York: Atherton, pp. 288–411.

TOMKINS, S. S. (1963b) *Affect, Imagery, Consciousness*. New York: Springer.

TOMKINS, S. S. (1964) *Polarity Scale*. New York: Springer.

TOMKINS, S. S. (1965) Affect and the psychology of knowledge. In S. S. Tomkins and C. Izard (eds.), *Affect, Cognition and Personality*. New York: Springer, pp. 72–97.

TOURANGEAU, R. (1973) An experiment in self-confrontation. Honors thesis: Department of Psychology, Cornell University.

TRUAX, C. B. (1963) Effective ingredients in psychotherapy. *Journal of Counseling Psychology* **10**, 256–263.

TRUAX, C. B. (1966) Reinforcement and non-reinforcement in Rogerian psychotherapy. *Journal of Abnormal Psychology* **71**, 1–9.

TRUAX, C. B. and CARKHUFF, R. R. (1967) *Toward Effective Counseling and Psychotherapy: Training and Practice.* Chicago: Aldine.

TRUAX, C. B. and MITCHELL, K. M. (1968) The psychotherapeutic and psychonoxious: human encounters that change behavior. In M. Feldman, *Studies in Psychotherapy and Behavior Change,* Vol. I, *Research in Individual Psychotherapy.* Buffalo: State University of New York Press, pp. 55–92.

TRUAX, C. B. and MITCHELL, K. M. (1971) Research on certain therapist interpersonal skills in relation to process and outcome. In A. E. Bergin and S. L. Garfield (eds.), *Handbook of Psychotherapy and Behavior Change: An Empirical Analysis.* New York: Wiley, pp. 299–344.

TURNBULL, C. M. (1972) *The Mountain People.* New York: Simon & Schuster.

ULLMANN, L. P. and KRASNER, L. (1969) *A Psychological Approach to Abnormal Behavior.* Englewood Cliffs, NJ: Prentice-Hall.

VAILLANT, G. (1974) Antecedents of healthy adult male adjustment. In D. F. Ricks, M. Roff, and A. Thomas (eds.), *Life History Research in Psychopathology,* vol. III. Minneapolis: University of Minnesota Press.

VALINS, S. and NISBETT, R. E. (1971) *Attribution Processes in the Development and Treatment of Emotional Disorders.* General Learning Press.

VINEBERG, S. E. and WILLEMS, E. P. (1971) Observation and analysis of patient behavior in the rehabilitation hospital. *Archives of Physical Medicine and Rehabilitation* 52, 8–14.

VON BERTALANFFY, L. (1968) *General System Theory.* New York: Braziller.

WACHTEL, P. (1973) Psychodynamics, behavior therapy, and the implacable experimenter: an inquiry into the consistency of personality. *Journal of Abnormal Psychology* 82, 324–334.

WADDINGTON, C. H. (1968) The basic ideas of biology. *Towards a Theoretical Biology.*

WADE, N. (1972) A message from corn blight: the dangers of uniformity. *Science* 177, 678–679.

WAHLER, R. G., SPERLING, K. A., THOMAS, M. R., TEETER, N. C., and LUPER, H. L. (1970) The modification of childhood stuttering: some response–response relationships. *Journal of Experimental Child Psychology* 9, 411–428.

WAHLER, R. G. (1972) The indirect maintenance and modification of deviant child behavior. Paper presented to a symposium (The Child in His Environment) of the Houston Behavior Therapy Association, Houston, Texas, May, 1972.

WALDMAN, R. D. (1971) *Humanistic Psychiatry: From Oppression to Choice.* New Brunswick.

WALLACE, B. (1972) *Essays in Social Biology.* Englewood Cliffs, NJ: Prentice-Hall.

WATKINS, J. W. (1960) *Confirmable and Influential Metaphysics.* Ind.

WATT, K. E. F. (ed.) (1966) *Systems Analysis in Ecology.* New York: Academic Press.

WATT, K. E. F. (1968) *Ecology and Resource Management.* New York: McGraw-Hill.

WATTS, A. (1969) The individual as man-world. In P. Shepard and D. McKinley (eds.), *The Subversive Science: Essays Toward an Ecology of Man.* Boston: Houghton Mifflin, pp. 139–148.

WEINMAN, B., GELBART, P., WALLACE, M., and POST, M. (1972) Inducing assertive behavior in chronic schizophrenics: a comparison of socioenvironmental, densensitization, and relaxation therapies. *Journal of Consulting and Clinical Psychology* 39, 246–252.

WEISSMAN, M. W. (1972) The depressed woman as a mother. *Social Psychiatry.*

WEITZMAN, B. (1967) Behavior therapy and psychotherapy. *Psychological Review* 74, 300–317.

WERNIMONT, P. F. and CAMPBELL, J. P. (1968) Signs, samples, and criteria. *Journal of Applied Psychology* 52, 372–376.

WESSMAN, A. E. and RICKS, D. F. (1966) *Mood and Personality.* New York: Holt, Rinehart & Winston.

WHITE, R. W. and WATT, N. F. (1973) *The Abnormal Personality.* New York: Ronald.

WICKER, A. W. (1969) Attitudes versus actions: the relationship of verbal and overt behavioral responses to attitude objects. *Journal of Social Issues* 25, 41–78.

WICKER, A. W. (1971) An examination of the "other variables" explanation of attitude–behavior inconsistency. *Journal of Personality and Social Psychology* 19, 18–30.

WICKER, A. W. (1972) Processes which mediate behavior–environment congruence. *Behavioral Science* 17, 265–277.

WILKINS, W. (1971) Desensitization: social and cognitive factors underlying the effectiveness of · Wolpe's procedure. *Psychological Bulletin* 76, 311–317.

WILLEMS, E. P. (1965) An ecological orientation in psychology. *Merrill–Palmer Quarterly* 11, 317–343.

WILLEMS, E. P. (1967) Behavioral validity of a test for measuring social anxiety. *Psychological Reports* 21, 433–442.

WILLEMS, E. P. (1969) Planning a rationale for naturalistic research. In E. P. Willems and H. L. Raush (eds.), *Naturalistic Viewpoints in Psychological Research*. New York: Holt, Rinehart & Winston, pp. 44–71.

WILLEMS, E. P. (1972a) The interface of the hospital environment and patient behavior. *Archives of Physical Medicine and Rehabilitation* 53, 115–122.

WILLEMS, E. P. (1972b) Place and motivation: complexity and independence in patient behavior. In W. J. Mitchell (ed.), *Environmental Design: Research and Practice*. Los Angeles: University of California at Los Angeles, pp. 431–438.

WILLEMS, E. P. (1973a) Behavioral ecology and experimental analysis: Courtship is not enough. In J. R. Nesselroade and H. W. Reese (eds.), *Life-span Developmental Psychology*. New York: Academic Press, pp. 195–217.

WILLEMS, E. P. (1973b) Behavior-environment systems: an ecological approach. *Man–Environment Systems* 3, 79 110.

WILLEMS, E. P. (1973c) Behavioral ecology as a perspective for man-environment research. In W. F. E. Preiser (ed.), *Environmental Design Research*, vol. 2. Stroudsburg, Pa.: Dowden, Hutchinson & Ross, pp. 152–165.

WILLEMS, E. P. (1973d) Changes in the micro-ecology of patient behavior over three years: direct observations of patient behavior. Paper presented to the American Psychological Association, Montreal, Fall.

WILLEMS, E. P. (1974) Behavioral technology and behavioral ecology. *Journal of Applied Behavior Analysis* 7, 151–165.

WILLEMS, E. P. Behavioral ecology as a perspective for research in psychology. In C. W. Deckner (ed.), *Methodological Perspectives for Behavioral Research*. Springfield, Ill.: Charles C. Thomas (in press).

WILLEMS, E. P. and RAUSH, H. L. (eds.) (1969) *Naturalistic Viewpoints in Psychological Research*. New York: Holt, Rinehart & Winston.

WILLOUGHBY, R. R. (1934) Norms for the Clark–Thurstone inventory. *Journal of Social Psychology* 5, 91–97.

WITTCOFF, R. H. (1973) The future of cities. *The Center Magazine* 6, 67–73.

WOLPE, J. (1958) *Psychotherapy by Reciprocal Inhibition*. Stanford University Press.

WOLPE, J. (1969) *The Practice of Behavior Therapy*. New York: Pergamon Press.

WOLPE, J. (1972) Behavior Therapy. Lecture presented at Cornell University Symposium on Behavioristic and Humanistic Approaches to Personality Change.

WOLPE, J. (1973) *The Practice of Behavior Therapy*, 2nd ed. New York: Pergamon Press.

WANDERSMAN, A. and POPPEN, P. J. (eds.) (1973) Special issue on Behavioristic and Humanistic Approaches to Personality Change, *Cornell Journal of Social Relations* 8.

WRIGHT, H. F. (1967) *Recording and Analyzing Child Behavior*. New York: Harper & Row.

WRIGHT, H. F. (1969–1970) *Children's Behavior in Communities Differing in Size*. Lawrence, Kansas: University of Kansas.

YATES, A. J. (1958) Symptom and symptom substitution. *Psychological Review* 65, 371–374.

YATES, A. J. (1970) *Behavior Therapy*. New York: Wiley.

ZELAZO, P. R., ZELAZO, N. A., and KOLB, S. (1972a) "Walking" in the newborn. *Science* 176, 314–315.

ZELAZO, P. R., ZELAZO, N. A., and KOLB, S. (1972b) (Letter) *Science* 177, 1058–1059.

ZIMBARDO, P. G. (1970) The human choice: individuation, reason, and order versus deindividuation impulse, and chaos. In W. J. Arnold and D. Levine (eds.), *Nebraska Symposium on Motivation, 1969*. Lincol, Nebraska: University of Nebraska Press, 237–307.
ZIMMERMAN, B. J. and ROSENTHAL, T. L. (1974) Observational learning of rule governed behavior by children. *Psychological Bulletin* **81**, 29–42.

Psychotherapy Cases and
Clients Discussed

Name Index

(Italic figures refer to entries in Reference list)

Subject Index

Affect, humanistic orientation grounded in positive, 214; in appropriate expression training, 223–226; "I feel" statements, 231, 387–388; relation to cognition and behavior, 256–257; appropriate, inappropriate, and conflicting labels, 257; teaching appropriate, 258–260.

Anxiety, in neurosis, 57; desensitization for, 58–63; free floating, 76–77; appropriate expression training for, 224; avoidance of arousal, 258.

Apathy, behavioral treatment for, 77–78.

Arousal, interaction with cognition and behavior, 256; threshold of, 256; labelling of, 256–257.

Appropriate expression training, (*see also* Assertive training, described), 64–65; developed from assertive training, 223–224; relation to humanistic goals, 223; theory of, 224–225; techniques, 226–227; use of role reversal and modeling, 229–230; "I feel" statements, 231, 387–388; directness, 231.

Assertive training, described, 223; compared to appropriate expression training, 223–224; research, 232.

Assessment, affective, 138–143, 158; self superior to clinical, 155.

Attribution, of power and strength to client, 37; of assumptions and judgment to experimental subjects, 166; attributions as psychotherapeutic goals, 256; blaming the victim, 366.

Autism, family setting for, 270.

Aversive conditioning, illustrated, 16; used to change reinforcing behavior, 16; for drug habits, 57; ethical problems, 196–197; least humanistic of behavior methods, 389.

Awareness, self, 132, 145; problem for conditioning theory, 137; of contingencies

determinant of action, 155–156; criterion for psychotherapy, 201; affect labels and insight, 257; ecological, 315; of reinforcement, 363–364; increases resistance to manipulation, 377.

Behavior, of therapist as basis for classification, 189, 194; abnormal, from behavioral viewpoint, 253–254; relations to cognition and emotion, 256; prosocial, 256; ecology of, 307; linkages, 336.

Behavior deficits, examples of, 12; abnormal, 253–254.

Behaviorism, scope, 4; criteria, 4; role of environment in, 4–5, 140, 147, 151, 152, 153; ideal type, 6; radical, 6, 362; social learning theory, 7–8, 361–379; humanistic critique, 46.

Behaviorism, affective, described, 220–221, conceptual base, 255–256; illustrated, 259–261; research, 261–263.

Behaviorism vs. humanism, main contrasts, 20; scientific vs. intuitive, 20–21; means (method) vs. ends, 21–22; external behavior vs. internal emotions, 23; behavior change vs. insight, 23–24; manipulation vs. humanization, 24–25; active vs. passive therapist, 25–26; direct control vs. indirect control, 26–27, 183.

Behavioral ecology, definition, 317; behavior and environment, 318–319; site specificity, 319–320; molar phenomena and non-reductionism, 320; behavioral focus, 320–321; transdisciplinary emphasis, 321–322; systems concepts, 322–323; habitability, 323–324; ecological diagnosis, 324; naturalistic emphasis, 325; distribution of phenomena in natural systems, 325–326; taxonomy, 326–327; small rates,

TITLES IN THE PERGAMON GENERAL PSYCHOLOGY SERIES
(Continued)